OUT WEST

Signs of settlement—the first days of the 1889 Oklahoma landrush. (University of Oklahoma Libraries)

By the same author:

First Overland: London-Singapore by Land Rover (George Harrap & Co., 1957; Signal Books, 2005)

Lying in State: How Whitehall Denies, Dissembles and Deceives (Aurum Press Ltd, 2003, 2004)

OUT WEST

Travels through the American
West—Past and Present

Tim Slessor

Interlink Books

An imprint of Interlink Publishing Group, Inc.
Northampton, Massachusetts

First American edition published in 2016 by
Interlink Books
An imprint of Interlink Publishing Group, Inc.
46 Crosby Street
Northampton, MA 01060

Copyright © Tim Slessor, 2016
Published simultaneously in the United Kingdom by Signal Books

Library of Congress Cataloging-in-Publication Data available

ISBN 978-1-56656-064-1 (paperback)

Production: Tora Kelly
Main cover illustration: Unknown (see Preface)
Maps: Sebastian Ballard

Printed and bound in the United States of America

CONTENTS

LIST OF MAPS

PREFACE

"The West is America, only more so ..."
Wallace Stegner, Historian

"Well, good luck, and mind you tell them that it was a whole lot more than just cowboys."

He was an oilman. We were both checking in at a motel in Casper, Wyoming. He asked me what I—obviously a Brit—was doing in those parts. Perhaps he thought that I was an oilman too. I explained. So, while the desk clerk dealt with our credit cards and gave us our keys, we stood and talked for a few minutes. Then we picked up our bags, said goodnight and headed for our rooms. But moments later, I was struck by his last, over-the-shoulder advice. It had a satisfying ring. It made good sense too. So, maybe I now had a clear focus, an overriding theme for my book. After all, the West is "a whole lot more than just cowboys."

⁊

I have some explaining to do.

First, everything in this book is true. And even if it isn't, it could be. You will soon see what I mean ...

Second, the chapters that follow are uneven and often partial. Given the enormous spread of the West, in both its geography and history, they could hardly be anything else. So please, don't expect a narrative that is neatly systematic. There are all kinds of omissions, bumps, diversions, and potholes along the way. But more than that, and for most of the time, my path heads toward the places (and their histories) that I have come to know. My enthusiasms go back to the days when, once upon a time, I lived and worked for a very happy year on the High Plains; later I was lucky enough to have a job making documentaries for the BBC that took me zigzagging across those parts, particularly across Nebraska, Wyoming, Montana, and the Dakotas. So, after a few broad-brush chapters, that is where we will be heading.

Third, you will ask how a mere Brit could have the nerve to write about something as quintessentially American as The West. That is a fair point, and thirty years ago, when I first started to write things down, I would have been too shy to attempt an answer. Indeed, I hid my early efforts in a bottom drawer for those three decades. But with increasing age, there comes a lowered embarrassment level—and I am now well into my dotage. Also, some of my American friends have suggested that I might have a different "take," a foreigner's angle, on certain well-worn subjects; it is encouraging of them to suggest it.

Fourth, who do I think I am writing for? Brits or Americans? The short answer is that I *hope* I am writing for both. But there is another possibility: maybe I am really writing for myself—putting together a sort of personal "thank you" to a people who, for over fifty years, have always made me welcome and whose history fascinates me. Therefore I have told my laptop that everything must be spelt/spelled in American. That task it has now learnt/learned, but of course it can't cope with "usage," which on one side of the Atlantic is sometimes different than/different from that on the other. So, Americans, please allow me occasional slips or perhaps some overly obvious perceptions. For instance, it is interesting for me to see that the Founding Fathers, when writing the Constitution, used the English spelling (originally from medieval Norman-French) for *labour* and *defence*. But if any of this is already familiar, please recognize/recognise that it may *not* be for many British readers.

Fifth, I make few claims for originality. Indeed, there is not much in this book that a diligent reader will not find in a good library. I don't apologize/apologise for that; I am not trying to assert my credentials as a researcher. So, only rarely have I gone back to original sources, because by now all the usual archives have been so thoroughly plowed/ploughed over that they are unlikely to provide anything new, let alone revelatory. After all, most writers of history, if they are honest, have distilled the works of a whole slew of earlier literary explorers and pathfinders. How could it be otherwise unless they were actually "there"—at Fort Laramie, Sutter's Mill, Wounded Knee, the Alamo, or wherever? Even then, one will often read almost as many different eyewitness accounts of what took place (especially if the event was controversial) as there were people taking part. So it seems to me that, once past a few basic and unarguable historical facts (the Union won the Civil War, Colonel Custer most certainly did not win at Little Bighorn), one is quickly into the much more interesting background of a given event: what were its causes and, even more important (given that we may still be living with some of them), what were its consequences? At which point there is, as often as not, a divergence of opinion among the different commentators. In short, we have moved into interpretation. And that, surely, is what makes history so interesting. In other words, except in its most basic elements, history is seldom merely what happened; it is, more often than not, what different people *think* happened, or sometimes, even more pertinently, what they *want* to think happened. I am arrogant enough to hope it is my *thinking*, my occasional original *opinions*, that will interest the reader, but that of course is for the reader to decide.

Further, and in connection with that last paragraph, I am told that in the eyes of some professional historians, a deficiency of detailed endnotes and source references labels one as someone of negligible legitimacy. So be it: I am resigned to being illegitimate. As already admitted, much of my information comes from a distillation of other people's books and articles; I have listed around 200 of them in the bibliography, and selected choice quotations for the chapter openings. Nevertheless, besides picking my way through other men's literary flowers, I have driven many thousands of miles (and walked a few) across the West, and I have visited many (though certainly not all) of the places I write about. I have also talked and listened to people who know far more about these things than I do.

Lastly, although at the end of this book I acknowledge in some detail the help I have had at so many points in putting the whole thing together, I want to say another "thank you" at this early stage as well. So, I thank everyone who responded to my questions and who offered advice, encouragement or simple kindness: like the warden-historians at the Little Bighorn Battlefield, or the highway patrolman who pulled me over for speeding (and then let me off), or the Kansas farmer who stopped his pickup on a back-country road to ask if I had a problem. When I explained that I had just pulled over to look at my map, I think he was mildly disappointed. I mention him (without even getting close enough to ask his name) because his concern was, and is, entirely typical of the hospitality one gets from complete strangers all over the West.

Tim Slessor
Wimbledon, 2015

P.S. At some point in my various travels across the West I came by the photo of the single cowboy that appears on this book's cover. To me, it is so evocative that I have taken the liberty of using it—without remembering who gave it to me. So, please, if the owner gets in touch (via Signal Books), not only will I be happy to pay the copyright fee, but at the same time, my conscience will be much eased.

HO! FOR
THE WEST!
NEBRASKA AHEAD!

VIEW ON SCHOOL CREEK FIVE MILES NORTH OF SUTTON NEB.

THE TRUTH WILL OUT!

THE BEST FARMING AND STOCK RAISING COUNTRY IN THE WORLD!

THE GREAT CENTRAL REGION, NOT TOO HOT NOR TOO COLD

☞ The facts about Western Iowa and Southern Nebraska, are being slowly but surely discovered by all intelligent men. The large population now pouring into this region, consists of shrewd and well-informed farmers, who know what is good, and are taking advantage of the opportunities offered.

The crops of Southern Nebraska are as fine as can be; a large wheat and barley crop has been harvested; corn is in splendid condition, and all other crops are equally fine. The opportunities now offered to buy

B. & M. R. R. LANDS

On long credit, low interest, twenty per cent. rebate for improvements, low freights and fares, free passes to those who buy, &c., &c., can never again be found.

There are plenty of lands elsewhere, but they are in regions which can never be largely prosperous. Southern Nebraska, with its fine soil, pure water, and moderate climate, is the right country for a new home.

PRAIRIE, TEN MILES EAST FROM LINCOLN, NEB.

Go and see for yourself. You will be convinced, as thousands have been before you.

☞ Low Round Trip Rates to all points and return, and the amount paid is refunded to those who buy.

I am now prepared to sell Round Trip Tickets to Nebraska and return. The General Office of the B. & M. R. R. is at Lincoln, the Capital of the State. I will sell tickets from Alton Junction to Lincoln and return for $24.90, and the fare is refunded to those who buy.

Write to me or call, for a circular and for full information, or for tickets to Lincoln or other points.

CHAS. A. GAISER, Edwardsville, Ills.,
Agent for B. & M. R. R.
In Effingham, Fayette, Bond, Madison, St. Clair, Monroe and Randolph Counties.

AGREE, BLACKMAR & CO. PRINTERS, BURLINGTON, IOWA.

1

FIRST THINGS FIRST

"We think so much of our state that if the Good Lord chooses it for His second coming, we'll be pleased, but not much surprised."

A notice over the mirror in a Scottsbluff (Nebraska) barber's shop

൮

More than fifty years ago, being disappointed with my boss, I left my BBC job, or, to use the vernacular in which I soon found myself, I "up'n'quit"—to go and work on the High Plains of the American West for 12 months. I had been there before; I have been back many times since. I was, and still am, fascinated by the place.

It is a well-worn cliché, but the West *is* much more than just an enormous spread of geography. As has often been observed, it is also a way of life, a state of mind, an attitude, a style, a way of saying and doing things. Westerners—the real ones, not the dudes—even walk, talk, and smile a little differently than the rest of us. And, more often than not, they think a little differently too—sometimes a lot differently. So, above all, the West is its people, past and present. They have always been rather special, and, based on my hither-and-thither travels around the rest of the world, I can tell you that they are also among the most open and hospitable. And one other thing: even though many of them hardly recognize it, they are conditioned by an epic sweep of history; I am thinking of the facts, not the fiction—though, at times, the two are (satisfyingly) not too far apart. Yet, intriguingly, if any of today's Westerners think about these things at all, their time-perspective is such that they are likely to regard "the taking of the West" (and much that followed) as having happened only a little this side of Magna Carta. Yes, I exaggerate. But not much.

After all, when the BBC first sent me filming "out west" in 1961, I found myself listening to an eighty-two-year-old Sioux who told me how, as a boy, just after Christmas in 1890, he had watched the 7th Cavalry (yes, the same 7th that, under Colonel Custer, had been chopped up only fourteen years before) riding out to bring in a minor chief called Big Foot and his small band of followers—an episode that ended in the so-called Battle of Wounded Knee. "So-called" because it was not much of a battle, more a massacre. I do not know if the old man was telling me the truth, but, given his age, there is no reason to suppose that he was not. Later and elsewhere, I met a gnarled old rancher who proudly told me that his father, as a lad, had ridden with Butch Cassidy; indeed, he had held the horses while Butch went into various small-town banks to make "some cash withdrawals." Further, he was adamant that, in his father's company, he had briefly met Butch in the early 1920s. So, Butch was not killed in Bolivia, but secretly came home to live out his days under a false name—until he died of cancer in 1937. (We will come to that intriguing story.) And then there was Mr. Roberts, born before the Civil War. At 101 years old, he still lived on the same Colorado acres that his parents had staked out as their homestead in the mid-1870s. Some ninety-two years later he was still grumbling about what he judged to be an ill-considered treaty under which some local "Injuns" had been given back their guns. Today, of course, fifty-five years later, he and those other old-timers are long gone. But, once upon a time, I met and listened to them; I still feel something between awe and great privilege that I did so.

Anyway, back in 1965, and some weeks before my wife and I and our two small children left London, a friend from New York was downright disbelieving. "But why do you want to go and live in Nebraska?" To him, as to many East Coast sophisticates, the place was not an appropriate destination for anyone except perhaps, well, Nebraskans. At the same time, an English friend said that, yes, he knew about New York, New Orleans, New Jersey, New Hampshire, and even New Mexico. "But come again, where's this place, New Brasker?" Perhaps he was joking; I hope so.

I at least knew where the place was. But I had no tightly drawn idea of why I wanted to go and live there for a year. I just did. Anyway, given that the land now 8,000 feet below us *was* Nebraska, it was rather late for introspection.

Earlier that day we had lifted away from a London morning, and then, pressurized and slightly queasy, we had arrowed through the stratosphere at something over 500 mph, nonstop for Chicago. There, dropping down into the sticky heat of a midwestern August, we presented ourselves at US Customs. "Any

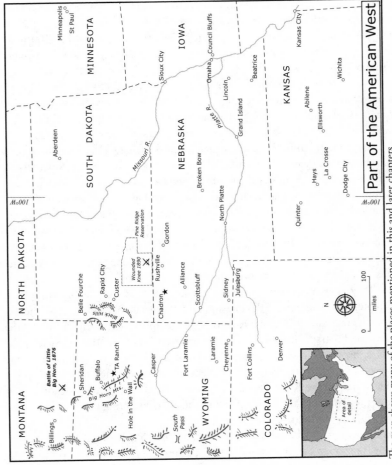

Part of the American West

The map shows many of the places mentioned in this and later chapters

fresh meats or agricultural products?" "Yes," my wife answered brightly, "we have a couple of apples for the children." The customs man's eyebrows went up and, throwing back his head, he hollered "A-a-agareeculchah!" (A statement of fact or of amazement?) Presently another man with a pair of long tongs appeared; with a "thank-you-ma'am," he carefully lowered the offending apples into a plastic sack. Clearly, we had arrived in the U.S. of A. With only 30 minutes remaining to make a connection, we ran to catch the next plane. "Just think positive, ma'am, and you'll make it," advised the customs man. So we flew another 300 miles to Omaha where, still thinking positive, we changed planes again, to Frontier Airlines.

Now, nearly fifteen hours from London, we were still flying west—though more slowly, and under mere propeller power. It was the same sun, swinging down into the sinking evening, that had risen that morning over our departure from Wimbledon. My still uncorrected watch showed an English midnight.

Every twenty minutes or so the plane, a workhorse DC3-Dakota, banked to glide into some town with a western-sounding name: Grand Island, North Platte, Scottsbluff. Coming in over the rooftops, one sees that there is not much that is European about these places; they have not grown higgledy-piggledy, slowly and organically down the centuries. A railroad track runs like tailored stitching down the middle. Beside the track tower enormous white grain elevators, like ultramodern cathedrals. The low sunlight flashes off the cars parked slantwise, like horses at a hitching rail, along Main Street. Less than one hundred years earlier most of these places had not even existed.

They grew up as depot towns in the late 1860s along the railroad which, searching out a route to the Rockies and to the Pacific far beyond, was hammering down its rails along the same rough trail taken in the years before, first by the westering fur-trappers, later by the wagons overlanding to Oregon, then by the Mormons, the gold-seeking Forty-Niners on their way to California, the Pony Express and, lastly, the continental telegraph. They all made their way up the wide valley of the River Platte, the greatest of all the highways leading west from the center of the continent. From the air, considering its place in history, it is a disappointing river. In the evening, it flashes silver as it trickles over the sandbars; then, as the flaps are lowered and the aircraft turns against the sun on its final approach, the water loses the slanting light and turns to mud. The Platte: "Too thick to drink, too thin to plow, and so muddy that the fish have to come up to sneeze." The early settlers often said things like that; sometimes their grandchildren still do.

The plane only stops for a few minutes. Maybe a cowboy gets off (well, he is wearing a cowboy hat, pointy boots, and a big-buckled belt, but he could be a local lawyer who likes dressing up); a bundle of the afternoon papers out of Omaha is dumped on the warm tarmac; a couple of businessmen get aboard, one of them unclips his tie and immediately goes to sleep. Then we fly on.

We are over the deep heart of the continent; the Atlantic is nearly 1,500 miles behind; the Pacific is almost as far away to the front. We have crossed the 98th meridian; in geography and history this is the line where the Midwest becomes the West, where the grass becomes shorter and drier, and away from the few rivers, the trees become almost nonexistent.

In the dusk, the wing-tip lights flashed red and green; we banked and then steadying gently we slid onto the runway. The flight hostess took down our coats and toys from the rack, opened the door, lowered the steps, and as we stepped down and thanked her, she gave us the gentle goodbye we were to hear so many, many times over the next twelve months. "You're welcome, and mind you take care now." We walked across the tarmac still radiating from the afternoon sun. Behind us, the DC3 turned and taxied back to the runway. Then, with an accelerating growl, it lifted off on the last leg of its schedule, north 100 miles to Rapid City.

So, in one very long day, we had come from Wimbledon to western Nebraska—to the small town of Chadron.

✂

I had first been west a few years before, filming for the BBC. When that particular assignment was almost finished I had phoned my wife to suggest she fly over and join me. Having no children at that stage, there was just enough money to spare. Over a three-week vacation we rented a VW Beetle out of Denver and saw enough of Nebraska and Wyoming to make us want to come back—one day. Two years later, I was lucky enough to persuade the BBC to send me back again to make a five-part series to be shown on the shortly-to-be-opened channel BBC2. By the time I got back from *that* assignment, I was completely hooked.

So now, with two small children, we had come back. We were going to live and work here in Chadron. Through a Nebraskan friend I had met three years earlier, I had been offered a job teaching English. I was nervously unqualified. But if I could hold my nerve, the job would, at the least, keep us in rent money and food for twelve months. Our son Jeremy was just four; our daughter Katy was nearly two. So they were old enough to travel, but not old enough to be at school. It seemed like the right time to take off. Indeed, we reckoned that if we did not go then, we probably never would.

It was a very good year. And ever since (well, until I retired over 30 years later) I was lucky enough to have a job that allowed me to go back—again and again. So, over almost half a century, I have grown to know as much about the West ("my" part of it, anyway) as many Americans, and more than most foreigners. Much of what I have picked up is not remotely significant, but I take an unreasonable pride in it. I know where one can still see the ruts of the overland wagons (just south of Guernsey, Wyoming); where there is a good cheapish motel in Cheyenne (The Scout); how to make the quickest time between Laramie and Casper (along the back roads of the Shirley Basin); what to do if stopped on a highway by a police car (keep still and don't get out until the officer tells you); where to look for arrowheads (in the miniature badlands five miles west of Chadron); how to play a passable game of horseshoes; when (and when not) to filter right on a red light; what to do when one of those yellow school buses slows to a halt on the highway (stop immediately, in both directions); how to keep the score when ten-pin bowling; what, in the matter of western headgear, is the difference between a Stetson, a Low Crown Topper, and a Montana Peak.

And, lastly, I know how to order a western breakfast in a roadside diner without even glancing at the menu. "I'll take a small orange juice, two eggs over-easy, four bacon strips, hash browns, and a toasted English muffin." And "Yes, I'll take my coffee now." (For British readers: the correct usage is "I'll take," never the supplicatory "Can I have?") To spread on the muffin (second cousin to a crumpet), you will be provided with some purple goop called Smuckers Grape Jelly. The best that one can say of the stuff is that, presumably, both the grapes and the good folk at Smuckers have done their best. Believe me, for a foreigner, ordering breakfast in a diner is a most practical skill—certainly worth a diploma in Basic American Studies. Incidentally, the coffee served in most of these places is so weak that it should be deeply ashamed of itself. Further, unless you specifically ask for "real cow milk," the coffee will come with a plastic thimble of white stuff; the label tells you that this is "non-fattening dairy-style cream substitute."

Anyway, let's get back to Chadron. Like all small western towns, it really is—as the old song had it—a place of "kind hearts and gentle people." But, in the wider scheme of things, one has to say that most Americans have never heard of it. It thinks it gets its name from a Breton fur-trader, Louis Chatron, who presumably made friends with the Sioux hereabouts back in the very early days. A brochure put out by the town's Chamber of Commerce—and wherever two or three small-town businessmen find themselves gathered together they quickly form themselves into a Chamber of Commerce—told us that this was The Forward City. No one I asked knew quite what that meant. But it did not matter; Chadron was a good place to live. It is unmistakably western and of the High Plains. If you look down any street, you can see grassy prairie in one direction and pine-dotted hills in the other. Within twenty-five miles there are places called Buffalo Gap, Mirage Flats, Hay Springs, and Dead Horse Butte. Within a further twenty-five, one will find Custer, Red Shirt, Wounded Knee, and Cheyenne Crossing. You really cannot get more western than that.

When we lived there, the town and the surrounding 1,600 square miles of Dawes County had three policemen, one traffic light and a population of about 4,000. That was fifty years ago. When I was back there in the fall of 2014 the place had grown, but not much. Main Street is as it has always been: four lanes wide, broad enough to turn a wagon and its team—useful in the early days. Downtown, behind the cars tethered nose-in to the sidewalks, are the shops and the stores. A few still have their original false fronts and peeling paint, some have neon signs hanging on modern facings of glass bricks and aluminum. Each building, one beside the other, is a different height and color; together they look like a row of very uneven teeth. Above, a complicated tangle of wires sag from pole to pole: power lines, telephone cables, street lighting. Chadron is not picturesque; few western towns are. But it has a functional charm.

At the northern end of Main Street, the tracks of the Chicago and North-Western Railroad cut across the roadway at a wide and ungated crossing. For over sixty years, people set their clocks by the rumble of the big black steamers that came hissing and sighing through the town once a day in each direction. But no more: because of competition from trucks, the last freight trains came through in the early 1970s; because of cars, the last passengers stepped down twenty years before that. Today, a line of wagons loaded with local wheat is hauled away two or three times a summer. And that, "railroadwise," is about it.

These days, the town's main artery parallels the railroad three blocks to the south: Jighway 20 begins in Chicago and ends somewhere beyond the Rockies. In the two-and-a-bit minutes that it takes you to drive through the town—and the speed limit of twenty-five mph is rigidly enforced—one has the choice of four gas stations, three used-car lots, seven motels, and five "eateries" (including a McDonald's, a Pizza Hut, and a place that offers Kidz Kuizine). And there are two supermarkets, a couple of laundromats, a car laundry (sic), and, for those who need these things, there is the Birthright Pregnancy Store and the Jeepers

Peepers Eye-Care Center. There is also a church with a sign that advises "If God is only your co-pilot, switch seats." This, for a small western town, is pretty much the standard compliment of such facilities (and advice). And, for shopping, if you can't find "it" in Chadron—whatever "it" may be—you had better try your luck in Rapid City 100 miles to the north or in Scottsbluff about the same distance to the south.

Chadron is a ranching center. Along the sidewalks strolls the occasional cowboy in town for the afternoon. Some of them really do have bow-legs and walk with at least one thumb hooked into a low-slung belt; those with Stetsons wear them with the brims as tightly rolled as tricorn hats, but these days many are (disappointingly) wearing baseball caps. I don't know about today, but back when we lived there, young "Native Americans" (one is not meant to refer to "Indians" these days, though they themselves don't seem to mind the word) would stand against the walls between the bars down on Second Street; some of them might have walked thirty miles from the reservation. They seemed sadly aware that many people in the area tended to see them as a "problem." And sometimes they were—though given their story since we whites first began to dispossess them of their land, their occasional sulky bad temper is neither surprising nor unjustified. At times there is even an altercation with some local drunks. But, apart from this, when we lived in Chadron, one of the more serious crimes was breaking that speed limit.

A paragraph back I wrote that the town is a ranching center. It is also the home of Chadron State College, a degree-granting "school" for about 2,600 students, mostly drawn from this western end of Nebraska. The college (though much smaller back in 1965) was why we had come; it had offered me a job.

When my wife and I had decided to take a year or so out of our patterned lives in London, I had written to several friends out west. Two weeks later one of them had phoned to ask if I would be interested in teaching something called "Communications" at the college. Surprisingly, the job seemed to be mine for the taking. As my friend Phil (he ran a local newspaper) was paying for the trans-Atlantic call, and as "Communications" seemed to be broadly my "trade" (journalism, radio, TV), we did not go into much detail. Besides, the job paid better than the likely alternative: stacking shelves in a supermarket. So I wrote a formal letter to the college. Back came a reply giving me the job at $660 a month, telling me to be there at the end of August, and enclosing my "assignment schedule." Reading it, I quickly realized that "Communications" had nothing to do with journalism, radio or television; it was just a rather American way of saying "English." This was a disaster because, in the teaching of English, I had no qualifications or experience whatsoever. Indeed, the truth was that I had no experience of teaching anything—period.

I phoned the college from London to explain that, in honesty, I could not take the job. But the dean seemed much less interested in my (his?) problem than in the fact that the call was coming all the way from London. He countered my "resignation" by saying, "I understand that you went to Cambridge and that you wrote a book some years back. And besides, it will be real good for our students to be taught by someone from the jolly old BBC." Lastly he added that the course only involved "teaching English at freshman level," as if that did not make things even more difficult. He would not take no for an answer. Given that I had already "resigned" from the BBC, I did not have much choice. So it was fixed. I hurried to a Wimbledon bookshop to buy a book or two on English grammar. Four weeks later we were on our way.

Dangling participles and misplaced modifiers gave me some problems at first, but my students were very patient. Once I had the basic grammar sorted out, it turned out to be a very special year. For an absurd $60 a month, the college let us have a small three-room house on campus. People we had not met three days earlier lent us pots and pans. During an early snowstorm, we borrowed some warm clothes—until our trunk arrived by sea and rail. We bought a "previously owned" Ford, only slightly smaller than an ocean liner, for $500. We opened a bank account where, after just three weeks, it was "Hi, Mr. Slessor. What can we do for you today?" (Back home in London, they were still checking my signature after more than two years.) We watched our son Jeremy make friends with other children, and begin to talk about candy in what we liked to think was a western drawl. And when his younger sister Katy called for what sounded like a "party," we learned that if we didn't hurry she would soon be needing a clean nappy. (Sorry, diaper.)

We settled in. At weekends and holidays/vacations we explored the country around us. We picnicked under Register Cliff where Forty-Niners, with more than another 1,000 miles still to go, paused to carve their names. We found our way to Hole-in-the-Wall, a remote hide-out sometimes used by Butch Cassidy and the Wild Bunch. We climbed the low hill at Wounded Knee where the last shots of the Indian Wars were fired. We went to rodeos, calf round-ups and town parades. We watched mirages, bears, rattlesnakes, and western sunsets. We made friends with cowboys, ranchers, and the local sheriff. We listened to the radio in February telling us that it was minus 33°F and, five months later in July, that it was "103 and goin' up." We learned the rules (well, we tried) of American football.

In the longer vacations (semester breaks) we took off for the Bighorn Mountains, Wyoming ski slopes, Black Hills ghost towns, and Denver shopping

9

malls. We got to know something of the West; or rather, a small part of it. And between times I got on with the job of trying to explain the difference between a gerund and a participle, between an allusion and an illusion. In a year we drove nearly 20,000 miles. The West is a big place.

We submerged ourselves in the social landscape (not a happy phrase, but I can think of no other). Looking back, our going west was one of the best ideas that we ever had. Friends sometimes ask why, as we enjoyed it so much, we did not stay. The answer lies in the fact that my trade and training was in documentary television and, let's face it, there is not much of that in small-town America. A year's self-imposed sabbatical is one thing; a lifetime's is something else. But I would go back any time. Fortunately, I sometimes do.

So, I am fascinated by the West, by its people, by its history, by its skies and by its scale, by everything about it. Well over a century ago, a traveling Englishman, Lord Bryce, wrote that the West "may be called the most distinctively American part of America because the points in which it differs from the East are the points in which America as a whole differs from Europe." That thought is no less true today, which, I suppose, is one reason for this book. Another, as I have partly implied, is that when one is thoroughly won over by a place, its people, and their story, one surely wants to tell everyone else about it.

2

LA VENTE DE LA LOUISIANE

"The day that France takes possession of New Orleans ... from that moment we must marry ourselves to the British fleet and nation."

President Jefferson's warning to Napoleon on his learning of French plans to re-establish an empire in North America.

✌

When I try to tell my American friends about the debt the United States owes to the British for an early, critical, and sudden expansion of their young Republic, they usually look doubtful. I have to admit that the story, in at least one respect, seems so improbable that I do not blame them. Anyway ...

✌

Back in January 2009, I made a phone call to the London bankers, ING-Barings; I asked to be put through to their archivist—if they had one. Presently, Moira Lovegrove came on the phone. I explained. "Yes indeed," she said. "We have many of the financial papers. Do you want to come and look at them?" Yes, please!

So the next day I made my way to an address in the heart of London's financial district. Mrs. Lovegrove met me in the lobby and took me up to a boardroom where, on the mahogany table, she carefully opened the file. There they were—nearly all the documents pertaining to what, today, we might call the nitty-gritty of the financing of what, back then, was referred to as La Vente de la Louisiane (which I will continue to refer to as La Louisiane, to save any confusion with the far smaller boundaries of modern-day Louisiana). On that table, there must have been nearly 100 items: letters, lists, and memoranda in French, in English, and (if I am allowed the distinction) in American. All were in beautiful copperplate writing.

Here was what I had heard about, and, as I carefully turned those pages, I could not help thinking that those American friends would be amazed to hear of this little-known but essential stage of the proceedings. How could they imagine the crucial role that a very British institution played in helping their not-long-independent nation to grow and, thereafter, to prosper? I am referring to the successful conclusion of what was, and still is, the biggest real-estate deal in history: the Louisiana Purchase. After all, without that colossal bargain whereby the then US more than doubled its size, how else might history have turned out? Who knows, but for the fact that a British bank advanced what was essentially the mortgage capital, there might never have been a wholly American West ...

ↄ৹

So where and how did the British play such a key role in the growth of the young Republic—apart from the small matter of having provided most of the forebears of its liberty-loving citizens in the first place? But wait: perhaps, on reflection, that was not such a *small* matter. Look at the names on the Declaration of Independence and, a little later, those of the delegates to the Constitutional Convention: Washington, Jefferson, Franklin, Hancock, Hamilton, Madison, Henry, Randolph, Adams, Jay, Scott, Bloodworth, Livingston, Gadsden, and more than eighty others. With just one possible exception (William Paca?) those would seem to be British names—English with a useful stiffening of Scots and Scots-Irish. The more intelligent among those British, whether at home or abroad, had never taken comfortably to restrictive edicts, peremptory taxes, arbitrary embargoes or heavy-handed, let alone undemocratic, rulers. That aversion is, after all, what prompted many of them to cross the Atlantic in the first place.

No taxation without representation. Absolutely. It was a typically English response—which is why the attitude of the "rebel" colonists was well understood and supported by large sections of the thinking population back in "the mother country." Among those thinkers, one can point to John Wilkes, Edmund Burke,

William Pitt, Charles James Fox and, of course, Thomas Paine, who must have been mentally drafting his seminal *Common Sense* before he had even stepped ashore in the New World. And in one further demonstration of where many of the rebels, to use a modern phrase, were "coming from," one can quote the Virginian George Mason: "We claim nothing but the liberty and privileges of Englishmen, in the same degree if we had still continued among our brethren in Great Britain."

Now let us get back to the purchase of La Louisiane with a question: how, specifically, did the British, nearly twenty years after American Independence, contribute to forging the key that was to open the West? Well, among a tangle of worries in Napoleon's mind, there was the clear, though latent, threat of the British navy, invoked and then, at a key moment, leaked by President Jefferson— as the quotation at the head of this chapter demonstrates. The last thing that Napoleon wished to see was any kind of alliance or cooperation between the Americans and the British. More specifically, the threat of a blockade by Britain's warships either in the English Channel or in the distant Caribbean now became such a concern in Napoleon's calculations that, in the end, he was forced to realize that he would have to abandon his grand design to re-build a North American empire from the distant bridgehead of New Orleans. Instead, and no doubt in sulky frustration, he decided that all those North American lands to which his country laid rather dubious claim were likely to become a draining liability rather than an imperial asset. They would have to be dumped—sold to the Americans. Of course there were negotiations and haggling, but on April 30, 1803, in one short Paris afternoon, to the squeak of several quill pens, the United States more than doubled its size, for $15 million. The fact is that Napoleon, knowing that the cannons of the British navy were primed to blast apart the supply lines that he would have needed to sustain any Louisiana "empire," had little choice but to abandon his plans. And the other contribution of the British? Well, believe it or not, given that Napoleon was unwilling to allow the Americans to pay off that $15 million in the form of a bunch of promissory notes to be redeemed, bit by bit, over the next fifteen years, it was a London bank that came up with the bulk of the "here and now, money down, $15 million" that he was demanding.

But first we need to go back 40 or so years *before* that afternoon of the quill pens. In the middle decades of the eighteenth century, Britain and France were at war: situation normal. In Europe, it was the War of the Spanish Succession or the Seven Years' War; in Boston and Philadelphia it was called Queen Anne's War; in the forests of the Alleghenies and the Adirondacks it was the French and Indian War or "*la petite guerre*." But it made no difference what it was called when, on a forest path, an arrow came singing in from twenty paces to take the next man in the throat. It was a vicious and bloody business. Both sides bribed the tribes to do most of the dirty work—paid off according to the number of scalps brought back. Generally, the British colonists suffered worst. In a series of hit-and-run raids, the French, reaching down from the St. Lawrence in the north, carried this ragged guerrilla war to within twenty miles of Boston; their Indian mercenaries burned, tortured, and terrorized all along the farming frontier.

The British replied at sea, where they had strength. Then for a few years there was meant to be a peace while treaties, truces, and armistices were argued far away in Europe. But in North America, those cease-fires were irrelevant; "*la petite guerre*" never really stopped. The French, seeking to outflank the British and, at the same time, to cut south from their St. Lawrence colonies to their Mississippi territory (based on New Orleans and St. Louis), came sneaking down the Ohio valley. They built a line of forts. This was something that the British had always feared. So, intending to introduce some class to the proceedings, they sent a General Braddock of the Coldstream Guards to tidy up. Nearing Fort Duquesne (Pittsburg) he and most of his command walked into an ambush and were overwhelmed by Indians, urged on by the French. The redcoats were not used to a close-quarter fight where they could not see the enemy coming. The general was killed, but one of his staff officers, a Major George Washington, despite having his horse shot from under him, got away—to fight another enemy another day.

Nevertheless, in the end Britain's navy won the victories that really mattered. Her captains stopped French troop-and-supply ships from reaching the St. Lawrence; they chased the enemy's Channel fleet and smashed it in Brittany's Quibéron Bay; they swept the Mediterranean; they landed General Wolfe and his grenadiers on the cliffs by Quebec. With the dawn, they were on the Heights of Abraham. The battle lasted three hours, and sealed the matter.

Three years later, in 1763, the Treaty of Paris stripped France of all her North American possessions. Her claims to lands all the way down the Mississippi, including New Orleans, went to Spain; all her Canadian territory, except for two very small islands off Newfoundland (why, even to this day, did she keep those?), were turned over to the victor: Britain. France, though not *Les Canadiens* (one thinks of de Gaulle's exhortation two centuries later: "*Vivre le Québec libre*"), was finished in North America. It was an extraordinary finale to more than two centuries of extraordinary Gallic endeavor.

Historians will roast me for such a skimpy summary. But for my sake, rather than theirs, I have to keep it simple. And I will not even try to cope with 1776 and all that, because the Americans tell that particular story much better than any Englishman could do; after all, they have a better story to tell. Anyway, except for the fact that the rebels (all right, the colonists) were deeply irritated, first by Britain's unreasonable attempt to bar them from pushing west into the virgin wilderness, and second by her much more reasonable attempt to tax them to help pay for the recent wars holding off their French and Indian enemies (another fact that some Americans are still slow to appreciate), the "first West" did not have much to do with the quarrel.

But the Western void was to have everything to do with the confused ambitions of the new and very loosely jointed republic once the matter of independence was finally settled. With the defeat of the British, the rebels-now-become-Americans belatedly realized that they had just come by an enormous windfall: all the land west as far as the Mississippi. Already they had heard from hunters and soldiers returning from the frontier wars about what lay beyond the mountain ridges. They had heard quite enough to start them dreaming.

Some dreamed of personal wealth, some of empire, some of an arcadian utopia. And some, the hardy few with little time for mere dreaming, followed pathfinders like Daniel Boone and got on with the business of working their way through the mountains to make new lives in the exploitable wilderness beyond: the first all-American West.

They broke through to the grassy parklands of Kentucky, they burned clearings across the piney uplands of Georgia, they chopped mule trails through the forests of Pennsylvania, they banged a few logs together and went rafting down the Cumberland, the Ohio and the Tennessee to see what they could find.

Those pioneers, afraid of no one and with total faith in themselves and in their ambitions, are easily recognizable as the archetypes of a new breed: the pure-bred American frontiersman. They were impatient and brashly practical men, highly mobile, single-minded, individualistic, acquisitive, thoroughly capitalistic (though they would not have known what that meant), and not in the least averse to taking the law (such as it was) into their own hands. As these early "Oh-yes-indeed-we-can!" loners hacked about in that first trans-montane wilderness, the Americans following on behind looked toward their first great inheritance: for the next 100 years, the knowledge that there were always virgin lands to win further on made the frontier much more than a westward-drifting line on the map; it was a social process which generated a state of mind that seeped into the young nation's evolving style and personality. The essentials of that driving temperament and character are not gone yet. One hopes that they never will be.

Before the end of the century there were nearly 200,000 Americans west of the Appalachians. The land was surveyed, pack-trails became wagon roads, fords were replaced by bridges, settlements grew to towns, Kentucky and Tennessee were admitted to statehood, and the forward scouts of the migration had reached all the way down to the bustling Spanish port of New Orleans; indeed, it was the Americans who did most of the bustling.

Like the branches of a huge tree, all the creeks and rivers of the mid-continent flowed into the trunk of the Mississippi; you could build yourself a cargo-raft somewhere near Pittsburgh and in three months drift 1,000 miles downstream to New Orleans and the sea. The journey home, of course, took much longer. Anyway, at New Orleans you traded off your resins, skins and grain for the hardware necessities of hinterland life. On the levées and the wharfs were traders from New England, sea captains from Europe, French-speaking fur-men from the far Missouri country, river-men from Tennessee. A generation before the first steamboats, New Orleans had become a bazaar for most of back-country America.

President Jefferson had long been both bothered and intrigued by the huge emptiness that began *beyond* the Mississippi. This vastness went by the name of Louisiane and, along with the port of New Orleans, was now claimed—under the terms of that earlier treaty—by Spain. In fact, Jefferson was not worried by any expansionist plans the Spanish might have had; they were too weak to have any. But in 1801 the Spanish did something he did not expect: they traded Louisiane back to France, its original "owners," in exchange for some obscure

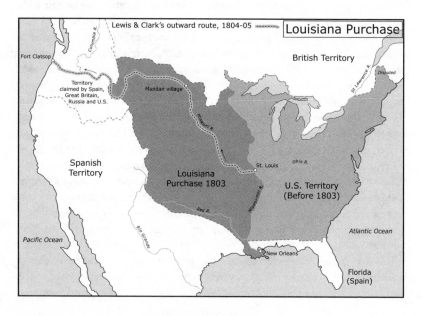

gains in Tuscany. One can assume that this transfer to France sent Jefferson straight to his maps. While he liked the French on a personal level, he did not trust them as a nation—not, at least, while they were led by Napoleon. He suspected that a French "retaking" of La Louisiane might presage an attempt to rebuild her North American empire. The British, for whom he had no great affection, but whom he seems to have trusted to behave with some predictability, might try to head off any French move by landing on the Gulf Coast first. Then, perhaps at the same time, to further thwart the French, they might push south from their Canadian territories. Jefferson feared that his infant republic would be hemmed in.

He had already sent word to his man in Paris, the diplomat Robert Livingston, that he should sniff around and keep him informed. His first concern was that the French would close the gateway port of New Orleans to all ships and cargoes other than their own, and thereby starve the upriver American settlements of both imports and exports. So he instructed his Paris emissary to see how the French would react to the idea of a straight cash offer for New Orleans ... say $2 million? Napoleon and his foreign minister, Talleyrand, were not interested.

Jefferson grew more worried. He seems to have felt that, of the two superpowers, France was the more likely to initiate a disturbance; the danger from Britain lay in her probable reaction. The young United States would lose either way. So, he decided that, if there were any trouble from France, he would have to make some loose alliance with Britain. In short, if a French army *did* land at New Orleans, "from that moment we must marry ourselves to the British fleet and nation." By way of a diplomatic leak, Jefferson made sure that Napoleon became aware of his thinking. In fact, Jefferson had diagnosed Napoleon's intentions exactly; French troops were already on their way to New Orleans; they had recently landed to gather their strength on a Caribbean stepping stone: San Domingo (present-day Haiti and Dominican Republic). It is said that this French army of more than 25,000 men was, up to that time, the largest seaborne expeditionary force in history.

However (without a sprinkling of "howevers," the writing of even simple history would be almost impossible), unknown to Jefferson, Napoleon now began to get increasingly wobbly about his plans for a new American empire. First, he had learned that in San Domingo thousands of his soldiers were being lost to yellow fever and to a Black revolt. Second, and just as important, before he had even heard of Jefferson's threat, Napoleon had already begun to realize that the shipping of munitions and supplies across the Atlantic to his expeditionary army in New Orleans, in the face of an inevitable blockade by the British navy, would be a very chancy business. After all, only a few years earlier he and his Mediterranean fleet had suffered a catastrophic defeat, at the hands of Admiral Nelson, in the Battle of the Nile (Aboukir Bay). As a consequence of that debacle, a French army of 20,000, recently landed to establish a French empire in the Levant, had been abandoned and left to rot. Napoleon could see that the same thing might happen again if he attempted to land an army at the mouth of the Mississippi. So, almost overnight, he decided to give up on his distant American adventure. He would sell to the Americans. That way, he could also raise some much-needed cash for priorities closer to home, such as rebuilding a fleet and fighting the British.

So, next time the American ambassador, Robert Livingston, came to call, Talleyrand and Barbé-Marbois (the treasury minister) asked how the Americans would feel about buying not just New Orleans but the whole of La Louisiane. Livingston, one imagines, could hardly believe his ears. Nevertheless, with admirable nerve, he murmured something about $5 million. He knew that Jefferson had recently authorized more than that for New Orleans alone. But a calculated lack of enthusiasm might persuade the French to keep the price down.

By now, Jefferson's special emissary, James Monroe, had arrived in Paris; he confirmed Jefferson's anxieties. So, despite some inevitable haggling with the French, an agreement was quickly in place: $15 million for what (if one does not include Alaska) would eventually turn out to be nearly a third of the present-day United States. Arrangements for actual payment took longer. The Americans made to transfer $3 million across the Atlantic as a down payment; they suggested that the rest, via promissory bonds, would be gradually paid off over the next 15 years. But this was an arrangement about which Napoleon was not at all enthusiastic. He wanted his $15 million, there and then. After all, despite a brief truce, another war with Britain was almost inevitable, and it would have to be paid for. But the US Treasury did not have anything like that amount in gold or silver in its vaults. As a consequence, the whole deal was in danger of coming apart. But, extraordinarily, just at this time there was that uneasy armistice (following the Treaty of Amiens) between Britain and France. The truce allowed the contract to be rescued by two banks acting in concert: Baring Brothers in London and Hope & Co. in Amsterdam. A Barings man was able to travel to Paris to negotiate directly with the French. Another Barings man was already in Philadelphia. In the end, the bankers bought the American promissory bonds at a discount of 13.3%. In short, they supplied the mortgage capital whereby the Americans were able to take possession of La Louisiane. The total sums involved were huge and there was much nervousness; indeed, Sir Francis Baring commented, "we all tremble at the magnitude of this American account." But in the end the French got their cash; the Americans got nearly 1 million square miles of largely unexplored territory (at less than four cents an acre); and over the next 15 years the British bankers got their profit.

Once the deal had gone through, Napoleon is said to have commented, "this accession of territory strengthens for ever the power of the United States and I have just given to England a maritime rival that sooner or later will humble her pride." He had a point. No blood had been spilled, the door to the Great West was now more than merely ajar, and, as Napoleon predicted, the United States soon became the only transatlantic power that mattered.

President Jefferson, in excusing the fact that he had fractured the US Constitution by not seeking the detailed approval of Congress and the individual states before the whole transaction was virtually a Done Deal, justified his action with the excuse that "it is the case of a guardian investing the money of his ward in purchasing an important adjacent territory, and saying to him when of age, 'I did this for your sake'." Talleyrand is said to have told Livingston and Monroe, "you have a bargain, make the most of it." The politicians of New England, when they found out, became distinctly grumpy and some of them even plotted secession—which, presumably, is the main reason why Jefferson had not consulted them beforehand. If he had let them in on his intentions before the deal with the French was completed, they might well have tried to scupper the whole project—for fear that the dominance of their states in the affairs of the nation might eventually be challenged by new states to the south and to the west. They would have had a point: the Louisiana Purchase almost certainly made inevitable the Civil War just 60 years later.

ℰℐ

As described at the beginning of this chapter, I was amazed to find myself sitting in the boardroom of one of London's leading merchant banks, being carefully guided through a file of documents that detailed the financing of the Louisiana Purchase.

Obviously, I felt wondrously privileged to be allowed to turn those pages. And, of course, I was surprised that the papers should be held in London. It would have taken me a week to study them all—even if I had appreciated the intricacies of eighteenth-century banking. Nevertheless, at its simplest there is something very intriguing about an English bank openly helping to bolster the finances of Britain's then current enemy. As a short brochure recently published by ING-Barings suggests, the story seems to provide an insight into the character of international banking before the more recent centuries of total war.

But, above all, there is something even more intriguing about the role of an English bank in such a pivotal event in American history. And one should not forget the role of Britain's navy. Who knows but without that bank and the threat of those warships, the history of the West might have turned out rather differently. Just possibly, there might never have been a wholly American West ...

That last paragraph was intended to end my version of *La Vente de la Louisiane.* However, sometime after finishing it, I learned that, while most of the diplomatic papers (as opposed to the financial ones) are housed in Washington, there was at least one significant document held far away to the west. Entirely appropriately, it lived in the very heart of the vastness with which, more than 200 years ago, it was directly concerned. So, I made a short transatlantic phone call to an old friend, John Gottschalk, in Nebraska. Yes, he confirmed, the 1803, 16-page, handwritten Proclamation of La Vente, signed by President Jefferson and Secretary of State Monroe—the means whereby the American people were formally told of the just-completed agreement with France—was in Omaha. It was owned by a notable Nebraskan businessman. If it could be arranged, would I like to see it, next time I was in those parts? Yes, please.

A few months later, in early 2011, Mr. Walter Scott explained to me how he had come to possess such an important fragment of his nation's history. Apparently, as soon as President Jefferson and Secretary of State Madison had checked and signed the document, it was dispatched to the government's official publisher. Then, once in print, it seems that the handwritten original was judged to be of no special significance. So the printer gave it away to someone who, most fortunately, had the foresight to suppose that, one day, there just might be some interest in the document—complete with its various addendums and deletions. Over the last two centuries it had occasionally changed hands, until Mr. Scott bought it at auction some years ago with the intention of eventually bequeathing it to Omaha's renowned Joslyn Museum.

So, there it was: the Proclamation in all its beautiful 16 pages, displayed in a sealed cabinet behind polished glass. I just had to stand and stare, and wonder at the privilege of seeing two sets of such priceless documents: the first in London, the second nearly 5,000 miles away in Omaha. Not many people can say that ...

3

LEWIS AND CLARK

An intelligent officer with ten or twelve chosen men ... might explore the whole line [of the Missouri] even to the Western Ocean.

From President Jefferson's confidential proposal to Congress in January 1801 that an expedition should be sent across the continent

❧

To President Jefferson, the blend of geographical ignorance and tall tales—rumors of prehistoric animals, a tribe of Welsh-speaking Indians, and, no doubt, mono-breasted Amazons—that came out from the mists of the continent's vague interior was too tantalizing to be ignored. So for some years, quietly and without advertisement, he had been planning an expedition of exploration—regardless of who, at the time, actually claimed ownership of the unmapped vastness.

To this end, two years before that fortuitous transaction in Paris, he had selected a young army officer, Captain Meriwether Lewis, to be his private secretary. This was a disguise: Lewis was really being groomed as the leader of the projected expedition. Accordingly, he was sent off to various savants and scientists in Philadelphia for crash courses in navigation, surveying, botany and geology. He was instructed to read anything that had even the remotest bearing on the project being planned. There was not much.

Lewis would certainly have studied the recently published account of Alexander Mackenzie's journey ten years earlier right across Canada to the northern Pacific. Both Lewis and his patron, the President, would have been

21

worried by the last part of Mackenzie's book in which he outlined British schemes for the far north-west. While predicting rich returns in fish and furs, he also forecast that the plans had "many political reasons which it is not necessary here to enumerate." This elliptical phrase added another purpose to Lewis' assignment: he must get to the far Pacific to plant the new republic's flag before the British. Elsewhere in Mackenzie's account, Lewis would have been excited to read that the Scot claimed to have made his journey across most of the western part of the continent by paddling from one river or lake to the next with only a few intervening portages.

Lewis would also have learned that in 1792, Robert Gray, the first American to sail around the world, had discovered the mouth of a huge river (the Columbia) and deduced, from its size, that its headwaters must be far inland. Lastly, Lewis would have known that French fur-men had, for several years past, been trading far up the Missouri. So the conclusion was obvious: a journey to the Missouri's headwaters (wherever they were) should place an expedition, via a modest portage or two, within reach of the headwaters of Robert Gray's Columbia. From there, surely, one would be able to float downstream to the Pacific. After that, it could not be far to China and the Indies. Helpfully, Jefferson suggested that if, on arrival at the far Pacific shore, the expedition found itself short of funds it should contact the American consul in Mauritius.

Even if the President had rather foreshortened ideas about global geography, his 2,000-word brief to his protégé was detailed and exact. "Your mission is to explore the most direct and practical water communication across this continent … make yourself acquainted with the names of nations … their language, traditions, monuments … their laws and customs … their diseases and remedies … the animals … the remains of any which may be extinct [Jefferson collected bones] … your observations are to be taken with great pain and accuracy … several copies … one to be written on the paper of the birch as less liable to damp … name a person who shall succeed you on your decease."

Captain Lewis must have been glad when, eventually, he could say farewell to his demanding patron. He took the traditional route west: to Pittsburgh, then down the Ohio River and out onto the Mississippi. Presently, he was joined by an old friend whom he had asked to come as co-leader of the expedition: Captain George Clark.

By Christmas, 1803, they had established a base camp on the east bank of the Mississippi, just opposite St. Louis and near the mouth of the Missouri. They would have based themselves in St. Louis itself, but its French governor had not yet heard that his domain had just been bought by the United States. He thought the sale was so improbable that he would not take Lewis' word for it.

The winter was passed in gathering stores and recruiting. Eventually, there were nearly 40 men in the party: soldiers, Kentucky hunters, French-speaking *voyageurs* with upriver experience, and Clark's black servant, York. They would travel in the keelboat which had brought Lewis down from Pittsburgh. She was nearly 60 feet long, had a small cabin aft, and was equipped with a large square sail and 22 oars; they also had a couple of large open canoes.

With ten tons of stores aboard, they pushed off on May 14, 1804. "Proceeded under a jentle brease up the Missourie." As the "brease" does not seem to have lasted, progress depended on their sweat—rowing, poling or, where possible, towing from the bank. They were plagued by "numerous and bad ticks and mosquiturs."

After ten weeks they had come only 500 miles. They tied up for a couple of days to "invite the Otteaus and Panies (Pawnees) to come and talk with us at our Camp." At the meeting, presents were offered, and several chiefs were informed that as result of a recent "Change of Government," they and their people were now subjects of the Great Father in Washington. The locals had no idea what all this meant but they willingly accepted the presents. And, because it seemed the obvious thing to do, Lewis called this meeting place Council Bluffs.

 confin

The site of that meeting is a few miles further upriver from today's city of Council Bluffs. But no matter. You can stand in the main street of Council Bluffs and look across "the wide Missouri" to Omaha's airport from where the jets go screaming off to San Francisco, Seattle, Salt Lake City, Chicago, New York … Incredibly, only 70 years after the expedition paused here, an iron railroad bridge would span the great river. You could then (with three changes) travel right across the continent, from New York to San Francisco Bay, from "sea to shining sea," 2,800 miles, ten days, and $200. I mention this detail because, coming less than a lifetime after Lewis and Clark passed this way, it seems an excellent illustration of the speed with which the vast interior of the continent was tamed.

Incidentally, the locals call the river the "Mizzurah"—no final "ee."

☙

Going on, the expedition was encouraged to find that the river bent away toward the northwest; they optimistically reckoned that they were now paddling in the right direction—toward the Pacific. They also knew that they were now entering the country of the unpredictable Sioux.

As they feared, the Sioux were full of "rascally intentions." Nevertheless, they thought it prudent to spend a few days with them. After all, it was just possible that the expedition might have to come back this way. There were peace pipes to be smoked, presents to be exchanged, and plate-size medallions to be hung round the necks of selected chiefs. In this last matter, Lewis and Clark were continuing a custom that the French had started more than 100 years earlier: first, to identify a few apparent leaders who seemed more amenable than the rest; then to present them with a badge of office. In this way they became the "official" chiefs through which the government could deal in any later negotiations. The system had worked well enough among the eastern tribes, where a hierarchical structure was more developed. But these tribes out on the plains did not work like that, and, down the following century, the system would cause endless aggravation to Washington's would-be treaty makers. For a start, the more tractable chiefs were often not the ones most respected by the tribe. Second, an agreement made with one group of chiefs was seldom regarded as binding by their rivals.

☙

Even today, in any negotiation with the Sioux (particularly with the Oglala tribe), it is important to know that one is talking to the right people. Some years ago, I wanted to film a short sequence of "Native American" dancing and music at a summer festival on Pine Ridge Reservation, the homeland of the Oglala Sioux. I negotiated a day or two in advance with members of the Tribal Council. The questioning was quite tough and I had to explain to a suspicious audience that my documentary, being made by the BBC, did not have a moneybag sponsor, nor, when it was eventually transmitted, would it carry remunerative advertising. Eventually it was agreed that *for $200 we could film for an hour. Willingly, I paid. A few days later we turned up at the festival somewhere in the back-country of the reservation. Entry was refused. I explained that our presence had been agreed—and paid for. I was told that the Tribal Council was made up of busybodies who had no jurisdiction over these proceedings and that I had been negotiating with quite the wrong people. Anyway, why should I be believed? "Never," I was informed, "trust a white man." Who was I to argue? Anyway, another $200 would be required. Maybe I was being ripped off, but given the way the Sioux have themselves been ripped off over the last 150 years, I knew that I was in no position to complain. My experience came as no surprise to those who think they know the Sioux. "So, what's new?" was the general reaction.*

In fact, though I did not know it at the time, I had naively run slap-bang into an enmity which had been developing between a dissident group and the Tribal Council. A few years later, this hostility was one of the causes of the second "battle" of Wounded Knee. We will come to that sad story ...

℃

As the expedition pushed on upstream it called on several other tribes until, in early November, it reached the country of the Mandan people. The river was beginning to freeze. So they tied up their boats, built a rough fort, and prepared to snug down for the winter. They had come over 1,500 miles, and this was about as far as all but a very few whites had ever penetrated.

The Mandans were a more or less settled people who probably saw, in the expedition and its guns, some protection against their enemies, the marauding Sioux. And the expedition had callers: French-Canadian traders. One of them, Toussaint Charbonneau, had recently taken a young wife from among the Mandans; it is probable that the expedition leaders thought that, despite the fact that Sacajawea was only just 16 and pregnant, she would be useful to them. First, they knew that Indian war parties never traveled with their women, let alone one carrying a papoose. So there was a fair chance that any roving Indians the expedition might meet would conclude that Sacajawea's companions did not have any hostile intentions. Second, she was not a true Mandan, but had been taken five years earlier from a tribe called the Shoshone who lived away to the west. Now, the two captains, thinking ahead, knew that when they eventually had to leave the river they might need horses. Sacajawea would be a useful interpreter and go-between. So it may well be that Sacajawea's husband really owed his engagement to the fact that he had a potentially useful wife. As for her pregnancy, she would have the baby at least two months before the expedition moved on; Indian mothers were quite accustomed to traveling within a very few days of giving birth.

Of course, the piquancy of just one girl among so many men has been altogether too much for some people. The situation particularly appealed to the Victorians, who saw Sacajawea as a curvaceous, high-bosomed, wasp-waisted, dark-eyed Valkyrie with twinkling rings on her toes, a dagger in her belt, and feathers in her waist-long plaits. And, of course, Lewis or Clark or both fell in love with her. The unsentimental truth is that Sacajawea seems to have been a quiet and modest young woman who became a thoroughly useful member of the team and, yes, in time everyone became fond and caring towards her and her baby.

By late March the ice was melting and they were ready to go. On an afternoon in early April, they watched their keel-boat with its 14-man crew drift away downstream. It carried a cargo of specimens and reports for their patron in far-away Washington. Then they loaded their own small dug-outs (built during the winter) and the two larger canoes that they had brought with them.

For the next few weeks, they bent their heads against the stinging sleet and hail of the spring storms—they were in present-day North Dakota. Then, as the weather got warmer, there were clouds of midges and more of those "mosquiturs." Details of all the creatures they met went down in the journals: grizzly bears, buffalo, antelope, rattlesnakes, cougar and, above all, beaver. Jefferson would be disappointed; he had hoped for mammoth elephants.

Jefferson was also going to be disappointed in the expedition's failure to find any of those Welsh Indians. (There were also rumors of Israelite Indians and Chinese Indians, but about these Jefferson was more skeptical.) This beguiling piece of Celtic lunacy had its origins in the legends of a Prince Madoc, who was supposed to have led his people across the Atlantic hundreds of years before. Always, according to the tales, the Welshmen had inconveniently wandered off somewhere "more west." A few years earlier, a single-minded Celt, John Evans, got as far as the Mandan villages looking for them. True, some of the Mandans were lighter skinned than most other Indians, and, yes, they built Welsh-looking coracles. But, no, they did not know what John Evans was talking about.

By early June they could see mountains on the western horizon. Then they came to a series of impassable cascades. These were the Great Falls of the Missouri. There was nothing for it but to drag the boats and all the stores around the rapids until they reached smooth water again. They must have been deeply frustrated. They had so hoped that, like Mackenzie away to the north ten years before, they would have been able to make their way right across the continent with only a few short and easy portages.

The biggest boat was too heavy; it had to be left behind. For the other boats, they made crude rollers with logs. For day after day they pulled and pushed. As soon as one load had been taken forward, they had to make the 18-mile hike back to get another. It took three weeks.

Once back on the river, they paddled, poled, and towed themselves as fast as they could manage. Soon, the river (they called it the Jefferson) became a mountain torrent; the canoes could go no further. Now it was urgent that they found the Shoshone—Sacajawea's people—and traded for horses. Lewis and three others went ahead to try to make contact.

"After refreshing ourselves," wrote Lewis on the third day of his trek, "we proceeded on the top of the dividing ridge from which I discovered immense ranges of high mountains still to the west of us with their tops partially covered with snow." Lewis must have been devastated: he could see that there was now no possibility of a convenient portage to take them across to some river that would lead them easily down to the Pacific.

༼༽

I was sitting in the departure lounge at Salt Lake City waiting for a flight north to the town of Great Falls, to make preliminary arrangements for a film about the wheat harvest. On my knees was a large road atlas and it was turned to the double-spread of Montana; I was trying to work out how close the flight path would go to the Lewis-and-Clark country at the head of the Missouri. Maybe the man waiting in the next seat thought I was trying to find some small town. Anyway, he said that he was from Montana and asked if he could help. Well, maybe he could. He doubted that we would fly quite that far west; we would miss those particular mountains by about 100 miles. But he was a western history "buff" himself and, being an executive with Western Airlines, he would ask the pilot when we got aboard. Then, while we were about it, how was "jolly old London," and why not fly Club Class with him, courtesy of the airline? Thank you very much.

An hour later the aircraft seemed to bank slightly. My friend explained that there was no question of the pilot diverting by more than the smallest fraction from the airline's normal routing, but he might, for a few seconds, drop the port wing slightly

Lewis and Clark, Sacajawea, her baby, and her husband Toussaint Charbonneau (Denver Public Library)

so that "we can get a better view." It was one of those blue, mountain days when one can see for 100 miles or more. Somewhere ahead was Three Forks, and away off to the west, sliding under the wing, were the very foothills up which Lewis had struggled on Monday, August 12, 1805. On the farthest horizon, partially covered with snow, were what I reckoned to be the Salmon River Mountains, probably what Lewis could see from the crest of his windy ridge.

At 28,000 feet and close to 500 mph I did not learn much except an even greater wonder at the nerve of those first explorers; and that the Rockies stretched away forever, range after range. It was enough. I would not have missed it.

A few minutes later we were over the wheat country of the plains. Then we passed the broken water of the Missouri and landed at Great Falls. From my map I could see that the runway was just across the river from the place where the expedition put its boats back on the river after that 18-mile portage. I remember that, on leaving the aircraft, I was allowed to put my head round the door to the cockpit to thank the pilot for what might have been a slight divergence from his normal flight path.

"Well, we dodged over a little-bitty to the west," and I'm sure he gave a wink, "'cause we figured on some clear-air turbulence to the east—and we always aim to give you folks a real smooth ride."

"It was great. Thank you very much."

"You're welcome."

ᆼᅩ

As Lewis and his companions went on, they began to realize that the valleys and the streams had a westerly thrust to them. In geography and in history, they had crossed the continental divide. More prosaically, they were running out of food. Then, just when they were about to turn back, they came on four women. Two of them ran away. But an old woman and a young girl were too frightened or too slow to run. The white men tried to reassure them by sign language, and by giving them some beads and a small mirror. Suddenly, with a rushing of hooves, the explorers found themselves facing 60 or more warriors. Lewis put his gun on the ground and walked forward. The Indians sat their horses and watched; some fingered their bows. This was the most critical moment of the expedition so far. Then the old lady shouted; she seemed to be calling out that these strange pale beings had given her some presents. She ran across to show the beads. The Indians rode slowly forward. Perhaps the chief leaned down from his horse and touched Lewis to see what kind of man this was. It was enough.

"The men advanced and embraced me very affectionately in their way, which is by putting their left arm over your right shoulder, clasping your back, while they apply their left cheek to yours and frequently vociferate ah-hi-e, ah-hi-e, that is 'I am much pleased, I am much rejoiced!' We were all caressed and besmeared with their grease and paint till I was heartily tired of the national hug." Given his luck, Lewis seems unreasonably grumpy.

They spent the night in the Shoshone camp where they were received with much dancing and mutual smoking of ceremonial pipes. But it took two more frustrating days of sign language before the Indians could be persuaded to go back to meet the rest of the expedition. When they reached the prearranged rendezvous with the main party, there was no one there. The Indians became very edgy, fearful of some treachery. Lewis was on tenterhooks lest they took off for some hiding place where he would never find them or their horses again.

Now comes the moment so beloved by all tellers of the expedition's story, whether they are romantics or dry old realists. The Indians pointed to three distant figures coming up the river; Lewis recognized them as Clark, Charbonneau, and Sacajawea. Slowly the three figures came on, unaware that they were being watched. Then Sacajawea must have seen them; she knew immediately that they were her own people and, scrambling forward, she embraced the chief. Lewis reports rather flatly that "Captain Clark arrived with the Interpreter Charbono and the Indian woman who proved to be the sister of the Chief; the meeting of these people was really affecting."

The next day was Lewis' 30th birthday. He spent it giving presents to the Shoshone. The main party had now come up. With no time for a rest, they hid their canoes and transferred their loads to a string of newly bartered horses. Then whites and Indians made their way back into the mountains. As they wound their way up, the whites questioned their guides, presumably through Sacajawea, about the best route to reach the great western river, the Columbia.

On one point the information was quite specific: the upper Columbia (in fact the tributary now called the Salmon) was impassable to any rafts. Nor would horses be able to find a footing on the sheer canyon walls. If this were true—and Clark set off to verify it while Lewis bartered for more horses—it could be a disaster.

Clark was away for four days. He found that the river was everything that the Indians had claimed. Now, not only was there no hope of making a quick passage through the mountains, but gone too was the chance of establishing a workable route across the continent to the Pacific. Perhaps there was some easier way that they had missed? Anyway, with winter coming, they would have to scramble forward as fast as they could.

They said goodbye to their Shoshone friends. The next few weeks were the hardest of the whole journey. Often they had to climb high up along the ridges in the wind and clouds, with only the mistiest idea of where they were going. They were always cold and damp. They could find no game, so they ate dog. Their clothing was quite inadequate, their boots and moccasins were ripped and torn. At night, there was never enough dry wood to build a fire; anyway, they were usually too tired to try. Most of them had dysentery at one time or another, either that or an aching hunger. This was no way to reach the Pacific.

Coming down, at last, into the beautiful and warmer valley of the Bitterroot, they met Indians again. These were the friendly Flatheads. They paused long enough to regain some strength (they called the place Travelers' Rest) and to buy more horses. They also transcribed many words of the local language. "They appear to us as though they had an impediment in their speech." Welsh, perhaps? Anyway, Lewis, conscientious as ever, was taking no chances and noted down "the names of every thing in their Language, in order that it may be found whether they Sprang or origenated first from the welch."

A few miles beyond the Flatheads, they climbed into more mountains, more snow, more dysentery, more frostbite. Often they only managed to make nine or ten miles in the day, but the wonder is that, somehow, they kept going at all. Perhaps Sacajawea had something to do with it. If a 16-year-old mother with a papoose on her back could take the hardships ... It was during this scramble over the Lolo Pass that the expedition really came to admire the uncomplaining spirit of the girl. They had grown fond of the baby swaddled on her back, whom they called Pompey; it meant "little chief" in his mother's language.

At last they limped down into the easier valleys of the Pierced Nose Indians (the Nez Percé). The Indians told them that they were only a few days from a large river. It turned out to be the Clearwater and, on the evidence of the salmon they could see, they reckoned that it must eventually flow into the Columbia and thence into the Western Ocean. So now they built another flotilla of canoes, and left their horses with the Nez Percé. The worst, they hoped, was now behind. They reckoned that they had come 300 miles since they had hidden their boats back on the Jefferson; it had taken eight weeks.

℘

Today, in summer, the map shows that one can drive the whole distance from the Jefferson to the Clearwater in about five hours. I have not made the journey (one day perhaps), but the road winds through the same mountains and over the same passes; it follows the expedition's route, sometimes exactly, always within a few miles. Dynamite and bulldozers have made the difference. True, you will need to fit chains to your tires in autumn—if the road is still open. In winter it is firmly closed: both the Lost Trail Pass and the Lolo Pass are blocked by snow and ice. All this you can learn from any worthwhile road map. And you can see too that the Flatheads still have their lands, a reservation now, just to the north of Travelers' Rest.

❧

our rout lay along the ridge of a high mountain
course S20.W.—18. me used the snow for cooking.
Thursday September 19th 1805.
        Set out this morning a little after sunrise an
continued our rout about the same course of yesterday
or S.20.W. for 6 miles when the ridge terminated and
we to our inexpressable joy discovered a large
tract of Prairie country lying to the S.W. and widen
ing as it appeared to extend to the W. through that
plain the Indian informed us that the Columbia
river, (in which we were in surch) run. this plain
appeared to be about 60 Miles distant, but our guide
assured us that we should reach its borders tomorro
the appearance of this country, our only hope for
substance greatly, revived the sperits of the party
already reduced and much weakened for the want of
food. — the country is thickly covered with a very

An extract from Lewis' diary recording the crossing of the continental divide on 19 September, 1805 (Historical Picture Service, Chicago)

On water once more, the party's morale revived. They had no accurate way of knowing how far they were from the Pacific. In fact, they had nearly 300 miles to go. But now, traveling with the current, progress was much faster. Sometimes, round the "smokey" evening fire (smokey to drive off the "mesciters"?) they even found time to relax and laugh again: "After dark we played the fiddle and danced a little."

When they came out onto the Columbia, they were amazed at its size; it was even wider than the Missouri at St. Louis. Now they paddled easily toward the sea on the Great River of the West; it had been flowing through Lewis' mind ever since he had first read the accounts of Mackenzie and Gray. But ... if only there were an easier way across or around those cursed mountains.

Now the river broadened to nearly a mile, and the Indians hereabouts, the Chinooks, had canoes larger than any they had yet seen. Then they met a chief who kept repeating a phrase someone deciphered as "son-of-a-bitch." A day or two later they came up with another chief who wore a scarlet coat and carried a sword. It began to rain. The dugouts dipped to waves. They paddled on. Now gulls skimmed the boats, and the river grew to an estuary so wide that they could hardly see the other shore. The water became too salty to drink; the wind blew damp and raw; the beaches on which they camped each night showed the flotsam line of tides. Yet they still had not reached the sea.

For the next three days they took a terrible battering from gales which, blowing up the wide and unsheltered estuary, almost swamped their boats. Then one morning they saw far ahead a line of breakers where the "great Pacific Octean" pounded across the bar. It was November 7, 1805. The pathfinders of the prairies and the mountains had come at last to that "which we had been so long anxious to See." In 18 months they had trekked 2,000 miles. In elation, they must have felt like Columbus when he first made landfall in his imagined Cathay. But, unlike him, they had some idea of where they were and what they had done. More or less.

"Ocian in view!" noted Clark. "Oh, the joy!"

❧

Conscientious as ever, the two captains had already decided that there were too many questions of geography on which they had failed. So even if a ship *did* come into the Columbia and offer them passage home, they would have to refuse. They would have to go back the hard way in order to fill in the gaps. But there was no point in starting yet; the high country would be impassable with winter snow. So they chopped down some trees and knocked together some rude shacks; they ran up the flag and called the place Fort Clatsop—after the thieving local tribe. From November to April, the coast of what, today, we call the Pacific Northwest can be a very wet place indeed: day after day, the sodden winds blow in from the sea. The expedition's journal tells that, in five months, it stopped raining for just twelve days. Even then, everything dripped.

Inside the fort, they were out of liquor, tobacco and salt. Outside, the opportunities for R'n'R were limited. A few of the more energetic souls ambled off to a nearby establishment run by a Clatsop matron and her six "nieces." One of the nieces sported a tattoo which read "J. Bowmon." So, in more ways than one, someone had already been here. The captains disapproved of these goings-on, but on practical rather than moral grounds: there was the problem of payment. They were going to need all the trade goods they still had, to "pay" the various tribes during their return journey. In the end, they handed out a few colored ribbons and hoped for the best.

Not surprisingly, they all grew heartily sick of Fort Clatsop. In spring, as soon as the rains eased, they got ready to move. Before going, they carved their names on a few trees, raised more flags and handed out proclamations to the natives. While all this undoubtedly had an element of "Kilroy Was Here," it was also part of the ritual of declaring to any subsequent passersby that these parts were now formally claimed by the United States. On such very slender assertions of ownership, the nation was to become more than merely argumentative with the British three decades later.

On March 23, 1806, they abandoned Fort Clatsop and headed east. Four weeks later, when they reached the easygoing Nez Percé, they learned that the snows were still far too deep on the passes ahead; they would have to wait 30–40 "sleeps." This enforced idleness was infuriating to the captains, because there was so much to be done once they got beyond those mountains. But for everyone else, the delay in the spring sunshine of the high country must have been a golden time. The longer they stayed, the more they appreciated the hospitality of their hosts. They were given horses for food without mention of payment; they learned enough of the language to ease the monotony of only speaking to each other. That skill must have been handy when fraternizing with the younger of their hostesses. Indeed, after a few weeks, several of the explorers were quite ready to quit exploring. Apparently, even today, it is still a point of pride among a few families in that tribe to claim descent from those times; some even suggest that Captain Clark might be their five-times-great grandfather. There is no allusion to this possibility in the captain's journal.

When the expedition eventually pulled itself together to move on, it had spent seven contented weeks on the Clearwater.

Now, each man had a horse to ride and a pack-horse to lead. For five days they scrambled up, down, and along the ridges. On the sixth day, almost before they knew it, they were coming down to the warmth of the valleys again, to the comfortable place that earlier they had called Travelers' Rest. Now, the plan was to split into three different parties for the next six or seven weeks, so that they could cover more ground in searching for a better route through the mountains.

Lewis reckoned to take six men directly east to look for an easier line back to the Great Falls of the Missouri. Meanwhile, Clark would take the rest of the expedition off to the south, to the place where, the year before, they had left their canoes and their stores. A part of this group would then take the reloaded canoes directly downriver to the Great Falls, while Clark would try to find the headwaters of the Yellowstone River. If he and his small party succeeded, they would build a raft and float 400 miles down the Yellowstone until it flowed into the Missouri. There, at the junction of the two rivers, the three different parties would rendezvous in about six weeks' time.

Astonishingly, the plan worked just as they had hoped.

℘

Halfway down the Yellowstone there is what my guidebook mundanely called "a point of interest." Without stretching things, the writer might have been more enthusiastic. He or she is referring to the one and only "in situ" remnant that, today, one can see of the whole long expedition. Three weeks into Clark's raft journey down the Yellowstone, he noticed a massive sandstone outcrop half a mile or so from the river. He pulled in to the bank; he scrambled halfway up the outcrop and, in a looping script several inches high, he carved his name: Wm Clark July 25, 1806. "I marked my name and the day of the month and the year." Today, one climbs 100 feet or so up a series of steep wooden stairways to reach a small platform. From there, one looks across a gap of about 12 feet to this simple piece of graffiti. It is guarded by a thick panel of plate glass. Clark called the whole outcrop Pompey's Tower. Perhaps, as Clark left his mark, Pompey sat on his mother's hip and watched from below. One would like to think so. Today, the place is known as Pompey's Pillar. The afternoon I was there, I had the whole place, including the Visitors Center at the base of the cliff, entirely to myself— time and peace to wander and wonder. And to be not a little moved.

☙

Three weeks after he had "marked" his name, Clark and his small party arrived at the junction of the Yellowstone with the bigger Missouri. He was ahead of schedule, so he settled down to wait for Lewis and his party. They came in just two days later. They'd had a narrow escape when they had bumped into a small party of hostile Blackfeet. In getting away, they had killed two Indians. So, fearful that the remaining Blackfeet would summon a very much larger group of their fellows and come after them, Lewis and his men had just made a forced ride of over 100 miles in the previous 24 hours. Now that the whole expedition was together once again, the fiddle came out, and they "went to dancing" around their cooking fires. Then, extraordinarily, just as they were pushing off downriver, they met two white men coming the other way. Dickson and Hancock were the first whites that the expedition had seen since leaving the Mandan villages 16 months before. They were the forward scouts of an extraordinary army of trapper-adventurers who, over the next 30 years, would beaver their way into every valley and over every pass of the western mountains.

The news the two newcomers brought from downriver was discouraging. The Mandans were feuding with the Arikara; the Minatarees were squabbling with each other, and the Sioux were being bloody-minded toward the world in general. The expedition would have to run this complex gauntlet.

Before they paddled on, the two trappers asked if anyone could be spared from the expedition to join them as a partner and guide. John Colter was keen to go, and asked for his discharge; perhaps he was one of those people who prefer the dangers of the wilderness to the comforts of civilization. Anyway, he collected his few belongings and headed back west again with his newfound companions. But we will meet him again, for John Colter was now taking his first steps towards becoming his own special legend.

When the expedition arrived at the Mandan and Minataree villages, the inhabitants were only too happy to see the white men again; they represented protection against their enemies. Charbonneau announced that he and his wife wanted to stay with the Mandans, where they had started. So please, could they have their wages, $500 for the last 17 months? Clark wanted to take Sacajawea's young Pompey, of whom he had become very fond, on to St. Louis for a white man's education. His mother said that perhaps she would bring him when he was a little bigger. After all, he was not yet fully weaned. They gave one of their guns to a local chief, "to ingratiate him more strongly in our favor." Then they pushed off.

One hopes that the Charbonneau family came down to the bank to wave goodbye.

Now there were only 1,500 miles to go. With the current behind them, they could make 50 miles a day and hardly raise a sweat. In the afternoons, the sun "warmed our backs." But, in the evenings, as always, "the mosquetors were excessive troublsom." (Of the two captains, Clark was the more inventive speller.) They paused several times for diplomatic meetings with various tribes. But when they came to the Sioux, they drifted past with their weapons leveled. The Sioux pranced about on the bank and shouted an invitation for the expedition to step ashore, so that they could all have a good fight. "We took no notice."

As they went on, Lewis and Clark must surely have felt some pride in what they had done. By their leadership and judgement, they had not only held their men together under the greatest hardships, but they had forged them into an extraordinarily efficient "Corps of Discoverie." In the whole long journey they had taken only two lives—those two Blackfeet. Even then, it had been "take or be taken." Above all, they were fortunate in each other: never once had they had a serious disagreement. So, it is entirely appropriate that in all the subsequent histories, one name is hardly ever mentioned without the other. Captains Lewis and Clark were a most remarkable pair.

There were more traders on the river than there had been two years before. Every few days the expedition would sight a new party and, to a shouted welcome, pull over to a sandbank and talk. The traders would have been astonished to see them; the whole party had long been given up for lost. Indeed, the river-men had been specially asked by President Jefferson to try to find out what had happened. Even to these hardened river-traders, the men who now clambered out of their canoes and waded across to ask for news of home must have seemed as if they had come back from the dark side of the moon. Burnt as brown as any Indian, they would have had a way of standing, talking and laughing among themselves which would have marked them as men who had been alone together for a very long time. To those other men, so lately come from "civilization," everything about this brotherhood must have been intriguing: their ragged but serviceable clothes, their questions, their stories, their music and songs, their jokes and ribaldries, even the Indian patois they sometimes used among themselves. They had been away for over two years.

Five weeks after leaving the Mandans, the expedition's flotilla steered out of the Missouri onto the Mississippi. A few more miles and they could see St. Louis—now under the American flag. After all that they had been through, their diaries for Tuesday, September 23, 1806 are marvelously matter-of-fact. "12 o'Clock," wrote one of the Sergeants, "we arrived in Site of St Louis, fired three rounds as we approached the Town ... then the party all considerable much rejoiced that we have the Expedition Completed and now we look for boarding in Town." So, they were back to the mundane reality of civilization: looking for lodgings. Sergeant Gass concludes, "We were received with great kindness and marks of friendship by the inhabitants, after an absence of two years, four months and ten days." Perhaps, for the time being, that was all that was worth saying. They seem to have been men of no recognizable pretensions.

And what of Sacajawea and young Pompey? Captain Clark wrote repeating his earlier offer to educate the lad. He even offered, if the family came down to St. Louis, to see Charbonneau set up as a small trader or farmer. In due course, the family arrived. Clark kept his promises. He looked after the growing boy and made himself responsible for his education. Later, while still in his teens, Pompey met the touring Prince Paul of Wurtemburg; he must have been a personable lad because the Prince took him back to Europe. By the time Pompey returned to the United States it is said that he spoke at least three languages. Sadly, other than working for a time as a guide, he then seems to disappear. His mother too poses a mystery. Most histories report her dying of "the bloody flux" while still a young woman, somewhere in what is now North Dakota. But to this day the Shoshone people, *her* people, insist that she lived to be over 90 and is buried on their reservation in western Wyoming. Her gravestone is there for all to see.

The fact is that Lewis and Clark's expedition had not found an easy or practical route to the Pacific shore or beyond to China; they had not discovered an obvious path for settlement; they had not laid an indisputable claim to new lands. But they had been to the Farthest Beyond, and returned; that was their achievement. In time, when the news spread, it would add immeasurably to their young nation's self-confidence and knowledge of itself. From now on, Americans would come to know that, despite all the difficulties, the journey right across the continent to the other ocean could be made—*had* been made. In time, other Americans, traveling by other routes, would be spurred to go themselves. Most of the continent was theirs—if they could take it. In the end, surely that was what mattered about Lewis and Clark; that was their achievement.

"I received, my dear sir, with unspeakable joy your letter of Sep 23 announcing the return of yourself & your party in good health to St Louis."
A letter from President Jefferson to Captain Lewis

4

MOUNTAIN MEN

"To Enterprising Young Men: the subscriber wishes to engage One Hundred Men to ascend the river Missouri to its source, there to be employed for one, two or three years."

An advertisement for would-be fur trappers, in a St. Louis newspaper of February 13, 1822

"A description of our crew I cannot give, but Falstaff's Battalion was genteel in comparison. They had little fear of God and none of the devil."

Jedediah Smith, one of those "enterprising young men," writing some years later

❧

It was a peculiarity of beaver fur that would bring about the animal's near extermination: just below the coarse and bristly outer hairs was an undercoat of fine, almost fluffy down. The fibers of this down were lined with microscopic hooks which, when the hairs had been plucked and matted together under a steamy pressure, held them together in a strong and glossy blanket. Apparently, there is no other animal whose pelt has quite this same felting property. Toward the end of the eighteenth century, the dandies of London, Paris, New York and Philadelphia demanded that their top hats and coat collars be covered with this shiny felt; army officers wanted tricorn beaver hats; ladies bought beaver trimmings for their cloaks. Given the hardships and dangers of the trapping, and then the immense distances involved in getting the pelts to the customers, it is no surprise that anything made with beaver fur was very expensive and, thereby, a symbol of status. So, among the wealthy it was a "must-have" item. Incidentally, mercury was an ingredient in the felting process and, in the final steaming and ironing, it gave off mind-bending fumes—which, apparently, is why we still talk about someone being "as mad as a hatter."

The demand for these beaver luxuries was such that the British Hudson Bay Company, even though it was reaching ever further to the west, could not keep pace. So the Americans could see no reason why they should not join in the business.

Among the first Americans that we know about were Dickson and Hancock—that pair who came paddling up the Missouri just as Lewis, Clark and Company came drifting down it. They knew as much about where they were going as, today, most of us know about the back of the moon. So, it made good sense to persuade John Colter to join them as a partner. He led them back to a place that Lewis and Clark had called Three Forks. There they trapped through the fall and into the winter. Then, in the spring, Colter left his two companions (he obviously didn't care for crowds) and went off trapping on his own. Later that summer he made himself a raft, loaded his furs and, alone, set off downstream for civilization. He had been in the wilderness for over three years. Two months later, somewhere on the lower Missouri when he was almost "home," he met one of the first of the big fur-parties coming upstream ...

When, only the previous autumn, the astonished people of St. Louis had turned out to welcome Lewis and Clark, the congratulations of one particular citizen had been mingled with some sharp-eared questions about trade, minerals and beaver. By the next spring, Manuel Lisa, having recruited several members of the Lewis and Clark party, was leading them upstream when he met Colter coming downstream. Lisa turned him around. He may have wanted Colter less for what he knew than for what, if he let him go back to St. Louis, he might tell any rival party coming on behind.

Lisa and his *engagés* (paid hands) made good progress and even persuaded the Arikara and the Mandan to harass any other traders who might be following behind. By the first snows the expedition had turned off the Missouri and reached up the Yellowstone. At the confluence of the Yellowstone and the Bighorn, Lisa decided to build a small fort, a trading post. (It would have been about the size of a tennis court.) While the place was being built, scouts were sent out to find Indians (probably the Crow) and to spread the word about the fantastic bargains—beads, iron pots, knives and rotgut whiskey—that were being offered for beaver pelts. Manuel Lisa knew that for an axe, some whiskey or a handful of bright beads which might have cost 25 cents in St. Louis he could now get two prime beaver pelts which when, eventually, he got them back to St. Louis would be worth $4 or $5 each. True, he had the dangers of that three or four-month journey upriver, and then the next summer two months downstream again. But if the Indians thought *they* were the ones who had got the best of the deal, everyone was happy. It was this prodigious, but life-risking profit that was to drive the beaver business for the next 30 years.

It seems doubtful that Colter was much bothered by thoughts of profit. He was just an archetypal loner. So now, in the fall, he set off alone from Lisa's fort on an amazing circular journey of more than 500 winter miles. (During this trek, he "discovered" the country that now forms Yellowstone National Park.) When he got back to the fort in late spring, he so convinced Lisa that the farther stretches of the high country were swarming with beaver that Lisa decided to go back the 1,600 miles to St. Louis to fetch more trade goods and to raise an even bigger expedition. Meanwhile Colter set off again on another lone marathon.

It was on this second trip that he fell foul of the Blackfeet—the same people from whom he and Captain Lewis had so narrowly escaped near the Marias River two years before. He was traveling with a band of friendly Crow and, in an ambush that turned into a running fight, he was wounded in the leg. Somehow he managed to escape and limp back 150 miles to the fort. As soon as the wound was healed he was off again. But for this trip, he teamed up with another old Lewis-and-Clark friend, John Potts. This time, somewhere near Three Forks, where only two years before there had been a complete absence of Indians, the Blackfeet struck again. Legend has it that just before the two whites were captured, John Potts shot one of the chiefs. So now, furious at this death and angered in any case by the way the whites had been trading arms with their Crow enemies, they took John Potts and slit him open. They threw his guts in Colter's face. Then, for sport, they stripped Colter naked and told him to run. Most men would have just prayed for a quick end—though the Blackfeet did not usually grant that mercy to their captives. Anyway, Colter ran.

After several miles, there was just one brave left in the chase. Colter could not shake him off. So at the last possible moment he turned and managed to snatch the man's lance. He ran him through. Then he dashed on. By now, totally exhausted, he dived into a river and, standing with just his mouth breaking the surface, he hid beneath some driftwood. By some miracle, the Indians never found him.

He came out at night. He had no clothes, no shoes, no weapons, no map, and, most people would reckon, no hope. He traveled mainly at night, he lived on roots and berries; he reckoned his course by the stars and by the rivers. He took nine days to hobble back to the fort; blood covered his legs and feet like thick varnish. "If God will only forgive," he is said to have vowed, "I will leave this country—and I will be damned if I ever come into it again." That spring, Manuel Lisa had been back to St. Louis to fetch more supplies and to recruit more trappers. Now, in late summer, he was on his way north again when he met a familiar figure coming downriver. And Lisa turned him around. Yes, it was John Colter. Already, he had forgotten that vow.

 C/)

In May 2011 I was in Billings, Montana. During an evening barbeque with friends (Western history buffs, of course) they told me they had something I should see. So the next morning we drove 30 miles east to the confluence of the Bighorn and the Yellowstone Rivers. This, it has long been known, was where Manuel Lisa had built his first fort-cum-trading-post. In two centuries both rivers have slightly changed their courses, so my friends' efforts to find the fort's exact location had been fruitless. Nevertheless, in the course of that search, they stumbled on something no less remarkable. A few hundred yards from the Bighorn, on the hidden and shady overhang of an enormous boulder, are two scraps of what one might call historic graffiti. Still faintly visible, in six-inch capitals which have defied the winter and summer weathering of two hundred years, are carved two names: M. LISA 1807 and, close by, COLTER 1810. All I could do was stare and wonder. Words failed me then, and they do so now —except to say that one would have to be historically dyslexic not to be moved by those time-distant and almost immortal scratchings.

C/)

During the next two years, Lisa's men pushed out further and further from their river bases. As long as they moved through the country of the Crow they were fairly safe. But, away to the northwest, where instinct fueled by rumor told them there were the best beaver streams of all, they were blocked by the terrible

Blackfeet. These warriors were savage enough in their own right, but they were also acting as mercenaries for the British—for the Hudson Bay and the North West Companies. So, anyone who thought to poke about too deeply to the northwest was taking an often fatal risk. At the same time, there was rumor of yet another competitor ...

In his paneled New York office, John Jacob Astor had been looking at his maps—maps not just of North America but of the world. Ever since he had arrived from Germany as a young man more than 20 years before, Astor had been looking for ways to make his fortune. Now he hatched a scheme to send a party overland all the way to the mouth of the Columbia, maybe using Lewis and Clark's recently published account as a guide. Once on the Pacific, his men would meet up with a store-ship sent around Cape Horn. Together, they would establish a fort from which they could spread out to harvest all the beaver trade of the far west; they would collar the sea-otter business of the Pacific coast, and then start a seaborne trading empire with the Chinese; the prices *they* paid for furs (particularly for those of the sea otter) were beyond dreams.

A man called Wilson Hunt was put in charge of the overland party. Arriving in St. Louis, he set about recruiting a crew of French-Canadian *voyageurs* and a stiffening of Kentucky hunters. This blend of the quirky and the dour seems to have become characteristic of the developing mountain trade.

Also in St. Louis was Manuel Lisa; he did his best to sabotage Hunt's recruiting drive by spreading tales of the danger and death that lay ahead. But Hunt and his crew of Astorians, as they came to be known, got themselves together and raced off up the Missouri ahead of Lisa. It took him 1,000 miles to catch up, and then the competing parties rowed along opposite banks keeping a close eye on each other.

Somewhere along the way, the Astorians heard of a quicker way of getting west. So they traded their riverboats to Lisa and he, thankful to be rid of these rivals, sold them some horses. They left the river and cut off overland in a direct line for the mountains. In seeking the far Pacific, the Astorians had an appalling journey. They lost men to cold, to starvation and, when they took to the rushing waters on the far side of the mountains, to drowning. Fifteen months after leaving St. Louis, the first stragglers came down the Columbia and found the ship-borne party waiting for them. Together, they built a fortified encampment and called it Astoria. Presently, another supply ship arrived from New York. So, in spite of the hardships and the huge distances, it seemed that Astor's imaginative strategy was going to work. From the comfort of New York, he had thrown a seed across to the far side of the continent.

But the seed withered. Maybe the feeling of isolation was too much; maybe their terrible journey and the knowledge of their utter dependence on the chancy arrival of an occasional ship demoralized them; maybe the news (brought by the second supply ship) that the Americans and the British were at war (the War of 1812), and that the British navy was coming to take them cracked their resolve; maybe they just realized that, even if successful, there was likely to be very small reward for them in the whole enterprise. Whatever the reasons, they crumpled almost as soon as the British North-West Company appeared on their doorstep. Eighteen months after building their fort they sold it (Astor never forgave them) for a few thousand dollars to the British, who renamed it Fort George. One month later, in November 1813, a British frigate arrived to take formal possession of all the Columbia shore.

In fact, well before this change of possession, a small party of Astorians had already left for St. Louis with dispatches for Astor. Attempting to find an easier route, they took a more southerly course than they had taken on their outward journey. In so doing, they hit on one of the very few reasonable passages over the continental backbone. A St. Louis newspaper later reported their discovery in a single sentence: "By information received from these gentlemen, it appears that a journey across the continent of North America might be performed with a wagon, there being no obstruction in the whole route that any person would dare call a mountain." They had discovered the South Pass.

❧

Stop your car on Wyoming Route 28 and stand in the middle of South Pass today in summer, and you can see only the most distant snowcaps. Despite the fact that you are at over 7,000 feet, so gradual is the ascent that you would not realize that you are on the continental backbone. But if you know where to look in the sagebrush (or can persuade someone to show you, as I had to do), you can still see some ruts made by the wagon wheels which, more than 150 years ago, well after the Astorians, rolled this way to California and to Oregon. And if you really strain your ears, you might hear the oxen of the Forty-Niners, the hooves of the Pony Express, the rattling hand-carts of the Mormons, and the wind singing in the wires of the Overland Telegraph.

All took this same path over the Rockies: up the wide valley of the Platte, along the Sweetwater, then over South Pass. Although the Astorians did not really appreciate it, the discovery of this new route across the continent was undoubtedly their greatest achievement.

⌭

John Jacob Astor had no crystal ball and so could know none of this. To him, his whole ambitious enterprise must have seemed a colossal waste of time. After all, to him the discovery of South Pass did not pay off in the only currency that mattered: hard cash.

By now, in the mountains, there was a scatter of itinerant freebooters who owed no particular allegiance to any particular company. We do not know much about them as individuals, except that many were of French descent and only a few survived long enough to reach even middle age. But we can assume that sometimes they would turn up in St. Louis to sell their pelts, then swagger off to the taverns to quench a thirst worked up over two or three years. They would brag of fights with grizzly bears, of escapes from Indians, of snakebites survived, of cold so fierce that your urine froze on its way to the ground. But, like fishermen who know a good hole, they did not talk too much about where they had been or where they were going. Yet word would get round of the money that could be made—if you kept your scalp and moved quietly.

⌭

I needed a few shots of beavers in their natural habitat for a sequence about the mountain men and the fur trade. But there are very few beavers left. Inquiries revealed that we might be able to find one or two in the protected environment of the Teton National Park. So, a few days later, a game warden led us to a beaver dam. We set up the camera. We waited for most of two mosquito-swatting days without seeing

45

a thing. Then we tried another dam. Again, no luck. As I really needed these beaver shots, and time was short, we got on the phone and eventually tracked down a man 300 miles away somewhere south of Salt Lake City. He ran a beaver farm and, yes, he could let us have a couple of beavers for $80 each. Cash. Half would be returnable, he said, if he got the animals back when we had finished with them. "Sorta Renta Beava, I guess."

So we drove their cages up to a mountain stream and then, standing just clear of camera shot, we let them go. After getting all the film we needed in ten minutes, we spent a muddy hour—with help from the beaver man—shooing them back into their cages.

Then down the mountain again. Some weeks later, back in London, the BBC accountants thought to query an item of my filming expenses: "Please explain the item 'Two beavers on sale-or-return, $80.'"

ᘒ

Always there were young men who would hear the challenge of the mountains, and wonder. So when, early in 1822, they read an advertisement in the *Missouri Gazette*, they did not waste time. "To Enterprising Young Men. The subscriber wishes to engage One Hundred Men, to ascend the river Missouri to its source, there to be employed for one, two or three years. For particulars, inquire of Major Andrew Henry who will ascend with and command the party. Signed: Wm. H. Ashley."

Within a month, Ashley and his partner, Major Henry, had all their men: a few of them already knew something of the beaver business; the rest were green recruits. Ashley was the Lieut. Governor of Missouri and had been watching the haphazard potential of the fur trade for some time. He himself had never been near the mountains, but his partner, Henry, was an old hand. Together, they discussed a modification to the normal methods of the mountain trade: instead of contracting trappers on a fixed wage at the going rate of about $300 a season, they would equip each man (with traps and the like) to go out and do his own trapping; at the same time the partners would announce a meeting place for the next summer. In short, each trapper would be paid according to the number of pelts he brought in to the meeting place. It was the beginning of the Rendezvous system.

Ashley's semi-freelance recruits—Ashley's Hundred, as they were known—had all the usual disasters going upstream. In the spring flood, the Missouri could be, and usually was, a bitch. Day after day, the men were up to their waists dragging the boats through the slacker and shallower water. Where a footing was impossible, they had to pole or row. Just occasionally, when the wind blew from behind, they could hoist a square sail. Then, when the river twisted away from the wind, they had to get back in the water again. The journey upriver could take four months, God and the Indians willing.

Sometimes the Indians were not willing, and the Almighty was not much help either. The enterprise was still young when it suffered an almost total disaster. Ashley was coming upriver with a year's supplies for his partner Major Henry, who, the previous year, had stayed to build a fort-cum-trading-post—a permanent rendezvous point. Ashley knew that the passage past the unpredictable Sioux would be tricky, but he hoped that, with some bluff and bribery, he could get by. In any case, he wanted to buy 40–50 horses from the tribe. On landing, he and his crew were cordially received. Presents were given, horses were traded, pipes were passed around. But, to the expedition's interpreter, a man who knew his Indians, everything was going far too smoothly. He told Ashley of his suspicions. The warning was taken seriously enough for half the men to be ordered to spend the night in the boats, anchored in midstream. The remainder camped on a sandy spit with the horses.

Some time after midnight, shouting was heard; then shots. The shore party, most of them inexperienced at this kind of encounter, tried to get themselves organized. In the dark the Indians crept closer. Then, at first light, with clearer targets, they began to pick off the whites one by one. Shallow water prevented the keelboats from going in to rescue them. Things quickly became desperate; the men on the bank were falling every few minutes. In the end, those remaining were forced to swim for it.

Ashley dragged aboard those of the shore party who made it, then ordered the anchor ropes to be cut. The boats swung away downriver. A head-count showed that 15 men were missing, presumably shot or drowned; 11 were wounded. They drifted most of the day until, after 30 miles, they anchored to take stock. Ashley was persuaded that the only way of rescuing his and Henry's enterprise was to turn away from the river and, while the Young Men of Enterprise still had enough horses and pack-mules, to make for the mountains directly, overland to the country of the more hospitable Crow. That summer the Sioux and the Blackfeet were quite unapproachable; all movement on the Missouri was stalled. Altogether about 25 whites were killed, and at least as many wounded.

Ashley's Young Men of Enterprise were the recruits who, only a few months before, had answered that advertisement in St. Louis. Yet within a few years, these greenhorns would become some of the most renowned (though not always the most loved) of the mountain men. They would lead extraordinarily dangerous lives: from hostile Indians, grizzly bears, rattlesnakes, drowning, near starvation, months of sub-zero temperatures, and all kinds of accidents far from help. There are tales of men performing their own amputations. Before they had reached middle age (and not many lived to reach even that modest level of ripeness) they would have trudged over every worthwhile pass, and poked their way into every valley, canyon, cranny and corner of their mountains.

At this point, and in parenthesis, the point must be made that historians have two rather different views about the fur trade and, more particularly, the men involved in it. To many, these were "knights in buckskin"—indeed, that is the title of a chapter in a book by Dee Brown, the western historian and author of the best-selling *Bury My Heart at Wounded Knee*. He and others, while accepting that the fur trade had a corrupting influence on the tribes, emphasize the epic style of the business and the cold courage of its participants. It is difficult to resist that interpretation. But a few others, for example John Terrell in his book *Land Grab*, take a different stance—though the criticism is aimed less at the trappers and more at the traders who organized the business. "In the code of the fur trader," writes Terrell, "cheating was a virtue. The greater his accomplishment in the practice, the more the trader was to be congratulated and envied ..." Elsewhere, he continues, "the industry that the Mountain Men represented was without a redeeming quality, and wherever they went corruption, disease and ruination were sure to follow." Yes, those are selected quotes, but they are representative. Perhaps the truth lies—if there is ever an objective verity in such things—somewhere between the two interpretations. But on one aspect all seem agreed: the gall, guts and unalloyed grit of the mountain men, entirely selfish though it often was, has had very few parallels—anywhere at any time.

Consider just one of those young Men of Enterprise: Hugh Glass. Somewhere on that overland trek to the mountains, he was out ahead of the main party looking for game. Going into a thicket, he surprised a grizzly with her cubs. She took him by the throat. Two other hunters heard his screams and she let go to chase them off. Two shots brought her down. By the time the main party arrived, Glass was dying. But the party could not afford for everyone to wait till he faded away. So the leader, Major Henry, asked two reluctant volunteers, Jim Bridger and John Fitzgerald, to remain behind until Glass's life finally gave out. Glass lingered for five days, then slipped into a seemingly lifeless coma. His two "carers" reckoned he would be dead within the hour. There was nothing more to do, and they had many miles to catch up; so they left him.

Four or five weeks later, and more than 100 miles away, he staggered down to the Missouri. Some Indians found him and, more compassionate than usual, took him to the nearest white men. He never talked much about his ordeal, but apparently he had recovered consciousness to find his guardians and his gun gone. So, deciding not to die, he dragged himself to a stream where he found some berries. He thought that he had lain there for about ten days; his wounds would not heal, but at least he gathered a little strength. Then he stumbled on. After two or three days he came on a buffalo calf not long killed by (presumably) wolves; he gnawed on the bones. He crawled on, living on roots, berries, anything that would keep him alive. At one point, he found some maggots in a decaying buffalo carcass; he used them to eat away some of his rotting flesh. It took five weeks to crawl those 100 miles.

After just two months of recovery Glass was off again, joining a small party of trappers who were determined to risk the passage up the Missouri. The Arikara caught and killed them; only Glass and one other managed to escape, but they became separated. Any normal man would have turned back; Glass went on. Over 400 miles later, on the last day of 1824, he walked into the camp of Andrew Henry and his original companions; they were wintering with the Crow. It is said that it was his obsession for revenge on the two men who had abandoned him that gave him the steel to survive. Maybe. But having at last caught up with Bridger and Fitzgerald, he forgave them both.

Now, at last, one might have thought that Hugh Glass would have settled down to do a little trapping. But within two months he was off again. In late February, Glass and four others volunteered to take a cargo of pelts 700 miles down the Platte River valley to Fort Kiowa on the Missouri. By the time they reached the upper Platte the ice had broken, so they built a bullboat—a large coracle covered with green buffalo hides. They swirled down on the spring flood until they passed a camp of friendly Pawnee. The Indians hailed them and invited them to stop for a feast. They accepted. While gorging themselves, some Pawnee women began to ransack their boat. Too late they realized that these were not Pawnee at all. They were Arikara, several hundreds of miles out of position.

Within minutes, two of the whites were dead. The other three escaped, but became separated. Glass had also lost his gun. So here he was once again, hundreds of miles from help, with nothing but the clothes on his back, a knife and a fire-making flint. Perhaps he reflected that, at least, this time he was slightly better equipped than he had been after that mauling by the grizzly. He took three months, often traveling at night and always on the look-out for possible enemies, to creep 600 miles down the Platte valley to a fort on the Missouri—the full length of present-day Nebraska. At the fort, he decided that he could do with some civilization. So he took a passing riverboat for St. Louis. But town life did not suit him. So he signed on with a wagon train bound for Santa Fe. Evidently, he worked in those parts for several years until he must have felt the call of the northern plains and the mountains once again. So back he came.

Somewhere up on the high plains—no one seems to know quite where—he bumped into his old enemies just once too often. The Arikara finally got him. Hugh Glass was not yet 35. The brave who took him could not have known it, but that scalp (if there was anything left of it) belonged to one of the truly great ones.

But lest one thinks that Glass was unusual, Jedediah Smith walked close behind. He too was caught by a grizzly. Besides several broken ribs, he was badly mauled about the head. He suggested that if someone in his party had a needle and thread, he would be much obliged if they would sew him up. A friend volunteered. "I put my needle through and through, and over and over. The bear had laid the skull bare ... one of his ears was torn from his head." In those days, alcohol was the only anesthetic. Jedediah Smith was a strict teetotaler. Within a few days, he had passed himself for duty—light duty, anyway.

Smith and his companions camped that autumn in a mountain valley with some friendly Crows. By late December, as always, it became too cold for trapping, and with the high-country rivers freezing, it was hibernation time for both beavers and humans. Inside the Crow tepees or in hurriedly built huts of pine logs (roofed with buffalo hides) the men could keep reasonably warm while they busied themselves with various winter tasks. The literate Jedediah, when done with his chores, wrote long letters home. "You may well suppose that our society is of the roughest kind. Men of good morals seldom enter into business of this kind. I hope you will remember me before the throne of Grace ... Pray for me."

Through the winter, the trappers worked at repairing their moccasins and clothing, casting lead into bullets, servicing their traps, sharpening their skinning knives, arguing and telling tall tales, and flirting with the Crow girls. In the evenings, someone might get out a book and read aloud to anyone (many of them were illiterate) who cared to listen. And always there would be discussions about what lay beyond those mountains away to the west. Which was the easiest pass? What was the temper of the tribes in that direction? Were there many beaver?

By late March, the cold was easing; the ice on the streams was breaking up; it was time to get down to business. First, one had to find the beaver—that was the easy part. The signs were fairly obvious: the enormous nest-like dams built across the streams, the newly chewed tree stumps, perhaps an animal or two scuttling about in the shallows. One had to wade through freezing water while laying the traps; one had to judge just the right places to put them below the surface; one had to bait the traps carefully with "castoreum"—not too little, not too much. This was an oily substance taken from the creature's anal glands; beavers would scent a supposed interloper and come to investigate. Then, the next day, if the trapper was successful, he had to wade out to kill his catch and reset his traps. Next came the labor of skinning the catch (a beaver could weigh up to 60 lbs) and stretching the skins on hoops of mountain willow. But the rewards were considerable. A good trapper might take 200–300 pelts a season; a prime one might be worth $3 at next summer's Rendezvous.

By now, the Rendezvous had become the established system; it allowed the trappers to stay out in the wilderness and have the St. Louis fur companies send out pack-trains to some spot arranged the year before. So, for a few weeks every summer, a chosen valley (or "hole," as they were often known) would become something between a sprawling bazaar and an orgiastic picnic. One imagines that if those involved were still sober enough to know what they were doing, the more formal business of buying and selling—pelts in one direction, supplies in the other—was quickly done. What really mattered was what followed: drinking, gambling, wrestling, fornicating, horse-racing, more drinking and, by all accounts, much brawling at a level well beyond mere fisticuffs. After all, many of the trappers—not much bothered by the conventions of polite society at the best of times—had been working in loneliness for most of the year. They had been looking forward to the Rendezvous for many months; some of them would have journeyed for several weeks to get there. Now, as they wound their way down from a pass with their pelt-laden mules trailing behind them, they found, spread out in smoky chaos across the mountain meadow below, everything long-isolated men might long for: companionship, news of friends (and enemies), whiskey and rum, sugar and coffee, singing and wild dancing, gambling and more whiskey, camp gossip and the latest "reports" from the far United States. And maybe an older trapper might find himself a new woman—more likely to augment the wifely duties of the one he had already than to replace her. Polygamy was common. The younger, apprentice trapper might also be on the look-out for an Indian girl who, according to most accounts, was also likely to be on the alert for a lasting liaison. Some of those relationships did indeed last a lifetime; others were over before the tepee poles had been lowered at the end of the Rendezvous.

For the trappers, once in the mountains, the Indians were seldom a problem. Probably, most of the mountain tribes were friendly because it suited them to be; the trappers brought them much useful "medicine": guns, lead shot, powder, pots, knives, fire-flints, blankets, mirrors, trinkets and, always, whiskey. As already implied, many mountain men married Indian women and became almost Indians themselves. Indeed, at least one writer has suggested that the phrase we use about someone "going native" stems from these times. Anyway, intermarriage further strengthened the bonds of mutual respect. Indeed, to this day, the Crow people of Montana seem to have many more "whiteman" names than, say, the Sioux—and seem to be more relaxed about using them.

But out across the plains, for a trapper or supply train trekking west toward the richer beaver country of the mountains, the risks were considerable; they stemmed from the sheer unpredictability of those more nomadic tribes. Last year's friends could be this year's belligerents. Horse stealing was almost a hobby, particularly among the Sioux. Without horses (or mules), one's chances of survival might be halved. Most of the fault lay with the whites. The tribes could reasonably accuse them of treachery—making agreements in the spring that they would break in the fall. Often, of course, it would be a different party of whites in the fall: a party who might not know of the pipes that had been smoked in the spring. Similarly it might be a different band of Indians. It was all very confusing, and risky. Often the whites were literally gambling with their lives.

Although, exceptionally, he was not a gambler in any normal sense, Jedediah Smith (he whose head had been "laid bare" by that grizzly) was one of the greatest risk-takers of all. Perhaps encouraged by the success of various earlier "journies of discoverie," and certainly by what was obviously his own innate curiosity, he now became the leader of an extraordinarily audacious expedition. While the declared motive was to find more beavers, Smith seemed to see himself as much as an explorer as a trapper. Some historians have rated him the equal of Lewis and Clark. Certainly, over the next few years, he would travel many more miles and add at least as much to the known geography of the west. And he did so without any government support or funds. For example, in 1826, starting from a Rendezvous well north of the present site of Salt Lake City, and aged just 26, he led a handful of companions through some of the most inhospitable terrain on the continent: across the desert of today's Nevada to a small adobe village near the sea that the Spaniards in those parts called Los Angeles. Having had to eat their horses, the party finished the journey on foot. Even today, the 700-mile journey southwest across Utah and Nevada into southern California, down Interstate 15, should not be undertaken in high summer without a reliable car, several bottles of water, a full tank of gas, and air-conditioning. Across the Mojave Desert the temperature can reach 130°F.

The Spaniards thought that Smith was a spy. So they took him to their Governor in San Diego. However, with the support of some American sea captains who were in port, he managed to persuade the authorities that he and his crew were just a bunch of inquisitive Yankees. The Governor let him go, on condition that he promised to return home the same way that he had come. Once out of sight, Smith and his crew cut north to what today is California's Central Valley. Early the next spring, leaving some of his crew behind to hunt beaver, Smith and just three companions headed inland from San Francisco Bay. Having forced a way through the snows of the high Sierras, they trekked out onto the aridity of today's Nevada and, eventually, across the salt flats of Utah. Again, they survived only by killing and eating several of their horses. Incredibly they arrived back exactly on time for the 1827 Rendezvous. In a year, Smith and his three companions had traveled over 1,700 miles.

The next year he set off again, on an even longer journey. Again, on arrival in California, he was arrested. Again, he was released on condition that he retraced his steps. Again, he slid off to the north and rejoined his crew from the year before. Now, instead of returning across Nevada, he and his men headed further north, trapping through the coastal forests for 700 miles to the estuary of the Columbia. Near the end of this journey they were attacked and lost 15 men, their horses and all their pelts. Jedediah and three others escaped—they had been traveling an hour or two ahead of the main party. A few days later they reached the Hudson Bay's trading post of Fort Vancouver, across the Columbia River from today's Portland. The Scottish factor at the fort promptly sent out a heavily armed party to recover the furs and the stolen horses. The sortie was successful. The Scot generously bought the recovered loot from Smith. So now, unencumbered by heavy bales of pelts, the Americans could make their way home relatively swiftly. By the time he and his small band eventually made their long way back up the Columbia to the Rockies, found their friends, and told of their adventures, Jedediah Smith would have traveled an amazing 4,000 miles, much of it on foot, in the previous two years.

By now, the boom years of the fur trade were passing. Over-trapping was the problem. So Smith, together with his partner Sublette (they called themselves the American Fur Company), beavered on for one more year and then, in 1830, they withdrew to St. Louis. Once home, Smith and Sublette counted their considerable profits and looked around for some other venture in which they might invest. They decided to buy 20 large wagons and load them to the gunnels with half a million dollars' worth of trade goods. They would enter the burgeoning trade southwest to Santa Fe; Jedediah would lead the caravan on its first journey. Four weeks into the trek, and somewhere on a dry stretch between the Arkansas and Cimarron rivers, he was riding ahead looking for water. A band of Comanche found him. His body was never recovered. He was just 31. If ever a man deserves a memorial, he does.

By the late 1830s the Rocky Mountain beaver trade had seen its brightest days. Fashion was moving on—to silk. And anyway, there were ever fewer beaver. The last Rendezvous took place in the summer of 1840 in the valley of the Green River in the west of today's Wyoming. Perhaps it was as wild a party as any of its predecessors, but one suspects that when the traders loaded the last bale of pelts and left for the long trek back to St. Louis without announcing the site of the next Rendezvous, most people knew that the glory days were over. Yet, in not much more than 20 years, the beaver trade had dissolved a nation's apprehension that the jumble of the "shining mountains" might mark a boundary to westward expansion. Someone later said that the map of the Rocky Mountains, and indeed much of the West, "was first drawn on beaver skins." He had it about right.

5

THE OVERLAND TRAIL

"Our ignorance of the route was complete. We knew that California lay west and that was the extent of our knowledge."

John Bidwell, in 1841, a leader of the first wagon train to California

They pursued their enterprise with the constancy that is characteristic of the Americans."

The Belgian missionary, Father de Smet, an observer of that first wagon train

౿ఎ

Perhaps, had they known what lay ahead, some might never have started. But ignorance, when blended with optimism and hope for a better life, has always made a powerful fuel for migration.

Some, young families mostly, wanted to find new lives and new farms on the free and distant lands loosely known as Oregon. Later, optimistic young men (and some older ones too), reckoned to strike it rich on the goldfields of California's distant El Dorado. Some, the Mormons, were trying to escape persecution by building their Earthly Kingdom in a remoteness where they would be left alone. A few, the missionaries, were looking to ensure their own salvation and, possibly, that of others by venturing out to preach The Word to the Indians and anyone else who would listen. Together, their journeys would become part of the largest and furthest migration since, some historians have suggested, the Crusades. In the 25 years up to 1867, when the railroad began to take some of the load, at least 350,000 people followed the 2,000-mile trail to California or to Oregon.

❧

The covered wagon was their symbol. Today, while there are still enough of them in museums, finding one that actually "works" is not easy. For the filming I was planning, I needed eight or nine of them and the mules to pull them. "Could be difficult," I was told. But, as always out west, if you ask around long enough, you can find almost anything. People want to help. It probably took half a dozen phone calls before I got lucky. Someone thought there was an outfit in a place called Quinter, in the middle of Kansas, that might help. I found it on the map. I phoned. Yes, the man said, restoring old wagons was his hobby, and in the summer he and some friends sometimes took them out onto the nearby prairie to give city folk and school children a feeling for what it must have been like in the early days. I explained what I had in mind. No problem, it was all fixed in five minutes: eight wagons for an afternoon at $70 each, including the mules and drivers. "And that's a 30% discount, as my wife's folks came from Wales." I did not question his generous non sequitur, and a few weeks later we got all our filming in a long afternoon. That was 44 years ago for a film I was making with Alistair Cooke about the story of the West. We sent the folk in Quinter a copy.

❧

It is reckoned that the first truly emigrant party came together in the spring of 1841 at a place called Sapling Grove, a few miles beyond the small Missouri town of Independence. John Bidwell, a 22-year-old New Yorker, seems to have provided the initial spark. He had already tried life in Pennsylvania and Ohio and now, with yet more miles behind him, he had come to temporary rest by the Missouri River. There, perhaps a little bored—he had tried farming, he had tried teaching—and now maybe wondering what to do next, he was tempted by the wondrous tales he had heard about far-away California. There, it seemed, January was as warm as June; the days were long and of perpetual sunshine, crops grew prodigiously, and no doubt the girls were beautiful beyond imagining. Young Bidwell soon found that there were other dreamers. They banded together and called themselves the Western Immigration Society. Everyone was required to be self-sufficient, to come with a wagon and team, a gun or two, and all supplies for a journey estimated at five months. In the event, early enthusiasms waned: some of those dreamers, when they thought about the distances and the hardships ahead, woke up with second thoughts. Others realized (rather late in the day) that California was not even part of the United States; it still belonged to Mexico. In the end just 68 people set out, including five women and ten children.

Years later, Bidwell wrote with beguiling honesty that, when they started, "Our ignorance of the route was complete. We knew that California lay west, and that was the extent of our knowledge." In the event, they were lucky: when just about to depart they were joined by a small group of missionaries. This party had engaged, as its guide and mentor, the recently retired mountain man, Thomas Fitzpatrick. Like a few others, with the beaver business now almost played out, Fitzpatrick looked around to find himself a new livelihood; he was about to become the first trail guide. He probably knew as much about what lay ahead as any man alive.

Over the first 1,000 miles, across the plains and then up to the mountains, this mixed party of greenhorn migrants and trust-in-God missionaries had its share of alarms. Spring rains swelled the river crossings (there were more than 30 of them); a tornado with hailstones as large as apples swept close, wagons broke down, draft animals went missing, there was sickness, and there were buffalo stampedes. Fitzpatrick was always there to advise and help, but he set a demanding pace. The convoy reached the remote trading post of Fort Laramie in exactly six weeks. They had come nearly 650 miles. That was a time seldom equaled by later migrations. Another three weeks and they were trekking across the high, open saddle of South Pass. Perhaps, once on the far side, their guide pointed out that all the streams now ran to the west. But one wonders if he added that there were still another 1,000 miles to the Pacific. They were only halfway.

A week later, on the Green River, they met a party of trappers. These mountain men (they must have been among the last of the breed) were gloomy about the ability of the migrants to cope with the onward route to California. There was no recognized trail, and, worse, there was a stretch of 400 miles which,

On the Overland Trail, a Mormon family takes a noon break by their wagons (Denver Public Library)

according to the few accounts that existed, would be across country that was only a little short of being a desert. Yes, the trappers probably knew that Jedediah Smith had managed the crossing 14 years before, and they might have heard of two or three others—experienced mountain men. But mostly it was rumors. And if that news was not disheartening enough, the migrants now learned that they were about to lose their guide. Fitzpatrick was contracted by the missionaries, but they were not going to California; they would be branching off for Oregon. Not surprisingly, thirty or so of the migrants—mostly families with children— quickly voted to take the safer option: they would go with Fitzpatrick. That left a party of 31 men, and an 18-year-old wife, Nancy Kelsey, with a baby. Led by young John Bidwell and an older man, John Bartleson, they were determined to push on to California, as had always been their intention. One of those missionaries, a Belgian émigré, Father de Smet, watched them depart. He later wrote admiringly, "They pursued their Enterprise with the Constancy that is characteristic of Americans."

In fact, for the next 700 miles, they would need much more than mere Constancy. As they toiled westward, mile after slow mile, theirs became an evermore perilous journey. They were never sure of where they were, or how far they had still to go; they got lost in dead-end canyons; they plodded towards mirages; they gagged in dust storms, and they found water so salty that it was undrinkable. "We could see nothing," wrote Bidwell in his diary, "except extensive arid plains, glimmering with heat and salt."

☙

Today, drive down Interstate 80 until 50 miles southwest of the town of Winnemucca (you'll be in the Humboldt Sink), then try walking out into the sagebrush desert. In high summer—as it would have been for the Bidwell–Bartleson party—you will get some idea of what it must have been like. And if you don't want your car to be an oven when you get back, best leave the engine and the air-con running. Yes sir, over the years, I have driven that stretch of I-80 three times – and there's not too much traffic.
One time I wanted to get an aerial shot of a Union Pacific freight train rumbling across this desolation, so we hired a small helicopter from Winnemucca. But it was very hot, and helicopters don't like extreme heat; their performance suffers. So, to lessen the load, the pilot landed briefly and made me get out, so that just he and the cameraman could chase after the train. Before leaving me standing in the remoteness of the desert, the pilot insisted on giving me a mirror—to flash so that he could find me on his return. I spent a shadeless 30 minutes polishing that mirror.

☙

The migrants suffered from thirst, from hunger, from heatstroke, from sheer exhaustion. They ate desert berries and snakes. Day after day, they were driven on by the fear that to give up or to turn back would be to die. Maybe they would die anyway. They abandoned their wagons one by one. Every few days they had to butcher one of their half-starved oxen for its meat and blood. Later, when there were no oxen left, they started to kill their mules. When, at last, they were across the desert, they had to find a way through a final range of mountains: the California Sierras. Now they abandoned their last wagon. But they were lucky: the snows were late that fall. Nancy Kelsey, carrying her baby and with her shoes worn out, walked the last two weeks with her feet wrapped in rags. But she, her husband, and their companions—all 33 of them—made it through to California. From Sapling Grove, it had taken them nearly six months.

In the years that followed, other migrants would follow, though at first they did so in only a trickle. It took time for the word to spread back to "the states" and, when it did, more wagons headed for Oregon than for California. (In those days, Oregon was the name applied to the whole of what today we call the Pacific Northwest.) The land in those parts was said to be well-watered, fertile, and free for the taking. As for California, while it sounded at least as attractive as Oregon once one got there, the deterrent lay in getting there. The two difficulties were the trek across the Nevada desert and then, as if that were not problem enough, there was the final haul up over the high Sierras. Nevertheless, despite the hazards, a number of determined and well-organized migrant groups managed to make it. And, of course, some came the long way round, by sea via Cape Horn.

૭૩

On that last, most difficult stretch, they had crossed the whole width of what would become, only 22 years later, the state of Nevada. Even today, once away from the string of sparkly gambling towns—Reno, Carson City, and Las Vegas—which range north–south below the eastern slopes of those Sierras, Nevada is still a very empty place. So empty that, in late 2007, somewhere in its vastness, the famous pilot and world adventurer Steve Fossett, flying a single-engine aircraft, without having first filed a flight plan, simply disappeared. Scores of aircraft went looking for him. His body and the wreckage were not found for nearly a year—in the Sierras.
A few months earlier, I was flying with an old friend (a Brit) who, with 25,000 hours in his 747 and Airbus log-book and now in sweet retirement, owned a small two-seat aircraft—a Globe Swift. Starting from the aircraft's home-base near Milwaukee, we were making a six-week circuit of the western states. The previous day, coming east

from San Francisco Bay, we had flown over the autumn snows of the High Sierras. Now we were crossing northeast from Carson City to Twin Falls in southern Idaho— about 400 miles across Nevada. From up there one looks out over a sun-baked immensity; apart from the very occasional irrigated oasis, it is part desert, part arid mountains, part dried-out salt lakes, part nothing. If anything mechanical were to fail, and you went down, someone had better find you—quick! Away from the black ribbon of the highway (Interstate 80) and the track of the Union Pacific railroad that parallel each other across the state and must coincide, in places, with the path taken (in the opposite direction) by that first wagon train, there is almost nothing. And very few people. Perhaps one needs to be at 8,000 feet to better understand and wonder at the achievement of 22-year-old John Bidwell, 18-year-old Nancy Kelsey and all those other single-minded souls who, over those early years, followed them.

℗

In 1843, two years after Fitzpatrick had led those missionaries and migrants to Oregon, nearly 1,000 people took to that same trail; among them were 130 women and as many children. They would have known, as they said goodbye to their mothers, father, brothers, and sisters, that they would probably never see them again. They were setting out on a journey of at least six months and nearly 2,000 miles, about which they could have known almost nothing. So, why? One answer seems to overarch all others: it lies in the faith and the curiosity that the Americans of those times, particularly those living near the frontier, had always had in the possibility of a Better Life Beyond. It was a stimulus that had already brought their pioneering parents and grandparents more than a third of the way across the continent. And, of course, it had earlier brought *their* parents and grandparents across the Atlantic. Even today, there still exists in America the often sardonic hope that if things don't Pan Out in the Here 'n' Now, one can always Pack-Up and Start-Over in Some-Place-Else. Old World skeptics interpret that as rootlessness; New World admirers see it as something rather normal. It is one of the traits that has made the nation what it is; it is in its DNA.

More specifically (and less philosophically), the lands along the western borders of the states of Missouri and Iowa were disappointing. Before railroads reached that far west, the land was too far from markets for anyone to make any cash. And another thing: summer malaria was endemic along the low-lying country of the Missouri valley. Lastly, many frontier farmers regarded their land as a commodity to be worked for a few years and then to be sold or even abandoned. After all, there was always more land or other opportunities—further west.

So if one had stood at, say, South Pass toward the end of July in 1845, one would have seen an almost continuous line of wagons going past for three or four weeks. That year more than 5,000 people made the crossing. If you had asked any of them where they were going, most would have told you that Oregon was their goal. The trail to California was certainly open, but mainly to the hardy few who knew (or quickly learned) what they were doing. They may have heard something about the fate, two years earlier, of the Donners.

The Donner party (named after its leader) consisted of 87 men, women and children. They set off from the Missouri too late in the year. In the months that followed they compounded that first mistake with unnecessary and unthinking delays, and then by being conned into taking an ill-advised "cut-off" which, while shorter on a map, added weeks to their journey. Eventually, later than ever, they reached out into the Nevada desert. By now, the oxen that were not actually dying were exhausted. So, one by one, the wagons and the supplies they carried had to be abandoned. The party split into factions, tempers frayed, a man was knifed, and another was abandoned to die. By the time they straggled out of the desert and up into the Sierras it was early November. They were in tatters and half-starved. They began the climb, but they were caught in early and heavy snows. Over the next three months, some died of cold, some of starvation, some ate parts of the dead, some survived. By the time rescue arrived in the spring, 37 had perished. The notion of Manifest Destiny had not worked for the Donner party.

Manifest Destiny has often been quoted as the stimulus, even the assertive justification, for the nation's thrust across the west. The term was first used by an editor in 1845: "It is our Manifest Destiny to overspread the continent provided by Providence." He seems to have interpreted something in the nation's psyche as both a historical imperative and a God-given right. Today it would be called a "mission statement." Nevertheless, back at South Pass, if anyone walking beside a wagon had been asked about their destiny (manifest or otherwise), he or she would have been totally perplexed. Both their ambitions and their concerns were infinitely more mundane, practical, and immediate.

Overlanding was not for the poor. Of course, a penniless young man might hitch a ride with a family in return for his labor on the heavier and more onerous tasks, but most of the migrants were people of some, if only moderate, means. They had to be; accounts show that a family needed at least $700 to equip itself properly with a wagon (if it did not already have one), with mules or oxen, and with enough food and all the other necessary gear. So, at a time when the average working wage was less than $20 a month, getting ready for the trail could be an expensive business. Most likely, an emigrant family had "realized" what capital it could by selling its farm or business.

It made sense to join a like-minded group—a Company or an Association. In the early years there might be 10 to 20 wagons traveling together; in later years there were up to 100. The Company would elect a committee which then drew up a set of rules and obligations. "We pledge ourselves to assist each other through all the misfortunes that may befall us on our long and dangerous journey." The committee would publish a scale of supplies that each wagon or family should carry. A decision would be made about when the journey should start: if it set off too early, the spring grass might not have grown enough to sustain the oxen, mules and horses; if too late, the grass might already have been eaten out by earlier parties. Also, if too late, the whole party might be caught and stalled by early snows at later stages in the journey, as happened to the Donner party. Once on the trail, the group would organize a rota of night guards. It might depute the best shots to keep the wagon train supplied with meat, from buffaloes and antelope.

On a more individual family level, there were decisions to be made about the wagon and the oxen or mules to pull it. With very few exceptions, the wagons chosen were the standard four-wheeled farm wagons of the time. These were not the great swaying "prairie schooners" imagined by many artists who never went beyond the Mississippi. The "schooners" were the famous Conestogas which, pulled by a team of eight or more oxen and carrying three or four tons of trade goods, traveled the easier and more level "road" southwest to and from Santa Fe. The farm wagons setting out for California and Oregon were much smaller; they might be strengthened with heavier axles or new wheels, and they would certainly be equipped with a canvas cover stretched over arching hoops. They could carry a load of more than half a ton, but the wise family did not push the load to the limit.

The main starting points were all on the Missouri river: Independence, St. Joseph, Belleview (just south of today's Omaha) and Council Bluffs. Here the travelers could find stores stocked with most of the things they might need. There were guidebooks too; they recommended what food supplies should be taken, what spare parts to carry for the wagons, which were the safe shortcuts.

Mules or oxen? The former were faster, but cost about $70 each; oxen were less than half that price, and they could pull heavier loads. Also, even if they were slower, they were said to be less trouble than mules. There were advocates both ways, but the balance was for oxen. Ideally, a wagon was drawn by a span of four animals. Additionally, there were usually a few saddle horses; they would be useful for scouting ahead of the wagon train and herding any cattle they had, or for riding out to find game for the pot.

Except where dictated by the terrain, it was unusual for the wagons to follow each other too closely in single file; the dust raised by the wagons in front was too uncomfortable for those behind. But any area of difficult badlands, or a particularly easy ford, might push the wagons together to follow directly behind each other. There are still today places like Deep Rut Hill near Guernsey in Wyoming where one can stand shoulder-deep in the "lane" cut in the bedrock by the succession of thousands of wagons that passed exactly that way. One imagines there must have been some frustrating traffic jams. And judging by the sketches that appear in some of the diaries, many landmarks are unchanged: Court House Rock, Chimney Rock and Scottsbluff (all in western Nebraska) are three of the more obvious. Most famous of all is Wyoming's Independence Rock, so called because, if all were going well, many of the wagons would arrive there on or about July 4. Some of the migrants climbed to the rounded top and scratched their names on the bare rock. Today, as one reads those names still clearly visible, and leans into the same western wind, one would have to be mentally numb not to be moved.

On the trail, the day began before dawn. While the women dealt with domestic chores and prepared breakfast, the men would pack up camp and help each other with getting the oxen or mules yoked and harnessed. Once under way, the men walked beside their oxen or mules; sometimes the women would walk with them; the younger children rode in the wagons. If the "going" was good, they reckoned to cover 12–15 miles by the evening, with a two- or three-hour break during the heat of the day. Across the almost treeless prairie, the travelers would collect any dry buffalo dung for cooking fuel. One pioneer observed that, with so much ash and smoke coming off the burning buffalo chips, there was no need for pepper. During the afternoon, a small party would invariably ride ahead to find a good spot for the whole caravan to bed down for the night. Obviously clean water and pasture that had not been eaten out by an earlier party were priorities. Each family prepared its own supper; the bachelors would have formed their own "messes" at the start. Afterwards, someone might get out a fiddle or a flute; there would be dancing and singing. But, given the pre-dawn start, people would bed down early.

Illnesses of every kind—pneumonia, measles, typhoid, malaria, mumps and whooping cough —were always a worry, especially to young mothers. Any medicines were just palliatives, rarely cures. Dysentery carried away babies and young children. But cholera seems to have been the most feared: it could strike out of nowhere, with death coming by the next morning. The dead were hurriedly buried in a shallow grave; perhaps someone made a wooden cross on which they scrawled a name and a date, and maybe someone said a prayer. There was seldom time for much more. No one really knows how many travelers died along the way in the 20 years that the trail was the highway to the Far West; estimates reach upwards from 10,000.

For the young it was maybe a great and carefree adventure; for the thoughtful it was a time of apprehension about what lay ahead; for the more energetic it was a protracted and tedious means to an end—the quicker they could reach their final destination the better. All the normal joys and sorrows of life traveled with them: new friendships, old enmities, laughter, tears, flirting, courtship, marriage, birth, death, good times and bad. One diarist describes an evening camp where at one end was a wedding (conducted by a missionary who happened to be along), at the other end the burial of a small boy who had been run over by a wagon, and somewhere between the two a woman giving birth. All human life ...

℘

There was one group of would-be migrants who were thoroughly atypical in their style and in their motives: the Mormons. They were different. That was their problem. It was not just their apparent prosperity and unashamed polygamy that stoked people's ire—or made them jealous (on both counts?). In the eyes of those who thought of themselves as good Christians, the Mormons were heretics. And compounding their heresies, they were also more industrious than their "gentile" neighbors; they banded together to work for the common good. Their enemies saw that habit not so much as mutual cooperation, more as that of a closed and secretive society practicing a form of proto-socialism. To people deeply suspicious of anything they did not understand, the Mormons were not merely distrusted; they were feared. Already, in their short history, rampaging mobs had driven them out of Ohio, chased them to Missouri, and then north to Illinois. There, near a town they had built and called Nauvoo (Hebrew for paradise), the leader and founder of the sect, Joseph Smith, and his brother were shot. Half the town was then torched. So in 1847, while thousands of gentile emigrants had already made the overland journey in the hope of finding a more prosperous life, a small advance party of Mormons set out to find something they counted as even more precious: a place where, far from possible persecution, they might have the freedom to follow their own gospel with its divergent style of Christianity.

Under a new leader, Brigham Young, the wagons of the Mormon vanguard (143 men, three women and three children) made their way west along the north side of the Platte, at a safe distance from the enmity of other migrants whose trail lay along the south side of the river. Once across the plains, Young led his people over South Pass, then he veered south away from the main trail. His path lay down a broad valley that overlooked the Great Salt Lake. They had come 1,300 miles. Now, with a minimum of pondering—or so the legend goes—Brigham Young looked around and then, with the certainty of an Old Testament prophet, he declared, "It is enough. This is the place." In almost the same breath, he ordered his people to start clearing the land, damming the streams, digging irrigation ditches, plowing and planting seed. A detachment was sent back into the foothills to cut logs; they needed to build cabins quickly to see them through the coming winter. Also fodder had to be gathered for the livestock they had brought with them: 66 oxen, 52 mules, 19 cows and a flock of chickens.

Brigham Young had chosen an unlikely spot. His fellow pioneers must have looked at each other and wondered. This was certainly not the verdant and clear-streamed wilderness of the migrants' dream. It was dry, hot and stony. It would take enormous toil to convert this sun-hard aridity to any kind of life-sustaining fertility. But Young knew exactly what he was doing. He had chosen this to be "the place" because he knew it would be unattractive to other, non-Mormon migrants. He was prescient enough to know that here, on the edge of the desert, he and his people would be left alone to build their New Zion. Irrigation would be the key. With relatively simple engineering (though much hard work) they could harness the springs and snow-melt from the mountains immediately behind them. Young judged they had all they needed to make this desert bloom. Anyway, they would put their trust in the Lord; no doubt, He would provide.

Now, in a wondrous act of faith, an order would go back east for the great Mormon migration to begin. Brigham Young himself would go back with the message. So, with a small escort, he made the 1,300-mile return journey, in just nine weeks.

The pioneers he had left at "the place," digging those ditches and building those cabins, needed all the faith they could find. Through the winter they came very close to extinction. Tales are told of grubbing for roots, butchering some of the weaker oxen, boiling hides for soup and stewing grass. But at last, come the spring, the wheat and corn they had planted late the year before began to sprout. Then, a few weeks before harvest, legend says that a great swarm of grasshoppers began to strip every stalk—until flocks of gulls flew in from the Great Salt Lake to feast on the hoppers. That miracle was, and still is, seen as proof of the Lord's endorsement of their labors: Trust in Him and He will provide.

In May 1848, from a gathering place they called Winter Quarters, close by the Missouri, the Mormons began the exodus to their Promised Land—led by their Moses. More than 2,400 of them started walking. Theirs was a colossal act of blind faith. They needed nearly 400 wagons to carry their supplies: sacks of flour, seeds, plows, saws, axes, beehives, chickens, geese, goats, and doves—everything that a whole community might need for self-sufficiency. And there were 1,300 oxen, 700 cows and some bulls, 140 pigs, 70 horses and a large flock of sheep.

In mid-September, the first of those wagons rolled down from the mountains and into the rough-and-ready settlement prepared by the earlier pioneers. One day this would grow to be Salt Lake City. Before he had departed the previous year, Brigham Young had chosen the exact place for a Temple. Again, like Moses, he had tapped the ground with a cane and said, "Here will be the temple to our God." By the time he got back nine months later, work had begun. But, within a few years, that first building was too small. So they started again, on a temple so large that it took 45 years to complete. Today, with its steeples soaring high above the traffic of Temple Square, while it is certainly not one of the most beautiful buildings in the world, it must surely be one of the most impressive in terms of the fortitude and faith of the people who built it. Alongside, and almost as striking, is the Tabernacle where, under a high and arching roof, they hold meetings and concerts. Although it was designed long before these things were properly understood, it is said by many experts to have acoustics as fine as any in the nation.

ↁ

I phoned the Tabernacle press office from London. I explained that the BBC documentary we were making about the settlement of the West must obviously include a passage about the Mormons. I had in mind several sequences, but at this early stage I wanted (please) to make arrangements for two in particular. The first, with the relevant permission, would involve filming something of the famous 350-member Tabernacle Choir in rehearsal. The second sequence would be the family farewells of a dozen or so young missionaries at Salt Lake City airport. These were (and still are) the polite and neatly-suited 19-year-olds who, as "apprentice" Mormons, are expected to go forth and knock gently on the world's doors: in Glasgow, Manchester, Toronto, Melbourne, Auckland, Oslo and beyond. Back then (maybe it is still the same today) the departures happened regularly on the second Tuesday afternoon of each month. Away from home for upwards of two years, those young men go to spread the Good Word and make converts—though, as readers will know if they have ever responded to their knocking, they are too well mannered to push their message too stridently. As for the choir, I especially wanted to film it in the Tabernacle singing the Mormons' unofficial anthem, a marvelous hymn that ends with the confident exhortation that "All is well. All is well!" The verses were written more than 150 years ago by a young English convert, William Clayton. Some say that he had the inspiration while walking beside a wagon over the last few miles of his long journey; he had crossed the Atlantic and now he had most of a continent behind him. At long last, as he came over a brow, he could see the lights of his New Jerusalem twinkling in the valley below. For him, all was indeed well—at last.

We got both sequences with maximum cooperation and minimum fuss. Months later, back in London to edit the film, we ran a sequence of families at the airport saying goodbye to their sons, followed by a long steady shot of the aircraft, with the young missionaries aboard, climbing away into the evening sky. As it banked toward the mountain, we laid the triumphant refrain, "All is well. All is well!" Obviously I am biased, but for me it was a sequence that "worked."

 confidence

Mormon missionaries have been seeking converts from the very beginning. Two of the first countries over which they cast their net were England and Wales. Indeed, three years before he led that exploratory trek, Brigham Young himself had been preaching in Lancashire. The cotton towns of that county became favorite Mormon targets. Perhaps that is where William Clayton came from.

The journeys of those converts were subsidized from the tithes that all

Mormons contributed to their church's treasury. But by the mid-1850s, so great were the numbers that the funds could not pay for all the wagons that were needed. So Young, uncompromising as always, decreed that the newcomers should "come on foot with handcarts or wheelbarrows. Let them gird up their loins and walk ..." So began the handcart migrations. The Mormons kept (and still keep) meticulous records, so they know that over 3,000 converts—rather more women than men—walked all the way from the Missouri to their new home. Each two-wheel cart was loaded with 400 pounds of food and supplies; each migrant was allowed just 17 pounds of clothing and personal possessions, less for the children. They traveled in regiments of 100 carts, with five people allocated to each cart. On eventually arriving down Emigration Canyon they were met with bands, celebrations and thanksgiving prayers. They had pulled and pushed for over 1,000 miles.

Within ten years of its founding, Salt Lake City had a population of over 10,000. After San Francisco, it was the largest city in the western half of the nation. Along the base of the mountains, for more than 50 miles from north to south, stretched a broad carpet of irrigated farmland. More than 200 miles of carefully engineered canals had been dug; four or five times that mileage in farmers' ditches carried the water out into the fields. Elsewhere there were similar, though smaller, Mormon oases. Irrigation was the key; it still is.

Brigham Young had 27 wives and 56 children. But far more significant in the Mormon story was his iron will. He was the man who had made it all happen. He was autocratic, even dictatorial, but only his enemies (and he had a few) would have accused him of being tyrannical. Perhaps he had no need to be; his reputation for astute judgment was enough to compel unquestioning obedience. Above all, he obviously possessed three of the most valuable of all qualities in a leader: a vision for the future, single-mindedness toward that end, and, most important of all, the ability to Get It Right. When in 1877 he died, 25,000 Mormons filed past his coffin. In short, without Brigham Young, who knows where the Mormons would be today? As it is, they can very reasonably claim that their people were among the first real settlers in the West.

They gave up polygamy more than a century ago. In fact, well before its abolition (the price they willingly paid to join the Union and for eventual statehood in 1896) most Mormons were already monogamous. True, even yet there is still a small rump of polygamists who, as they see it, have remained faithful to what they call the "plural marriage" doctrine of the early Church; they are members of the breakaway Fundamentalist Church of Jesus Christ of Latter-Day Saints. They number a few thousand and tend to live secluded lives in the arid back-country of southern Utah, northern Arizona and northwest

Texas. Mainstream Mormons regard them as an embarrassment in which the media, out of prurience, is far too interested. If you ask about them you will be rather briskly told that they are a tedious irrelevance. Today, "normal" Mormons fly Old Glory with as much pride as anyone else. And, no doubt, they pay their state and federal taxes with as much resigned grumbling.

We'll find for us the place which God for us prepared,
Far away in the West,
Where none shall come to hurt or make afraid;
There will the Saints be blessed.
We'll make the air with music ring,
Shout praises to our God and King;
Above the rest, these words we'll tell –
All is well! All is well!

6

THE GOLD RUSH

"Oh, Susanna, don't you cry for me. I'm off to California with a wash-pan on my knee."

A line from a popular song of the time. The wash-pan was a prospector's most basic piece of equipment

~

For the first seven years of the overland trail, the overriding motive of the migrants was to find new land on which to build a new life. If, after a few years, a family's labors began to pay off, then the earlier sacrifices and remembered hardships would have been seen as worthwhile. But this simple equation would change in 1848. The change was sparked by a discovery in the western foothills of the California Sierras.

On the bend of a river in those foothills, a carpenter called James Marshall had not long finished building a small water-powered sawmill. Every few days he would clear the clogging buildup of silt from the end of the tailrace. One morning, in the delta of gravel, he noticed several particles about the size of very small peas; they were a dull yellow. When he bashed them between two small stones, they did not shatter but, being malleable, they merely flattened. Years later, Marshall was to say that he then sat down and "thought mighty hard." A day or two later he took the particles fifty miles downstream to his boss, Johann Sutter—the man whose mill he had been building. Together, they did some simple tests and concluded that, yes, these were indeed tiny nuggets of gold. They surmised that, back on the American River, there must be more of the stuff. Yet, rather than being delighted, they were troubled. Indeed, realizing the almost inevitable ramifications, they presumably both now sat down and did some more "mighty hard" thinking.

Sutter was a Swiss émigré, an expansive ex-bankrupt who, arriving in California ten years earlier (via Hawaii), had persuaded the Mexican Governor to give him lien over a small empire of land. Now this part trader, part venture capitalist and part amiable conman was busy creating his own private barony; it was centered on a small fort and trading post at the confluence of the American and Sacramento Rivers; much later this was to become the site of California's present-day capital. With a hundred or so employees working across a spread of 80 square miles, Sutter had established fields of grain, herds of cattle and pigs, flocks of sheep and goats, an orchard and the beginnings of a vineyard. He had commissioned that sawmill (on land which did not belong to him) because he needed sawn timber to extend his trading post. He was on the edge of a quiet prosperity. But now he realized that if word of the gold got out, the ensuing stampede would most likely end his pastoral dream.

In fact, there were already rumors. Marshall's assistant at the sawmill, Henry Bigler, was no unobservant dimwit. He wrote in his diary (held today in a California archive) for January 24, 1848, "This day some kind of mettle was found in the tail race that looks like goald." A few days later he wrote, "Our mettle has been tride and proves to be goald … we have pict up more than a hundred dollars woth last week." Bigler kept his day job at the mill but, after work and on Sundays, he and a friend sneaked off upstream. They became California's very first prospectors. Surprisingly, their secret held for several weeks. But there was no way it could hold for much longer.

Sutter was soon complaining that his men were deserting him to head upriver to find their fortunes. Within a month the news had reached the small port of San Francisco and the provincial capital of Monterey—though, contrary to the popular myth, there was initially some skepticism. Indeed, there were several weeks of delay before the newly appointed Governor of California—the territory had only just been won from Mexico—decided to take a trip upcountry to check the rumors for himself. A young Lieutenant, William Tecumseh Sherman, accompanied him. By the time they reached the American River, passing vacant farms, abandoned fields, and empty mills along the way, they found, by their reckoning, three thousand hopeful gold-seekers at work.

When he got back to Monterey, the previously disbelieving Governor wrote an official report "… $30,000 to $40,000 worth of gold, if not more, obtained daily." Then, presumably by way of proof, he carefully filled his tea caddy with gold dust and some tiny nuggets that he had bought on the diggings. He gave the report and the caddy to a Lieutenant on his staff—to take to Washington. Three months later, the young officer made his delivery; he had journeyed first by ship to Panama, then on mule-back across the isthmus, then by sea again to New Orleans, and finally, after a succession of stagecoaches, to the nation's capital. Although there had already been a number of unofficial letters and word-of-mouth rumors coming back East via the overland route, one might reasonably suppose that it was the governor's formal report and, no doubt, his tea caddy (quickly put on display, under guard, in the lobby of the War Department) that really detonated the phenomenon that became the California Gold Rush. El Dorado was now official.

Of course, back out in California, the rush (official or not) was already a fact. In San Francisco Bay, crews were walking off their ships, merchants were closing their stores, soldiers were deserting their barracks, farmers were abandoning their fields and livestock. Up in Oregon, some of the migrants who had only just arrived were now tempted, once more, to hitch up their wagons for a journey south to join the fun. Even the Mormons, some of them anyway, were temporarily forsaking Zion and trekking across the desert to try their luck. Along the newly named American River and, now, along other streams as well, shantytowns of canvas and wood were being hammered together almost daily. Always there was an enticing rumor that someone somewhere had struck it rich again—just yesterday or even that morning. And it would be the same tomorrow. Gold fever was highly contagious, and there was no known antidote. There still isn't …

Way back east in "the States," it was already winter—too late to make a start overland. But time enough to make plans. First, the fortune-seeker had to decide how he (there were very few women at this stage) was going to get to California. There were three choices. Without waiting for the spring, he could make an early start by taking a square-rigger all the way round Cape Horn. Shipping companies in Boston and New York optimistically advertised passages of a mere four months to San Francisco. The truth was that, owing to the prevailing winds, it was a voyage of over 16,000 miles, and it could take six months; sometimes it even took eight. Alternatively, the fortune hunter could catch a ship down to Panama; then having crossed the 75-mile isthmus by mule and canoe (and risked dying of yellow fever), he needed another ship (if he could find one) north to San Francisco. Or, lastly, he could wait for spring and then take the already-pioneered overland trail. The decision would largely prompted by where he lived. If his home was in New England, he might be inclined to go by sea—either round the Horn or via Panama. If he were a Midwesterner (though, obviously, the term was near meaningless in those days) he would almost certainly go overland. But the choice also had a good deal to do with how impatient he was; it was not just the gullible who believed that there were only so many easy shovelfuls of gold to be won before the winning would become more difficult. Thus, even if the young hopeful lived in the farthest reaches of New England, there were railroads and riverboats by which he could get to any of the recognized starting points on the Missouri within a couple of weeks.

So, given that patience was not a characteristic trait among the Argonauts (a name they proudly adopted) it is not surprising that most of them chose what they thought would be the quickest and cheapest route: the overland trail. As in earlier years, the same informal rules applied; some were based on common sense; some were based on feedback from earlier travelers: if you did not already have a wagon, buy yourself the stoutest one that you can afford, and start with strongest teams you can find. Lay in adequate supplies, but don't overload the wagon (a difficult balance); get the timing right—set off neither too early nor too late; husband your strength and resources for the more difficult later stages of the journey; don't assume that there will be plenty of buffalo meat along the way, nor should you rely on picking up any supplies on route. Lastly, and perhaps most important, for mutual help when things became difficult (as they surely would), form an Association with thirty or forty like-minded travelers. In this, the gold-seekers were no different from earlier migrants—except that, now, many such groups first gathered together in their hometowns long before they set off toward the west. If they were wise, they would send a small party several weeks ahead—to buy wagons, oxen and stores in the river towns along the Missouri. Often too, they set themselves up as joint stock corporations with, say, a compulsory $500 "investment" from each member. The records list outfits like the Washington City Company, the Boston Joint Stock Company, The Sacramento Company of Massachusetts, the Iron City Rangers (from Pittsburgh), the Helltown Greasers (from where?), the Spartans, the Pioneers and many more. They were prone to appoint "officers," kit themselves out with self-designed uniforms, and to draw up formal rules and legalisms that owed much in length, rhetoric and aspirations to the Constitution of the United States itself. On the day they left their hometowns there was usually a parade, a party and, no doubt, among the family men, some brave farewells. "Now, all we have to do is to get to Cal'forny."

In 1849, at the small military post of Fort Kearney, a few hundred miles up the Platte River (near the south bank), they kept a tally. On one day, May 28, 460 wagons passed. No wonder that the migration became known as the Gold Rush. Indeed, by the time the last train had gone through, in the third week of June, nearly 6,000 wagons had been counted. And there were reckoned to be at least a further 1,000 that had bypassed the fort by taking a trail along the other (northern) bank of the river. Given that a wagon was usually home to between three and four people, there must have been some 24,000 people on the move. Other sources show that about 8,000 migrants went via the Panama crossing; rather fewer took a ship all the way. In the second year, 1850, the numbers on the trail nearly doubled, and there were many more women and children. It was much the same in 1851. With the possible exception of the Israelites' flight from Egypt, this may well have been most concentrated migration in history—though many more started than finished.

Despite all their preparations, there were some problems that no amount of prudence or planning could prevent. At the river crossings, there were deaths from drowning—in those days, most people could not swim. There were wounds, sometimes fatal, from careless gun handling. There were the usual accidents under wagon wheels and, occasionally there were altercations with Indians. As with the earlier migrations, sickness was always a worry. At one time or another, almost everybody went down with dysentery. While it was rarely fatal, it could be very debilitating, making the sufferer a wagon-bound invalid for days, even weeks. And, again, as in the days before the Rush, cholera was a constant fear. Rum laced with gunpowder was one remedy; but judged by the number of deaths, the prescription was not very effective. About half the patients died. Some years later, a diarist wrote that the succession of graves, many hundreds of them, marked the trail as effectively as signposts.

By the time the wagons had passed Independence Rock and were on the high sagebrush country beyond South Pass, they had been on the trail for nearly three months. From this point on, three topics seem to recur in both the diaries of the time and in the interpretations of later historians. First, the novelty of the adventure was obviously losing some, if not most, of its shine; people were tiring. Most were impatient to get to California as quickly as possible; mere irritability at the grating habits of one's slower companions was, by now, giving way to outright bad temper and arguments, even fights. "Some of our men are dissatisfied," wrote one diarist, "and they talk of disunion &c. Much occurs to stir men's baser passions. Our Captain thinks they could not be all pleased were the Good Being himself to direct affairs."

Some of the companies that had started out in undying brotherhood were coming apart. In the volatility, factions were splitting off and wanting to go their own way. Indeed, even among those companies which remained united, *which* way was a source of discussion, even disagreement. There were choices. They revolved around the various shortcuts or, as they are still known in the West, the cut-offs. By 1849, the first year of the Rush, while some of the cut-offs were fairly well established by earlier travelers, others were still chancy. There were always some less-cautious souls who were willing to take risks and thus save time. Sometimes they were right, sometimes they were wrong. While a cut-off might be geographically shorter, it could be so wearing on the wagons and the teams that, subsequently, everyone would have to shed gear to ease their loads. It might have been wiser and, ultimately, quicker to have gone the long way round. One diarist grumpily wrote, "Never take no cut-offs."

Ten days beyond South Pass (if they did not take Sublette's cut-off) they came to Fort Bridger. Built by Jim Bridger, the old mountain man, this was a caravanserai where, with a forge and carpenter's shop, repairs could be made. If they were wise, the migrants called a rest for a day or two. If they were lucky they could trade in their more exhausted or footsore oxen and replace them, at a price, with fresh ones. The "replacements" were probably someone else's ailing oxen of a few weeks before. Now, allegedly refreshed, they were reckoned to be ready to go again.

Before leaving Fort Bridger, the captains had to decide if they were going to dip south through Mormon country—a route which would then take them looping round the bottom of the Great Salt Lake. Or they could choose the easier but longer route to the north—arching right up into today's southern Idaho before eventually turning again for California. Either way, if they had done their homework, they would have known that the most exhausting part of their journey lay ahead—420 miles of it. Within three weeks, by either route, they would be into what their inadequate maps called "Desert." The maps were not far wrong. As with the earlier Overlanders, there was only one practical way across—down the course of the Humboldt River. For 360 of those 420 miles, the river would be their lifeline. Indeed, without this river, the overland Rush might never have grown beyond a mere trickle. True, there were other ways of trekking to California, but they were long, lonely and far more hazardous. A few gold-seekers had made it from the Missouri to Santa Fe; then across the mountains and aridity of Arizona to southern California. They used pack-mules rather than wagons. But, on arrival in California, they found that they still had another 300 miles to go—north to the goldfields. Another group, arriving from South Pass and then crossing into Mormon country, realized that they were running very late. They knew that they were unlikely to make it over the desert in time to get through the Sierras before the snows of late autumn filled the passes. So, instead, they went southwest—to cut around the southern end of the Sierras. With difficulty and three deaths, they crossed the desert, only to find themselves trapped in the waterless wastes of Death Valley. Thirteen more died.

So the Humboldt was really the only way to go. Grass and water, as always, were the priorities. For the early wagons, the river had both. But by mid-

September, when the traffic had built up to more than a hundred wagons a day, the grass was almost gone. And if conditions away from the slowly flowing stream were anything like they are today, the desert sagebrush was no help. With very few exceptions, the aridity began (and still begins) within a few yards of the stream. Even in late summer, temperatures could (and still can) reach over 100°F/37°C. The sun's shadeless glare and heat, the flat sameness of the terrain, the dust storms, a wobbling wagon wheel or a sick wife, and, always, the growing exhaustion of the oxen or mules would have strained the spirit of even the most sanguine of the gold seekers. As the teams grew less willing, the way became littered with a jetsam of dumped supplies: stoves, cooking pots, clothing, saws, axes, even mining tools—anything to lighten the load. Sometimes, even wagons would be abandoned; maybe something had broken that would take too long to repair. The oxen might then be used to carry packs. Even if there were no breakdowns, and you managed to plod fifteen miles each day (some wagons traveled at night to escape the heat), the journey down the Humboldt would still take more than three weeks. But there was worse to come. It was not so much that, after 300 miles, the river suddenly ended in the Humboldt Sink, a desolation that was part drying lake and part marsh; it was the fact that beyond the Sink lay the Forty Mile Desert—no water at all. In growing dread, they would have talked about this barrier during the preceding weeks, but probably they pushed the subject away in order to deal with some more immediate problem. Now there was no escape.

The word was that, halting at the margins of the Sink, you should cut as much grass as you could carry, you should fill every possible container with water, and, once started, you should not stop. It was best if you left at sunset because, in a crossing of about 36 hours, two-thirds of the journey would then be away from the heat of the day. Even so, one diarist wrote that, along the whole way, even at night, he was seldom beyond the smell of rotting oxen and mules. Mostly, by now, it was every family for itself. Nevertheless, there are some tales of charity: someone stopping to help repair someone else's broken wheel; someone else helping some walking children (yes, there were a few) into a passing wagon, even a family sharing its short rations with another who had nothing. But, at the same time there were some sharp operators—shysters who came back into the desert from the Truckee and Carson Rivers with water at $20 or $30 a pitcher.

That same diarist who recalled the smell also wrote that when he eventually reached the Truckee River, the relief was such that he felt "as near Heaven as anyone could reach in this world. Tongue cannot express the joy we felt when we see that we was safe over these deserts."

Such was the reputation of the Forty Mile Desert that late in the summer of

1849 more than a thousand gold-seekers were seduced into taking what might be called a long-cut. This alternative route led away to the north. Within a few days, as the going became increasingly dry and difficult, they must have cursed their misinformation. But they pressed on, always hoping that things would get better. They never did. Today's road maps show that their route led across what is called the Black Rock Desert and, although there are at least a dozen lakes marked in this northwest corner of Nevada, their names (Alkali Lake, Mud Lake, Mosquito Lake, and others) are all followed by the single bracketed word: Dry. Even today, in this sun-baked desolation of 8,000 square miles, there are just two very lonely settlements: Empire and Gerlach. They have populations of 300 and 130 respectively. Further, it is said that when, in the 1950s, the US authorities were looking for a remote spot to carry out various underground nuclear tests, this part of Nevada was rejected; it was deemed to be *too* remote ...

Somehow those misdirected fortune-hunters struggled across the Black Rock Desert and managed to reach the mountains beyond. Now, terribly weakened by their ordeal and almost out of food, they came to an exhausted halt. Then, too early, came the first snows. But they were lucky. On the far side of the mountains, the Governor of California had become alerted (by some unexplained premonition?) to the plight of those misguided Argonauts. Remarkably, in an era not much noted for official benevolence, he used government funds to equip two relief expeditions. One of the expeditions found and rescued the snowbound wagons, but not before several deaths. Thereafter, very few people risked what came to be called Death Road. Even today, if you decide to drive north along Highway 447, you had best take more than normal precautions.

Back on the "approved" trail, once the Forty-Niners were across the Forty Mile Desert, and had arrived safely at the Truckee or, alternatively, the nearby Carson River, men and animals needed to recover their strength for the final trial: the High Sierras. The mountains began 70 miles further on. It was an unforgiving uphill haul—starting a few miles west of the site of today's divorce capital: Reno. In places the way became so steep that it was often necessary to yoke two teams together—to pull the heavier wagons over the passes. By now, after nearly 2,000 miles, the men and their animals were tired almost to exhaustion. But, if they were through before the snows (and most of them were), the knowledge that they were now "almost there" must have given an exhilarating lift to everyone's morale. After all, in another week or two, any one of them (or maybe several of them) might have "panned out" a small fortune. Or even a big one. El Dorado was just over the next pass—at last. Who knew what riches might be in store?

Certainly, a lucky few found fortunes beyond even their most optimistic hopes, and, in the process, fired everyone else's dreams; that was how the contagion of gold fever worked. Nuggets rather than mere gold dust were what everyone was after; most of the nuggets were smaller than a pea, but a few were the size of a small pebble, and even fewer were the size of an egg. Very rarely one as big as half a brick would be unearthed. Finding just one of those, a man (and his family if he had one) could be "comfortable" for several generations. But, for most of the Argonauts, especially those who arrived after the initial rush, life was mostly one of hardscrabble. They found that most of the easier alluvial deposits along the streams had been worked out. The days were gone when a man working alone might make $10 a day with just a shovel, a pick, and a pan. Now men worked the diggings in teams; sometimes they formed partnerships; sometimes they worked for wages. They quarried in pits; they dug drift mines—horizontal tunnels back into the river banks. They brought the spoil down to the running water and ran it through perforated drums and rocker boxes. It was not yet an industrialized process, but it was going that way.

Today, the old mines and diggings with their wonderfully optimistic (or sardonic?) names like the Wish-Us-Luck, the Never Sweat, the Try Again, the Hurry Up, the Lord Knows, the Don't-Laugh-Yet, the Goodness Gracious and the Glory Be are long gone—collapsed, eroded, filled-in, overgrown. But echoes of the Forty-Niners are still with us: we still "stake a claim" in the hope that a venture will "pan out." We still hope to "strike it rich" rather than to wind up "stony broke." We still sing "Oh, my darling Clementine." The California State seal carries the one-word motto "Eureka"—Greek for "I have found it." And the world wears Levis, first sewn and riveted from heavy-duty sailcloth brought round Cape Horn by a 22-year-old emigrant, Levi Strauss. He planned to make miners' tents. But they did not want tents; they wanted pants. So he sent for more sailcloth, and slowly stitched and riveted his way to a fortune. And, one can say, to a long and worldwide recognition.

Young Levi Strauss was typical. Most of the time, it was not the miners who wound up with the money; it was the storekeepers, traders, entrepreneurs, and, as always, the lawyers and the bankers. One-year loans were made at rates of anything up to 50%. A consignment of $2 picks and shovels, freighted round the Horn at $1 each, would sell in the gold country for $10 a time. Similar profits could be made on almost anything (including tent cloth) that the miners needed. Young Bidwell, who led that first emigrant train back in 1841, had been working as a foreman for Sutter when, like everyone else, he caught gold fever. He got in early, struck it moderately rich, and then got out quickly. He promptly invested his takings in a spread of land on which to raise beef cattle. Within two years he had made a small fortune selling meat to the miners. Then he parlayed that small fortune into a much bigger one; he wound up the owner of 20,000 acres of irrigated farmland; he became a Congressman and even ran for President (as a prohibitionist). Another man who looked to local appetites was Philip Armour. He had walked all the way to California and, after a few fruitless weeks with a wash-pan, he too decided that beef was the business to be in. He opened a butcher's shop, raised some cattle on the side and, after five years, he went home with $8,000. Using his Californian savings and experience, he opened a small slaughterhouse and meat-packing business in Milwaukee. In time, Armour Inc. became the biggest meat packer in the world.

Other migrants realized that, unless they were very lucky, there were surer ways of making money than with a pick and a shovel. Spotting a gap in the market, one of them started a carpentry shop. He would make wheelbarrows. After some years, like Mr. Armour, John Studebaker took his considerable earnings home— to rescue his brothers' failing wagon-building works. Thereafter, one might reasonably say that for the Studebaker family, one thing led to another.

Nevertheless, on the actual diggings, it was not *all* sweat and frustration. There was always a spot somewhere that, after months of disappointment, suddenly yielded an unlikely jackpot. The dream was kept enticingly alive by the news that, for example, only that very week a lad barely into his teens had panned out gold worth nearly $3,000. Or that a loner just down from some stream high in the Sierras (and he wasn't saying where) was, even now, weighing out a prodigious "take" at the bank down the street. Then there was gossip about the folk who, somewhere in the next valley, had dug out a nugget weighing over twenty pounds. Or the rumor that someone thought that they had found the Holy Grail of miners the world over: a motherlode. Always, there was someone who, down to his last few dollars that morning, was standing drinks for everyone in the valley that same evening. You hoped that *your* luck might turn; incurable (almost) optimism was what kept the whole marvelous adventure turning.

So, life on the diggings was always unpredictable, frequently ironic. A miner who had hacked away for, say, six unrewarding months might, one day, look up to see a newcomer digging out a rich seam of pay dirt after only a week. Then, a day later, when on the edge of quitting in disgust, the first miner might find that he too had struck it rich—at last. Suddenly, he had been blessed with the Midas Touch. But that Touch was something with which Sutter and Marshall, the two men who could claim to have started the whole thing, were never blessed. Sutter, as he had feared from the very beginning, had been swamped by the stampede. Without staff to guard his livestock, he was robbed blind. Then he found that, under US jurisdiction, the original Mexican title to his land was invalid. He himself tried "excavating for a mine"—without success. He became an alcoholic and then a bankrupt until, eventually, the state legislature took pity and granted him a pension of $250 a month for five years. Sutter grumbled that it was not enough. He lived on until 1880, long enough to see California become one of the richest states in the Union—its wealth triggered and, in its early years, sustained by gold. He died a pauper. James Marshall, the man who had spotted those yellow peas in the tail-race, was no more fortunate. He too tried the diggings. Then he tried setting up as a blacksmith. Later, he earned a thin living as an itinerant lecturer—expounding, no doubt, about "the early days." He too took to drink. Penniless, he outlived his one-time boss, Johann Sutter, by a few years. His burial, paid for by the State (honor at last), was on a slope overlooking the site of the mill where he had once sat down and done that "hard thinking." Later, some public-spirited Californians put up his statue; it is said to have cost them a prodigious $25,000. Now there *is* irony for you ...

&

There is still money to be made in California's gold country. But these days most of it comes out of the tourists' pockets. For $10 or $20, at places like Rough-and-Ready and Coloma, they will teach you how to pan for gold; you keep what you can find—which won't be much. Afterwards, you can have your photo taken holding a shovel and clutching a small sack labeled Gold; for an extra dollar or two they will tint it to look like an 1850s daguerreotype. At a nearby bar, to a jukebox playing "Home Sweet Home" and other gold rush hits, you can imbibe a Forty-Niner, a Bourbon Bonanza or a Prospector's Special. Maybe you will order a Wagon Wheel Pizza. Then, by following along State Highway 49, you will arrive at the site of Marshall's mill, or, a little further on, you can put on a hard hat and go into a mine. Later, you might sleep off your exertions at the Golden Nugget Inn or the El Dorado Motel. Or, who knows, you might hightail it down to the lights of Sacramento or even San Francisco that same evening.

ɞ

All through the decade that followed the first exuberant years, the migrants kept coming. But many, disappointed to find that the easier gravels had long been worked out, resigned themselves to quieter lives—reverting to the mundane trades and professions they already knew, but which they thought that they had left 2,000 or more miles behind. Nevertheless, they helped to build California. By the late 1870s, the gold business was becoming mechanized. It needed heavy equipment for burrowing deep into mountains; it needed pumps and water jets to sluice through hundred of tons of overburden—to get at the gold-bearing gravel underneath. It all took capital. So now, the mining engineers, the accountants, the lawyers and, yes, the pawnbrokers and the bankers were taking over. Many of the original Forty-Niners and those who came soon after found themselves employed as simple shovel-hands. Or not employed at all. For a few (still dreaming), that was not what life was about. They took off. For the next half-century, as prospectors, they ricocheted all over the mountains and deserts of the west. They found silver in Nevada, Arizona and Idaho; they found gold in South Dakota, Colorado and Montana; they reached north into Alaska and Canada's Yukon; they sailed away for Australia's Bendigo and Kalgoorlie; they searched across the high country of New Zealand and the veldt of South Africa. As always, chasing gold was a wonderfully chancy business. A few made sizeable fortunes; some just rubbed along, most never made a bean. But one can surely guess that, in the mining camps of Arizona, Alaska, or Australia, around an evening bottle or two of cheap whisky, they would be telling each other, perhaps a little sourly, that gold was only where you found it.

7

THE HOSTILES AND THE MILITARY

"You will not receive overtures of peace and submission from the Indians, but will attack and kill every male Indian over twelve years of age."

An order by General Patrick Connor prior to his abortive military sweep of the Powder River country in the spring of 1865.

☙

The whites wanted North America; it was their "Manifest Destiny," even though that convenient term was not invented until the process was long under way. The slow war with the Indians (as they have long been known and, despite the recent inroads of political correctness, the way they still often refer to themselves today) had begun in the forests "back east" more than three centuries earlier. But the most bitter struggle of all—involving the tribes of the northern plains—really began only 150 years ago. Mostly they were the several tribes of the Sioux nation and their allies, the Cheyenne.

With their adoption of the horse, the people of the Plains had become true nomads, wandering continuously in pursuit of the buffalo herds—which gave them their food, their clothing, their shelter, their fuel, their needles and thread, their water carriers (the dried stomach of the animal), and even the strings for their bows. Between times, for summer fun, they raided other tribes. That was how it was until they saw the white invaders. At first it was the trappers, later it was the wagon trains. But they were only moving *across* the plains—to find gold in California or to start farms in Oregon. And if they killed a few buffalo along the way, well, there were plenty more. Besides, the slow-moving convoys gave easy opportunity for the occasional excitement—a raid on a party that was under strength or straggling, a running fight with a military escort, maybe the chance to take a scalp or a few guns or a mule or two if the raiders were lucky. It could be a grim game and lives were lost, but it was far short of war.

But whenever actual settlement, temporary or permanent, encroached along the margins of their land and, thereby, the buffalo were driven off, the tribes were wont to strike back in murderous bad temper. The Santee Sioux suddenly rampaged through central Minnesota back in the summer of 1862; they killed several hundred settler families and more than sixty soldiers. Thirty-eight Sioux were caught and publicly hanged on one huge scaffold.

Two years later, another tribe living in what is today's western Kansas became irritable. These were the Southern Cheyenne. The buffalo had been driven off over a swath of territory by the constant traffic of miners and supply wagons rolling out along the broad Smokey Hill Trail to the gold strikes in the eastern foothills of the Rocky Mountains. The Cheyenne became resentful of the need to ride ever further to find their food. One story has it that to redress the balance, braves drove off some cattle from a ranch just outside the small mining town of Denver. Another story tells of several families, including small children, being killed and mutilated in Cheyenne raids. Denver's *Rocky Mountain News* led the call for a quick and bloody revenge. Several hundred local citizens quickly formed themselves into an ad hoc regiment; they called themselves the Colorado Cavalry. This bunch of rough-riders was led by a self-righteous Methodist pastor, the Reverend "Colonel" Chivington. "I believe that it is right and honorable to use any means under God's heaven to kill Indians."

Presently, word came that there was there was a sizable Cheyenne encampment on the plains about 120 miles southeast of Denver. The fact that this was known to be an uncharacteristically peaceful group of Cheyenne was irrelevant as far as the men of the Colorado Cavalry were concerned. After a forced ride through the snow, they fell upon the unsuspecting tepees at dawn. It is said that most of the slaughter was done in ten minutes. But, for the rest of the day, the volunteers killed anyone they could find hiding nearby. By late afternoon, they were reasonably satisfied; the body count had risen to nearly 200. Regrettably, 300 had escaped.

It was no secret that, only a month earlier, the military commander for southern Colorado had met with this band of Cheyenne; he had given their leader, Black Kettle, a guarantee that they could safely make winter camp along a stream called Sand Creek. But, given that his headquarters, Fort Lyons, was a hard day's ride to the south of the proposed Indian camp, he would surely have known that he would be in a very weak position to honor his protective assurance. Black Kettle, too trustful by far, had assumed that he and his people were safe from attack; he was even flying the Stars and Stripes outside his teepee.

The Colorado Cavalry claimed that some of the now-dead Cheyenne had been involved in the earlier hostilities. Quite possibly. It often happened that way: with winter coming, the ponies would become too thin and weak to chase the buffalo; it was time to make camp until the spring. So, wandering bands would make their way to the nearest fort where the elders would haggle with the military until some uneasy agreement was reached. No doubt, many of them really did want peace, but sometimes, four or five months later, the warmer days of spring would rekindle the younger hot-heads to "paint up" for just one more summer of raiding. In short, one cannot be sure if everyone in that Sand Creek encampment, under their genuinely peaceable leader, Black Kettle, really wanted to stay clear of the hostilities, or whether some of them only wanted a convenient cessation through the winter. In any event, either possibility would have made no difference to Colonel Chivington. He proclaimed that all Indians were vermin. "I want you to kill all, big and little." His men were only too willing to obey. Immediately after the massacre—for such it was—the colonel sent a dispatch back to Denver. "Attacked a Cheyenne village of from nine hundred to a thousand warriors ... Killed between four and five hundred. All did nobly."

When he and his volunteers were later criticized for the disproportionate number of women and children killed (some said that, altogether, there were more than 150 slain as compared with sixty braves), he replied that the women had fought back as hard as any of the men and, anyway, his men would willingly have killed more of the men if there had been more to kill.

Maybe there was some truth in the accusation about the women. But what is undisputed is that many of Chivington's volunteers ran amok; after burning the camp to the ground, they took scalps (later displayed in a Denver theater) and mutilated many of the bodies—cutting breasts from the women and scrotums from the men. It was recognized on the frontier that the skin of those organs, when cured, made supple pouches. A very old man once showed me something that looked like a congealed wodge of black tissue paper; he said it was his grandfather's tobacco pouch. It could have been.

To some later commentators Sand Creek rates as an unpardonable Mi-lai of the plains. But, at the time, back in Denver, Chivington and his men were honored citizens. One wonders what the colonel would have made of the fact that in 1996, the General Conference of the United Methodist Church passed a formal resolution apologizing "for the atrocities committed at Sand Creek by one of our own clergy." More relevantly, one wonders what today's Cheyenne Tribal Council made of the apology.

❧

Today, just after you cross the Big Sandy on Colorado Highway 96 there is a roadside marker to the incident. It calls it "One of the regrettable tragedies of the West." Perhaps there is not much else that it can say. A mile or two further on, the road runs past a derelict gas-station, a school house whose roof has fallen in, and three or four deserted shacks. There are a few cottonwood trees, a rusting tractor and a notice which says "Chivington, Pop 12." On the afternoon I passed by, I would reckon that that number was an exaggeration—by about 100%. The only living creature I could see was an old horse.

The site of the actual massacre lies five miles north along a seldom-traveled dirt road. Here too there is a small monument which, in 2007, along with the actual battle site, was taken under the jurisdiction of the US National Park Service. The monument itself, a slab of concrete rather like a big gravestone, sits on a low and windswept hill looking down over the sagebrush to the cottonwoods of Sand Creek. Lying on and around the monument was the detritus of plastic flowers, a child's pink slipper, a scatter of coins, a necklace of colored beads, some tobacco in a plastic pouch, a small US flag, a crucifix and chain, a pen knife, a baseball cap and two scruffy and sun-bleached teddy bears. My notebook asks, "Teddy Bears? Why? From where did the western world get this maudlin "thing" for all these bloody bears? Shades of poor Diana."

❧

The repercussions of Sand Creek were not long coming. As soon as the weather eased, the Cheyenne erupted. Across western Kansas and into Colorado, they went on the rampage. After what had happened to Black Kettle and his people there was obviously nothing but danger in trusting the whites, whether military or civilian. All freight and stagecoach traffic in and out of Denver was halted. Outlying settlements and stage stations were overwhelmed, fleeing wagons were sacked, and the men were killed, scalped and filled with arrows. Any women still alive were dragged away as captives; some killed themselves, some were eventually bartered back to the whites. A few were deranged for life.

Away to the north, in the vastness that is now Montana, Wyoming and the Dakotas the situation was quieter. It was not that the tribes of the Lakota (also known as the Sioux) were naturally inclined to peace. Far from it. But being only occasionally disturbed by small army expeditions, they were not much bothered. In any case, during the Civil War, the Army—such as it was out West—had better things to do than to provoke the Hostiles (as they were becoming known). Meanwhile, as far as the tribes in those parts were concerned, there were still plenty of buffalo to hunt, and there was the equally satisfying pastime of raiding their ancient (and weaker) enemies, the Crow, and pushing them off their lands to the west—the Powder River country of today's Wyoming.

Of course, the Sioux heard of the troubles away to the south and drew their own conclusions—conclusions which were confirmed when some of those Southern Cheyenne came drifting north. They arrived with the plunder of the stage stations they had sacked; they displayed the cavalry horses and mules that they had taken, they demonstrated the rifles they had captured, and, one supposes, they boasted how weak the whites were when really confronted. The temptation for the Cheyenne and their more numerous Sioux allies must have been powerful. Perhaps they would go south to see what they could take from the travelers moving up the broad valley of the Platte River—along the Overland Trail.

These possibilities were not lost on the Army commanders who were, anyway, stirred by the recent humiliations. For them, the Civil War had ended at just the right moment. Now, with the promise of additional troops, plans were made for a major expedition into the very heart of the Sioux hunting grounds—the country along the Powder River.

"You will not receive overtures of peace and submission from the Indians, but will attack and kill every male over twelve years of age." That was part of an order issued by General Connor who would have overall command of the campaign. He planned that three columns totaling more than 2,000 soldiers would converge to push the Sioux and their Cheyenne allies into an ever-tightening killing ground. The telegraph between Fort Laramie and Omaha clattered day and night as details were coordinated. On both Connor's mental map and on the one in his Fort Laramie headquarters, there were three confident axes of advance; it must have looked a very workable plan.

In the event, things started to go wrong before they had even started. The catalog of errors and misfortunes is interesting because it explains a great deal about the problems of "Indian fighting"—problems that the Army was to face again and again over the next 20 years. These problems owed little to the tribes. Too often, the Army was the author of its own misfortunes.

First, rivalry—or something close to it. Before the column detailed to advance from the Missouri had even started out, it received countermanding orders from a Major General who had immediate command in that quarter. Perhaps piqued that he had been passed over for command of the whole campaign (by General Connor), he ordered his immediate command away to the north side of the Missouri. Examples of such rivalries occur too often in the story of the Indian Wars. In this particular case, the consequence was that the column spent two months crisscrossing the prairie on the wrong side of the river, without ever seeing a tepee.

Second, morale—or, rather, the lack of it. Many of the officers and even more of the enlisted men had no experience of the plains. They were frightened or mutinous. Or both. Further, many of the rank-and-file argued that they were volunteers who had enlisted to fight the Confederacy. "Indian fighting" had never been a part of their plans and, now, with the Civil War won, they demanded to be discharged. At best, they were unwilling combatants. At worst, they became deserters. Three hundred of Connor's men—a third of his immediate command—disappeared within two weeks of the General's column setting out northward from Fort Laramie. Quite where they went no one seems to know; maybe they just walked south until they came to the Overland Trail and then hitched a ride to California or Oregon. In short, inexperienced officers and deserting soldiers were a recurring pattern on the plains. Rather better, by some accounts, were the "galvanized Yankees." These were ex-Confederate prisoners who had earlier been released from Union prisoner-of-war camps—on condition that they volunteered for duties on the frontier.

Third, staff work or, again, the lack of it. General Connor seems to have done nothing to ensure that any of the three columns took experienced guides with them. Thus, any hope that they might synchronously converge at some designated meeting point hundreds of miles away was likely to be a remote one. Also, the columns had no means of supporting each other, and no means of exchanging any intelligence they might gather. To be fair, that latter failing owed more to the immense distances than it did to military inadequacy.

Lastly, logistics were always a problem. Reaching far out from their bases, columns had to carry all their supplies with them. This meant there had to be an accompanying wagon train—which severely hampered both the speed and flexibility of operations. On the only occasion when Connor's own command found a sizable Sioux camp and, with the advantage of surprise, put the Hostiles to flight, the officer involved was unable to follow up because his men were out of ammunition; they had ranged too far ahead of their supply wagons. In passing, it is pertinent to emphasize that, all through the Indian Wars, while the

Army's speed and mobility were always limited by its supply "tail," the Indians—except in winter—were almost entirely free of such a constraint.

Eventually, after getting lost several times, Connor's column turned around and made its way back to Fort Laramie. Some of the soldiers were barefoot. Many were in tatters.

For the Sioux and the Cheyenne it had been a good summer. They had avoided any major confrontations. But, falling on stragglers, they had taken rifles, bugles and a variety of supplies. And they had added to their own herds with a number of cavalry mounts and mules. Always a proud, even an arrogant people, they were now quite confident that they could bargain from a position of strength with the whites. Consequently, when they heard a few months later that the whites (who had evidently rethought their strategy) were summoning them to a treaty meeting at Fort Laramie, they sent back messages saying that they would think about it. Why should they be in any hurry?

But by the spring, curiosity seems to have got the better of them—that and the hope that the whites would be handing out the bribes which had become an expected part of such proceedings.

Fort Laramie, though adequately garrisoned, was not stockaded; it was spread out—stables, barracks, stores, officers' quarters—around a well-worn parade ground. In preparation for the meeting, carpenters had built a wooden stage and knocked together a spread of low benches in front of the commanding officer's two-story house. Colonel Maynadier must have been well pleased; his messengers, sent out some weeks before, had obviously managed to persuade most of the chiefs who mattered to come in. Undoubtedly, the promise of an issue of clothing, blankets, axes, sugar and tobacco had helped—and curiosity about what the whites had in mind.

In fact, there were now more than 400 tepees scattered across the grassy plain around the fort. One can picture the scene. Cooking smoke, drifting with the dust of the pony herds, smudges the stillness. Old men sit in the sunshine smoking their long pipes and swapping stories of their valor. The women pound new buffalo hides to soften them, and patch the worn footings of their tepees; later, they will take their children and wander off to have a look at the white man's fort. The young men, the braves, are out in the open meadows, galloping their ponies, showing off to each other and, no doubt, preening themselves for the benefit of the girls who stand off to one side.

The tribal elders are gathered in the shadow of a tepee; they discuss the meeting they are about to have with the whites. They would still have been unsure of the meeting's exact purpose, but, whatever it might be, they would have concern that they should not allow themselves to be divided. And they discuss the rumor that there is a regiment, some say 1,000 men, coming up the Platte valley. What for?

There are no records of the conversations that Colonel Maynadier would have had with Commissioners Taylor, Wistar, and McLaren who had just arrived from the East. But one can surely assume that at some point they went through a list of the various tribal elders in order to work out, on the basis of vague intelligence, who would be the likely hawks and who the doves. One imagines too that they discussed the purpose of the infantry regiment that the Commissioners would have overtaken on their own journey up the Platte.

So what was that purpose? Quite simply, the regiment was to build and then garrison a fort in the middle of the Sioux's favorite hunting ground, the Powder River country. The reason for this proposed incursion was equally simple ...

Prompted by the mining lobby, the Government—anxious to replenish the nation's near bankrupt coffers after the Civil War—had been looking at its maps. It wished to open a shortcut to the burgeoning gold mines that lay along the eastern margins of the northern Rockies (in today's Montana). The existing route was far too long; it was also expensive. In shallow-draft steamers, it began on the Missouri at St. Joseph or Council Bluffs. But, frustratingly, the river looped far away to the north before eventually bending to the west. So, even with good piloting, the journey—against the current for over 1,500 miles—could take two or more months. The head of navigation, in the spring when the river was full, was Fort Benton. From there, the last 200 miles was by wagon. What was needed was an overland "road" that cut the corners and ran more or less straight cross-country.

The fact was that such a shortcut had already been pioneered. Just before the Civil War, a small party of prospectors had found a way across the *terra incognita* of the Powder River country. A few other brave souls had followed them, and the route was now referred to as the Bozeman Trail, after one of the original pathfinders. But without military protection it was a very risky journey and, consequently, little used. Now, with the end of the war, the government was keen to establish the trail as the "official" route for the Montana goldfields. Thus it hoped to encourage more miners to head for Montana, and so to refill more rapidly the national treasury.

But there was a problem: the Sioux. As in Vietnam exactly a century later, and in Afghanistan more recently, there were two theories (amongst others) on how best to achieve "pacification." Broadly, in the late 1860s there were those who advocated an aggressive tactic of "search and destroy." But, given that this tactic had not, on the few occasions the Army had tried it, been notably successful, official thinking was now more inclined to the less ambitious concept of the

Red Cloud, leader of the Oglala Sioux and an arch-enemy of Colonel Carrington (National Archives)

"defended enclave." This meant the building of a fort, or forts, far out in the wilderness from which, once firmly established, roving patrols might assert what, today, we would see as a combination of muscular pacification with a policy of winning hearts and minds. (One can see reflections of both these approaches in recent Afghanistan.) The second of these policies was recommended by the War Department to Congress in February 1865. "The permanent cure for the hostilities of the Northern Indians is to go into the heart of the buffalo country and hold forts until, the trouble is over ..." In fact, "the hostilities of the Northern Indians" had been at a relatively low level during the Civil War—which was just as well because, of course, military manpower at the time was concentrated on other targets.

When the Sioux leaders wrapped their blankets around their shoulders and walked up to the fort to take their places on those benches in front of the colonel's house, they were, as always, distrusting. Commissioner Taylor started proceedings. To make interpretation easy, he spoke in short sentences: "The Great Father in Washington is sad when his children make war ... he does not want his children's land ... soldiers only come when the Indians make war ... the Great Father has many soldiers ... he has a great wish for a treaty with his red children ... they would be wise to listen to the Great Father."

No doubt the Indians listened impassively. Then the treaty itself was read out. After the legalistic and meaningless (as far as the audience was concerned) preliminaries, the commissioner got around to what the treaty was really all about: a right of way through the Powder River country. Immediately the Indians bubbled with annoyance. Two chiefs, Man-Afraid-Of-His-Horses (his name was really "Men are afraid of *his* Horses) and Red Cloud began to argue with the commissioners; they grew increasingly frustrated at the delays of interpretation. They pointed out that the tribes had "touched paper" before, but that it had not stopped the whites from killing the buffalo and driving off the game. Anyway, why did the Great Father always want more land?

Commissioner Taylor explained that the Great Father did not want more land; he merely wanted a safe right of way, and he promised that "travelers will not be allowed to disturb the game in the country through which they pass." Taylor must have known that this was an impossible commitment. The Indians certainly knew it. With a good deal of bad temper the council broke up, to meet again the next day.

That same evening, five miles to the east, the 18th Infantry halted and formed its wagons into a large square within which it would camp for the next few days. The regiment had marched 350 miles from Fort Kearny; the men were looking forward to a rest. Presently, a small band of Sioux rode up; their leader was taken to the colonel. An interpreter was summoned. Standing Elk came quickly to the point: where were all these soldiers going? Colonel Carrington, who was as honest as he was naive, replied that his regiment was on its way to guard a new road through the Powder River country.

According to Colonel Carrington, writing a year later, Standing Elk just looked at him and said, "There is a treaty being made just now with the people who hunt in the country where you say you are going. You will have to fight if you go there." Doubtless, Carrington replied that he hoped fighting would not be necessary. But, as far as the Indians were concerned, the news would have spread as soon as Standing Elk got back to the tepees.

The Sioux were not fools. Already angered by the meeting earlier that day, they now became thoroughly antagonistic; the Commissioners were obviously forked-tongued double-dealers; while asking for a right of way, they were, in any case, planning to take it by force. The Commissioners, of course, would not have seen it that way; they would easily have persuaded themselves that they had come in good faith to negotiate. After all, once the Sioux agreed to the new road, soldiers would be needed to enforce the agreement against the inevitable hotheads who existed on both sides. But the truth was that, in the event of the Indians being unwilling to "touch paper," there was no alternative plan. The forts would be built; the road would go through.

The Council gathered again on the parade ground the next morning, but the Indians, now knowing that the proceedings were a charade, came to vent their anger rather than to negotiate.

Colonel Carrington, who had ridden over to the fort to oversee the issue of some much-needed supplies before he moved on, was formally introduced to the chiefs. A few acknowledged him. But Red Cloud and Man Afraid, both Oglala-Sioux (then, as now, according even to other Indians, let alone whites, the most stubborn of all the seven tribes that make up the Sioux nation), took the introduction as an added insult. The story goes that the two of them stood up and, shaking their rifles at the whites, one or other shouted, "I trust only in this and in the Great Spirit." Then they turned their backs and, taking their followers with them, stalked angrily away. Within a few hours, Red Cloud and his people struck their tepees and were gone.

It would have been wholly in character for some of the younger braves among the Oglala-Sioux to take immediate vengeance on the Great Father's agents—perhaps a raid on the tempting herds of cattle and horses which were part of the Army's expedition. The fact that there was no such raid suggests a cooling influence. It almost certainly came from Red Cloud. Perhaps by instinct, perhaps by calculation, he seems to have realized that there was a much more important issue than any immediate retaliation against the whites' double-cross. With a regiment poised to enter its homeland, his tribe's very existence as a sovereign people was at stake. What lay ahead had to be a purposeful campaign.

He was right. But for a Sioux, particularly an Oglala, he must have been an unusual man. After all, his people were not much given to working out consequences, let alone strategies. The "long term" was not a concept that much concerned them; in their nomadic life they had little need for it. By custom and culture, they did not so much analyze a situation as react to it.

&

"I apprehend no serious difficulty. Patience, forbearance and common sense in dealing with the Sioux and Cheyenne will do much with all who really desire peace." A comment by Colonel Carrington in a dispatch shortly before he left Fort Laramie for the Powder River country on 18 June 1866

&

There was no way that over 700 soldiers and civilians, more than 200 wagons, and a herd of at least a 1,000 cattle could move on from Fort Laramie without the now-alerted Sioux knowing their exact whereabouts. The summer dust would have been visible for miles. Nevertheless, the Sioux held back from mounting any attack; they seem to have realized, again almost certainly on Red Cloud's advice, that it would be better to wait.

So, the 18th Infantry Regiment marched routinely toward the wilderness of the Powder River country. This was obviously not an expedition equipped for offensive campaigning: there were too many heavily loaded wagons, too many civilians, too many new recruits. This was a force whose purpose was to establish two forts from which, somehow, it was then hoped to protect the proposed trail to those Montana goldfields.

In the growing light of dawn, as he watched his men stamping out their breakfast fires, Colonel Carrington probably wished he had not been burdened with so many under-trained recruits—more than half of his total command—and only 12 officers to lead them. He certainly would have wished for a larger detachment of cavalrymen. But in other respects, he should have been reasonably content. His chief scout and advisor was Jim Bridger, an ex-mountain man and, as such, one of the most experienced westerners ever. The cattle, even allowing for reasonable losses, would keep the battalion in beef for the next twelve months; in those 200 wagons there was sack upon sack of flour, coffee, beans, molasses, salt and hard-tack—enough to sustain the command until it could be re-supplied the following spring. His quartermaster had boxes of vegetable seeds, and there were milk cows, pigs, and poultry. There were mowing machines to cut hay, a horse-driven sawmill, axes, saws, nails, and augurs with which to construct the fort. There were carpenters, blacksmiths and wheelwrights; he had three doctors and a 25-man band, and even a dozen rocking chairs. Lastly, as if to confirm that this was a garrison force rather than one for combat, the officers had been officially encouraged to bring their wives and children, hence his own wife, Margaret, and their two children, Jim and Harry, for whom there was a schoolchest of books, chalks, slates, and a globe. Colonel Carrington should have been a satisfied man for he liked to do a job with much more than mere efficiency. He was an experienced administrator, a by-the-book headquarters officer who planned to build the finest fort west of the Missouri.

Five days after leaving Fort Laramie, the vanguard of the column splashed through a head-water stream of the Powder and rode up the low bluffs on the far side into the furthest outpost of the US Army. Most of the small garrison were "galvanized Yankees," or ex-Confederate prisoners who had been released on condition that they served a term out West. They had been cooped up and forgotten for the last eight months; food had almost run out, scurvy was taking hold, and morale was low. They greeted the incoming column as long-overdue deliverers. They wanted nothing more than to get out and go home. Fort Connor had been hurriedly built, ill-supplied and under-garrisoned; it was in the middle of nowhere. Colonel Carrington and his men were welcome to it.

A day or two later, Carrington left a detachment of his own troops at the fort in order to give himself a halfway house on what would be his ever-lengthening line of communication back to Fort Laramie. On the day the column moved on, the afternoon temperature rose to over 100^0F (38^0C). The dry heat on this and several preceding days had so shrunk the wooden wagon wheels that sometimes their iron tires were falling off. The mules and horses had become irritable and hard to handle. The men—those who were not somnambulant with heat exhaustion—became murderously bad-tempered.

❧

By way of a back-country road, I have taken no more than an hour to drive the 70 miles that it took the battalion the next five days to cover. It was an early autumn day, when the sky was the bluest and the highest I had ever seen. But the glare seemed to reach back behind my eyes, and you'd be a fool to be out without dark glasses; even the occasional cowboy wears them. The only trees were a scatter of pines along the ridges and a line of cottonwoods strung along an almost dry watercourse. The grass was parched to a brittle brown, and one doubts if it had ever been green.

The upper basin of the Powder is still empty country. Occasionally the road runs past a clutch of "nodding donkeys" pumping oil from hundreds of feet below. But it seems entirely possible that nowadays there are fewer people living in these parts than there were Sioux and Cheyenne before Carrington's arrival. As one drives on, one presumes that someone somewhere must own all this land, though for many miles there are no ranch houses, just a straight ribbon of gravel or "blacktop" (tarmac) running away ahead. (In fact, most of this is Federal land.) Sometimes the distant road detaches itself from the ground in the quiver of a mirage. If you stop and switch off, the only sounds are the rush of tires and the slipstream which go on singing in your ears.

Then you might notice on the distant westward horizon that there are some thin white wisps between the blue sky and the darker land. They are too steady to be a mirage; five minutes further on, these feathers seem too smooth to be clouds. You glance at the map and realize that the white must be snow lying along the extreme tops of the highest of the Bighorn Mountains, nearly 30 miles away. After another 15 or 20 minutes the air seems a little cooler; you are climbing slowly, there are trees in the middle distance, the grass is no longer brown. In those few miles it has gone from late-summer-dry to spring-like green. Mrs. Margaret Carrington wrote in her diary: "The transition is like the quick turn of a kaleidoscope."

❧

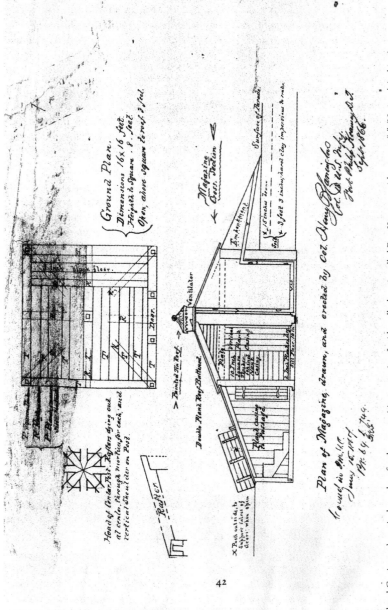

Colonel Carrington's meticulous plans for the ammunition magazine. Incidentally, he misspelled Fort Kearny—with an extra "e" (National Archives)

As their progress brought them into the shadow of the mountains, Carrington and his men would certainly have sensed a kinder countryside. Today, though the wolves, the buffaloes, and most of the bears are gone, there are still antelope, deer and sage hens in the foothills; the grass is lush; wild plums and berries grow in the valleys.

Just before noon on Friday, July 13, the column wound through some cottonwoods and out onto a meadow beside a stream they would call Piney Creek. Carrington ordered his men to make a tented camp. Here was what he had hoped to find: water, pasture, and pine timber. "At last," wrote his wife in her journal, "we have prospect of finding a home."

The colonel went to work immediately, surveying the country around for a site for his fort. By Sunday morning, after prayers and a hymn, he ordered some wagons to be driven a mile or so up the valley. There, on a broad shelf overlooking the Piney, the teamsters drove their wagons back and forth along the four sides of a rectangle to mark the perimeter of the fort. By the afternoon, a horse-powered sawmill had been set up, and the first timbers were being cut. It was his enthusiasm for the task rather than any fear of lurking Indians that drove Carrington with such speed and energy.

Today, one can walk across that same grassy shelf; there is a modest parking lot, a small museum (open in the summer months), and a short section of stockade—an exact facsimile of the original. The outline of the fort is marked with wooden palings. From contemporary records and the colonel's own drawings we know almost everything about the layout of the place that would be called Fort Kearny. The colonel's first priority was to build a perimeter stockade, so pine logs were cut and stood vertically side by side in a trench three feet deep. Then the earth was re-packed solidly around them. A narrow platform, five feet down from the top, ran around the inside of the wall; this was a walkway for riflemen who, if a direct attack ever came, could aim through slits cut along the top of the wall. The stockade (150 yards by 120 yards) made this one of the very few fully enclosed forts built in the West. Inside, Carrington planned barracks, quarters for married and single officers, a hospital, company offices, stores, latrines, and an ammunition store. Within a few days, the colonel was sufficiently pleased with progress that he could send a dispatch 700 miles (by courier and then telegraph) back to army headquarters in Omaha. "In thirty days this post can be held by a small force against any force."

Throughout the now shortening summer days, the digging, sawing, and hammering went on. The colonel was anxious to get his men out of their tents and under solid cover before the first snows. Everything was secondary to the construction; there was certainly no time to send patrols into the surrounding country; there was not even time given to drilling the men in the effective handling of their weapons

In fact, of course, just as they had watched Carrington's slow westward march, the Sioux now watched the building of his fort. Indeed, only two days after those wagons had flattened the grass, a small party of warriors approached under a truce flag. Carrington saw his opportunity to make an impression. While the band played, the visitors were escorted past a small parade and welcomed by the colonel and his officers in hurriedly donned full-dress uniforms. A howitzer fired some rounds onto a nearby hill. The visitors seemed impressed. The visitors were Cheyenne. They said that they had come for an assurance that, if they were attacked by any Sioux, they could expect protection from the Army. In fact, we know from later accounts that, within hours of their departure from the embryo fort, the Cheyenne were being debriefed by Red Cloud. His reaction to what they told him was immediate. He attacked early the next morning.

Even if he did not lead the raid himself, Red Cloud was certainly the author of it. In a galloping swoop, a small band of Oglala Sioux drove off 175 mules and horses. When, eventually, a detachment had saddled up to give chase, the soldiers rode out in a straggle. This was just as the Sioux had planned and, in a series of running skirmishes over 15 or so miles, they killed two soldiers and wounded three others. The cavalry managed to recover just four horses. The first graves were dug that evening.

The Sioux had made the first move. To say that the colonel had lost the initiative would be to imply that he ever had it in the first place. But what else could he do? Certainly, the fort he planned and into which he now put so much energy was (with hindsight?) too elaborate. He would probably have argued that he was following a standard military principle: first establish a secure base from which, later, to move out to patrol and pacify. But the fact remains that he ignored two other important principles: first, if at all possible, gain and then hold the initiative; second, find time for training—especially if one's soldiers are green.

Training: from it flow discipline, confidence in oneself and in one's comrades and, thus, morale. For example, to load and fire the Civil War's Springfield rifle required, according to one manual, seven sequential actions. A highly trained soldier might fire three shots a minute; a green recruit might get the thing jammed. And many of Carrington's men were very green. They got hardly any training drills, and no target practice. Carrington's subsequent reasoning was that there was a shortage of ammunition. Maybe. But his underlying problem was that all his thinking was focused on building his fort.

It soon became apparent that the colonel had another problem: there was not enough timber in the immediate area to supply the construction crews.

Furthermore, there was the need to start laying in a large store of firewood for the coming winter. Soon, logging parties would have to work well away from the protection of the fort. But, for the time being, Carrington may have been lulled into a sense of some security; the Sioux had disappeared.

In fact, they were busy elsewhere. Several war parties had moved off to the south in order to harass the single supply line that led from Fort Connor (now renamed Fort Reno) to the fort that Carrington was building on the Piney. The narrative of one of their ambushes could have been written as a screenplay. Indeed, it has been—many times. But, be that as it may, the story of this one small incident is worth examining because it demonstrates some of the inadequacies exhibited by *both* sides in what was to follow over the next few months. And years.

A small detachment of reinforcements was making its way up the trail: nine wagons and drivers, five officers, ten enlisted men, three civilians hoping to reach the Montana gold diggings, a chaplain, a surgeon and a young photographer. There were three women—two army wives and a black maid. The officers had saddle horses. They had had a tiring but uneventful journey of a week or so from Fort Laramie to Fort Reno/Connor. Now, after a couple of days' rest, they set off on the last 70 miles. On the afternoon of the first day they came on the mutilated remains of a cavalryman, presumably a courier. This, quite apart from the warnings that they had been given only that morning at the fort, should have alerted them.

Now, early on the second day, they came over a low divide and could see, a mile or so ahead, the cottonwood trees that marked the line of Crazy Woman Creek (a tributary of the Powder). On the far side of the creek, they could see some buffalo. So two of the officers decided to ride ahead, to shoot fresh meat. Lieutenants Daniel and Templeton were half a mile ahead and out of sight among the creek-side trees when the main party heard war whoops. In alarm, they managed to scramble their wagons into a rough circle on a low hill.

Presently, Lieutenant Daniel's horse came tearing back to the wagons; its saddle was flapping under its belly and a couple of arrows were lodged in its neck. A few seconds later, Lieutenant Templeton came galloping in; he had an arrow in his back. He fell from his horse in a state of collapse. As best they could, the men started to dig scrapes under the wagons. Extraordinarily, the photographer looked around for a good spot from which to shoot the anticipated action. "I desired," he later wrote, "to make some good instantaneous views." One imagines that the enthusiastic Mr. Glover was told that there were other priorities.

The Indians had a few muskets, but mostly relied on their bows. Small groups would race in to 70–80 yards away. Then, circling the wagons at a gallop, they would drop down to the further side of their ponies and loose off arrows from under the horse's neck. This style of attack was characteristic; it was seldom accurate. But it did not need to be. If only one arrow in fifty found a mark, it was enough. Every now and then a soldier's curse told that a target had been found.

At one point, a brave pranced about just out of accurate rifle range. He was wearing Lieutenant Daniel's tunic and hat. By now despair must have been very close: a sergeant had been killed and more than a third of the defenders were wounded; they had little water and the temperature would have been in the high 90s. They were surrounded by more than 200 Sioux. They knew that to surrender was not an option; prisoners were only taken so that their living bodies might then be mutilated until they died in (and of) agony. With that terrifying prospect, even the greenest soldiers knew that they had to hold on till the last bullet—which they kept for themselves. By late afternoon four more men had been seriously wounded; coughing and spitting blood, they were dragged out of the rifle scrapes and laid under that central wagon where the women were already doing the best they could for those wounded earlier.

"Our condition was now so desperate that a council of war was held. It was decided that in case it came to the worst that we would mercifully kill all the wounded and then ourselves." The chaplain, who by all accounts had been a rifle-toting inspiration all day, was not keen on this decision and, even though slightly wounded, suggested that while there was still an able horse, he should try to break out and race back to Fort Reno for help. A private volunteered to go too.

Only the most brazen screenplay would dare to invent all this: the circling Sioux, the dead Lieutenant's clothes, the diminishing ammunition, the women tearing up their petticoats for bandages and, finally, the escape of this Man of God. With the dusk, the people at the wagons watched as their two messengers disappeared at full gallop over a ridge, pursued by a small band of braves. Lieutenant Wands, the man in charge, would have estimated that if either of the two messengers got through to Fort Reno it would be well into the next morning before a relief column could arrive. The Sioux, even if they did not attack during the night, would start again at first light. The exhausted band set about deepening their scrapes, checking their rifles, reinforcing the wagons, and making the wounded as comfortable as possible. They could hear ululations down by the creek.

Then, in the last glimmer of the day, someone pointed to a dust cloud away to the north. Yes, it was a detachment of cavalry. They had been sent south from the embryo Fort Kearny to find and escort an expected supply convoy. It was chance that brought them, at just that moment, to Lieutenant Wands and his party. After the hubbub of relief and welcome, the newcomers took over the night guard. The Sioux had gone. In the morning, down by the river the soldiers found Lieutenant Daniel—stripped naked, full of arrows and with a stake driven into his anus. Later that morning, they were joined by another detachment of cavalry, from Fort Reno. The chaplain and his companion were with them.

With a military historian, Robert Murray, I have wandered among the cottonwoods of Crazy Woman Creek, and while we both pondered the exact geography of the engagement, there were other more fundamental questions that my knowledgeable companion raised. In working out the answers, he pointed to certain conclusions, truths even, about the different "cultures" of the combatants—which is why this small incident is worth narrating.

First, what were those two officers thinking when they rode out ahead of the main party? After all, only that morning they had come upon the bloody remains of a courier. Second, why, in a fight that lasted most of the day and in which the Sioux outnumbered the soldiers by seven to one, did they only manage to kill two soldiers—and one of those (Lieutenant Daniel) before the action had even begun?

The answers explain much of what followed over the next 20 years in the frequently muddled encounters between the Army and the Hostiles. First, most of the officers and men now being posted for duty on the western plains were quite unfamiliar with what was involved in "Indian fighting." If they had any military experience, it had been gained in the relatively large-scale engagements of the Civil War. Consequently, too many officers had little feeling (if any) for these seemingly empty plains; they had little appreciation of the way the Sioux could suddenly appear from nowhere. So, those two officers could blunder forward to look for their buffalo. It was not the first time and it was certainly not the last that officers would be prompted by a blend of over-confidence and inexperience. Indeed, out west, such "blundering forward"—and not just by junior officers—was to become something of a habit. It would cost lives.

And the answer to the second question? That the main party survived in the face of probably as many as 200 Sioux is largely due to the fact that it was up against an enemy who had little taste for direct assault. The most notable exception to this generalization occurred if, when under enemy attack, warriors found themselves compelled to defend their women and children; under those circumstances they were prepared to fight to the death. Otherwise, when out on an all-male war party, the individual brave rated glory as more important than collective victory. And glory depended on being alive at the end of a fight in order to win the admiration of his fellows. Such prestige was not much good if you were too dead to enjoy it. So, against even a hurriedly prepared defense, there was usually a lack of volunteers to charge into a final and inevitably bloody assault—one could get killed that way. Additionally, their weapons were relatively primitive. The killing range of their small bows, designed for handiness on a horse, was surprisingly short: about 70 yards. Beyond that distance, an arrow might inflict a nasty flesh wound but it seldom had enough penetration to kill.

In short, the fight at Crazy Woman Creek was a fairly typical encounter: a blunder by some over-confident officers, a quickly mounted ambush by an ad hoc war party, some ordered panic by the whites, a great deal of shooting and shouting by the warriors, a fair number of wounded (but relatively few fatalities) among the besieged and, finally, as each side eventually withdrew, an outcome that was inconclusive. So, while the Sioux could be lethal when attacking stragglers or small parties of careless travelers, when up against a force of any strength, they seem—like most guerrillas then and since —to have relied on two main tactics: a quick hit-and-run raid or a decoy-and-ambush. But, as often as not, their war-parties were too impetuous for a hidden and patient wait by a trail or a river crossing.

All the same, despite those deficiencies (and who is to say what might have been the outcome if the cavalry had not come riding to the rescue), the fact is that the Sioux had everyone guessing. Their skirmishing accelerated to become a constant, if ragged, war. With the cooler days of September, they really increased the pressure, as the catalog of just one week demonstrates ...

At dawn on Monday, September 10, a raiding party drove off 42 mules from an army supply column that had arrived at the fort from Fort Laramie the evening before. That same afternoon, picking on another herd, they made off with more than 100 horses and mules. As usual, a mounted detachment galloped out in pursuit, only to return bad-tempered and empty-handed. On Wednesday, the Sioux attacked again—twice. First, they rode in on a party of hay-cutters; they killed three of them and wrecked one of the mowing machines. The same day they stampeded one of the beef herds, and 200 steers were lost. On Friday, they turned their attention to the horses again and drove off a number of cavalry mounts; two sentries were wounded. Saturday passed quietly. On Sunday, another haying party was ambushed and one man lost. That afternoon, Mr. Glover, the young photographer, wandered off from a wood-cutting crew. His body was found later; he had been scalped and his back split open by a tomahawk.

The next few weeks were not much different, but toward the end of October the tempo of attacks eased off. Maybe the Sioux were away hunting buffalo against the coming winter. Now, inside the fort, there was muttering among some of the officers that their Colonel was wasting his chance for retaliatory action. But his mind was still on other things. He had ordered a wood-cutting detail to find two particularly high pines; lashed end to end, they would make a 120-foot flagpole. At the same time, the band was commanded to practice various patriotic airs. Over in the stores, the quartermaster's staff were opening bales of new serge jackets. The carpenters were building a platform at one side of the parade ground. The wives were cooking cakes and pies, and shaking out their best dresses and shawls.

Despite all his problems and anxieties, Colonel Carrington was pleased. By any standards, his fort *was* a remarkable achievement—though whether, in detail or in principle, it was appropriate to the needs of that time and place is surely (even without the benefit of hindsight?) doubtful. Anyway, the colonel was determined that now, before the first snows, would be the right time for a ceremony.

The afternoon of Wednesday, October 31 was cloudless. The garrison wheeled onto the parade ground; the band played; guidons flapped; brasswork flashed in the sun. The colonel, chaplain, and ladies stepped up onto the platform. The proceedings began with the chaplain asking the Lord's blessing on the work just completed. Next, the colonel stepped forward and unfolded the speech he had been preparing over the last several days. His wife had helped him—which is how we know what was said. He began by paying tribute to the battalion's dead: Lieutenant Daniel, Infantrymen Terrel, Livelsberger, Gilchrist, Johnson, Fitzpatrick, Oberly, Wasser.

"They have given their lives to redeem our pledge never to yield one foot of advance, but to guarantee a safe passage to all who seek a home in the lands beyond … The steam whistle and the rattle of the mower have followed your steps in the westwards march of empire …" He talked in similar tones for a further half hour; one can guess that some of the troops fidgeted inside the stiffness of their new jackets. Then, when he had finished, the band played the national anthem, an artillery piece fired a salute, and the flag was slowly raised. It was huge: 20 by 36 feet. Waving gently in the breeze, it was the highest and the biggest flag that anyone had ever seen.

The Sioux saw it too. Attracted by the noise, some of them had ridden in from their camps and now, in clear view but out of range, they flashed their mirrors at each other and into the fort. The adjutant knew that he would have to order a strengthened guard that night.

That evening, the officers and wives were received by their Colonel and his lady. Amidst the small talk, one can reasonably surmise that some of the officers wandered across the room to ask "what now?" of their commander. Did their questions embarrass him? After all, throughout his army career, he had been a headquarters officer; he had never fired a shot in anger. Perhaps, just within his hearing, some of his subordinates reminisced (a little too loudly?) about their active service at Shiloh, Kennesaw Mountain, Stone's River, Jonesboro, Gettysburg, the march through Georgia ... The not-so-subtle implication would have been that the colonel should now let them get on with their proper work: taking the fight out to the Sioux.

Lack of confidence was seldom a problem in the frontier army.

Captain Fetterman was to become one of the most famous soldiers in the story of the Indian wars. But his fame did not come in a way he would have chosen ... (National Archives)

8

NO SURVIVORS

"Give me eighty men and I will ride through the whole Sioux nation."
A comment allegedly made by Captain Fetterman a few days after he arrived at Fort Kearny

Two days after the speeches and the flag raising, reinforcements arrived. Among them was the man appointed as Carrington's second-in-command: Captain William Fetterman. Here was an officer with an impressive combat record who, during the latter part of the Civil War, had temporarily commanded this very regiment. Indeed, he had reached the rank of Lieutenant Colonel, and had frequently been cited for courage and zeal under fire. That first night, in the officers' quarters, he would have been given a warm welcome.

He had come West at his own request. In the much-reduced postwar army, he had been compelled to accept demotion. Now, as a mere captain, he would have felt rather cheated. After all, that showman Custer, even though two years his junior, had just been given command of his own regiment. So he would have calculated that (as in Vietnam exactly a century later, or in Iraq and Afghanistan today) heading for "where the action is" was a necessary course to gain promotion.

Carrington and Fetterman might, just, have made a complementary pair: the one a careful logistician, the other a competent and ambitious man of action. But, within days, Fetterman would have been less than human if he had not been concerned about his Colonel's lack of aggression. This, he must have thought, was no place to regain the higher rank he had come west to win. Despite his total lack of experience of Indian fighting, he is said to have impatiently claimed that, with just one company of 80 men, he could "ride through the whole Sioux nation." That statement, whether he actually made it or not (and the evidence is uncertain), has long become so central to what one might call the Fetterman legend that it cannot be ignored. On the evidence that has come down to us, it seems reasonable to suggest that, even if he never actually made the comment in such specific terms, it was characteristic of his thinking.

Anyway, within days of his arrival, he dreamed up a scheme that made good sense: to stake out some horses one evening in an exposed position near the fort. He and a posse of cavalry would hide in some cottonwoods nearby. They waited all night and, just as they were bringing the decoy horses back the next morning, the Sioux made off with some mules from the other side of the fort. He came up with another more personal tactic, which made rather less sense, of quietly voicing his impatience to some of his brother officers. He would have found some willing allies; they would be useful witnesses if things came to a head, and if General Cooke back in Omaha ever held an inquiry into what was going wrong. Almost certainly, when he himself had paused in Omaha on his way west, he would have heard rumors that the general had doubts about Colonel Carrington.

In fact, every infrequent mail from Omaha contained some peremptory order for action from the general. The incoming mail of November 25 was typical:

"You are hereby instructed that so soon as the troops and stores are covered from the weather, to turn your earnest attention to the possibility of striking the hostile band of Indians by surprise in their winter camps ... You have a large arrears of murderous and insulting attacks by the savages upon emigrant trains and troops to settle, and you are ordered, if there prove to be any promise of success, to conduct or to send another officer on such an expedition."

As the second-in-command, Captain Fetterman would surely have seen that order. He would have been most anxious to be that "other officer," before the winter closed in. But, for Colonel Carrington, the order would have demonstrated that the general's staff, 700 miles away in the comfort of their headquarters, were quite unappreciative of his problems, particularly his shortage of officers and sergeants.

If all this were a melodrama of the period, the second act would begin with the curtain rising on Red Cloud's winter camp. "Sound of Indian drums. Red Cloud and other chiefs are seated around a fire inside a tepee." And, for all we know, it may have been like that. Certainly we can conclude that, after a last buffalo hunt to top up their winter larders, Red Cloud and his allies were now discussing how best to rid themselves of the white intruders ...

Before first light on Wednesday, December 5, more than 400 Sioux were on the move; that evening they camped a few miles short of the fort. Early the next day they split into three groups and quietly rode forward to take up position. One group hid itself just behind the ridge-line overlooking a valley; the second group did the same just behind the ridge-line on the other side of the same valley. The third party, smaller than the other two (this was the decoy group), made its way three miles further south and hid in a thicket within a few hundred yards of the trail running from Fort Kearny up to the wood-cutting area.

It is fairly certain that Red Cloud was in command—so far as any Sioux was ever in command. It is said that, peeping over one of those ridges, he watched the distant "firewood" trail through a captured telescope. In time, when he saw some wagons and their escort creaking towards the timberline, he knew that the decoy party would shortly show themselves.

The first the fort knew about it was the distant crackle of rifle fire. The colonel immediately ordered Captain Fetterman to take a detail of about 50 infantrymen up the trail to relieve the wood-cutting wagons. Just as they were leaving the fort, he told Fetterman not to pursue the Sioux too sharply; he wanted time to get around behind the enemy with his own detachment. Then, a few minutes later, he himself led a group of cavalry (about 40 men) off at an angle from the trail in order to get across the line that he reckoned the enemy would take to escape Fetterman's advance.

In the event, all sides failed in their purpose. Fetterman's soldiers marched too quickly toward the Sioux decoy party, who started to retreat just as they had planned, enticing the soldiers to follow. Then, typically, this same decoy party had second thoughts: seeing that they were being pursued by only 50 men, they thought to grab a bit of glory for themselves. So, instead of enticing their pursuers into the trap, they turned to skirmish. Meanwhile, a mile or so away, several of the waiting ambush party jumped the gun and, emerging over the ridge, raced towards Carrington and his men. For a few minutes there were two separate fights—until the decoy warriors, hearing firing behind them, thought that they might be missing the main show. So, scattering, and followed by Fetterman's posse, they raced away again.

Meanwhile, the colonel's group had dismounted and was now in some difficulty. The Sioux were all around, and for a few minutes there was some very bloody close-quarter fighting. The cavalrymen had some of the recently issued breech-loading carbines and, with these, they just managed to hold off their attackers. But it was the arrival of Captain Fetterman and his men that saved the day. The Sioux, probably discouraged by the way their plan had gone awry, melted away.

Neither side could claim any honors. According to some accounts, Captain Fetterman, who, ironically, seems to have been the single subordinate on either side to have carried out his orders almost to the letter, now became even more dismissive of his colonel. And Jim Bridger, the old mountain man turned civilian scout, reckoned that everyone was to blame. "These men are crazy," he reportedly said. "They don't know anything about fighting Indians."

The soldiers' casualties were two killed and seven wounded. Both sides learned some lessons. Carrington determined never again to be drawn beyond the ridge to the north of the wood trail. As he still needed firewood, he ordered the doubling of escorts up and down the trail, and the intensive drilling of his men in quickly turning the wood wagons into a tight defensive corral. All the garrison's horses—at least all those that were still fit, now only about 50 of them—were to be saddled every morning and held in readiness until all the wood-cutters were safely home in the evening. And once again he wrote to Omaha for reinforcements and, pathetically, for mittens. It might be the last mail out for several weeks, what with the Sioux and the snowdrifts.

The Sioux would have had their debriefing sessions too. What had gone wrong? Not much, except that a few impetuous braves did not understand the reason for patience and collective discipline—which is hardly surprising given that, to this day, it is said that no exact translation exists for either concept in the Sioux dictionary. Anyway, next time it would be different. And one can reasonably assume that if Red Cloud had anything to do with it, there was going to be "a next time." In fact, it came just two weeks later.

Again, a decoy party attacked the wood wagons. Again, the fort heard the sound of distant firing. But this time the colonel dispatched a very cautious officer, Captain Powell, with strict instructions to drive the attackers off but not then to pursue them. And this time no flanking party was sent out to cut off the retreating Sioux. The decoys withdrew just as soon as they were sure that the soldiers could see where they were going. But the soldiers did not follow. The whole engagement was over in less than an hour, and there were no casualties on either side.

There is no record of what Captain Fetterman thought of the afternoon's events, but one can guess. As he surely would have seen it, this was a deteriorating situation that cried out for decisive leadership. He must have reasoned that, unless met by timidity, the Hostiles always turned and ran; he had seen it for himself. Carrington's caution was not only personally exasperating, but it would reduce the regiment to an object of ridicule throughout the Army. And how then would he, as the second-in-command of such regimental nervousness, ever gain promotion? It seems entirely reasonable to suppose that he reckoned that he had to Do Something.

His chance came just two days later. The Sioux and their Cheyenne allies were certainly persistent. Twice they had tried to lure the troops into a decisive battle; now they tried a third time. Once again, there was the sound of distant firing. Once again, the colonel gave his orders to the cautious Captain Powell. But this time, Captain Fetterman interrupted. As second-in-command he asked (some say he demanded) that he be given command of the relief column. The colonel acquiesced. Perhaps he simply wanted to avoid a showdown, and anyway he could assume that even Fetterman would stick to the very specific orders he now gave him. "Relieve the wood train. Do not under any circumstance pursue over Lodge Trail Ridge."

By now Fettermen's infantrymen, their breath misting on the freezing air, were drawn up at one side of the parade ground; a hurried inspection of arms, a quick volley of orders, and they were on their way. A few minutes later, a detachment of cavalry under Lieutenant Grummond raced to catch up with Fetterman's infantrymen. Captain Fetterman had command of 81 men. From the fort, the colonel could see that the column was not moving straight along the wood trail, but, as he had himself done three weeks earlier, it was striking off at an angle—presumably to attack from the flank, or even from behind.

Presently, Fetterman saw a party of Sioux some way ahead. He would have been disappointed and annoyed because, obviously, they had gotten wind of his attempt to cut them off. Now they were breaking off their attack on the wood-train, in order to escape. Not if he could help it ... Although the range was extreme, he ordered some of his infantrymen to open fire. He thought that he might have hit a few. Certainly, one of the Hostiles was now lagging behind his fellows; he seemed to have a wounded horse. But, strangely, the others also appeared to be in no hurry to ride off. Maybe they were trying to distract and delay the soldiers while the main war party made its escape. Fetterman moved forward in pursuit. In their eagerness, the cavalry under their impetuous leader, Lieutenant Grummond, raced ahead; the Sioux moved away, just keeping their distance.

By now, the far end of Lodge Trail Ridge sloped away into a further valley. Given that the terrain has obviously not changed over the intervening decades, one can see that there is no way that Fetterman would not have realized that, while he had not actually crossed *over* the "forbidden" ridge, he had chased over the rising ground at the far end of it. Maybe his concern was to help Lieutenant Grummond and his cavalrymen who, having rashly galloped ahead, could now be in some danger. Perhaps, too, Fetterman thought that unless he hurried, the Sioux might get away. But they had no intention of escape; they rode to and fro, shrieking and yelling, just out of effective rifle range. They were drawing the soldiers on.

Suddenly there came a sound from nowhere—and everywhere. It must have been like a crescendo roll of muffled drums: thousands of hoofbeats on the hard-frozen ground. From half a mile away, erupting over the crests of the hills on either side, hundreds of Sioux and Cheyenne came galloping down on them. It must have happened so quickly that there was time for only a flash of thought: no way out, no cover.

A good deal is known about how they died: from where the bodies were found, from accounts given years later by the Sioux, and from minute debris—bullets, arrowheads, buttons—found by metal detectors up to the present day. We know that Lieutenant Grummond and his men (racing ahead to catch the decoys?) were the first to be overwhelmed. We know that Fetterman's infantrymen made a desperate scramble for the side of a rocky hill off to their right. There they held off the Sioux as long as they could—maybe ten minutes? We know that they were almost out of ammunition, and they would have known it too. We know that very few of them were killed by rifle shots; mostly by arrows and clubs. There must have been much frantic courage, and, no doubt, some panic, and even cowardice too. But by whom, or how, or where, we do not know.

And the Sioux? Unless, years later in their old age, they were making it all up, we know the names of most of the decoys: Dull Knife, Big Nose, White Bull, Little Wolf, Young Man Afraid, American Horse and, most daring of all, the one with the "wounded" horse, Crazy Horse. We know that there were at least 1,000 warriors in the ambush; some say twice that number. We know that Red Cloud planned the trap, but, strangely, we cannot be sure that he took part in it. We know that in the immediate aftermath the Sioux, their blood high with victory, were still unsatisfied. They began an orgy of mutilation.

Back in the fort the soldiers had heard the distant firing. The colonel had immediately ordered Captain Ten Eyck and a detachment of 75 men to march out and, if possible, to reinforce Captain Fetterman. He also sent two wagons with them, in case there were wounded to bring in. Ten Eyck was nobody's fool, and he determined first to gain some high ground from where he might get a clear view before he straightened course toward the sound of the rifle fire.

As they climbed away from the fort, Ten Eyck's detachment paused every now and then to "locate" the distant noise of the now intermittent shooting. Then the noise seemed to stop. Either Fetterman had pulled off something spectacular or … or what? By now it was late in the day; already the temperature was well below freezing; the sky was darkening. Perhaps a snowstorm was coming. Both the Sioux and the soldiers knew that, without shelter, few would last the night. The Sioux turned from their plundering of the bodies and rode away. The soldiers crept forward to see what they could find.

☙

Just to the east of the Bighorn Mountains, Interstate Highway 90 swoops along a line that follows or parallels what was once the Bozeman Trail. Not many people pull off at a rather insignificant exit road to drive ten minutes to a small parking lot. At one end is a rough stone monument carrying a large bronze plaque. As one reads it, squinting against the summer sunshine, it is difficult to imagine the carnage of that mid-winter's day all those years ago. And yet, one wonders, is it really that long ago?

On this field on the 21st day of
December, 1866,
three commissioned officers and
seventy
of the 18th
2nd U.S. Cavalry, and four citizens,
Captain Brevet-
Lieutenant Colonel William J. Fetterman
were killed by an overwhelming
force of Sioux, under the command of
Red Cloud.

There were no survivors.

That last line is in larger lettering than the preceding lines. If the plaque is correct, in all, there were 78 people killed that day. Yet some accounts tell of 81 people leaving the fort.

Recently, a small subsidiary notice has been put up at the foot of the memorial. It points out that "there are several inaccuracies ... and some language reflects the racial feelings of the times." Clearly it is referring to the last line on the memorial plaque, which claims that "there were no survivors." In fact, of course, there were a large number of survivors—among the Sioux.

☙

The day had almost gone when the colonel saw Ten Eyck's column coming home. He would have known, from the way no one rushed ahead with an answer to the unspoken question, that the worst had happened.

They brought back 49 bodies; there was no room in the wagons for more. The dead were unloaded into the guardroom. There was no time to do anything else, because, for the living, the situation was now urgent: surely the Sioux, exultant with success, would not wait too long before they attacked again. In the growing darkness, everyone worked with ordered panic. Ammunition had to be allocated, defenses shored up with extra timber, rifles checked, the howitzers placed and readied, and a message dispatched to the outside world.

Two civilians on the quartermaster's staff, Portugee Phillips and Daniel Dixon, volunteered to take the message south to Horseshoe Station, 190 miles away. It was the nearest point on the military telegraph. What with the Sioux and an approaching blizzard, their chances of getting through were very uncertain. Perhaps they were tempted by the promise of $300; perhaps they reckoned that the blizzard was more of a blessing than a hazard, as it would give them some cover. While they prepared themselves and their horses, the colonel wrote his dispatch. If its tone borders on the frantic, it is surely forgivable:

"Do send me reinforcements forthwith…. I have today a fight unexampled in Indian warfare. I hear nothing of my arms that left Fort Leavenworth September 10. The additional cavalry ordered to join me has not been reported; their arrival would have saved us much loss today…. Promptness will save the line, but our killed shows that any remissness will result in mutilation and butchery beyond precedent … Promptness is the vital thing. Give me officers and give me men …"

Presumably each of the two couriers carried a copy and each planned a slightly different route—to double the chances of one of them, at least, getting through. The colonel watched them go and then turned back to the next task. He had all the available wagons turned on their sides as a defensive barrier around the ammunition store. He ordered a powder barrel to be primed and fused. If the worst came to the worst, and the enemy climbed in over stockade, they would blow themselves up.

If anyone slept that night it would have been from exhaustion. Toward dawn, a favorite time for Indian attacks, everyone was manning the stockade walls. They watched and waited. No attack came.

With the benefit of what we now know of their collective personality, one can reasonably say that the idea of a follow-up immediately after their victory probably never occurred to most of the Sioux. But one wonders about Red Cloud. Maybe it was another example of their inability to plan more than one move ahead. Either that or it was just too cold. Nor did they set another ambush in the area of those dead who were still unrecovered. Carrington had every right to assume that they would set such a trap around the remaining dead. Surely it would be unwise to venture out; but not to go might be equally unwise, for it would tell the enemy very clearly just how weak and frightened the garrison had become.

So, with 80 infantry and a few cavalry, Carrington himself went out. It was a brave thing to do. The bodies were frozen hard. Lifting them into the wagons must have been like stacking logs. The butchery was terrible. "We walked on top of their internals and did not know it. Picked them up, that is their internals, did not know the soldier they belonged to. So, the cavalry man got an infantry man's gutts and an infantry man got a cavalry man's gutts." That was a cavalryman's account. The colonel's more detailed description was suppressed for 20 years.

Slowly the wagons hauled their cargoes back to the fort. That night the blizzard, which had been threatening for the past two days, finally swept down from the mountains. By dawn the snowdrifts were, in places, almost up to the level of the stockade. The Sioux would not even have had to climb over; with snowshoes they could have walked in. For the next two days, Christmas Eve and Christmas Day, the storm blew and made burial impossible. Everyone in the fort knew that somewhere out there Phillips and Dixon would be struggling— if they were still alive.

Strangely, we know nothing more of Dixon. But Phillips made it. Moving mostly at night, in temperatures that were always far below freezing, hiding along the creek bottoms by day, taking care to travel where his horse's tracks would be quickly obliterated by the drifting snow, he rode nearly 200 miles in three days. He arrived at Horseshoe Telegraph Station early on Christmas Day. The operator tapped out a shortened version of the dispatch to Fort Laramie and beyond to General Cooke in Omaha. But Phillips, though exhausted, must have been conscientious to a fault; he called for a fresh horse and, in temperatures that had fallen to 40°F below freezing, battled on a further 40 miles to Fort Laramie. It was just as well he did, for the earlier telegraphed message was so garbled that, at Fort Laramie, they had not believed it. Legend has Phillips staggering in on the officers' Christmas dance. What is more certain is that he now delivered the papers to the garrison commander and was then helped to the post hospital where he spent the next few days recovering from exhaustion and frostbite. Afterwards it was said that he always walked with a limp. In 1899, after 33 years, his widow was awarded $5,000 dollars in belated recognition of one of the great rides of the west.

In distant Omaha, General Cooke reacted immediately to the message that eventually came down the wire. He relieved Colonel Carrington of his command and ordered Fort Laramie to send four companies of infantry and two of cavalry to Fort Kearny as soon as the weather allowed. He then sent an edited version of Carrington's dispatch to the War Department in Washington, together with a covering signal of his own. "Colonel Carrington is plausable (sic), an energetic, industrious man in garrison. But it is evident that he has not maintained discipline and that his officers have lost confidence in him." Obviously, Cooke was not going to defend his subordinate. But, for all that, his comment was not too unfair.

On the plains the blizzard blew on. It was not until New Year's Day that the relief column was able to set out. It arrived at Fort Kearny 16 days later. En route it had not been attacked once; it was too cold for even the Sioux. At the fort, they found Captain Wessels in command. It must have galled Carrington to be replaced by an officer who was markedly his junior. He would have brooded on the injustice of it all. If only Fetterman had obeyed orders. If only he himself had gone out to relieve the wood train. If only General Cooke had given him even half the help he had asked for. But now that he had to go, he wanted to be away from the place as quickly as possible.

Because he was taking several women (widows) and children with him, he waited for the weather to improve. But, after a week, he could delay no longer. For three days his convoy of wagons and its mounted escort crept south through the snowdrifts to Fort Reno. On arrival, two of his men had to have frostbitten fingers amputated by the post surgeon. Then on they went. Somewhere along the way he was redirected to another post further east. It became obvious to the poor man that he had been made the scapegoat for the Fetterman disaster. It was a comfortless zigzag journey that, in a sense, he was to take for the rest of his life.

The press, then as now, love to create a villain. Carrington, it was said, had looked on from the walls of his fort while his men were chopped up in front of him. He had ordered his rival to his death. He had even given away arms to the Sioux. Some of the more imaginative reports were by "eye witnesses." There followed army courts of inquiry, Senate investigations and unofficial tribunals in every officers' mess in the land. All the loud-mouthed politicians who had ever seen a redskin, and a good many who had not, had a theory.

Rather surprisingly, Carrington was eventually cleared of all blame by both the Army and by the Senate—partly on the testimony of old Jim Bridger, the scout who had spent nearly 50 years on the frontier. But the official reports were given very little publicity, and Carrington's military career was finished. He became an academic. He had been neither hero nor villain. He had been ordered to protect the Bozeman Trail without, if possible, provoking the Sioux. At the same time, and in contradiction, he was ordered to bring them to heel, but was denied enough trained men to do so. In short, lacking adequate men and supplies he was ordered to fight a limited war—which even at the best of times is one of the more difficult military assignments.

And Captain Fetterman? Had he lived, he would have faced a court martial. He might have pointed out that he felt compelled to go to the aid of the impetuous Grummond and his cavalry. And anyway, he had not pursued *over* that ridge; he had pursued over the rising ground at the far end of it. A hair-splitting alibi? Maybe. But he might have persuaded a court that the interpretation of the order, on which depended either his career or Carrington's, was capable of more than a single meaning.

Interestingly, even today, opinion is still divided about the relative culpability of the main players in what the nation quickly called the Fetterman Massacre. Fetterman, in the judgment of some historians (a judgment undoubtedly triggered by that alleged "Give me 80 men" outburst), was an over-confident boaster who, despite a total lack of relevant experience, held a catastrophically low opinion of the Hostiles. If those historians are right, Fetterman's assessment of the enemy was only echoing that of many in the Army's high command, particularly Generals Cooke and Sherman. That Fetterman also held a low opinion of his commanding officer is something we know with some certainty from at least one private letter he wrote at the time. So he may have thought that he could (should?) disregard that order not to chase off beyond that ridge. Well, his critics sniff, he surely got his comeuppance, and then some. Pity he took so many good men with him! To other commentators, Fetterman was a disciplined officer who became concerned, sometimes even exasperated, at what he (and some others) saw as their colonel's fixation on the detail of fort building, at the expense of going after the Sioux.

The problem, as is almost always the case following a debacle, was that everyone quickly began playing what today we call the Blame Game: personal reputations are best protected by pointing at someone else, preferably someone else lower down the chain. Right at the top, the president asked difficult questions of General Grant, the head of the Army. Grant demanded answers from General Sherman; Sherman quietly disowned General Cooke; Cooke impugned Carrington. In support of Cooke's contention that the fort was not, as Carrington complained, ill-supported with supplies and soldiers, Cooke was able to quote an optimistic dispatch that Carrington had sent him only two days before the massacre: "Indians appeared today and fired on the wood train but were repulsed. They accomplished nothing, while I am perfecting all details of the post and preparing for active movements."

In the years that followed, the colonel's wife, Margaret, had much to do with her husband's rehabilitation. With its interestingly female perspective, her book, *Absaraka, the Experience of an Officer's Wife on the Plains,* sold widely. Shrewdly, she dedicated it to General Sherman. In her text, she was also careful not to denigrate the dead hero, Fetterman. Indeed, she paints him as a man of integrity and character who was, nevertheless, compelled to "reach for laurels that were beyond his reach." Then, by emphasizing the clarity of her husband's order about crossing that ridge, she subtly implies Fetterman's ultimate disobedience. One suspects that she had some help from her husband.

The debate surrounding the events at Fort Kearny is still alive today. Read Dee Brown's book, *The Fetterman Massacre,* or General "Slam" Marshal's *Crimsoned Prairie,* or any of the several articles by Robert Murray, or (most recent of all) Shannon Smith's deeply researched *Give Me Eighty Men* in which she rides to the rescue of Fetterman's reputation. All have been published more than a century after the events. To quote the old dictum, "You pays your money and you takes your choice."

ℂ

It is surprising that Hollywood has never made a film about those five months at Fort Kearny. After all, they have made at least three full-length movies of varying accuracy about Colonel George Armstrong Custer and the Battle of the Little Bighorn. But, if ever they do get around to the story of Carrington and Fetterman, the opening shot must surely be a long, slow pan across some of the most beautiful scenery in the West: the eastern slopes of the Bighorn Mountains. No music; just a low wind. Gradually, as the camera pans, it will "find" and then zoom in on a small crowd of people and their buggies. Except for some ranch hands at the edge of the crowd, the men are formally dressed in the suits and high white collars of the period; the women hold parasols against the July sun. They are clustered near the top of a small craggy hill listening to an old man in a brass-buttoned army uniform. As we get closer, we begin to hear what Professor Henry Carrington is saying.

"... I did not come here after a journey of 2,500 miles, and at my advanced age, for my gratification. I am here to do justice to the living and the dead ... This

In 1908, Colonel Carrington returned to speak at the dedication of the memorial to the Fetterman massacre – 42 years after the event (Wyoming State Archives)

monument fashioned from the gathered stone nearby is a very poor testament to the valor of those it honors ... Yet it is, in its very roughness, an exponent of their struggles for you ... Thank God, who gave us such men so loyal ... In regions where all was peace, as at Fort Laramie, twelve companies were stationed, while in regions where all was war, as at Fort Kearny, only five companies were allowed ... I will tell you how this monument happened to be erected on this hill ..."

And tell them he does, for nearly an hour. He has waited 42 years to put his side of the story. Yet toward the end of his peroration, he makes a simple statement in reference to Captain Fetterman. It is rather remarkable—not quite magnanimous, yet not bitter; it is succinctly to the point: "Life was the forfeit. In the grave," he said, "I bury disobedience."

With his speech finished, the crowd moves to a flagpole. Another old man steps forward. William Daley, back on October 31, 1866, performed the same duty with the biggest flag he or the garrison had ever seen. Then the colonel and six of his old soldiers lead the crowd in "Nearer my God to Thee"; they end with "Auld Lang Syne."

Perhaps, as the flag is raised, the camera should pan and zoom in to settle on the plaque, and tilt slowly down those final words, "There were no survivors." Now, holding those words full frame, we might go through a slow dissolve to a faraway line of infantry, cavalry and wagons moving west across a vast, empty horizon. The distant figures shimmer in the heat. A caption is superimposed: "Wyoming Territory 1866." Now, at last, we might indulge in some appropriate music ...

Hollywood might find this all too drawn out. But one hopes that room would be found somewhere for Red Cloud's telegraphed regret, sent from a distant reservation. He was sorry, but he was now too old to come to the ceremony. Extraordinary.

9

THE RAILROAD

"We are on one side at the extreme of the world. Build this railroad and we are of the center—with Europe on one side and Asia and Africa on the other."

A comment by Asa Witney, one of the early lobbyists for the building of a transcontinental railroad

"One of the most marvellous undertakings of modern times."

A comment by *The Times*, the London newspaper, on hearing that the transcontinental line had been completed

&

Perhaps it is just a good story, but the railroad buff who passed it on to me thought it better than that. Me too.

When, in the late 1940s, the western railroads began to replace their steam locomotives—and they had some of the biggest in the world—with diesels and diesel-electrics, westerners soon complained that they missed the wonderful wailing cadences of the old steamers. After all, the call of a distant train had been with them for at least 80 years. They set their clocks by it. It went deep into the western soul.

So one company, thinking to combine modernity with nostalgia (at no extra cost), planned to replace its diesels' dismal hooters with the tonal whistles of the past. Instead of steam, the whistles would be powered by compressed air. But the idea did not work. They had forgotten that it was not only the virtuosity of the engineer (he was never called the driver) on the whistle's lanyard that gave that old peculiar wail. Even more, it was the blast of super-heated steam through the copper whistle, and the consequent rapid expansion of the metal, that did the trick. A chill rush of mere compressed air only produced a single steady note—which was back where the whole plan started. So, no longer do folk out on the prairies and in the mountains hear "that lonesome whistle blow." They just hear an ear-jangling toot.

৩

Priorities change. So, for a moment, let us go back to the shift of military thinking in the summer of 1867. The plain truth was that, up in the Powder River country, Red Cloud and his Sioux had won their war; the soldiers garrisoning Fort Kearny could hardly guarantee their own safety, let alone that of civilian travelers on their way to look for gold in Montana. So the Bozeman Trail was abandoned, and the soldiers were ordered to withdraw in order to fulfill a strategic necessity away to the south: the guarding of the construction crews of the transcontinental railroad who were, by 1867, hammering their way towards the mountains.

Already that summer some Cheyenne had waylaid a train at a place called Plum Creek. They cut the telegraph line, pulled up a rail and then sat down to see what would happen. A few hours later a handcar came along the line, to repair the broken wire. The Cheyenne killed four of the crew; the fifth, an Englishman called Thompson, was scalped and left for dead. Then they sat down again to await a bigger prize. Presently they were rewarded: a locomotive hauling supplies came clanking along the track; it hit the gap and rolled over, snorting and wheezing like a dying buffalo. The war party watched in pleased disbelief. Then, after they had killed the crew, they broke into the wagons. Among other cargo, they found whiskey, clothing and bolts of cloth. The story goes that they got roaring drunk, put on the clothes and then, having tied the bolts of cloth around their ponies' necks, they went galloping off with the cloth unwinding chaotically behind them. Incidentally, Thompson survived, though it is said that he chose to wear a woolly cap for the rest of his life.

There were other times when the actual construction crews were molested. Some lives were lost. These disruptions, when reported back east, raised doubts in the nation's self-esteem. After all, people were being told that this was the biggest engineering project since the building of the pyramids. So it stood to reason that no bunch of savages should be allowed to interfere with the nation's march towards its Destiny. Which is why the Army was called in.

Five years earlier, in 1862, when President Lincoln signed the Pacific Railway Act, there were many who said that the undertaking—building a line nearly

2,000 miles long—was so massive that it would never be completed. Not in that century anyway. Perhaps, when faced with a national ambition that reached far beyond all previous experience, there was nothing unusual in that skepticism. After all, there were similar doubts when, amazingly only 100 years later, President Kennedy had the vision (and the confidence) to promise Americans that they would see at least one of their countrymen walk on the moon by the end of the 1960s. As well as the sheer scale of the two endeavors, there are other parallels. Indeed, it has been calculated that the earlier project would, in the end, consume a greater proportion of the country's wealth. And its progress would seem to have been just as closely followed by the nation; its eventual completion would be met with the same pride and celebration.

Both visionaries and pragmatists had been urging a transcontinental railroad since the late 1840s. True, if you were wealthy, determined, and in a hurry you could get to California by stagecoach, but it took a punishing five weeks. Starting from St. Louis, the approximately once-a-week service would cost you a colossal $200. During the 2,000-mile journey, down across the deserts of the southwest (this was the "all weather" route) to Los Angeles and then north to San Francisco, you paid extra for your food and accommodation—if there was any. In fact, the passengers were rather an afterthought; it was the carriage of government mail that mattered. The contract had been won by John Butterfield; he ordered 100 specially strengthened stagecoaches and more than 1,000 horses and mules; he established 120 stage stations along the route. With loans from the banks, it cost him over $1 million. But one day Mr. Butterfield's company would, via myriad mergers and takeovers, grow to become known to the world as American Express.

It is little wonder that there was pressure to build a railroad. After all, by the middle of the century the nation well understood the technology; indeed, it had already laid more than 12,000 miles of track—about a third of all the track in the world. But that was all in the eastern states. Now, surely, it was time to build westward. "We are on one side at the extreme of the globe," wrote Asa Witney, one of the earliest lobbyists. "Build this railroad, and we are of the center—with Europe on one side and Asia and Africa on the other."

That was the language of geopolitics, and, while the pragmatists saw the project as making more secure the nation's transcontinental reach, others saw it as a first thrust for an American imperialism that might, one day, reach out across the Pacific. But, while the dreamers and the romantics talked about "a road to the Indies," the moneymen and the promoters, who were more astute or more cunning (it came to the same thing) than the dreamers, saw the whole enterprise in much simpler terms: it would be a splendid way of amassing huge personal fortunes. Their whispered reasoning was that, in a project that was obviously going to cost as-yet uncalculated millions, and on which the accountancy would largely be under their own control, there would be some very rich and easy pickings.

The route that the line should take was much argued; it depended (as, to this day, do many big federal projects) on the home states of the lobbyists. But, in the end, what one might call a "central route" was chosen—on the entirely reasonable grounds that it would be the most easily engineered; it would follow, for much of the way, the relatively easy gradients that had been used for the preceding 20 years by the Overland Trail to California.

So, in 1863, in the middle of the Civil War, under the compelling slogan that this was to be "The Grandest Enterprise under God," the first westward rails were laid in Omaha. Over 1,800 miles away, in Sacramento, work also began. The government's thinking was that two companies—they called themselves the Union Pacific and the Central Pacific—would build toward each other until, one day, they would join their rails somewhere in the middle. The men in control of each company, many of whom were visionary rogues, had long recognized that it would be many years before the volume of traffic would be sufficient to bring them any significant dividends from their holdings of company shares. So, instead, they would have to take whatever they could finagle in the shorter term. Contracts could be rigged, funds siphoned, specifications fiddled, stock manipulated, congressmen bribed, auditors persuaded, escrow accounts milked, and promises broken. At the Union Pacific end, the arch-villain was Thomas Durant; the tricks he and his conspiring colleagues played were still being unraveled in lawsuits 60 years later. Indeed, even to this day, financial historians argue about some of that cabal's more esoteric maneuvers. Shades of Enron.

In California, the birth of the Central Pacific was in the hands of four men. All were merchants who, during the preceding decade, had already made small fortunes in the goldfield supply business. Over the next 20 years, Stanford, Huntington, Hopkins and Crocker would accumulate much greater wealth. Maybe the Big Four (as they were known) were not quite as grasping as the men at the top of the Union Pacific, but they seem not to have been far behind. Their names are still honored all over California: on banks, hotels, universities, beaches, and countless streets, parks and boulevards.

In the end, perhaps the venality of the promoters ("their scrupulous greed and dishonesty," as one commentator neatly put it) did not matter too much. Indeed, perhaps the thinking of those financial sharpshooters was exactly what the nation needed because, spurred by the temptation of such prodigious pickings, they bent all their energies to making sure that things happened.

To spur the two companies, the government had agreed to hand each of them enormous tracts of land—land that it did not bother first to appropriate from the owners, the Indians. For every mile of completed track, the companies would get a strip of land (including all mineral rights) running away from the railroad line on alternate sides; each strip would be one mile wide and ten miles deep. Further, for every mile of track across the plains, the government would hand out bonds worth $16,000; this would rise to $32,000 in the more difficult foothills, and then to $48,000 through the mountains.

With inducements like that (and, incidentally, I once got into a genial argument with a Republican westerner who claimed that the building of the railroad was a supreme example of unsubsidized private enterprise), it is no wonder that corruption was endemic and, at the same time, that a race should develop between the two companies to build as much of the line as possible. Because there was no designated point at which the two lines would meet, it was in each company's interest to lay rails as quickly as possible over as many miles as possible, and thereby to collect the maximum reward. Each hoped that its rival would run into some major and delaying problem.

In fact, both companies had problems right away. Out in California, quite apart from the cost of bringing all the rails and locomotives around Cape Horn (more than 20 cargoes were on the high seas at any one time), progress was slowed to a crawl by the mountains and snows of the California Sierras, only 70 miles up the line from the optimistic start in Sacramento. At the Omaha end, over 1,800 miles away, work was stalled for over a year, partly by the Civil War, and partly by poor organization and squabbling among the promoters. When, at last, the Union Pacific got its internal problems sorted out—largely because the impatient government pushed it into appointing an army engineer, General Grenville Dodge, to take charge—progress accelerated until, by the summer of 1867, the line was being hammered across the flatlands of Nebraska at the rate of nearly a mile a day.

To reach that pitch, a whole slew of management decisions had to be implemented. Thousands of laborers had to be recruited, some to work at the Omaha supply base, others to be railed out to the ever-advancing end-of-track. Out there, they had to be supplied with everything from water to tobacco. Beef herds had to be bought up and then driven cross-country to the rail camps; the workers expected a diet of at least two pounds of meat a day. Back east, contracts had to be negotiated for enormous quantities of rails; locomotives and rolling stock had to be designed and commissioned; shovels, picks, hammers, crowbars, wheelbarrows, earth-scoops and a hundred more tools had to be ordered. Then, all these thousands of tons of hardware had to meet at Omaha on the far

Missouri. From there everything had to be fed along the single track to the west.

Out on the plains, at the railhead, there was an even greater need for disciplined organization. Today, the proceedings would, no doubt, be the subject of "critical-path analysis" and "system logistics" regulated by a bunch of stop-watched consultants poring over flowcharts. Back in those days, it seems that General Dodge and his lieutenants just got on with the job. Those lieutenants were the Casement brothers, two ex-Army engineers. Jack Casement was responsible for the day-to-day progress of construction out at the railhead. His brother Daniel, back in Omaha, was the logistician. Once a day, he would dispatch a loaded train up the line. On arrival at the railhead a day or two later, its 400-ton cargo (enough for about one mile of track) would be quickly dumped onto the ground alongside the track. Then, empty, the train would reverse until it met the next train; they would pass each other on a temporary stretch of double track laid for this specific purpose. Meanwhile, the just-delivered rails and all the other bits of hardware would be dragged forward by a continuous stream of mules.

Far ahead were the surveyors. Behind came armies of pick-and-shovel men who, with wheelbarrows and mule-drawn scoops, leveled the right of way, preparatory to the men who actually laid down the rails. These were the iron men, chosen for their sheer physical strength. In gangs of six, they would manhandle each 700-pound rail into its final position. They were paid $2 a day—big money in those days. Sometimes, they were offered double wages to work even harder and longer than normal. With that inducement, on several occasions they managed to bang down four miles of track in a single day. Once they laid nearly six miles.

> *Oh, it's work all day,*
> *No sugar in your tay,*
> *A-workin' on the U-pee Rail-way.*

They made up many such songs, presumably more grunt than melody, to help them with the straining rhythm of their labors. One can guess that the big investors back east sang an even sweeter song as they collected the $16,000 and the 6,400 acres for every completed mile.

At 80- or 90-mile intervals a supply camp would spring up. Some have long since grown to respectable towns—places like Grand Island, Lexington, North Platte, Sidney, Julesburg, Cheyenne, Laramie, and Rawlins. Others just faded back into the sagebrush when the railhead moved on. But whether they grew or died, for a few weeks these were the wildest places in the West. It was not just the

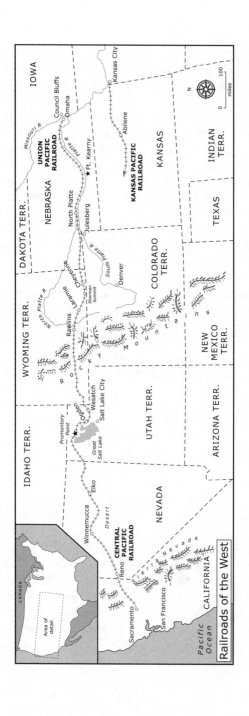

Railroads of the West

railroad gangs that made them so. There was a whole population of parasites who came sweeping up the line from Omaha: gamblers, girls, saloon-keepers, quacks, cardsharps, pickpockets, gunmen, and all kinds of itinerant ne'er-do-wells. They all had the same aim: to separate the railroad gangs from their pay as quickly as possible. They brought their accommodation with them: prefabricated wooden shacks with canvas roofs which could be erected overnight and just as quickly disassembled and moved on to the next Hell-on-Wheels. Along with the R'n'R provided by these temporary settlements, it is said that murders ran at the rate of one a day, or double on holidays—though there were not too many of those.

Usually the railroad company would set up its supply camp on one side of the line; the makeshift bars and brothels would bed down on the other. Perhaps that is why, even today, the railroad track running through many a western town is still seen as the dividing line between the respectable and the raffish, between the right and the wrong side of the track. But back in the late 1860s, mere "raffishness" would have been a wholly inadequate description of a place whose sole purpose was gambling, drinking, brawling, and fornication. Listen to Henry Stanley (yes, he of Dr. Livingstone fame) writing about Julesburg in 1867: "This is the wickedest city in America…. Civil law is as yet too new to be an impediment to the unwashed canaille [rabble], and it certainly offers no terror to the women who travel about undressed in the light of day…. These women are expensive articles. Everyone seemed bent on debauchery and dissipation."

એ્

One of the first and wildest of all those Hells-on-Wheels established itself at a spot they called North Platte, 300 miles up the line from Omaha. Unlike some of those places, it never died. Indeed today, 140 or so years later, a couple of miles west of its now respectable Main Street there has grown what they claim as the largest marshalling/shunting yard in the world. The Bailey Yard, bang in the middle of the continent, is the hub of the Union Pacific network. It was surely worth a visit—the more so as my map showed a Visitors' Center with an observation tower from where one could, presumably, look out over the enormous spread of a railroad going about its daily business. Unfortunately, after a 150-mile drive I found that the Visitors' Center was closed, for "major refurbishment." So they suggested instead that if I drove back a mile or so, "You'll get a real good view from the highway overpass on

Buffalo Bill Avenue." Well, given that I had driven all morning to get there, it was that or nothing. But a marshalling yard, from whatever vantage point and no matter how big, does not really lend itself to lyrical description. So, instead, here are a few statistics: the place is four miles long by one mile wide (about 2,500 acres) and it contains over 300 miles of track; over 2,500 UP employees, working night and day, handle (sort out? rearrange? shuffle?) up to 15,000 freight cars (empty and loaded) every 24 hours. In that time as many as 150 trains come throbbing slowly through the yard. Some stop to be "sorted." Others rumble straight on to destinations over 1,000 miles away. So vast is this spread that many of the movements of the shunting engines, and the switching of the trucks from one track to another, are radio-controlled—no drivers. The cargoes? Everything imaginable: grain, cars, lumber, newsprint, heavy machinery ... you name it. But coal, millions of tons of it (in 36–40 trains every day) is the biggest load. And I will come to the intriguing "how come" of that a little later.

❧

On the far side of the continent, the Central Pacific was in financial difficulties, even though someone paid the state geologist to certify that the more or less level terrain of the line's first 70 miles out of Sacramento was so steep that it qualified for the "mountain payment" of $48,000 for every mile. The problem was that, presently, as the line really did rise through the foothills of the Sierras, the rate of advance dwindled to just one or two twisting miles a week. Now, reaching right into the hard-rock mountains, daily progress was sometimes measured in mere yards. Even with the by-now-legitimate mountain subsidy, the backers were still losing money.

In summer, the mountain terrain was difficult enough; but in winter, the workers had to contend with freezing temperatures, blizzards, landslides and 30-foot snowdrifts. The line was surveyed to crest at over 7,000 feet, but well before that altitude was reached it was obvious that the line would have to be protected with nearly 20 miles of wooden "tunnels" to hold off the weight of drifting winter snow, at the prodigious cost of $2 million. (The line is still protected by over 15 miles of such snow sheds.) And there was another problem: even if conditions had been easier, many of the construction crews were not much attracted by the idea of working for $2 a day when, instead, they might gamble on making much better money on the nearby Nevada gold and silver fields. They deserted in hundreds. At one time, there were fewer than 1,000 workers left from the 5,000 who had started. Work almost stopped.

This desperate problem had to be met with a desperate solution. Charles Crocker, a leading partner in the whole enterprise and the man who had assumed overall command, looked around for an alternative source of labor. Mexicans were a possibility, but their legendary inertia was held against them. However, by this time there was a scattering of Chinese in California; many had come to make a living by picking through the abandoned tailings of those miners who had now moved on to richer pickings in Nevada. Crocker put the "Chinese idea" to the construction boss, a bad-tempered Irishman called James Strobridge. He was downright scornful. Those weedy, rice-eating "orientals" would, he said, have neither the strength nor the stamina to stand the pace. Maybe Crocker reminded Strobridge that the forebears of these same rice-eaters had managed to build the Great Wall. Anyway, with more desertions every day, the track boss was forced to take a chance on a crew of just 50, for a week's trial.

Almost immediately, they proved to be harder working and more reliable than the deserting whites. At $1 a day they were cheaper too. (Ethnic equality, let alone political correctness, had not yet been invented.) Within a few days, Strobridge was asking Crocker for more of the same. Within a few weeks, the Central Pacific had found a further 4,000 of these fragile rice-eaters and, within months, in response to advertisements back in Canton, 10,000 more had been shipped in. Initially, among the remaining white workers, there was resentment and even riots against what they saw as scab labor. But the management solved the problem by sacking most of the more bad-tempered whites and promoting the rest from pick-and-shovel workers to foremen. Strobridge had been won over; indeed, he became an ardent advocate of his new workforce. In the end, partly by sheer weight of numbers (15,000 Chinese were working on the line), and partly by their stoic determination, they broke through the Sierras. It had taken three years. In the process, though no one bothered to count, it is reckoned that at least 500 Chinese workers perished—in accidents, in snow slides, and sometimes in the subzero cold. And some were lost to a new and unstable invention known as "blasting powder." The Sierras saw the world's first significant use of nitroglycerine, a compound recently "invented" by the Swedish chemist Alfred Nobel.

We foreigners do not think of sunny California as sometimes being beset by heavy snows. It is true that much of the place has never seen a snowflake. But I can recall how, some years ago, when I was directing a documentary sequence about the overland wagons coming through the High Sierras, we ourselves had to take refuge in the comfort of a motel for a full 36 hours. The road in and out was closed until the storm passed and the snow plows could do their work. We were within a mile or two of the railroad; occasionally, despite all those snow sheds, that too is closed.

✑

Once onto the Nevada desert, with what was now a well-tuned workforce, backed by an assured supply route coming through the mountains, the Central Pacific raced away. There was much time to make up. And every mile completed was money in the pockets of the promoters. True, there were still some problems: desert temperatures were frequently above 100°F, every drop of water for both drinking and for the locomotives' boilers had to be railed in, and the Chinese, sensing their worth, were asking for a pay rise of an extra $5 a month. After some haggling, the Chinese (Crocker's Pets, as they were now known) got their money. Deservedly.

Far away, on the other side of the continental divide, the Union Pacific had not long celebrated its first 500 miles; it was now working west from a Hell-on-Wheels called Cheyenne. Within months, this makeshift scatter of shacks, tents, and muddy roads would become the capital of Wyoming Territory. But right now, once the sun went down, it was still "a bibulous bacchanalia of booze and bawds."

✑

Today in downtown Cheyenne, just across from the Union Pacific depot (dee-poh please), there stands a giant black locomotive. It sits on rails which do not go anywhere; it could do with some paint, and its firebox has been cold for nearly 50 years, but it is still quite magnificent. It and its 24 brothers (sadly, all but two have apparently long gone to the scrapyard) were designed in 1940; their primary task was to haul freight trains up and over Sherman Summit, a job they did for almost two decades. In that direct and attractive way that Americans often have, the locomotives were always referred to as the Big Boys. They were almost certainly the largest and most powerful steam locomotives ever built, and therefore, if size and power are the criteria, they must surely have represented the ultimate development of steam locomotion. I once met, all too briefly, a man who had crewed one of these glorious machines; I think there were tears in his eyes. There is reportedly just one Big Boy left in semi-working trim, at a place in New Hampshire called Steamtown.

Some details for enthusiasts: the Big Boys had a wheel pattern of 4-8-8-4. Not including the tender, they weighed 344 tons and had mechanical stokers for a 150 cubic ft grate. Working pressure was 300 lbs/sq. in. with an evaporating surface of 5,755 sq. ft plus a super-heating surface of 2,043 sq. ft. They had four cylinders of 24 in. by 32 in. driving sixteen 5 ft 8 in. coupled wheels. Maximum tractive power was about 135,400 lbs. There are no official figures for horsepower, but estimates put it at about 9,000 hp. An empty tender weighed over 120 tons; it could carry 80 tons of fuel and about the same of water. The whole rig was 132 ft long. They normally operated with a crew of two.

By way of comparison, in the 1860s the steam locomotives of the UP and CP weighed 30–40 tons; their working pressure was about 120 lbs/sq. in.; their horsepower would have been in a range of 150-250hp.

❧

Back in the spring of early 1867, the Union Pacific, by way of some quite steep grades, was hammering over the Medicine Bow Range between Cheyenne and Laramie. At more than 8,000 feet, Sherman Summit was, for some years, the highest point on any of the world's railroads. Once out onto Laramie Plains, a management crisis came to the boil: Durant and his cronies wanted to sack General Dodge. Their complaint was that he was being unnecessarily professional, though they would never have put it like that. As they saw it, the problem was that he was too often laying out a track along what he considered to be the most direct alignment, even though it might be more expensive than a more meandering and, perhaps, flatter course. They always wanted the longer route because, that way, there would be bigger mileage payments and larger

When building the railroad, the Union Pacific would replace their temporary wooden bridges with more permanent stone constructions, as here in 1868 (The UP Railroad)

land grants; though, again, they would never have put it like that. For example, Dodge might have chosen a longer, gentler route through the Medicine Bow Range, or even have avoided the range altogether. That would have added, say, 80–100 miles to the track and thereby brought Durant and Co. more of that mileage money.

The problem was that Dodge was a brusque engineer. Fortunately for him and for the railroad, just when the dispute came to a head, General Grant was taking a swing out west, to review progress on the railroad and to check on the Indian problem. Indeed, he had just been trying to negotiate, together with Generals Sherman and Sheridan, yet another treaty with Red Cloud and the Sioux. Now he and his fellow generals had moved on to Laramie, to bang heads together in this matter of the near-terminal tensions between the UP's chief engineer and its general manager. (Incidentally, Laramie and Fort Laramie, the scene of the negotiations with the Sioux, are different places, about 100 miles apart.)

General Grant was running for the Presidency and, given that he was favored to win, Durant had to be careful. Furthermore, Dodge and Grant knew each other from their time in the Civil War. Anyway, Grant listened to both sides. Durant, at some length, charged Dodge with all kinds of money-wasting and autocratic decisions. When it came to Dodge's turn, he simply said (according to his own later account) that if he suffered any more interference from any source, he would quit. Maybe that was enough because, after only the briefest of intervals, Grant let it be known that "the government expects the railroad to meet its obligations. And it expects General Dodge to remain with the road as its chief engineer until it is completed." True, Grant was not "the government"— yet. But Durant knew when he was beaten. And Dodge? One report says that within three days he was back working with his survey crews 400 miles to the west, to cheers from workers along the way.

Within another week or two he was even further west, to meet with his opposite number on the Central Pacific. They needed to decide where their respective lines would join. But, given that each company was determined to build as much line as possible and thereby collar the maximum in mileage payments, agreement was impossible. Indeed, the mileage rewards were such that each company doubled their workers' pay, to keep them building through a winter when the temperatures frequently fell far below freezing.

By the spring of 1869, the competition had become absurd; across northern Utah the two companies were grading their roadbeds in parallel and right alongside each other—in opposite directions! Indeed, the workers on one line were sometimes showered with the rock debris of a blasting operation on the other line.

In the end, Grant, by now the newly elected President, had to intervene. He decreed that if the two managements could not agree, then the government would order an investigation into the financial affairs of both companies. The threat was enough. Within days, it was agreed that the "joining of the rails" would take place four weeks later at a place called Promontory Summit.

The top brass of each company now readied themselves for the long journey to Promontory Summit. Special trains were prepared. A military band was arranged. An enormous national flag was ordered. Champagne was shipped. A cross-tie of laurel was carpentered and varnished. Gold and silver spikes (to hold the final rail to that special tie) were cast. Photographers were engaged. The overland telegraph was temporarily rerouted to the meeting place, so that the whole nation would know when the job was finally completed. And, no doubt, the whiskey merchants laid in extra stock and readied their tents.

The dignitaries started to arrive at Promontory. The two sets of rails were still a few hundred yards apart; the final closing of that gap would provide some curtain-raising entertainment. Everything was ready for the following day except for the unexplained absence of the Union Pacific Special that was bringing Durant and his party to the celebrations. Then it was announced that the Special had been delayed by heavy rains and spring snowmelt somewhere back in the mountains of Wyoming. Parts of the track had been washed away, and repairs would have to be made. The official ceremony would have to be postponed.

In fact, besides some flooding, there was another truth behind the delay. Perhaps because of the Union Pacific's embarrassment at the time, there is even today some confusion in the accounts that have come down to us. Certainly there had been heavy rains, but, more or less coincident with the weather, Durant and his party had been kidnapped. A group of disgruntled workers had waylaid his train and demanded that they be paid some long-overdue wages. Indeed, they uncoupled Durant's carriage and chained it to the track. For two days, the telegraph line hummed with urgent requests from Durant to his bankers back east to release funds so that the men surrounding his carriage could be paid. Eventually, the money (some say more than $250,000 in cash) arrived; the captives were released.

May 10 was bright and sunny. Now, with Durant and his entourage safely arrived, the nabobs of the Central Pacific, who had been kicking their heels, were impatient for the business of the day to begin. First, an engine from each company, "Jupiter" for the CP and "Engine 119" for the UP, clanked slowly forward until, wheezing gently, they faced each other about 80 feet apart. Between the two, spectators then pressed forward to form a hollow square with a line of infantrymen lining one side. Behind the soldiers, sitting on the two engines and standing all around, were straggles of workers and other hangers-on. One of the more candid accounts speaks of some "dissipation" among these spectators—not too surprising, given that they had been waiting for several days with nothing much to do other than to "repair" to the whiskey tents. Off to one side was the band of the 21st Infantry Regiment; one assumes that at appropriate intervals it umpah-umpahed patriotically. Now the last two rails were brought up and laid in position, one rail by a crew of UP iron men and the other by a crew of much smaller CP Chinese. There was a deal of speechifying; at least one speaker made the point that they were about to complete the work "begun by Christopher Columbus," and another reminded anyone who could hear him above the hubbub that this was now "the new way to the Indies." Then, rather late in the day, someone remembered that perhaps the Almighty should be involved. A Rev. John Todd, who was doubling as a reporter for an eastern ecclesiastic journal, volunteered. He ended his prayer by neatly asking of the Heavenly Father that "this mighty enterprise may be unto us as the Atlantic of thy strength and the Pacific of thy love. Amen."

During these various events, the telegraph operator, a Mr. Shilling, was conveying to an audience of several hundred other operators across the nation what must be reckoned as the nation's first coast-to-coast networked commentary. Then, shortly after 12:40 p.m., he tapped out a rather perfunctory "Stand by. We have got done praying. The spike is about to be presented." Various dignitaries stepped forward to hammer home one or other of those special spikes, to fasten the last two rails ceremonially onto that laurel tie. To drive the final spike, someone handed a silver-plated sledgehammer to Leland Stanford of the CP. He swung, and missed. Thomas Durant of the UP stepped up to do the job for him and also missed, at which point one imagines that those spectators suffering from that earlier "dissipation" would have contributed some well-judged ruderies at the expense of the two frockcoated worthies. Further, one can guess that Mr. Shilling, fingers on his key, could have endured no further suspense. So he just tapped out "Done." It was 12:47 p.m. local railroad time.

The "electro telegraph" carried the news across the nation. In Philadelphia they rang the Liberty Bell; in New York and Omaha they fired hundred-gun salutes; in Chicago they held a seven-mile parade; on Wall Street they banged the gavel to suspend trading for the day; in San Francisco they announced (typically) the forthcoming annexation of the United States; in Sacramento 30 locomotives, with steam raised specially for the occasion, blew their whistles in discordant unison. Right across the nation crowds turned out to cheer and wave flags; bells were rung and banquets held long into the night. Even in far-away London, *The Times* editorialized the next day about what it called "One of the most marvellous [English spelling] undertakings of modern times." It was, too.

Back at Promontory Point, the two engines had inched forward until their cowcatchers were touching. Perhaps that was the moment when, with speeches done and those ceremonial spikes replaced with ordinary iron ones, the magnitude of what they had done really came home to both the workers and the dignitaries, when everyone congratulated everyone else—even if, for many of the workers, it meant that they would shortly be unemployed. It was also the moment when the two "official" photographers (A. J. Russell and his assistant, S. J. Sedgwick) took some of the most wonderful pictures in all the rich history of the United States.

> *What was it that the Engines said,*
> *Pilots touching, head to head,*
> *Facing on the single track,*
> *Half a world behind each back?*

What Bret Harte's poetic engines might have said ("spoken slightly through the nose, with a whistle at the close") was something that is little mentioned, perhaps understandably, in most of the writings that flowed from that marvelous day. Engines Jupiter and 119 might have complained about those bridges and trestles where they were limited to speeds of less than 10 mph, and about those stretches of line along which they dipped and rolled like ships in a heavy swell. The fact was that long sections of the line had been banged down so hastily—pushed by the priority of garnering as much money-per-mile as possible—that they were unstable, even dangerous, at any but the very slowest speeds. The fact is that, within the first two years, the government inspectors (where had *they* been all this time?) demanded that hundreds of miles of rails be re-laid, bridges be rebuilt and, in some places, the line itself be re-routed.

There were other disappointments. For the first year or two, the promoters found that the money did not roll in at the rate they had hoped. Freight was light, there were too few passengers, and, beyond the first 200 miles through eastern Nebraska, the sale of railroad land to would-be settlers was very slow

The famous joining of the rails: the Central Pacific meets the Union Pacific just after noon on May 10, 1869 (The UP Railroad)

137

as the Indian "problem" in those parts was not yet resolved. As for the long-dreamt land route west toward the East Indies, this was thwarted by the Suez Canal being opened just a year after the celebrations at Promontory Summit. It then proved cheaper to ship cargoes from the East Indies westward through the Canal and across the Atlantic to New York than to route them eastward across the Pacific to San Francisco and then across the continent by rail. Nevertheless, despite these early hesitations, traffic picked up and, by the mid 1870s, the moneymen (crooked and straight) were beginning to see some rewards.

In 1870 a first-class ticket from Omaha to Sacramento cost $100; second class cost $75. The journey was advertised to take five days. There were numerous stops along the way as the locomotives needed to take on water and fuel and the passengers needed to eat and, presumably, get to a latrine. Strangely, none of the contemporary accounts mention this matter of "wayside" sanitation. Perhaps, with 60–70 passengers all making for the same facilities, we do not need to know the details. Time at these stops (usually about 20 minutes) was determined by how long it took the engineer to pick up fuel and water for his locomotive. So food was rushed and, apparently, without variety. One traveler wrote, "It was necessary to look at one's watch to tell whether it was breakfast, dinner, or supper." Once underway, the trains made speeds of between 8 and 30 mph, depending on the condition of the track. Within three years, back east, a line (with a bridge across the Missouri) was completed from Chicago to Omaha. So now, at last, it was possible to buy a through ticket for $200 in New York for the 2,800-mile journey from "sea to shining sea." But, as the route was operated by three different railroad companies, the passenger had to change trains and stations in Chicago and Omaha. The journey took ten days.

Within 30 years of the driving-of-the-spikes at Promontory Point, three more transcontinental lines were built, plus two more across Canada. To generate income, and thereby to bring in the profits they reckoned to be their due, the promoters of these western railroads set out to attract migrants from within the US and from abroad to take up land beside their tracks. Like other companies, the UP set up a so-called Land Department; it placed regular advertisements in more than 2,000 newspapers across the eastern states; it set up promotion booths at state fairs and national expositions, it sent agents to every country in Europe. On offer to thousands of land-hungry peasants (many of whom were still living as feudal tenants) were cheap land and free rail travel to a chosen destination, with the railroad doing most of the choosing. Within a decade tens of thousands came, and kept on coming for the next 30 years. To this day there are clearly recognizable settlements of Swedes, Norwegians, Poles, Russians, Czechs, Slovaks, Swiss and Germans scattered all over the western plains and into the mountains. They are all solidly patriotic Americans, but at the same time they still proudly remember their origins and, more often than not, the customs, costumes, flags, and songs of their great-grandparents. The English, responsive as always, came up with an enterprising scheme to send their about-to-be-released convicts across the Atlantic so that they might take advantage of the railroads' generosity. When Washington realized what was planned, an official grumble was dispatched to London complaining about "these acts of discourtesy."

Over the years since, much opprobrium has been thrown at the so-called "robber barons" of that railroad-building age. Doubtless they kept a Bible by their bedside, just in case. Maybe they even said their prayers. But money was their only real god; its pursuit their only religion. They made massive fortunes by every manipulation, fair or foul, that they could devise. Self-interest was their guiding star. Yet, one can argue that it was that very self-interest which generated the prodigious energy that, in turn, eventually really opened up the West. Without that driving force, the process might have taken another 30 years. In short, despite the almost endemic corruption of those tycoons, were they not ultimately—despite (or because of?) their rascally ways—national benefactors?

꽃

Today it would take a pile of doctoral theses to detail the myriad takeovers, buy-outs and mergers that, over the last 140 years, have made the Union Pacific not only the largest railroad system in North America but also the largest non-nationalized railroad in the world. The Central Pacific, the California Pacific, the Southern Pacific, the Kansas Pacific, the Missouri Pacific, the Missouri-Kansas-and-Texas, and a host of smaller lines all now come under the umbrella of the UP. Omaha, where it all began, is still the operational headquarters. There, in a very large low-lit room rather similar to that of Houston's "mission control," sit 70 men and women; each watches a group of computer-like screens: from a total of 32,000 miles of UP line across the nation, each person controls 500 miles of track via a series of micro-wave links which, with barcodes on each train, signal that train's progress. The controllers in Omaha talk quietly to the driver/engineers who may be over

1,000 miles away; they can redirect a train to a new routing; they can switch another onto a siding so that a mile of empties can slide past; they can check the speed of four trains coming down the Platte Valley. They are in complete control; the engineers do their bidding.

❧

While being shown the control room, I was told that in any given month the number of trains being handled across the UP system was a fair indication of the economic health of the nation: less than 24,000 trains a month and things were not looking good; more than 28,000 and things were lookin' up. What an indicator . . .

❧

When driving across Nebraska or Wyoming, if you come to a set of flashing red lights and a lowered barrier you had best be patient, very patient. The train that comes rumbling and hooting along the track may be 1½ miles, or 150 wagons, long. It is in no hurry; at 30 mph it takes three minutes to pass. The UP runs some of the longest trains in the world; a few stretch out for 1¾ miles. They are usually carrying Wyoming coal, over 22,000 tons of the stuff at a time. There are two huge and grubby yellow diesel-electric units pulling at the front and two more pushing at the back. The ones at the back have no crew; they are radio-operated by the engineer in front. If the controller sitting 600 miles (or more) away in Omaha wants the train to stop, he had better instruct the engineer to start the process three miles back up the line. The UP alone (other railroad companies are also in the business) has at least 30 of these coal trains rolling somewhere across the US at any one time, on their way to power stations from Texas to Maine, from Georgia to Wisconsin. Most of them will be routed through that marshaling yard at North Platte.

The coal comes out of the Powder River Basin of Wyoming, from strip mines at Black Thunder, North Antelope, Belle Ayr and a dozen more. In terms of the

Blank No. 1. 0177

THE WESTERN UNION TELEGRAPH COMPANY.

The rules of this Company require that all messages received for transmission, shall be written on the message blanks of the Company, under and subject to the conditions printed thereon, which conditions have been agreed to by the sender of the following message.

THOS. T. ECKERT, Gen'l Sup't, } NEW YORK.   WILLIAM ORTON, Pres't, } NEW YORK.
O. H. PALMER, Sec'y, }

Dated *Promontory Utah via Omaha* 186 9

Received at *May 9*

To *Oliver Ames*

Prest.

You can make affidavit of Completion of road to Promontory Summit.

G. M. Dodge

Af Engr

11.400 Coll

Rec'd May 10

The telegram that announced that the work was finished (The UP Railroad) *heat it generates, this is not high-quality coal. But in these days of worries about atmospheric pollution, it has one great advantage: it has a very low sulfur content, so power stations love it. Some 30 years ago they had hardly heard of it. Yet today the US derives about 25% of its electric power from Wyoming coal, much of it brought out from the Powder River country by the Union Pacific. And incidentally, air-conditioning now means that the US needs more of that coal to generate more of that power in summer than in winter.*

In the time it took you to read those two paragraphs, less than half of that coal train will have passed by.

❧

Lastly, it must surely be of some relevance to try to judge the moment when the US first began to become a world power. Some might look back to the very birth of the nation, to the time when the rebel colonists (sic), following on from their Declaration of Independence, broke their English chains. After all, one can argue that until that moment they were not, except in the sense of geography, even Americans. But from that time on, that is what they became, in every way. So everything since achieved by the United States, not least its march to being the world's only superpower, begins from that moment of irritable birth. Other commentators might point to that spring day in Paris when, on Jefferson's orders, the Americans bought "Louisiane" and thereby doubled the empire of their young nation. Or why not, much later, choose the nation's decisive entry into the First World War? Again one can assert that, from that time on, no other nation could afford to disregard American muscle, industrial or military. The Japanese tried in 1941. But what about a moment in between? What about 12:47 p.m. on May 10, 1869? One remembers Asa Witney who, long before that moment at Promontory Point became a reality, had looked into the future and seen the time when, by God's Good Grace—in close alliance with that of Union and Central Pacific Railroads—the United States would move to stand at the center of the world. Surely, from that moment, much follows in terms of the nation's history. In the world's, too.

10

CUSTER AND LITTLE BIGHORN

"My every thought was ambitious—not to be wealthy, not to be learned, but to be great. I desired to link my name with acts and men as in such a manner to be an act of honor to future generations."

George Armstrong Custer, aged 27, from his book *My Life on the Plains*, written while campaigning in Kansas in 1867

❧

The brief report just in from somewhere far out in the West was not believable. Generals Sherman and Sheridan, both in Philadelphia for the nation's celebration of its first centennial, quickly dismissed it. Yes, no doubt, just as they had planned and hoped, there had been a major engagement. Excellent! And there would certainly have been some casualties, probably some killed. Inevitable ... But nearly half a regiment knocked out, including the colonel? Ridiculous. It couldn't happen.

On the evening of July 4, 1876, a telegraph operator in Salt Lake City started to take down an unscheduled message coming in from the Montana gold-town of Helena nearly 400 miles to the north: five companies of the 7th Cavalry, together with their colonel, had apparently been wiped out somewhere on the northern plains. The news had arrived in Helena a few hours earlier, via a civilian courier named Muggins Taylor. A week earlier,

Taylor had been riding with a military column that had been ordered to converge with the 7th Cavalry. It had indeed converged, but with a scatter of dead horses and over 200 mutilated corpses. Then, a few miles further on, it found the rest of the 7th Cavalry in a huddle on a hilltop. Taylor was detached to ride 200 miles westward with a first brief dispatch. From Montana, via Salt Lake City, the news was wired 2,000 miles east. It was in response to this short report that those two generals had made their denials. As they pointed out, there was nothing official from the Army's regional headquarters in St. Paul. All the same, as they no doubt quietly admitted to each other, it *was* worrying.

The generals did not have to wait long. Late the next day, a lengthy dispatch started to come in (via St. Paul) from the frontier town of Bismarck, in Dakota Territory. General Terry, the man in the field and in overall charge of the campaign that summer, had sent two dispatches. A short and immediate one had gone west with Muggins Taylor; another much more detailed one went east in the river steamer attached to the campaign, 700 miles down the Missouri to Bismarck.

To a nation which that very week was celebrating its 100th anniversary with flags, bands, parades, speeches, and fireworks, the news from out of the west was devastating. Judged by contemporary reports, the disaster seems to have been not far short of the Pearl Harbor or the 9/11 of its day. One of the nation's most famous regiments, allegedly highly trained, dedicated to Indian fighting, and led by one of the Army's brightest stars, had been chopped up by a bunch of faraway redskins. How? Why?

So what, indeed, had gone so catastrophically wrong for George Armstrong Custer? The short answer: just about everything. The slightly longer answer was that the colonel, over-confident as always, took on too many Indians who then did the opposite of what he expected them to do. But, as one might guess, there is a yet longer answer. It has engaged hundreds of historians and military commentators ever since. (I am well aware that adding my own ten cents' worth won't make any difference. Nevertheless ...)

The disaster had several connected causes. First, Custer was deeply apprehensive that, if the Indians learned of his approach, they would flee and scatter. Second, if he allowed them to get away, not only would there be no glory for him but, even worse, he would be blamed, and his military career (already under a cloud, as we will see) would be finished. So, third, he rushed forward with no idea of the terrain ahead and no idea of the numbers he was up against. Lastly and fundamentally, the "hostiles," instead of scattering—as, on experience, he certainly had a right to expect—swarmed out to attack.

In that brief analysis, one hopes there is not much ground for dispute. But beyond that, when we get to a detailed examination of what went wrong, we are looking at one of the most argued incidents in all of American history. Perhaps that is not too surprising. After all, the sole survivor of Custer's immediate command of 215 men was a horse. And live horses can tell no more of what they have seen than can dead men. True, there were plenty of Sioux and Cheyenne who, later, had tales to tell. But their accounts were not trusted. Some of them still aren't. Elsewhere that day, four miles distant, there were some hilltop officers who, having survived, quickly realized that they might become scapegoats; so they looked to their own reputations rather than to an objective analysis of the debacle. Consequently, within weeks, the narrative became muddied and, to some extent, has remained so ever since. In short, once past the basic analysis that there were too many Indians who behaved uncharacteristically, there is almost endless room for questions, debate, and conjecture. Which is why, over the years, there have been more accounts (over 2,000 of them—books, pamphlets, papers, and theses—totaling many millions of words) written about Custer than any other military leader in history except for Napoleon.

So, to tease out some answers and to understand the conjectures (as far as we can), it is essential to look at the "education" of the man in charge because, if ever the tactical thinking (or the paucity of it) of an officer was the product of his earlier experiences, namely those accumulated during the Civil War, it has to be in the thinking and personality of Custer. Further, if ever the fate of a regiment was to be finally centered on one man, the regiment was the 7th Cavalry and, again, the man was Custer. So, to understand him as a military character, we must see what made him, what molded the man. In short, in order to decide whether Custer, from his earliest military days, was *always* riding for that final fall, we must go back nearly 20 years. (Dare I say it, but too many books about Custer start their narratives *after* the Civil War; one might as well attempt an analysis of Winston Churchill's wartime leadership by ignoring all of the man's life before 1940.)

ço

"Tim, as a Brit, what do you know about Isandlwana?" He was smiling—so maybe he was anticipating my ignorance.

"Well, not much … Wasn't it a battle somewhere in the Zulu wars? Didn't we Brits get rather badly chopped up? Why do you ask?"

"Because if you think that Custer got things wrong, I have to tell you that it was nothing compared with the mess that your Lord Chelmsford got into just three years later. He lost over 1000 men. Custer's 250 or so was bad enough—but while the world is fascinated by Little Bighorn, it knows almost nothing of Isandlwana. Odd. But maybe you Brits are better at forgetting these things." He laughed.

Bob Murray was a professional historian with a particular interest in the military story of the northern plains. He took a dim view of Custer's competence— as had become obvious during the afternoon we had spent wandering over the site of the colonel's final engagement. Now we were driving home to Bob's place in Sheridan, Wyoming. That was over 20 years ago and so I don't remember word-for-word exactly how our conversation went. Sadly, Bob is no longer around. But those few sentences are a fair approximation. Apparently, with British imperialism in full flood, General Lord Chelmsford led a force of more than 1,600 men into Zulu land to discipline the locals and to plant the flag. It would be "a military promenade" according to one of the officers. They casually set up a tented camp on the slope below an outcrop called Isandlwana. The next morning 20,000 Zulus, armed with clubs and short stabbing spears, came round the corner. In less than two hours a battalion of the South Wales Borderers and over 500 native levies had been wiped out. And Chelmsford? He was away somewhere else—with part of his divided command.

And some people think that Custer got things wrong. Yes, Bob—point taken.

❧

George Armstrong Custer was the son of a blacksmith. Thus he was with horses from boyhood. From his early teens, he wanted to be a soldier, a horse-soldier. At just 18, in 1857, he surprised everyone (except himself?) by being accepted for West Point. He twice came close to being expelled for an accumulation of minor breaches of military order: "late at parade," "unmilitary conduct," "room grossly out of order," "idle and talking," and many more. He obviously had a problem with discipline; it was a handicap that he never really overcame. Except in his horsemanship, he was a notably poor cadet, academically and militarily. After three years, he graduated last in his class of 34. Yet, less than a week after leaving West Point, this most unpromising young man was posted to a front-line regiment.

In fact, the regiment already had a full complement of officers, so Custer found himself without a proper role. Disappointed, but a willing volunteer for anything exciting, he became a "balloonist"; he quickly gained a reputation at being rather good at spying out enemy positions from on high. So he was sometimes winched up two or three times a day. Between times, he galloped hither and thither on various errands, or took part in quick sorties into Confederate territory. In short, he offered himself for any project that caught his interest, the closer to combat the better.

An incident in the early summer of 1862 was typical. A Union column was held up at a river over which an important bridge had been destroyed. While a cluster of senior officers huffed and puffed about what should be done, the young Custer pushed forward and spurred his horse into the water, to see if the river was fordable. With the water up to his saddle, he could easily have been picked off by an enemy sniper. But he made it to the far bank and back. The story goes that the general in charge was so impressed that the next day he gave Custer the honor of leading the first cavalry company across the river. Once on the other side, he and his detachment put some local Confederates to rout. It was a first instance of something that would, in time, be called "Custer's Luck."

Over the next few months, he began to gain a reputation that would be with him for the rest of his life: for limitless energy and impetuous courage. He was, after all, one of nature's cavalrymen and, as such, he was always fretting for action. Armed with pistols and sabers, cavalrymen were for speed, for smashing through the enemy, for creating chaos, and for what today, in an age of Humvees and Bradleys, is called "shock and awe." To a young cavalier like Custer, courage and dash were far more important than forethought; after all, too much thinking might lead to too much caution.

In short, he was deeply impatient. His chance came at a place called Aldie. Two senior officers were out of the battle early; one was killed leading a charge and the other had his horse shot from under him. Custer rushed forward to take command, by example rather than by rank. Against the odds, he and the men following him swept through the enemy's lines. Casualties were high; they usually were. But Custer had helped turn the battle. The General commanding the Cavalry Corps was deeply impressed. Indeed, so keen was he to make Custer's vigor and leadership an example throughout his rather ill-disciplined corps that, ten days later, this young lieutenant was surprised beyond even his ambitious dreams.

Returning from some minor assignment, he was handed an envelope: it was addressed to Brigadier General George A. Custer. Even he did not believe it; it must be a joke. But the contents were genuine. Suddenly, less than two years out of West Point, he had been chosen to leap over a whole host of more senior officers. He was aged 23; it was unprecedented. Indeed, the records apparently show that he was the youngest American officer ever to have reached that rank, before or since. Custer's Luck?

The contents of that envelope told General Custer that he was to take command of four regiments of cavalry; they were stationed over 40 miles away. He immediately made the night ride. Within a day or two of his arrival, he was demanding something that he detected to be a missing ingredient in his command: discipline. He had become a convert—where others were concerned. Of course, among a few of his older officers, there was whispering about someone whom they saw as an over-rewarded and overconfident young pup. (Damn it, the man had even designed his own uniform: all velvet, gold braid, a red scarf, and a big floppy hat: "like a circus rider gone mad," wrote a fellow officer.) Nevertheless, no one could accuse the Boy General, as he was becoming known, of not leading from the front. Standing in his stirrups, he would draw his saber and calmly walk his horse to the front where everyone could see him. Then he would turn and call for the bugler to sound the charge. Now, with a shout and a whoop, he would start forward at a trot, with his men in a broad echelon reaching away on either side. Nearing the enemy, the pace would quicken through a canter to a full gallop; then, a saber-slashing mayhem. One could get oneself killed that way. But not Custer.

At Culpepper, he was slightly wounded in the thigh by a piece of shrapnel, and his horse was shot from under him. But, as he had done before, and as he would do again, he had exactly judged both the place and the moment to attack. During the next two years, it is said that at least six more horses were shot from under him. Yet, in leading at least a dozen full-tilt charges and many more hot-blooded skirmishes, he was wounded just that once. Custer's Luck? Perhaps. But there was more to the man than just good fortune. A senior officer summed him up: "He might well not conduct a siege, but for sudden dash it's Custer against the world."

Early in 1864, Custer persuaded his commanding general to give him three weeks' furlough to return to his hometown, Monroe in Michigan. He planned to marry his sweetheart, Elizabeth Bacon. Earlier her father, a judge and one of the town's prominent citizens, had disapproved of his daughter's suitor; social lines in Monroe were rigid and a blacksmith's son did not "measure." But now that the young man was a Brigadier General, Elizabeth's father gave his willing consent. The wedding was a grand affair with most of the town cheering the young couple on their way. After a brief honeymoon in New York, they went south to Washington. Then Custer rode out to rejoin his command.

By all accounts, once in the saddle, he was not only careless of his own life, but also that of his men. But then most generals of those times were. Perhaps, to hold their rank, they had to be. In the Civil War, the toll of casualties (on both sides) was always high; it seems to have been almost a point of pride with some officers, including Custer, that it should be. After all, heavy casualties demonstrated what a hard-won battle it had been. He wrote to Elizabeth (more usually known as Libbie) more than once about the exultation of a full-blooded attack. "Oh, could you but have seen some of the glorious charges that were made ... while thinking of them, I cannot but exclaim Glorious War!"

After the battle at Winchester, for "gallant and meritorious service" he was promoted to Major General; he was 25 and the most widely recognized young officer in the Union Army. In any war, what we now call "the media" prefer their heroes to be young, successful, somewhat eccentric, and then either disarmingly modest or charismatically flamboyant. With long blond locks, a self-designed uniform with braid from wrist to elbow, a big hat, and a pistol tucked into a boot top, the Boy General looked the part. And he knew it.

When at last the war was over, he led his men into Washington to join what today would be called the victory parade. Coming down Pennsylvania Avenue, some way short of the reviewing stand, his high-stepping horse became disturbed by the shouts of acclaim (that, at least, was *his* story) so that, with a tattoo of prancing hooves, it carried him alone and theatrically past President Johnson and Generals Grant and Sherman, to further amused cheers from the thousands of bystanders. Both his friends and his skeptics, when they heard, would surely have thought it typical of the man. The former presumably just smiled indulgently, the latter probably rolled their eyes heavenwards and muttered something about "grandstanding again."

For General Custer, it had indeed been a Glorious War. But more importantly, in terms of the years that followed, he had been indelibly shaped by the experiences gained and the promotion won. Above all, he had become a personification of the chancy dictum that success comes to those who take risks, to those who dare. Or, to coin a cliché (with which he would surely have agreed), one should never look too hard before one leaps lest one hesitates and, perhaps, never leaps at all.

Although the Civil War years had been so formative, the young General and his wife now discussed his leaving the military. After all, where would be the fun, let alone the glory, in a peacetime army? But then, following a short and rather boring posting in Texas, he was offered the command of a cavalry regiment that was being formed on the western plains. True, in the now much reduced army, he would have to drop rank to a mere colonel. Nevertheless, the high opinion he already had of himself would have been even further boosted by the knowledge that he, Custer, had been singled out, again. He and Libbie set off.

The 7th Cavalry was forming on the eastern edge of the Kansas plains at a place called Fort Riley. (Today it is the site of one of the biggest army bases in the US.) On arrival, Custer was disappointed: he found that too many of his men were untrained recruits. Further, among his officers were a few obvious time-servers, neither inspiring nor inspired. But, for the time being, that hardly mattered because they all had a task that kept them busy: training those recruits in preparation for a campaign in the coming spring, under the overall command of General Hancock.

Toward the end of the week between Christmas and the New Year (1866–67), the fort would have heard rumors of the Fetterman Massacre far away to the north-west. One imagines that the news gave a shocked urgency to the regiment's training. Anyway, by late March, all was ready and General Hancock started westward with a column of 1,400 men and a supply train of more than 100 wagons. Custer and his 7th Cavalry were in the van.

Against the mounted tribes of the western plains, Sioux, Cheyenne, Kiowa (it made no difference which), speed and mobility were everything. Hancock, with his plodding column strung out over three miles, might as well have tried to bring down a distant brave with a howitzer. True, some of the Cheyenne were persuaded, by a local official of the Indian Bureau in whom they had some trust, to "come in" for a powwow with Hancock. But, already apprehensive, and now seeing the forces poised all around them, they became frightened and belligerent. When Hancock threatened them with punishment for any future bad behavior ("insolence," he called it), they were gone so quickly that they did not even delay to pack up their tepees. Hancock promptly burned their village and everything in it—an action that was unlikely to persuade the hearts and minds of the Cheyenne toward the paths of peace. Custer and his men were ordered to go after the "insolent fugitives." But like all tribes when pursued by a superior (even if slower) force, they had scattered in a dozen different directions. This was not Aldie or Culpepper.

In revenge, elusive war parties of Cheyenne now killed more than 100 whites, including women and children. Custer lost a number of stragglers. In trying to catch the Cheyenne, Custer marched his men till some of them and their horses dropped. Characteristically, he reasoned that if he could stand the pace, so should they. Equally characteristically, and peremptorily, he had some would-be deserters shot. By the time they pulled into a huddle of tents called Fort Wallace on the western fringes of Kansas, the men of the 7th Cavalry had zigzagged well over 1,000 miles, achieving very little. Custer's orders from General Hancock were waiting; he was to replenish his supplies and immediately get back to chasing the Hostiles.

But Custer now did something unprecedented. He had heard a rumor that, back in Fort Riley, there was an outbreak of cholera. Concerned for his dearest Libbie, he abandoned his regiment with the excuse that he personally must return east to arrange for more supplies. So, with a company of his fittest horsemen for an escort, he set off to cover the 300 miles back to Fort Riley as quickly as possible. On the second or third day, two of his troopers dropped behind because their horses could not keep up with their Colonel's desperate pace; he refused to go back for them, such was his personal haste, but some Cheyenne caught and killed them at a place called Downer's Station. In the event, he found Libby in good health. Many years later, as a widow, she wrote, "There was in that summer of 1867 one long, perfect day. It was mine and, blessed be the memory, it is still mine—for time and eternity." One is almost won over.

But the fact was that her husband had deserted his command. The next day, a message from General Hancock came over the wire: Custer was under open arrest. Two months later, in Fort Leavenworth back by the Missouri, he faced seven charges. The one that really mattered was the abandonment of his command. His admirers (yes, there were quite a few) put it about that he was being made a scapegoat for General Hancock's notably unsuccessful campaign. Be that as it may, he was found guilty on all counts and suspended from rank and pay for a year. In some disgrace, which they pretended to ignore, he and Libbie went home to Monroe. He began his memoirs.

Back on the plains, through the iciest months of that winter, the Indians and the Army went into hibernation; it was too cold to do anything else. But with the spring the tribes were back on the warpath, more vigorously than ever. Within two months, along the Smoky Hill trail leading across Kansas towards the Rockies, they killed another 100 whites: soldiers and civilians. The unsuccessful Hancock was relieved. General Sheridan took over, and shifted his headquarters out to Fort Hays in mid-Kansas, to be central to the campaign he now planned. He knew who he wanted at the sharp end of those plans: he sent a telegram to Washington asking that Custer be reinstated, and another to Monroe. "General Sherman and myself, and nearly all the officers of your regiment, have asked for you. Can you come at once?" Given that Custer, the previous summer, had achieved no more than anyone else, one wonders what prompted Sheridan.

Perhaps he remembered Custer's manic energy in the Civil War. Perhaps he reckoned that the man would risk anything to rescue his damaged reputation. For Custer, it must have been very satisfying. One imagines him turning to Libbie: "See! They can't manage without me."

He was in Fort Hays within a week. "How soon do I start?" is reported to have been his first question. He and Sheridan recognized that chasing Indians in the summer, when they were scattered and highly mobile, was a waste of time. So instead, they would hit them in mid-winter when they were clustered together, when the ponies on which they might escape were weakened by lack of feed, when the cold itself was immobilizing.

In mid-November the 7th Cavalry, nearly 700 strong, set off south from Fort Hays. After 100 miles, it established a supply post called, appropriately, Camp Supply. Four days later, nearing the Washita River, the scouts picked up a confusion of trails in the snow that led toward what they judged must be a large encampment. Moving quietly through the hard-frozen night, Custer split his command into four in order to surround the village and stop its inhabitants from trying to flee. At first light, on hearing the band strike up, each detachment was to attack simultaneously. There was no attempt to send scouts ahead to gauge the size or the geography of the village.

Despite the fact that, with no reconnaissance, the attack was tactically haphazard, it was successful. Against a sleeping enemy, it could hardly be anything else. The main action through the village, with the troopers shooting or cutting down anyone who moved, was over in minutes. Custer counted the Battle of the Washita, as it came to be called, as a personal triumph. Estimates varied as to the number of Indian dead: some said 100 braves were killed, some said 200 or even more. A number of women and children were captured; given that Indians were always concerned for their families, these captives would be useful hostages against any subsequent trouble. The cavalry's casualties were light: one officer killed, one seriously wounded. There was some confusion as to the whereabouts of a detachment of troopers under the regiment's second-in-command, a Major Elliott.

What Custer did not know, because he had not bothered to find out, was that this village was just one of a string of large encampments scattered along the Washita valley. Again, estimates vary, but one calculation put the number of warriors within five miles at more than 3,000. Anyway, Custer was soon alarmed to see several hundred armed warriors lining a distant bluff; more were joining them. Uncharacteristically, he decided to withdraw, making apparent to the enemy the presence of his "hostage" captives. He later explained that he was low on ammunition. More likely, he realized that he had no idea of how many

Indians might be lying in wait up or down the river. So for once, he was being careful. He may also have been worried about the safety of his supply train, which had been left some miles behind. Anyway, before moving out, he ordered that the camp be burned and the Cheyenne's means of summer mobility be destroyed: their herd of more than 500 horses was to be shot. He surely could not have been *that* short of ammunition.

Elliott and his men did not come in to rejoin the column. Custer sent out a small search party, but in the wrong direction. Once again, as back at Downer's Station, he was in a hurry: in this case, to get back to Fort Supply. Weeks later, 20 frozen and mutilated soldiers were discovered. In chasing after some Indians fleeing from the Washita, they must have been cut off and overwhelmed. Some of Custer's officers never forgave him for what they saw as a second instance of his deserting his own men.

But General Sheridan, now waiting in Fort Supply, was delighted when advance couriers brought him Custer's news. At last, a real success. Two days later, he turned out to take the salute as the 7th Cavalry, with sabers drawn, paraded into the fort. One imagines that the colonel was also well pleased. His critics maintained that his record at the Washita did little to demonstrate his prowess and, given that the Cheyenne were all asleep, a raw recruit could have directed the attack. That is probably putting it too strongly, and it is certainly not the way Colonel Custer would have seen it.

On the contrary, he judged himself a thoroughly proven success as a fighter and conqueror of Indians—an attitude of overconfidence that goes a long way to explain the mind of the man in what follows.

❧

Early in 1873, there came the order that Custer had been hoping for: he was to take his regiment north to Dakota Territory, to guard surveyors who would be working on the alignment of the second transcontinental railroad, the Northern Pacific. This, he knew, was the country of the bad-tempered Sioux. Well, he would show them ...

Nearly five years earlier, in the protracted aftermath of the Fetterman disaster, the US had no alternative but to negotiate. Under the second

Fort Laramie Treaty in 1868 (the first had been aborted two years before, after that dramatic exit by Red Cloud), the government had been forced to abandon its forts along the Bozeman Trail and, moreover, it had been forced to recognize that the Sioux had rights over all the land stretching west from the middle Missouri to a line well beyond the Black Hills. This vast tract of land, into which all white incursions were now banned, came to be known as the Great Sioux Reservation. It was to the ill-defined northern reaches of this vast expanse that Custer was now sent to protect the incursion of those surveyors.

Now, a short digression: in the second half of the nineteenth century, Washington's Peace Commissioners journeyed west to negotiate any number of treaties with the tribes. In "touching paper," the problem on both sides— whether in the deserts of, say, New Mexico and Arizona or on the high plains of Wyoming and Montana—was always the same: neither side was in a strong position to deliver that which it had just guaranteed. The government might promise to hold off trespassers from some vast tract that it had just patronizingly "recognized" as Indian land, but it knew that it would seldom be able to enforce its side of the bargain, even if it wanted to. The tribal leaders, for their part, might agree that whites traveling (or settling) outside the treaty boundaries would not be molested. But, given the frequency of white trespass, the tribes did not have the collective discipline (or will) to hold back their hotheads from revenge. Nor, just as importantly, did the tribes have leaders in the hierarchical, white man's sense of the term. So, for example, when Red Cloud sulkily agreed to that second Fort Laramie treaty, there were any number of Sioux far away in the Powder River country who would have denied that Red Cloud, or anyone else, had their agreement to "touch paper" on their behalf. In short, there was a developing schism between the "reservation" Sioux (the Friendlies) who had grudgingly begun to appreciate the power of the whites, and their cousins out in the back-country (the Hostiles). So whatever the whites might write on those bits of paper that they called "treaties," the Hostiles would have felt no inhibitions about attacking anyone who came too close. In any case, the idea that anyone could *own* land, let alone "trade" the stuff, was a concept wholly outside their culture. Land was something across which the buffalo roamed; the Indians hunted and depended on the buffalo; the whites were destroying the buffalo. Simple. Except, of course, it was *not* simple—as history and a number of lawsuits still being brought, even today, by the Native Americans will confirm.

But back to Custer: one can reasonably say that the rights and wrongs of his assignment in Dakota Territory that summer would not have concerned him in the least. But to the Sioux, the railroad surveyors and their military guardians were in direct violation of that earlier treaty. There were several sharp engagements, and lives were lost. On one occasion, Custer extricated his command from what might have become an encircling ambush by resorting to the Civil War tactic he had always trusted and understood: the full-blooded charge. The Indians broke and fled. To Custer, it would have been confirmation yet again that, when subjected to a bold and direct attack, the Hostiles would always turn, run and scatter.

At the end of the summer, the regiment returned 300 miles east to its recently completed home by the Missouri river; Fort Lincoln had been built right on the edge of the treaty lands. Again, Libbie and the other wives joined their husbands. For the Custers and their immediate entourage, the winter must have passed easily. They kept open house: their guests included Captain Tom Custer (a younger brother), Boston Custer (a civilian and his youngest brother), and Lieutenant Calhoun (his brother-in-law, married to Custer's sister). And beyond the family circle, favored officers would join them for musical evenings, charades, cards and, when the weather allowed, rides and picnics on the prairie. Between times, Custer busied himself on what his wife called his "literary work": articles about army life for newspapers and for *Galaxy* magazine, a New York monthly.

With the coming of spring, the regiment began preparing for what would be known as the Black Hills Expedition. There had long been rumors of gold "in them thar hills." And as the government was anxious, as always, to bolster its treasury, it could not allow a likely source of national wealth to stagnate. Never mind that the Black Hills were, by treaty, in the heart of the Sioux domain and that they were especially sacred to the tribe. So, perhaps to ease its conscience, the government put it about that it was mounting an expedition of "geographic exploration," a mere mapping party. Anyway, whatever it was labeled, in early June, with the band playing their colonel's favorite tunes, "Garry Owen" and "The Girl I Left Behind Me," he led his column out of Fort Lincoln. In addition to ten companies of the 7th Cavalry, there were two companies of infantry, three of the new Gatling machine guns, an artillery piece, 100 Indian scouts, four journalists, two miners, a geologist, a cartographer, a botanist, and a photographer—over 1,000 men in all; plus, it is said, one woman: Calamity Jane. Custer's orderly later said that "she did not smell good." Supporting the column were 100 supply wagons and a large herd of "beeves." All this to do some mapping?

Four weeks later, they found gold—of course. Some of Custer's more opportunistic troopers immediately formed themselves into joint stock companies. Custer sent off a dispatch: "… gold among the roots of the grass." Well before the expedition was back in Fort Lincoln, the nation had the news, and miners were on their way. By the following spring, the trickle had become a continuous stream. The Sioux boiled. The Army made several half-hearted attempts to turn back the rush. But within 18 months there were 6,000 people around a place that is still called Custer, and at least as many again were prospecting elsewhere in the hills. (During the decades ending in the early 1950s, the nearby Homestake Mine became the most productive gold mine on the continent.)

The Thieves' Road was what the Sioux called the path first opened by Custer. A worried government sought a way out of its treaty obligations; it sent its Commissioners west once again, to buy the Black Hills. After all, only the year before the US had bought the whole of Alaska from the Russians for less than $8 million. So now, for the Black Hills, they were offering what they judged to be an overly generous $6 million. But the "reservation" Sioux (the Friendlies), in a series of irritable meetings with the Commissioners, made it clear that the offer was not nearly enough. In any case, when the Hostiles out in the Powder River country heard what was going on, they let it be known that they were against *any* kind of a deal for *their* hills. Indeed, under the young Crazy Horse and the older Sitting Bull, they were prepared to go to war if necessary. Indeed, they might go to war anyway.

In the end, the government justified what it called "the annexation" of the Black Hills by claiming that the Sioux, particularly those who had certainly been responsible for a number of minor raids, had obviously not been keeping *their* side of that earlier treaty. General Sherman bolstered that thinking. "Inasmuch as the Sioux have not lived in peace," he wrote, "I think Congress has a perfect right to abrogate the whole of the treaty ..." The Indian Bureau agreed. Of what it called "certain wild and hostile tribes," the Bureau wrote, "The true policy is to send troops against them in the winter, the sooner the better, and whip them into subjection." The Army could hardly wait.

The plan was simple: a major campaign would be mounted that winter when the "hostile" encampments were at their most vulnerable. So, in early December 1875, Indian couriers were sent to all the outlying Hostile bands; the message they carried was simple: anyone who had not peaceably reported in to one of the several Bureau Agencies scattered across the Great Reservation by the last day of January would be liable to attack without further warning. Some of the bands sent back word that when the snowdrifts of winter had gone and when their ponies had recovered their strength, they would think about it—but that could not be before the spring. Others never got the message and a few, defiant and contemptuous, did not bother to send back any reply. Interestingly, some of the messengers did not themselves get back until after the deadline, such were the winter storms.

The truth is that the authorities had already calculated that many of the Hostiles would ignore the summons. To that end, the Army had been planning its winter campaign for several months, since well before that "deadline" message had been drafted. It was judged that the Hostiles would be in winter camps somewhere in the lands that were loosely known as the Powder River country, between the Black Hills and the Bighorn Mountains. So the intention was for a two-pronged advance. The distances were considerable: 150 miles for General Crook coming north from a base (Fort Fetterman) on the Platte, and twice that for Colonel Custer coming west from Fort Lincoln. In the event, the prolonged snows, sub-zero temperatures and a shortage of supplies stalled Custer before he had even made it off the parade ground. General Crook did manage to get away and make slow progress until a blizzard (at 40°F below freezing) stopped his command for four days. A week later, his scouts reported a medium-sized village; the ensuing attack went badly awry and the Hostiles got away. By now the fight was against the weather rather than the Sioux; snow-blindness, frostbite and diminishing supplies (as usual) were the problems. Crook turned round and struggled back to base.

So now a spring campaign was planned. This time there would be *three* converging contingents. Crook would again come up from the south. Custer, again starting from Fort Lincoln, would close in, as planned before, from the east. A third group, under Colonel Gibbon, would advance from the west, from Montana down the line of the Yellowstone River. During his preparations for this renewed attempt to "whip the Sioux into subjection," Custer found himself suddenly ordered back to Washington. This interruption seems to have had a real (though sometimes under-recognized) influence on Custer's behavior two months later. Were it otherwise, the tale would hardly be worth telling ...

For some years, Custer and other officers serving on the plains had become evermore irritated at what they saw as increasing corruption high up in the War Department. The Department gave licenses for civilian traders to set up shop (literally) in its army forts and Indian Bureau's Agencies across the West. In the more isolated encampments and forts it was a lucrative monopoly: selling the officers and enlisted men all the "civilian" supplies that they might need, from clothing and "extras" for enhancing their army rations to soap, whiskey, and tobacco. The prices charged were high; they had to be because a number of senior officials back in Washington expected their cut for both the initial granting of the license and, thereafter, on the retail turnover.

An unsigned article about the scandal had recently appeared in *The New York Times*. Many thought that Custer was the whistleblower, if not the actual author. But, whatever his precise role, he was summoned to Washington to give evidence at an official inquiry. Once in the capital he was, as was his habit, more impetuous than he had need to be. He implicated one of President Grant's closest cronies, the Secretary of War, General Belknap. The chairman of the inquiry, who was no friend of President Grant or General Belknap, led Custer on. His further testimony pointed at Orvil Grant and his wife. Orvil was the President's brother. In short, elements of President Grant's administration were allegedly rotten. Grant was furious. So when, with his testimony delivered, Custer set off back to Fort Lincoln, he was ordered off the train, on the direct order of the President. He asked to see Grant. Indeed, uninvited, he hurried to the White House and sent in a note asking to be allowed to return to his regiment. In agony, he waited all day in an anteroom. Grant's door stayed shut.

Desperate to get back, and hearing a rumor that another officer might be nominated to command *his* regiment, Custer secretly left Washington on the next train. Changing trains two days later in Chicago he was arrested on orders direct from the President. Now, even more desperate, he appealed to Generals Terry and Sheridan to intercede on his behalf. Reluctantly, they did so. Eventually, Grant relented—even more reluctantly. He had been pushed by *The New York Times* and other newspapers that were sympathetic to Custer and his allegations of corruption. But the President ordered that Custer should no longer be in overall command of both the northern contingents, as originally planned; General Terry would now fill that post. One can imagine Custer's reaction. Anyway, less than a week after Custer rejoined his regiment, he led it out of Fort Lincoln. The wives and children waved them off. There were some tears. Beside the cavalry, there were three companies of infantry, three Gatling machine guns, a wagon train, a hundred or so pack-mules, and a small beef herd. As civilian helpers with the pack train, Custer's youngest brother, Boston, and his nephew, 17-year-old Autie Reed, went along too.

Even for the northern plains, that spring was unusual: first there was driving rain, then snowstorms into early June. The terrain also slowed the column: too many swollen streams to cross and the contorted geography of some badlands to negotiate. In the event, it was five weeks before Custer and General Terry eventually met up with Colonel Gibbon coming from the west. Also arrived was a steamer, the *Far West*. Loaded with supplies and under the command of a skillful skipper, Grant Marsh, she had navigated 700 difficult miles from Bismarck and nearby Fort Lincoln, up the Missouri and then the Yellowstone. Now Terry held a council of war in the ship's small saloon.

It was assumed that many of the Sioux would be camped in one extended village; that was their usual summer custom. Further, the officers all agreed that, having first found the village, the overriding problem would be how to prevent the Hostiles from scattering. Even at this stage, despite the mutterings of several civilian scouts—old hands who knew the Sioux well enough to guess what, following the invasion of their Black Hills, would be their reaction— the possibility that the quarry might stand and fight did not occur to any of the assembled officers. And even if it had occurred to one or other of them, the boast among regimental commanders was always much the same: any regiment, even at sub-strength, could "whip" (a favorite verb) any provocation from the Indians, any Indians in any strength. Additionally, there was the assumption, despite further mutterings from the scouts, that they were unlikely to find more than 700–800 warriors in the village.

As they leaned over their rather inaccurate maps, Terry and his officers would have wondered how far General Crook's converging advance from the south had come. But there was no way of finding out because, even assuming that Crook was already on the move, the intervening distance (of over 100 miles) was far too dangerous for any scout to go to find out, let alone then to return. So, as far as planning was concerned, any possible contribution from Crook's column had to be ignored.

More immediate was a lack of intelligence about the exact whereabouts of the Hostiles. Nevertheless, partly based on the direction of a large and recent trail found some days earlier during a short probe to the south (under Major Reno, second-in-command of the 7th Cavalry), the conclusion was that the Sioux were probably camped on one or other of two of the Yellowstone's north-flowing tributaries: the Rosebud or the Little Bighorn. Although the area of search was fairly large (at least 40 by 40 miles), the strategy worked out some time before would still apply: Custer and his regiment, by first going south and then swinging west, would get "below" the enemy. Then, with any luck at all, by picking up tell-tale trails, Custer would be able to get a reasonable fix on the village. Gibbon and his infantry, having been ferried across the Yellowstone by the *Far West*, would advance southward and thus, with luck, be "above" the enemy. When the Sioux attempted to flee from one or other of these two forces, they would find themselves running into the other face of the vice. That, broadly, was the plan.

With hindsight, the plan had several weaknesses. But one stands out: it did not/could not take account of the possibility (the probability?) that the glory-hunting Custer might be working to what today would be called "his own agenda." What if he made contact with the Sioux first—as he had allegedly told

Colonel Custer was always having his photo taken; here he poses beneath one taken earlier (National Archives)

a few of his closest friends he had every intention of doing? The Sioux, thus alerted, might flee north toward Gibbon. But Custer certainly would not have seen himself as a mere "beater" flushing the quarry onto someone else's guns. Where was the prestige and acclaim in that? And he must have had another concern. What if the Sioux did not flee directly away from him, north toward Gibbon, but, much more likely, went sideways—west and then south toward their nearest sanctuary, the Bighorn Mountains? They would escape altogether, and he would get all the blame. The answer in his mind (the evidence surely lies in his actions four days later) must have been that he must find the enemy first and then hit them with such sudden force and surprise (shock and awe again) that they would simply not have time to escape—in any direction. That way the victory and all the acclaim would be his. Did he look back to his success, based entirely on surprise, at the Washita? Or, in his mind, did he go back even further, even subconsciously, to those thundering charges at Brandy Station, Aldie, or Culpepper?

Whatever else he may have been, Custer was very human. So, in addition to his inherent thirst for glory, one can surely assume that he was also still harboring something between resentment and dismay at the humiliation so recently thrown at him by President Grant and his cronies. So now, all the more reason why he should want to show his critics and his enemies (in and beyond the Army) how wrong they had been. But, to do that, he would have to get there first and, above all, he would have to take the Indians by surprise—so that they could not run.

Shortly before the column set off the next morning, Terry handed Custer his orders—confirmation, one assumes, of the decisions taken at that meeting in the *Far West*. They ran to two handwritten pages. There are two passages that have long been the focus of debate. "You should proceed up the Rosebud in pursuit of the Indians whose trail was discovered by Major Reno a few days ago. It is, of course, impossible to give you any definite instructions in regard to this movement, and were it not impossible to do so, the Department Commander [Terry is referring to himself; this arcane use of the third person is still common in the American army] places too much confidence in your zeal, energy, and ability to impose upon you precise orders which might hamper your action when nearly in contact with the enemy." Custer must have been delighted; he had been given what he wanted: a blank check, so far. But then Terry goes on: "You should proceed up the Rosebud until you ascertain definitely the direction in which the trail spoken of leads. Should it be found, as it appears almost certain that it will be found, to turn toward the Little Bighorn, he thinks that you should still proceed southward, perhaps as far as the headwaters of the Tongue, and *then* [emphasis added] turn toward the Little Bighorn ..." In other words, having found the trail, Custer should not immediately and directly follow it to the Indian camp, but should proceed for another 25 miles or so (a day's march) and *then* turn toward the camp. But why would Terry wish to send Custer this further distance? It has been suggested that he wanted to place Custer firmly across the path of the Indians who, if Gibbon were to make first contact, might try to escape south-westward to the fastness of the Bighorn Mountains. But this assumes that Gibbon, with his slower-moving infantry, was going to find the village (or its outliers) before Custer's cavalry. This was never very likely. Surely, the more probable reason for putting an extra day into Custer's itinerary was to delay him until Gibbon's slower infantry (as compared with Custer's faster cavalry) could take up a blocking position to the north of where the village might be. In short, Terry did not want Custer to attack until Gibbon was in position. But, again, he seems to give Custer latitude; he only "thinks" that Custer should proceed a day or so further before turning toward the Hostiles. Experienced soldiers will maintain that, then as now, when a commanding officer says that he "thinks" something should be done, it should not be regarded as a mere suggestion; it is very close to an order. But why was Terry not more direct? Why so polite? The answer may be that Terry was conscious that he himself had had no experience of Indian fighting, whereas Custer (as he would have made very clear) had been on and off the western plains for some years. Nevertheless, Terry was the man in charge, so his deference to Custer is rather curious.

Equally curious is Terry's lack of detail about the timing of the convergence of the two columns (Gibbon's and Custer's) on the Little Bighorn. We know from others who were involved that the date decided was June 26. Perhaps the plan had been so much discussed that Terry did not think that detail now had to be spelled out. But no one has ever doubted that a significant degree of coordination was intended. Confirmation lies in a much-reported incident when Custer mounted his horse and took his final leave. Gibbon is alleged to have called out, "Now Custer, don't be greedy; wait for us." To which, as he rode away, Custer is said to have shouted back, "No, I won't." Did he mean that he would not be greedy? Or did he mean that he would not wait? Given that there is no way of knowing, Gibbon's "wait for us" is the more interesting part of that exchange; it implies (confirms?) that there was the intention that his column and Custer's would start tightening the vice on the Indian camp from north and south at the same time. But Custer would have known that, if he hurried (and ignored Terry's "thought" that he should proceed further up the Rosebud), he would reach the enemy well ahead of what he undoubtedly saw as Competition.

Custer's desire for speed, and thereby the sole glory, would seem to be further confirmed by his rejection of Terry's offer of those Gatling guns. Heavy, awkward, and of little use in a swiftly developing attack, they would just slow him down. He was right in that analysis. Yet on that first day, because of a late start, the 7th Cavalry only made 12 miles. If there is any doubt about the imperative of Custer's haste, it is surely now resolved by the pace he subsequently demanded of his men. On a forced march, a cavalry regiment and its supply column of pack-carrying mules might cover 35 miles in a day, but to require the 7th, as Custer now did, to average that kind of distance, in noon temperatures of over 90⁰F (32⁰C), for each of the next *three* days meant that some men and their mounts would be near to exhaustion. Furthermore, by the second day there were increasing signs of recent Indian presence. Nerves would have been tightening.

By the third day, the trail they found—made by the Indian ponies and the furrows of their dragging tepee poles—was becoming fresher and broader; in places it was over half a mile wide. (The freshness of pony droppings indicated the recentness of any trail.) Both the white and Indian scouts were now nervously revising the numbers they thought were ahead: they reckoned that this was a trail made by maybe 4,000 adult Sioux; that could mean well over 1,000 warriors. Then the trail swung away from the Rosebud and lifted up over the higher ground that lay between the valleys of the Rosebud and the next-door river, the Little Bighorn. This intervening divide often appears on maps as the Wolf Mountains, but the terrain is really just a range of high pine-clad hills.

It was evening and they had already come nearly 35 miles that day. But with the fresh trail now so clearly before him, Custer's blood was up. He would abandon Terry's tentative "thought" that he should continue on further to the west—if indeed obedience had ever been part of his calculations. Instead, the regiment would follow the trail through the night until they were a little short of the crest of the divide. There they would hide and rest during the following day while some skilled scouts were sent ahead to locate the enemy, preliminary to a "shock and awe" attack at dawn the following day. The Washita again?

The night march was not easy. They were already very tired and now, in the dark, there was much stumbling, confusion, and bad temper. Even so, they managed to reach a point somewhere just short of the crest. They had come ten miles, and it was well after midnight. At dawn, someone reported that one of the mules and its cargo had gone missing during the night march. A small detachment was detailed to go back. They found the mule's load. It was being examined by four Sioux. The Sioux made off.

It seems that Custer was not immediately informed of this small incident because he had been called forward to a lookout point high on that ridgeline. Earlier, from that lookout and in the sharpness of the early morning light, the Crow scouts reported that they could see, across 15 miles of country, indications of what they said was a very large village. From the lookout (since known as the Crow's Nest) one can, today, see what the scouts could and could not see. They would *not* have been able to see the village itself; it would have been hidden behind a long, low bluff. But what they could observe was the dust of a very large pony herd. Indeed, they claimed that they could see part of the herd itself and, rising from beyond that distant bluff, a smoky haze seeping up from what could have been a host of cooking fires. That much pony dust and smoke would have indicated something about the size of the village. Already nervous, they were now even more so. But when Custer came up to have a look an hour or two later, he was dismissive. It seems that while Custer accepted that the position of the village was now more or less fixed, he was quite unpersuaded about its size. After all, his Indian scouts had been jumpy ever since leaving the Yellowstone. They were likely to be exaggerating.

೮/9

Guided by a friend, Emerson Scott, who has long studied the geography and the history of these parts, I recently stood where those scouts once stood: the Crow's Nest. It is a lonely spot, well away from any road; one needs a 4-wheel-drive to get there. From the piney knoll of the Crow's Nest, looking out over those 15 miles, one can just see the slow-moving dot of the occasional truck making its way north along the four-lane highway that is Interstate 90; the highway passes right over the ground on which that pony herd would have been grazing. There is a small cairn at Crow's Nest; the plaque tells one that "When General Custer came here and scanned with his field glasses he saw nothing." Would it be more accurate to say that, even with field glasses, General Custer said he saw nothing? Who knows? Maybe it is fairer to give him the benefit of the doubt. By the time he looked, the sun would have lifted and the morning haze may indeed have been too smudgy.

❦

In coming down from the Crow's Nest and rejoining the main column, Custer was told about those Sioux and that missing mule. Then, more bad news; he learned that other Indians had been seen. Obviously, the enemy village would now be warned. He had lost the vital element of surprise (if, indeed, he had ever had any right to expect it). Even now, the Sioux might be packing up and, to use Custer's own word, "scatterating." Suddenly he knew that his plan to wait a day in order to carry out a reconnaissance, prior to attacking with the next dawn, must be abandoned. If he were to catch the Indians, he must ride forward at once—and to hell with any plans to send scouts forward to reconnoiter.

The regiment was on its way within minutes. The scouts went out ahead. When they were in rolling country some way beyond the divide, they came upon a very recently abandoned campsite. Indeed, they could see the occupants, about 40 of them, galloping away in the direction of the village. To Custer, this would have been yet further confirmation of his obsession: he must attack immediately, before the now-alerted enemy had the chance to get away. His Crow scouts did not share that analysis; again they warned him that this was likely to be a very big village with thousands of warriors. Again, Custer ignored them, and now, as the regiment cantered down the upper reaches of a small stream (since called Reno Creek) which ran towards the Little Bighorn, he briefly halted. He divided his command: Captain Benteen was ordered to take three companies (between 120 and 130 men) away to the southwest, to cut off any escapers who might head that way toward the Bighorn Mountains. Benteen is said to have suggested to Custer that, in light of the unknown possibilities ahead, might it not be better for everyone to stick together? Custer is alleged to have cut him short with an abrupt, "Major, you have your orders." Another three companies were assigned to Major Reno; he was to lead them down the left side of the stream. Custer, with five companies, would ride down the right side. One company, under Captain McDougall, was detached to guard the mule train which would follow more slowly.

Custer's orders were quick and peremptory; as always, he led more by physical example than by verbal explanation. Consequently, on this crucial and, as it would turn out, perhaps fatal decision to split his command, some historians have complained that we lack strong evidence as to just *why* Custer did what he did. But surely his rationale is obvious, given his first conviction, that what lay ahead was just a medium-sized village; and second, that now the village knew

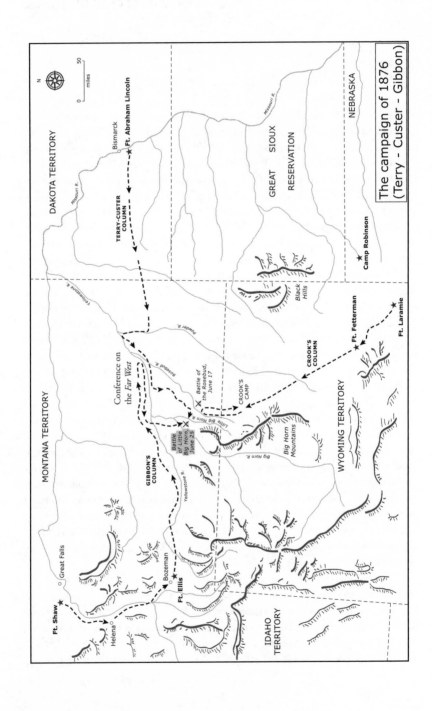

The campaign of 1876
(Terry - Custer - Gibbon)

of his approach, its inhabitants would be preparing to flee and disperse. His mistake lay in those two convictions. Plus, if one is still unpersuaded, there is the important fact (maybe it is the deciding element) that the man had the self-confidence of a gambler who had never lost yet—Custer's Luck.

They rode on. Presently Custer sent his adjutant across Reno Creek with a further instruction for Major Reno: he was to chase those Indians still running ahead of him and, once he was onto the river flats (having forded across to the far side of the Little Bighorn), he was to charge any village that might lie across his front, "and you will be supported by the whole outfit." Custer seems to have intended that, whatever the size and spread of the village ahead, Reno would charge in from the front while he, Custer, would ride on for some distance behind a line of bluffs which closely paralleled the east side of the river and which, at this point, still blocked his view. Somewhere down there, maybe in a couple of miles or so, he would find a ford. He would then cross the river and attack the village from the rear or from the side. Major Reno was certainly not informed of this part of the plan; he had reason to assume that Custer's promised "support" would be both closer and more immediate.

Knowing what we know now (but what Major Reno could not have known then), Custer obviously planned that, once across the river and into the village, he would cut across the path of the panicking hordes he expected to be fleeing from Reno's frontal assault. Custer had used the same tactic back in the Civil War. Anyway, a two-pronged assault of this kind has been a standard stratagem since at least the time of the Romans. But perhaps it is not quite so standard when a commanding officer is unknowing of what lies ahead. And Custer was in total ignorance because the intervening terrain blocked his sight line. In short, when he made the decision to divide his command, he could not see the village. So he could have had no idea of its size, despite those earlier warnings back at the Crow's Nest. Nor could he see the ground over which he intended to lead his flanking and "supporting" detachment. Nor did he know if the river would be easily fordable lower down. Nor did he know if the enemy would be alert to the possibility of his launching an attack at that point. But again one has to make the point that throughout his life of soldiering Custer had taken risks, successfully.

But, risks or not, he was unknowing of three other factors for which he must be excused; there was no way he *could* have known of these. First, he did not know that, only eight days earlier, the Sioux and Cheyenne had decisively repulsed the advance of General Crook. The battle had occurred not many miles away, on the upper reaches of the Rosebud. (If Custer had obeyed his order to proceed further up the Rosebud, he would have come upon some evidence of that battle and, who knows, he might have been more careful thereafter.) As far as the Sioux were concerned, they had come away from that full-day encounter as the clear victors. They had every right to that view: having killed some soldiers and wounded a number of others, they had seen Crook and his considerable force of about 900 troopers (plus 300 civilian muleteers and scouts) turn and go back the way they had come. Now, a few days later, the Sioux were, to use the modern term, still "on a high." Their exultation would have been further boosted by the news that one of their most respected spiritual leaders, Sitting Bull, had recently had a particularly strong vision in which he had clearly seen the easy slaughter of more soldiers than he could count. In short, everyone who mattered was in a state of confident euphoria. This is sometimes held as the reason for their casualness in not posting outlying pickets to give warning of any approaching soldiers. But it has to be said that "posting outlying pickets" was just not their style, and never had been. It is more likely that they simply did not expect the Army to mount another thrust quite so soon.

There was another thing Custer did not know. It seems likely that the trail he had been following up the Rosebud had been made by Sioux (some of whom had come away from the Reservation over the preceding weeks) who were intending to join up with their fellow tribesmen who were *already* in the region; the latter had, after all, had their encounter with Crook a whole nine days earlier. In short, the Indian encampment may have been even bigger than even the pessimists (the realists?) had reckoned.

And there was still one other thing Custer did not know: the Sioux were much better armed than he would have calculated. Not only had they accumulated a whole variety of ancient firearms over many years (though he would have known about that), but they had also recently bought a useful consignment of much more modern rifles from traders and gun-runners. These included at least 200 Winchester and Henry (lever action) "repeating" rifles which could be pre-loaded, with up to 16 rounds. While they were not long-range weapons, they were excellent up to 150 yards and adequate for another 100 yards beyond that; they could be fired from horseback at the rate of a round every 2–3 seconds. The 7th Cavalry had no Winchesters or Henrys; they had single-shot, breech-loading 1873 Springfield (45/70) carbines with a maximum rate, in the hands of an expert (of which the 7th was short) of possibly eight rounds a minute. But even an expert would have problems if, in reloading, he was also trying to control a nervous horse. For this reason cavalrymen often chose to dismount when hard-pressed by an enemy. Anyway, it seems that upwards of 200 Sioux were better armed than any of the soldiers. One further thought: in the time it took a dismounted soldier to load his next shot (say, seven seconds), a mounted Indian could be on top of him from 80 yards away. Then, unless the soldier could quickly bring his revolver to bear, or was closely supported by his immediate colleagues, a deftly swung club might be all that was needed.

Anyway, as events developed over the next half hour, one wonders who were the more surprised: the Indians when they first learned that soldiers were much closer than they had anticipated, or Custer when he began to realize that this might be a far bigger village than he had expected. In fact, this was probably the largest Hostile village ever assembled on the northern plains. Weeks later, after the Sioux had long disappeared, a military party counted the number of tepee circles (i.e. where the grass had been flattened under each tepee). There were more than 1,500 of them. Further, there were several hundred "wickiups"—rough shelters put up by single men, or men who had left their families back on the Reservation. It was usually reckoned that there would be 5–6 Indians (including women and children) to a tepee and that at least one of them, more often two, would be a warrior. So, including the wickiups, simple arithmetic shows that, opposing the 7th Cavalry, there would have been at least 2,000 warriors. Some say that there were half as many again. But it must be stressed that even today, more than 130 years later, this matter of numbers is still debated—it still fascinates. For example, Edgar I. Stewart, a much-respected author on the Custer story, devotes a footnote which runs to three pages of small print (over 2,000 words) to the "numbers" debate. He quotes more than 20 sources; a few even agree with each other. Not surprisingly, some historians accuse the military of subsequently exaggerating enemy numbers, in order to mitigate the disaster. Perhaps. But if one averages out the more reasonable estimates, one arrives at a figure of between 1,500 and 2,500 warriors. Whatever … it was enough.

Anyway, back to the narrative. Maybe, as Custer had always hoped, the Indians were taken almost unaware. But, if so, they did not then follow the second part of his script: they did not turn away in an attempt to escape. On the contrary, no doubt bolstered by their recent success against Crook, and confident in their numbers, hundreds of them swarmed out to block Reno. So Reno's advance, let alone the intended charge, was brought up short. Reno had just 112 men. With the warriors now aggressively riding to and fro across his front, and kicking up an obscuring dust cloud, the major shouted for his men to dismount and form a skirmish line, with several yards between each man.

Reno's under-strength command now came up against some very serious difficulties. These problems were not new; they had occurred before when, for example, Indians swept in from an ambush. Cavalrymen could suddenly find themselves (as Reno's men did now) deployed as infantry. In other words, while their horses gave them mobility across country, much of the actual fighting (especially in any tight, defensive situation) throughout the Indian wars had to be done dismounted. This was largely due to a limitation in the cavalry's principal weapon, that single-shot Springfield carbine. It was a difficult weapon to use on horseback because, after each shot, the spent cartridge case had to be ejected and a new round pushed into the chamber, then the "trapdoor" breech had to be closed and the weapon cocked. Certainly, at anything above a gentle walk, the task of controlling one's horse (with shooting and shouting all around) while, at the same time, following the sequence involved in reloading a Springfield (the task needed both hands) was difficult. Further, the firing of a carbine from horseback with reasonable accuracy at any but the closest range was thoroughly chancy. As a partial solution, each of Custer's cavalrymen carried a Colt revolver; some carried two. (They had left all their sabers back in the *Far West*.) Each Colt could be loaded with six rounds, but their range was limited to what one might call close-quarter fighting. Even then, once he had fired his six rounds (or twelve), the cavalryman would have to dismount to reload.

There were two further problems, and Reno's men would have been nervously aware of both. Dismounted as infantry, if a man were fully trained (and in the 7th Cavalry, that was a big if), he could load and fire his Springfield seven or even eight times a minute with a degree of proficiency and accuracy, provided someone held his horse while he and his fellow cavalrymen were banging away. The standard practice was that every fourth cavalryman became a horse-holder for three of his colleagues. Not only did this reduce a unit's firepower by a quarter, but, in all the shooting and shouting, any horse would be difficult to control; holding four of them (even at some distance back from the firing line) was very difficult. Indeed, it had become a standard Indian tactic to try to frighten those horses, to "spook" them, to drive them off. This did nothing for the confidence of the three riflemen; each was likely to have at least one eye nervously turned to check that his horse was still there, in case an order was given to move. To be left behind without one's horse was to face almost certain death.

The other problem was inherent in the lack of training. Such was the parsimony of the War Department, or more accurately the US Treasury, that funds only allowed for each soldier to fire at most a couple of dozen rounds a year in target practice. Indeed, it seems that some of the newer recruits of the 7th Cavalry had only fired ten rounds since joining. The lack of firearms training had a significant side effect. It seems that no one of sufficient seniority had noticed that in battle (as compared with the slow and measured firing on a practice range) a prone or kneeling trooper would sometimes remove several rounds at a time from his belt-bandoleer and lay them on the ground immediately in front of him; that way, reloading was quicker than reaching (or fumbling?) into his cartridge belt each time. But the rounds (specifically, the copper cartridge casings), for a reason no one had bothered to examine, could become slightly sticky. So, laid on the ground, they might pick up a minute piece of dirt. Further, copper expands quickly with heat. So if the weapon had been firing at the rate of six or seven rounds per minute (likely in battle but very unlikely on the practice range), the chamber would get hot, and thus the copper casing would expand. Extracting the empty casing could be difficult; if there were flecks of dirt involved, it could be even more difficult. In short, in the literal heat of battle, the weapon might jam until a knife was used to lever out the offending casing.

We know from subsequent reports that some troopers had earlier complained about this problem. Some months later, it was realized that the "stickiness" was caused by a chemical reaction between the copper of the casing and the leather of the belt-bandoleers; it produced a thin deposit of tacky verdigris. The solution later adopted was, first, to make the bandoleers out of canvas rather than leather and, second, to modify the metal composition of the cartridge casings. Interestingly, to this day, there is some debate about this jamming problem. How frequent was it, and what significance might it have had for the battle's outcome? The answer must surely be that even if every rifle had been entirely reliable, the final result of the battle (given all the other "mistakes") would still have been much the same. Nevertheless, the thought that his weapon *might* let him down must have had a serious effect on a man's morale and confidence, and therefore on his fighting ability.

Anyway, in one way and another, Reno's companies were about to pay for these various problems and shortcomings. Dismounted, his men were strung out in an irregular line over several hundred yards, facing toward the village and maybe half a mile out from it. In that intervening space the Sioux were riding backwards and forwards, taunting, shouting, screaming, shooting. Every now and then, a cavalryman's shot would find a fleeting target through the dust, and sometimes a cavalryman would fall, from arrow or bullet. Reno must have wondered about Custer's promised support. Soon it became obvious that some Sioux were closing round the open, western end of the skirmish line. Indeed, a few of them were already firing from the rear.

Reno yelled an order to remount and pull back a mile or so to a large area of cottonwoods nearer the river: supposedly better shelter, better cover. It was neither. Again, after perhaps 20 minutes, concerned that ammunition might be running low and with the enemy creeping ever closer (the cover of trees and brush was at least as useful to the attackers as it was to the troopers), Reno shouted again. Some never heard him. For those who did, the retreat was a gallop across some open ground and then a scramble through the river and a climb up a very steep slope of about 300 feet. Some were caught and clubbed, or shot in the water; some, riding two to a horse, made it. From the top of that bluff, exhausted, they could overlook the enemy; but they were missing nearly 50 men. Strangely, the Sioux did not chase them up that slope. Quite suddenly, they had disappeared. Maybe something else had attracted their attention ...

And Custer? As far as anyone now on Reno's Hill (as the hill just behind the crest of that bluff has been known ever since) could guess, Custer and his five companies had ridden off to the north, on a line roughly parallel to (but hidden from) the river. Presently, firing could be heard in that direction. Presently, too, Major Benteen and his men arrived at Reno's Hill. He had given up on what he saw as a pointless excursion. Now, at least, there was some safety in numbers. Then the pack train straggled in; now there was more ammunition. In some confusion, Reno and Benteen organized a defense. Reno was the senior of the two; but some subsequent accounts say he was indecisive. Surprisingly, this was Reno's first serious encounter with Indians; and he was still spattered with the blood and brains of a man who, standing just beside him, had been shot in the head when they were down by the river. Some historians think that this last occurrence had left him in shock, traumatized. But there is also strong evidence (from at least a dozen witnesses after the battle) that he had been trying to steady his nerves with whiskey.

There was talk of riding towards that distant firing. Maybe Custer was, even now, whipping the Indians. Maybe he needed help. Maybe they should go and find out. Reno was not enthusiastic. But, regardless of Reno's indecision, a Captain Weir and about 40 troopers set off. They rode north for well over a mile to a high point (now called Weir's Point) near the northern end of those bluffs. From there, looking across more than two miles further to the north, over flatter country, they could make out hundreds of mounted Sioux milling around in a low cloud of smoke and dust. The firing had almost stopped. Then they realized that they had been seen and that some of those warriors were now racing toward them. They turned, to find that the rest of the command was now coming up behind them. They all turned. Perhaps 15 minutes later they were back on Reno's Hill, frantically trying to scrape out some defenses. They had very few digging tools, just five small spades and some axes that had come up with the mules. The men used cups, mess tins, knives, and their bare hands to make shallow trenches. They used saddles and boxes and even dead and dying horses to form thin barricades. Fortunately in the middle of the hilltop was a low depression, a degree of shelter for the wounded.

The Sioux were quick to surround the hill—at a distance. So now, from their own hills 300–400 yards away, their best shots aimed to take out any soldier who showed himself. The Sioux were in no hurry; they knew something the soldiers

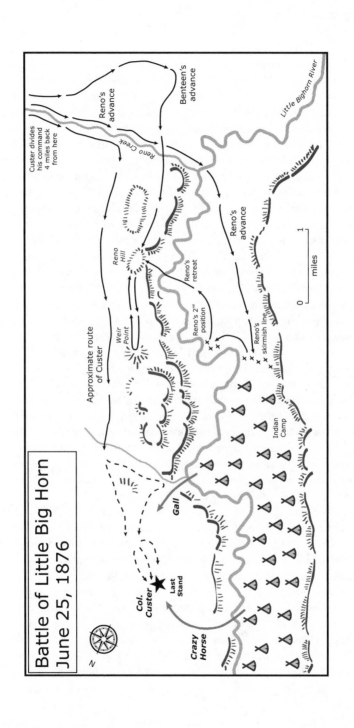

Battle of Little Big Horn
June 25, 1876

Custer divides his command 4 miles back from here

Reno's advance

Benteen's advance

Reno Creek

Reno's advance

Reno Hill

Reno's retreat

Reno's 2nd position

Reno's skirmish line

Little Bighorn River

0 1
miles

Approximate route of Custer

Weir Point

Indian Camp

Gall

Col. Custer

Last Stand

Crazy Horse

N

did not: Custer and his command were finished. But to those near-desperate men hunkered down on their hill, there must have still been the faint hope that Custer would be back, once he had dealt with the enemy. Or did some of them suppose that once their ammunition was exhausted, they too—like Major Elliot and his detachment back at the Washita—would be left to their fate?

So what *had* happened to Custer and his five companies? Unlike those men waiting up on their hill, we now know some of the answers. True, there were no survivors, and as a consequence there are many details that are still debated, but quite enough can be deduced to provide a broad sequence of events. Earlier, Custer and his command would have had an unopposed ride along a line back from (but parallel to) those bluffs which, in turn, paralleled the river. Somewhere along that line (his exact path is debated) he rode across to the crest of a bluff from where he could see out over to the village. Presumably, surprised (shocked?) by the size of the village he now saw before him, he sent a Sergeant Kanipe galloping back to fetch the mule train which was carrying the regiment's reserve ammunition. A few minutes later, he ordered his Italian orderly-bugler to ride back to Benteen with a message that he, Benteen, should join up with the mule train and escort it forward as quickly as possible. Because the orderly, Giovanni Martini, was a recent immigrant (four years earlier he had been serving with Garibaldi) who spoke imperfect English, Custer's adjutant thought it prudent that Martini should carry the message in writing: "Benteen. Come on. Big village. Be quick. Bring Packs. PS Bring pacs [sic]." Martini rode off. He was the last man to see Custer and all his immediate command alive. (Today, that famous and iconic scrap of paper is preserved at West Point.) There is a small but interesting question inherent in this "bring packs" scenario. How and where was the Italian orderly meant to find Benteen—last ordered to proceed away to the southwest, with no indication of when or where he was to turn round to return? None of the standard accounts are much help with an answer to this intriguing question.

Anyway, having dispatched his message, Custer rode on. He would have been looking to his left for a way down to the river and a ford, so that he could cross the river and get into the village. Presently he found what he was looking for: Medicine Tail Coulee. Only 200–300 yards long, it is more of an extended gully than a valley, and leads directly to the Little Bighorn. How far he or his leading company got down this coulee—maybe even to the river itself—is one of those details still debated. It does not much matter. The fact is that, either at the ford or some way short of it, his leading companies must have run into such strong opposition that they were forced to turn back.

Now, surely, when Custer first saw the numbers and the vehemence of the enemy as they came streaming across the river, and heard the exultation of their war cries, the realization of what was happening must have been heart-stopping. Suddenly, he would have known that he had placed himself and his men in an almost suicidal predicament. Advance was impossible. Retreat was the only option. But where to?

If, today, one stands somewhere near where Custer may have been when he first recognized what was unfolding, one looks north over a rolling and broken terrain of sagebrush and coarse grass. The land rises slowly away from the river toward a rather unimpressive ridge rather less than a mile to the northeast. We do not know how orders were given to ride for that ridge. Maybe there was too much noise for orders. But from where the bodies were later found (marked by small marble slabs today), it seems that there must have been a running fight all the way. Today, military men would say that there was an ever-increasing degree of "tactical disintegration." Those marble markers come closer to each other as they get nearer to the ridge. Elsewhere, sometimes hundreds of yards from the main grouping, there are other markers. Some are in small clusters; some are on their own. It seems that many of the troopers got separated and had to fight their own lonely battles. Some were shot, some were run down and clubbed to death. We don't know how long the killing lasted. One would guess that it was not long, maybe less than 30 minutes. We know from Sioux accounts that, at times, the firing was almost continuous or, as one of them said later, it was like the sound of the tearing of a blanket. We know that most of the warriors, having first repulsed Reno, then dashed back through the village to meet the new threat. Together with others who joined them, they surged pell-mell across the river and up across that sagebrush. We know that Crazy Horse and his people crossed the river lower down and then came galloping round to take the last pocket of soldiers from behind. That final pocket has long been called the Last Stand. That is where they found Custer. Some think that he may have shot himself; it seems unlikely that he found it necessary, such would have been the weight of incoming fire. One can reasonably assume that he was one of the last of his 215 men to go. Like most of them, he was stripped naked. Unlike most of them, including his two brothers, his nephew and his brother-in-law, he was not scalped.

On their hill, Reno and Benteen would have known nothing certain of what had already happened nearly four miles to the north. They had problems of their own. The incoming fire was frequent and, given the range, surprisingly accurate. Several troopers were killed, others wounded. It was fortunate that the Sioux did not know just how weak were the hilltop defenses. But gradually, with the fading light, the firing faded too. Soon it was dark. They could hear drumming and shouting from the village; they could hear the off-key squirling of a bugle. During the night some missing troopers came in; cut off in the retreat, they had been hiding in those cottonwoods down along the river.

Sioux drawings of the battle of Little Big Horn (Colorado State Historical Society)

The Sioux and Cheyenne snipers were back at first light. But the scrapes and shallow trenches that the troopers had made the previous evening, and further strengthened during the night, were enough—just. The Indian sharpshooters seemed to concentrate on the horses. All morning and into the afternoon, the siege went on. How would it all end? What had happened to Custer? For the troopers, the problem of thirst was becoming almost as important as dodging the bullets. Some of the wounded were already delirious. In desperation, a small party risked their lives in creeping down to the river to fill as many canteens as they could carry. But among so many, that water could only last so long. The fact that the besieging Indians chose not to guard against that water "break-out" confirms again their lack of strategic forethought. (Subsequently, the water carriers were each awarded a Medal of Honor.)

Presently the soldiers realized that the shooting had slowed, and then stopped. Perhaps the Indians were gone. Slowly and very cautiously, suspecting a trap, a few crept forward to a point from where they could overlook the plain and the village. In the evening light they could see that the Indians, in their thousands, were packing up and moving out. Long lines of them were trailing away to the southwest, toward the Bighorn Mountains. The reason for the Indian departure became partially apparent early the next day (June 27). They had seen a cloud of dust coming slowly towards them from the north, and they were low on ammunition.

Within a few hours, men from Gibbon's command climbed the bluffs; they told that they had found Custer and his men. By the time they finished counting, they concluded that Custer must have lost 215 officers and men; several bodies were never found. Reno had lost 53 killed and 52 wounded; 32 of them were killed down on the valley floor and in crossing the river. Some of the wounded would die within a few days. The Indian losses have never been assessed; guesses hover between 50 and 150.

So why, one might ask, with the exultant wind of a great victory behind them (to say nothing of their earlier defeat of General Crook) did the Sioux and their Cheyenne allies not stand and fight Gibbon and his advancing infantrymen? They themselves may have been imprecise about the reasons for their withdrawal; after all, although they had leaders—Crazy Horse, Gall, and Sitting Bull come to mind—the making of what today are called "command decisions" was not an Indian way of doing things. If they had stayed, who knows what might have happened? Gibbon's regiment of infantrymen was smaller than Custer's. Perhaps the Indian withdrawal was prompted by a certain weariness, and a feeling that they had done enough for the time being. Also they had lost some brave warriors. Further, with so much ammunition now expended (including that at the earlier fight with Crook), they needed time to rebuild their reserves; this was probably the key reason. And they may have sensed that, before many moons, a far bigger force would come looking for them; retribution was almost inevitable. Anyway, it was time to restock their food supplies and to move their pony herds on from what would have become a very worn-out pasture. Whatever the reason— probably a combination of all those possibilities—the fact is that, within a very few days, the Indians had scattered themselves over hundreds of square miles. They would never again come together in such numbers.

Over the next three days, Reno's wounded were carefully carried to the *Far West*; she had come upriver as far as her shallow draft allowed. Then, at a speed and with a skill never repeated, Captain Marsh took her the 710 miles down the Yellowstone and the Missouri to Bismarck and Fort Lincoln in just 54 hours (13 mph). She flew the national flag at half-mast. And she carried a long dispatch from General Terry, for telegraphing to the Army's command in St. Paul. Libbie Custer and her sister-in-law, Margaret Custer Calhoun, were given the news. Margaret had lost her husband, three brothers, and a nephew. Then the two women had to find and comfort 37 other wives who were also widows.

So that narration, with certain compressions and omissions (but I hope not too many inaccuracies), is my version of what is still the most debated battle in the nation's history. Over the years, many historians, while readily acknowledging the fascination of what happened, have been dismissive of its significance. It did not, they say, change anything that was not going to change anyway. They are probably right. The defeat made a humiliated army determined to finish off the Hostiles once and for all. In pursuing that focused end, nothing and nobody would be spared. Thus astonishingly, within less than 12 months, the Sioux and the Cheyenne, as free-roaming and independent peoples, were finished for all time. In short, the battle accelerated by a few years what many, even at the time, saw as inevitable—and had been from the moment the first white settlers came ashore on the continent.

So while, to the world, what happened is often known as Custer's Last Stand, it might be better recognized as the Last Stand of the Sioux. Therein, surely, lies its real significance. Yet, strangely, that does not fully explain why the battle is so famous, why it has held the imagination for so long. For part of the answer one must look to the terrible drama of that afternoon: a drama that Hollywood has often embellished beyond recognition. Another part of the answer lies more seriously in the questions that surround Custer's immediate conduct of the affair: questions to which, by definition, there are no finite and final answers, and which therefore, even today, more than 130 years later, *still* provoke almost endless debates, questions and intriguing "what ifs?."

What if Custer had not been in such a hurry? What if, as ordered, he had gone another day up the Rosebud and then turned to arrive at the southern end of the village in concert with Gibbon coming from the north? Answer: it would probably have made no difference because, in fact, Gibbon did not arrive at the site of the village until a day later than planned. What if Reno had pressed home his charge? The likelihood is that he and his three companies would have been swallowed up in that vast village and all would have been killed. One of Reno's men later said that had Reno not been a coward, "We all would be dead." Was Reno a coward? Well, he was no hero, but, given that he found himself quite unsupported and in real danger of being outflanked, did he have any choice but to retreat? Anyway, rather more than half his command lived to tell the tale—which is more than Custer, for all his guts, managed for *his* command.

Why did Custer not support Reno as he had promised? Because he seems never to have had immediate or *close* support in mind. Rather, he intended to give more or less simultaneous support by attacking from the right flank. Was this made clear to Reno? No, but to be fair to Custer, such a two-pronged attack is a fundamental tactic, still taught to cadets at West Point and Sandhurst. But it is also taught that a proper degree of coordination between the two prongs is essential. Custer entirely ignored even the most elementary pre-planning. What part did Custer's wish to rescue his reputation (after what he saw as the injustice heaped on him following his "Belknap" evidence) play in his thinking and in his impatience? Custer himself might not have been able to define an answer to that question. But that it played some part seems almost certain.

What would seem to have been Custer's biggest single mistake? Answer: apart from his careless trusting to Custer's Luck, it was surely his overconfident decision to divide his command into three units (four if one includes the pack-train). He thereby ensured that no single element was capable of coping with the enemy's superior numbers, on which he had disregarded his scouts' estimations. What if he had not divided his command? Who knows? It seems just possible that the 7th Cavalry, all eleven companies (not counting the one escorting the pack mules) charging as a single unit, might, despite heavy casualties, have succeeded where Reno's much smaller charge failed. Why did Custer not carry out a reconnaissance? Answer: apart from the fact that he had never been a strong believer in looking too hard before he leaped, he judged that, with his approach discovered, he had to attack before the Sioux and Cheyenne had time to flee. Given that this was by far the most important determinant of his tactics, he has been much criticized for his assumption that the Indians *would* flee, and thus escape. But, if one is fair, that criticism must be measured against the general assumption among *all* senior Indian-fighting officers of those times that, faced with an attack by a sizeable force, flight was almost invariably what could be expected of the Indians. The generals and, more importantly in this particular context, Custer had every right to base their (and his) tactics on that assumption. So perhaps his misjudgment, though serious, was less of a key factor behind the disaster than the fact that, quite unprecedentedly and in overwhelming numbers ("too many Indians"), the Sioux and Cheyenne did the very opposite of what almost everybody (except a few of his scouts) had a right to expect. Custer's Bad Luck? Or is that too charitable?

There are so many more things one could say. One could detail the obvious and touching devotion of Libbie for her husband, and his for her. They wrote many-paged letters to each other almost every day. She wrote three books about their life together, and she vehemently defended his reputation until the day she died, aged 90, in 1933. Consequently a number of informed critics of her husband hung back in deference to her, but died before she did. She was buried next to him at West Point. One could sift through the intricacies of the Court of Inquiry that was held three years later at the request of Major Reno in response to the whispers (some of them quite loud) about cowardice; he was cleared, but he died a broken man. One could turn to the confidential reports of Generals Terry, Sheridan, and Sherman and their estimations (in places rather self-serving) of what had gone wrong. One could quote from the many accounts given in later years by some of the warriors who were there and saw it all happen (well, most of it); the last four (all in their late 90s) turned up as honored guests to reminisce on the battlefield 75 years later, in 1951. One could recite from the conflicting editorials, reports and reflections in the journals and newspapers of the day; many of them blamed government policies rather than Custer. One could examine the many-stranded nature of the debates that even today, more than 130 years later, still exercise the experts; they will discuss every aspect of the affair, from the flaws in the overall strategy to the possible reasons why Custer was not scalped. One could look at reappraisals about the final 60 minutes of Custer and his immediate command, as prompted by archaeological evidence: some of it uncovered by metal detectors after recent grass fires. Finally, one might attempt to summarize the conclusions of the 50 most outstanding (and contrasting) books on this almost endless subject, which would require some very subjective judgments—yet that is more or less what I have just done.

∽

If you drive to the battlefield, just before turning off the main road you will find the Crow Trading Post (where they do excellent burgers); and there is the Little Bighorn Casino and Motel. Nearby, Colonel Sanders has established himself (one might guess that he was probably a mere corporal in 1876); in his wake is a Kentucky Fried Chicken house, the Song Bird Child Care Center and a Jim Cuts-the-Hair barbershop. There is also an office of the Bureau of Indian Affairs and, across the road, a neat white church whose pastors are Anita and Duane Bull Chief. Overlooking the whole scatter is a magnificent hospital of the Indian Health Service. This is land belonging to the Crow tribe, and one is told that they zealously guard against any suggestion that their old enemy, the Sioux, have anything but visitors' rights.

It used to be called the Custer Battlefield. Then, a few years back, in deference to the large number of Native Americans who were also involved (and they most certainly were) the name was changed to the Little Bighorn Battlefield. The land is owned by the nation; it is administered by the National Parks Service, and the Stars and Stripes fly over it. In the summer, the parking lot alongside the visitors' center is usually full. The spring or the fall are the times to go: the staff have more time to answer your inquiries, and to any half-sensible question, their patience is remarkable. Indeed, you get the feeling that they are at least as interested in your questions as you are in their answers. Or are they just being polite? Anyway, I have phoned them from London with some question, and found myself still listening 20 minutes later, despite calling long-distance.

☙

One can spend all day (and then some) wandering the nearly four miles between the site of the Last Stand and Reno's Hill. Unlike many battlefields, this one looks very much as it must have done on that day in 1876—except for those white markers. The geography of the place has not changed. So if you have done a little homework and are not too worried about the minutiae of exactly who was where when they fell, you can work out, more or less, how it all happened, or at least how most of it happened. Not that this is quite the same as saying you can work out why it all happened ...

Each time I go, I notice something different. For example, the authorities have recently replaced the rather inadequate wooden markers that indicated where various Indian warriors were found. Normally, the Indians carried away all their dead, but for a few—perhaps, in all the confusion, they were missed—their last resting place was where they fell. Anyway, markers of red granite (exactly comparable to the soldiers' white marble) now poke through the sagebrush; remembered are warriors like Noisy Walking or Lame White Man.

One of those red stones states that "Long Road, a Sans Arc warrior, died here while defending his homeland and the Sioux way of life." Well, yes and no. He was certainly defending his way of life, but the claim that he was defending his homeland is, except in the broadest sense, stretching things. If this particular homeland belonged to anybody, it belonged to the Crow. The bullying Sioux had pushed the Crow off through the first half of the nineteenth century. So there is both justice and irony in the fact that the site of the most famous Sioux and Cheyenne victory is now just an enclave surrounded on all sides by land belonging to their old enemies, the Crow.

૭๑

"White man, Custer died for your sins."

A bumper sticker sometimes seen on Sioux pickup trucks. The slogan is also the title of an incisive book by the Sioux author, Vine Deloria.

11

TOWARDS
WOUNDED KNEE

"One of the American Indian tendencies that led to our distress was their abiding passion for survival. The Indian developed an immunity to extinction."
A comment by John Steinbeck

"There was no hope on earth, and God seemed to have forgotten us."
Attributed to Chief Red Cloud sometime in the 1880s

ϛ

If one assumes that the Indian warriors saw Little Bighorn as a great victory, one can wonder if some of them, even as they packed up and rode away, might also have sensed that it had been just too great. Did they, even dimly, foresee that there was now no way that the Army, humiliated far beyond mere embarrassment, would or could accept that it had any choice but to finish them, the Hostiles, once and for all? One hardly needs hindsight to see that that battle was crucially definitive: it signaled the accelerated, inevitable, and final end of the Sioux and Cheyenne as sovereign peoples.

Nevertheless, if one were concerned with the minutiae of the next few months, one could catalog for several pages the many miles of marching and ineffective counter-marching that characterized most of the military endeavors through the rest of that summer. For the soldiers, the problem was that the Sioux and Cheyenne, although still moving in bands of some size, were proving difficult to find. Perhaps a single example of military frustration will make the point: General Crook, with more than 2,000 soldiers, advanced from the south while General Terry, with 1,600 (neither of them would seem to have been taking any chances), came down from the north in an optimistic but ill-coordinated attempt to sweep and then trap the Hostiles between them. But the Sioux and Cheyenne had "scatterated," as guerrillas or partisans are wont to do when chased by more heavily armed forces. It is reported that when, in mid-August, the plodding columns of those two generals eventually met face to dusty face, neither had sighted a single Indian. Maybe.

Anyway, back east, Congress was in something of a panic and quickly funded what today would be called a Surge. It voted funds for 2,500 more soldiers. After minimal training they were sped west by rail, river steamers, wagons, and foot. Their arrival coincided with the cooling weather of fall.

With the approaching hardships of winter, several hundred Sioux were persuaded via a combination of promises and threats to come in to the alleged comforts of various agencies. But, once arrived, they found themselves quickly hemmed in by soldiery with the demand that they surrender their guns and ponies. One doubts that this was an effective way to entice other groups, still undecided, to follow. Indeed, a number of potential Friendlies took the hint and promptly turned around—to rejoin the Hostiles.

Out in the back-country, the known militants, particularly Crazy Horse, Sitting Bull, and Dull Knife (a Cheyenne), were judged by the generals to be the leaders who would have to be brought to heel if the Army's honor was ever to be restored. The coming winter would be the time … With temperatures headed to somewhere far below mere freezing, with the war ponies growing thinner, and travel (let alone hunting) becoming increasingly difficult, the quicksilver wanderings of those scattered bands would slow down until, coalescing into semi-static camps, they would become vulnerable. Against the rigors of the coming campaign, the troops were issued with buffalo-skin coats, fur caps, gauntlets and heavy-duty leggings. They would need them.

The Army's first success came with the first snows of late October when Colonel Miles, a vain but competent officer, met with Sitting Bull. A truce had been arranged as a result of a message from the Indian saying that he wanted to parlay. He came quickly to his unrealistic point: he wanted the whites to get out of his country—forever. Colonel Miles countered by demanding that Sitting Bull and his followers, numbering over 2,000 (say 600 warriors), should surrender and then make their way to the Reservation. Indeed, Miles is alleged to have told Sitting Bull that he had 15 minutes to think things over. "Surrender," he said, "or fight." Shouting that he would never become a Reservation man, Sitting Bull swung onto his horse and galloped away to rejoin his warriors. The truce was over before it had really begun.

There followed a chase which lasted two days over a distance of about 40 miles. The Sioux put in several counterattacks, but Colonel Miles, aided by his skillful deployment of some light artillery, always came out on top. It was not a resounding victory, but it was enough. Several hundred Sioux surrendered, to be directed south to the Reservation. The rest had already scattered. Eventually, led by Sitting Bull, many of them would escape to Canada and the protection of Queen Victoria, the Great White Grandmother.

Away to the south and a few weeks later, in a snowy late November, the Army had a more definite success, against Dull Knife. It was the result of incoming intelligence followed by a confirming reconnaissance; the Army was learning. A sizeable winter camp of the Cheyenne had been located, tucked away in a canyon-like valley of the southern Bighorn Mountains. (Less than 25 years later, these parts would become known as the Hole-in-the-Wall country: a sometime refuge of Butch Cassidy and the Wild Bunch.) The troops, more than 1,000 of them (including 200 turncoat Sioux "scouts" temporarily recruited at 40 cents a day from among the reservation Friendlies), moved up quietly and then attacked at dawn. Most of the Cheyenne were asleep. Grabbing their rifles, they scrambled half-naked from the tepees. Some were shot or cut down, but enough managed to scramble up the valley walls from where they fired on the troopers below. As usual, the concern of the warriors was to cover the escape of their women and children. They soon saw that there was no way they could retake their village, which was then torched by the soldiers—after they had recovered a number of articles taken from the Little Bighorn: uniforms, revolvers, boots, bridles, saddles, even a 7th Cavalry guidon. Meanwhile the already freezing temperature was dropping; a blizzard was on its way. Over the next few days those native families, in flight and without shelter or proper clothing, are said to have lost a dozen or so young children and babies to the extreme cold. Some of the elderly and the wounded were lost as well. For the next ten days, Dull Knife led his people—what was left of them—on a miserable trek north through the mountains until eventually, after 140 miles, they managed to find Crazy Horse.

There were other skirmishes and engagements that winter and into the early spring (1876–1877). For the Hostiles, ammunition was low, food was short, hope was thin, and their war seemed unwinnable. The news that even Sitting Bull, an inspirational leader right across the Sioux nation, had sought refuge in the land of the Great White Grandmother was deeply demoralizing. So it was that a growing number of Sioux and Cheyenne began to argue among themselves: might it not be better to parlay with the military and, if terms could be arranged, join their brothers who were already on the Reservation? But there was a twofold problem. First, among the hardliners like Crazy Horse, the peace-seekers were abused as traitors. A second problem lay in the Army's insistence that any surrender would have to be unconditional; movement would be circumscribed and all pony herds and weapons would have to be handed over.

It was not until those unimaginative demands were eased that some of the more recalcitrant Sioux began to come in. As a further incentive, General Crook now sent a message that, if they behaved after their surrender, he would see to it that a whole new Reservation would be established in their favorite buffalo hunting ground along the Powder River. It was this particular assurance, plus the illness of his wife (it seems she had TB), that seems to have persuaded even Crazy Horse to move toward the Reservation. But, defiant to the last, when in early May he rode in at the head of several hundred mounted warriors, it was as if he were leading a victory parade. All were resplendent in war paint and feathers; all were chanting battle cries and shaking their weapons aloft: guns, bows, and war clubs. This was no meek capitulation. The officer who formally received Crazy Horse that day later wrote that he found him "remarkably brave, generous, and reticent … a pillar of strength for good or evil." In sour contrast, an agent of the Indian Bureau thought him "an incorrigible wild man … silent, sullen, lordly, and dictatorial." At different times, it seems that he could be both.

It is near unbelievable that the seven tribes of the Sioux nation could so quickly have fallen so far. And in just four more months, Crazy Horse himself would be dead. The reasons for his death are still discussed, but not least among them must be the fact that Crook proved unable to honor his promise of that new, buffalo-rich Reservation out on the Powder. He had certainly lobbied the Army's high command and the politicians in Washington. But he was up against both apathy and antipathy: there was ill will towards a Sioux chief who was widely seen as the leading tactician behind the disaster of just a year earlier. Additionally, even among the Sioux—always a fractious people—there were tensions and rivalries. Some seem to have felt that, at their expense, Crazy Horse was receiving too much deference from the military. Certainly, his presence on the Reservation stirred deep jealousies. Indeed, there were those who would have welcomed his comeuppance; sadly, they included his old comrade Red Cloud, who, not long back from a trip to New York and Washington (and reluctantly impressed), had now become a full-time collaborator with the white authorities. Anyway, when the news came through that Crook was unable to deliver on his earlier assurances about a new Reservation, Crazy Horse became resentful and bad-tempered. Soon there came a rumor that he was planning to make a last run for freedom and, no doubt, more mischief. So Crook ordered his arrest— by other Sioux. Initially, thinking he was being invited to negotiate, he came in without much fuss. But when he realized that he was about to be locked in a guardroom cell, he reacted violently. In the ensuing scuffle, he was stabbed or bayoneted by a soldier. Within a few hours, this greatest of all the Sioux was dead. He had never lost a battle; he had never signed a treaty. He was just 37.

It was surely more than mere coincidence that, with the passing of Crazy Horse, the last remaining spirit finally ebbed from the Sioux. In effect, they had to recognize that they were now a captive and wholly dependent people. The Army had won.

&

What about Sitting Bull? From the beginning, the Great White Grandmother's local representatives, her Northwest Mounted Police, had treated the refugee chief and his followers with a cold correctness. After all, diplomacy demanded that the sensitivities of the United States, where Sitting Bull was viewed as an unsurrendered Hostile and a likely source of future trouble, had to be recognized. So the Canadian authorities were not sympathetic when the old chief began demanding that he and his people be given their own permanent Reservation. Nor, when the hunting was poor, were they more than minimally responsive to his call for supplementary rations. As refugees, he and his followers were tolerated as long as they were not too demanding. Meanwhile, the Americans were becoming increasingly worried that, sitting just out of reach, there was an enemy who, as they saw it, might come south again at any time to spark all kinds of trouble among the now "pacified" tribes. So they sent officers north to persuade Sitting Bull to return to his homeland, where they could keep a closer eye on him. He refused to meet the Americans, until reminded by the Mounties that he was a guest who did not have much choice. So although Sitting Bull had to obey, he refused to shake hands with the visitors. He accused them of coming north only to tell lies of which, over recent years, he had heard too many already. The Americans went home.

In fact, Sitting Bull and his immediate band of followers stayed in Canada for another four years. Perhaps it was a diminishing supply of buffalo meat, the Sioux staple, that finally tipped the balance; the local herds were being hunted by both Sioux refugees and the nearby Canadian tribes. The latter were becoming resentful at having to compete for their food with the late arrivals. In the end, Sitting Bull realized that a long-term future in Canada, let alone a permanent one, was unlikely. So, in July 1881, he decided to take his chances; he would go home.

Having crossed the border, he was escorted to Fort Buford, along with 45 men, 67 women, and 73 children. But still unwilling to take part in the ritual of a formal surrender, he gave his rifle to his eight-year-old son, who took it to the fort commander. A few days later they were all put aboard a steamer heading down the Missouri for a larger fort. Most of the party were then released onto the nearby Reservation. But the authorities were not ready to let the last and greatest of the one-time Hostiles out of their sight; Sitting Bull was held at the fort for two more years.

In time, the Great Sioux Reservation (very approximately much of today's South Dakota) would be reduced, squeezed, and subdivided into five much smaller reservations. Across them, all Sioux hostility was finished. At the top of the Army, General Sherman could write with confidence on his retirement: "I now regard the Indians as substantially removed from the problems of the Army."

The psychological weight of their defeat must have been very heavy. They knew that they would never again hunt buffalo; there were hardly any buffalo left to hunt. Never again would they ride out to intimidate their enemies; never again would they exult in their freedom. All excitement was gone. Under white supervision a few tried farming, but it didn't work; the land was too poor. After all, it was mostly land that the whites did not want. So there was nothing to do on the reservations except to turn up every few weeks at the nearest agency for an issue of rations: some beef, a sack or two of flour, a little sugar, a blanket or two, maybe some tobacco. Between times there was nothing to do—except to grumble that the scale of rations was far below what they had been promised in various treaties and agreements. They were being continually shortchanged— partly through corruption, partly through policy: keep them hungry, and thereby docile. So these once proud people were now physically and mentally destitute; their undernourished children and old people were dying daily of malnutrition, measles, diphtheria, whooping cough and flu.

A people in despair will latch onto any hope, however remote. For the Sioux, a people whose lives had always been in thrall to visions, prophesies, magic, and a whole panoply of the supernatural, deliverance—if it lay anywhere—would surely come from the spirit world. But, as the years went by ... nothing. Then, in the late 1880s, they heard rumors of a mystic who lived somewhere far away in the deserts to the west. Apparently, on a day when "the sun had died" (a time of powerful "medicine," but, in reality, a solar eclipse), a Paiute shaman had had a powerful vision. In his trance, Wovoka had been lifted up to paradise. He had been shown many things up there. Now, down on earth again, he prophesied that, by performing a few simple rites, the white man would be swept away forever; dead relatives would come back, the buffalo herds would be reborn, the blind would see again, the old life would return. To find out more, eleven Sioux

Waiting for an issue of rations on Pine Ridge Reservation (Smithsonian Institute)

emissaries made the long train journey west to Nevada. They met Wovoka and were deeply impressed; they saw hope of deliverance. They learned how to do a particular dance which was the central feature of what, within months, became a new religion.

On arriving back at the Sioux Reservations, those eleven apostles spread the word, and the dance. The theory was that, if performed often enough and with sufficient verve, it would bring about a resurrection of the Old Life. Salvation was coming: probably in the spring, with "the greening of the grass." So, through the fall of 1890, the dance became an obsession performed by hundreds, perhaps thousands, of Sioux on all their Reservations. Because it invoked the spirits of dead ancestors, worried white observers called it the Ghost Dance. For many dancers, the seemingly endless repetitiveness of chanting and stamping could, if they did not first fall to exhaustion, induce a wondrous level of hallucinatory visions—a phenomenon that would, after all, be repeated in the white man's marathon dance competitions only 40 years later during the Depression.

At some point an addition was made to Wovoka's gospel: the Ghost shirt. Its "medicine" lay in the mystical patterns painted onto the garment; they made it impenetrable to the white man's bullets. Not surprisingly, this talk of bullets, along with a marked rekindling of Sioux morale, alarmed the whites both within and beyond the Reservations. So word went out that the more truculent among the Sioux leaders were to be brought in to the Agencies, where they could be guarded and watched. The Army was mobilized to do the policing.

Sitting Bull was high on the official "wanted" list. Some years earlier, he had been released to live on the Standing Rock Reservation. Since then he had been recruited to tour, for an enormous $50 a week, in Buffalo Bill's Wild West Circus. He was a target of curiosity wherever he went, a national celebrity. In 1887 he was even asked to travel with the circus to England and to perform at a command performance (in the Earl's Court arena of the day) to celebrate the Golden Jubilee of his one-time guardian, Queen Victoria. If indeed he was asked, he declined: either because he thought that he was too old for such a long trip, or else he just wanted to stay at home. (But one can't help thinking of the photograph that could have been: the old Queen and the old Chief.) Anyway, at home on the reservation (though deliberately living some distance from the relevant agency), he was now suspected of being a focus of potential trouble. Indeed, a nervous agency boss, Major Laughlin (a former army officer), had already had several run-ins with the old rebel. Now, taking no chances, the major gave the order for his arrest. Buffalo Bill, who was one of the very few whites that the old chief trusted, volunteered to journey from Chicago and, in peace, to persuade Sitting Bull to come to the agency. But the offer was turned

One of the few photos of a Ghost Dance, taken at Pine Ridge on December 25, 1890, a few days before the massacre at Wounded Knee (Smithsonian Institute)

down; the major wanted no help from a mere showman. A party of Indian police was sent out instead. As with the arrest of Crazy Horse 13 years earlier, things quickly went awry. A protective crowd had gathered round Sitting Bull and, in the ensuing mêlée, he was shot dead. So were six policemen.

Tension, already high, now became even higher as news of the old chief's death spread. Among the whites, both within and beyond the reservations, there was near panic at the thought that the Indians, in their anger, might well be arming for the warpath. Indeed, the settlers of the newly created states of North and South Dakota wired Washington requesting the urgent dispatch of enough rifles to arm every able-bodied male. One congressman, more perceptive than most, suggested that it might be better to send a full complement of promised rations to the semi-starving Sioux. For their part, the Sioux soon became even more alarmed when they heard that the Army, in strength, had been ordered to intervene. In their fear, many surrendered. Others, perhaps as many as 3,000, headed for the protection of the Badlands: an easily defended tangle of eroded cliffs and gullies well away from the agencies. It became known to the whites as the Stronghold.

Now, there were nervous trigger fingers on all sides. A detachment of the 7th Cavalry was dispatched to bring in another allegedly troublesome chief, Big

Foot. It was rumored that he and his people were heading to join forces with those other malcontents already in the Stronghold. However, when the soldiers caught up with him, an obviously ailing Big Foot (it turned out that he had pneumonia) professed peace, though less than boundless goodwill, towards the soldiers. In the face of an obviously superior force, he agreed that he and his followers (about 120 men, and 230 women and children) should be escorted to the agency settlement of Pine Ridge, a trek of about a day to the south. That, he said, was where he was heading anyway. Although accounts vary, it seems that during the journey the Indians, none of whom had been disarmed, gave no trouble; one narrative even has some of them joking with the cavalrymen and smoking their cigarettes. By evening, with about 15 miles to go, they stopped and made camp at a place called Wounded Knee. The cavalry commander, not convinced by the Indians' apparent calm, and quietly planning to disarm them next morning, positioned the two Hotchkiss rapid-fire artillery pieces that he had with him, plus two troops (about 80 men), on a low hill overlooking the area where the Indians, in the freezing twilight, were now erecting their tepees. The rest of his men (about 180 cavalrymen and 50 scouts) were stationed in a series of strong points encircling the Indian camp. This, of course, alarmed the Sioux. They became even more alarmed when, soon after dark, the soldiers were joined by four more companies of the 7th Cavalry; they had ridden out from the Pine Ridge Agency. The colonel of the regiment, George Forsyth, now assumed overall command. He added his two Hotchkiss guns (with shrapnel ammunition) to the two guns already on the hill.

The next morning, shortly after reveille, Colonel Forsyth sent a message into the tepees. All the men, more than 100 of them, were to come out unarmed; they were to assemble in front of the main cavalry position. When they were gathered, wrapped in their blankets against the cold, the colonel brusquely ordered them to go back to their tepees, 20 at a time, to fetch their guns. There was, as one might expect, much muttering at this command. They claimed that they had not been told the previous day that this was a condition of their surrender. Yet now they were surrounded, with no choice. But an Indian's rifle, especially if it were one of the new lever-action Winchester carbines, was his most valued possession. If they refused to disarm, what would the whites do? More importantly, given that many of them were wearing those bulletproof shirts, what would they do? Their medicine man, Yellow Bird, was quietly advising them.

Presently the first group returned from the tepees, carrying just two guns; both had obviously been unused for years. Big Foot was lifted off his sickbed and carried out of the tent which, together with a stove, had been provided by the cavalry the evening before. When told to advise his people to cooperate, he

Sitting Bull, a year or two before he was killed. (Nebraska State Historical Society)

said that they had already done so: there were no more guns. Colonel Forsyth decided that more direct action was needed. He ordered detachments of his own men to go and search the tepees. The braves, who were already restive, now became even more agitated. But they were under the guns of the soldiers. Perhaps they wondered if their bulletproof shirts would also be impregnable to the shells of those cannons up on the hill.

Sure enough, the search parties found some of the rifles they were looking for. Many had been hidden by the women, some in bedding, some under their long, full skirts. But the number found, less than 40, was suspiciously low. During the rummage, the soldiers were nervous, rough, and in a hurry. The distress of the women could easily be heard by their menfolk. The colonel was sure that there were more rifles to be found, so he ordered the Indians to come forward in ones and twos and open wide their blankets. A few old men shuffled forward: no weapons. Then suddenly, back in the crowd, one of the younger men shook a Winchester high above his head. Two soldiers moved towards him. He fired a shot in the air. Yellow Bird threw up a handful of dirt.

There has always been debate as to whether the shot and the dust constituted a prearranged signal. Indeed, there are varying interpretations about almost all the events of that morning: their sequence and their significance. In short, like so much throughout the Indian Wars, there can be no single version of what happened. Everything depends on who is telling the story.

So who fired first? We do not know, but it seems likely that within just a second or two of that "signal," those warriors who had rifles inside their blankets leveled them and fired. The soldiers could see what was happening, before it even happened. So, almost simultaneously, they too opened fire, nearly 100 of them, at a range of less than 50 yards. The immediate carnage, on both sides, must have been terrible.

So close was the fighting that, for the first minute or two, the crews of those Hotchkiss guns up on the hill had to hold their fire for fear of hitting their own men. But as the fighting below became more spread out, the gunners began to make their contribution; each of those four guns could fire a round of shrapnel every three seconds. The Sioux now found that their shirts were no more use against the exploding shells than they were against rifle bullets. Within minutes, most of the tepees were in shreds. The women and children, those not already killed or wounded, were running away to find shelter under the eroded banks and coulees along Wounded Knee Creek. Many of the warriors followed them.

For the next three hours and within a radius of several miles, the soldiers hunted down any Indian they could find. At one point, one of those rapid-fire Hotchkiss guns was moved in order to target its shells onto some of those groups sheltering along the creek. The shrapnel did not discriminate between women and children, or their still-armed menfolk.

By early afternoon, it was all over. The temperature, already well below freezing, was dropping by the minute; the wind was increasing. All the signs were of an approaching ice storm. So it was imperative to get the wounded back to the military hospital in the agency village at Pine Ridge as quickly as possible. They were quickly helped into wagons, along with the bodies of their dead companions. Of the soldiers, 39 had been wounded and 25 killed; some had almost certainly been hit by "friendly fire." Of the Indian dead: their bodies were not counted, but they included Big Foot and Yellow Bird. They were just left behind while the wagons and the column of cavalry moved off. This was late afternoon on December 29, 1890.

It was New Year's Day before the blizzard blew itself out. Only then did a detachment of soldiers, together with a group of workmen, a posse of journalists, and a photographer, get back to Wounded Knee. After two days of subzero temperatures, the scattered bodies were frozen solid. Big Foot's grotesquely twisted corpse was among them. The workmen dug a large pit into the top of the hill that, only three days before, had been the site of those Hotchkiss guns. It is generally reckoned that more than 150 men, women, and children were thrown, one on top of another, into that pit. It is also reckoned that the bodies of another 20 or 30 men and women, lying further afield, were not recovered until days or even weeks later. The photographer took a set of pictures that, even today, are a shocking record of the whole tragic episode.

And, given that it might have been avoided, it *was* a tragic episode. It is also one that, in terms of the participants' motives, responsibilities, and blame, is still debated. Among some of the soldiery there was almost certainly a wish to avenge old scores. This, after all, was the same regiment that, under Custer, had lost nearly half its men just 14 years before. Indeed, several of the officers and enlisted men still carried memories of that terrible day. For all they knew, some of the Indians in front of them might have been involved in that encounter. And further, from the moment that the shooting started that morning, there certainly would have been anger among the soldiers at what many would have seen as treachery. Why else would the Indians have hidden their weapons, if not suddenly to throw aside their blankets in a preplanned attack?

Among the Sioux, there would have been deep resentment that, having peacefully surrendered the day before and then behaved themselves, they should later be surrounded, bullied, and told to hand over all their firearms—something that had not, as they understood it, been part of the earlier agreement. They would have wondered what the whites, with this demand for total disarmament, had in mind. Perhaps they had hidden their guns not because they had plotted to use them that day, but because they had long learned not to trust the whites. They had good cause, for, although they could not know it, it seems that the true intention of the military was not to take them to Pine Ridge, but to march them to the railhead at the small Nebraskan town of Gordon; from there they were to be shipped by train hundreds of miles south, perhaps to the desolation of what is today's western Oklahoma.

One could go on with various conjectures. But what is certain is that nerves on both sides were so taut that it would take very little to detonate a two-way explosion. That single shot from the brave waving his Winchester was enough. From this distance in time, it is easy to say that Colonel Forsyth, with an overwhelming body of 500 troops at his disposal, could have been more sensitive. Maybe he could have ordered a cease-fire when it became apparent that the Sioux were finished, instead of allowing his men to chase after every remaining survivor. Perhaps and maybe …

The Sioux have long insisted that it was not a battle; to this day, they call it the Massacre at Wounded Knee. Again, they have cause. For its part, the Army was quick to ease its conscience by portraying the engagement as a wholly legitimate police action, triggered by treachery. To justify this version yet further,

The burial pit at Wounded Knee (Nebraska State Historical Society)

the authorities quickly distributed 13 Medals of Honor—one of the highest accolades for courage that the nation can bestow. Apparently there have never been so many such awards consequent on any single engagement, before or since. The Sioux have long referred to them as Medals of Dishonor, and in recent years have petitioned Congress to have them rescinded, without success.

Wounded Knee was the site of the last major "battle" of the Indian Wars. By the end of the 1890s, any mention of Wounded Knee beyond the Sioux would have generated interest in only the most concerned Americans.

೮౨

We were waiting in a departure lounge at Denver airport. There were nine or ten of these characters; they all seemed to know each other. They were heavily built, crew-cut, rather pasty-faced, and several of them chewed their gum too nervously. They were not Westerners—you could tell that by their dark and rather baggy suits and their black lace-up shoes. As we filed through the departure gate I tried to eavesdrop on their sporadic conversation. Evidently they were Federal Marshals; they had left Boston that morning and now, having just jetted 2,000 miles to Denver, they were boarding this small Frontier Airlines flight on the penultimate leg of a journey to South Dakota. They were on their way to the Sioux Reservation at Pine Ridge, "to wrap things up good." I doubt that any of them had ever been on the plains before. Certainly, they had some strange ideas about what they were going to find.

"Told my wife I was going to get myself a real short haircut—nobody's gonna take my scalp."

"They do say that these guys are mostly weirdoes or commies."

"Well, I hear that it's a real nothing place. Anyways, they've got us all booked back home next week, and no replacements. Must mean something."

I got off the plane an hour and a half later at Chadron, and was met by old friends. The marshals also got off; they drove away into the evening in a government bus.

In fact, it was another nine weeks before the 60 or so Indians (mostly Sioux) who had taken over and dug themselves in around the "nothing place" called Wounded Knee were finally persuaded to give in or melt away. But not before there had been several killings. The so-called "rebellion" was an ironic echo of the only other time that Wounded Knee made the nation's headlines.

℘

For the eight decades after 1890, few people would have known where to find Wounded Knee on a map. Indeed, on most maps it was not even marked.

What started to put the place back on the map, almost literally, was a growing militancy known as the Race Relations Movement, or the struggle for Civil Rights. Looking back, one remembers places like Selma, Little Rock, Montgomery, Birmingham, and more than a dozen others. In our minds they are indelibly associated with the campaign by Black people for equality and justice. But at the time another, rather smaller minority was looking on with more than a passing interest. Black Power? So why not Red Power?

In November 1969 a small group of Indians invaded Alcatraz, the disused but highly visible island-prison in the middle of San Francisco Bay. They held the place for 18 months and, with an ironic sense of history, generated some sharp publicity. For instance, taking a cue from the Dutch who, more than 300 years earlier, had bought the island of Manhattan (New Amsterdam) from the local tribe for a scatter of bright baubles, the Indians on Alcatraz now offered (via their Radio Free Alcatraz) to sell "their" island to the whites for a similar handful or two of glass beads; they even offered to set up a paternalistic Bureau for Caucasian Affairs to look after interests of the three white caretakers of the island. For a month or two the media lapped it up. Maybe it stirred a few white consciences; it certainly got people talking about some of the most ignored people on the continent.

The following year, 1970, on the other side of the country, a party of Red Skins (sic) boarded a replica of the Mayflower; they timed the takeover for Thanksgiving Day so that they could then pose an elegantly provocative question: for which particular benefits, apparently bestowed on them since the arrival of the Pilgrim Fathers, should all right-thinking Indians be expected to give Thanks? Again, it was a stunt, but it made people think.

The year 1970 also saw the publication of a book called *Bury My Heart at Wounded Knee* by Dee Brown. This history of the Indian Wars (with a title from the last line of a well-known poem) quickly became a bestseller. Now Wounded Knee was not only back on the map but was also planted in the nation's consciousness.

One year later, in growing militancy, a host of Indians were winding their way right across the country towards the nation's capital. Some of them had started on the far side of the continent; more joined along the way. They called the route of their motorized cavalcade "The Trail of Broken Treaties." They pointed to the fact that they had long been the most forgotten and the most impoverished people in the nation; they had the highest infant mortality, the highest unemployment, the highest suicide rate, the highest level of diabetes and of alcoholic addiction, and the lowest life expectancy. On any measure that mattered, they were at the wrong end of the scale.

By the time they reached Washington in early November 1972, their numbers had grown; estimates varied between 1,000 and twice that number. From the beginning there was, all too typically, a deal of infighting and ego-tripping among the different factions which, while having more or less common objectives, had very different ideas as to how best to achieve them. At the militant end were members of the American Indian Movement (AIM). They were in the lead when the procession broke into the headquarters of the white-dominated and deeply unloved Bureau of Indian Affairs (BIA). Once inside, they barricaded all the entrances and refused to leave. There were reports that a minority was not only armed but was ready to soak some of the upstairs carpets with gasoline, to torch the place if the authorities should mount a heavy-handed assault to reclaim the building. Up the road in the White House, President Nixon declined to meet a Broken Treaty delegation; he was preoccupied with the early rumblings of the Watergate scandal. But fortunately someone on his staff had sense enough to advise the police and others to adopt a softly-softly, wait-and-see posture. In fact, it was eight days before an evacuation was negotiated in return for various promises that AIM's list of demands would now be taken seriously. By then, the media and thereby the nation were losing interest in what was becoming an increasingly static story. And the occupants were very tired. It was later estimated that $1 million worth of damage had been done. As a gesture of goodwill, the Federal Government agreed to subsidize the cost of everyone's journey home.

Today, around 40 years later, it is difficult to work out what, in any specific terms, was actually achieved. Certainly among the leaders of AIM, in the weeks and months that followed, there seems to have been as much impatience and anger as ever. In fact, only three months later, this pent-up frustration was to manifest itself at a remote crossroads hamlet far away on the Western plains. Yes, it was that "nothing place" called Wounded Knee. Given its place both in history and now in Dee Brown's bestseller, it was the obvious place for a showdown. The leaders of AIM pointed to a long list of both national and local provocations …

High on the local part of that list was the hostility of the Oglala (Pine Ridge) Reservation's Tribal Council towards AIM. By a narrow vote, not only had the council contributed nothing to help the Trail of Broken Treaties, but it had then gone out of its way to be deeply critical of what it called "the recent and unjustifiable actions in Washington DC." In this, the council was voicing the personal views of its dictatorial mixed-blood president, Dick Wilson. He portrayed AIM as being led by Communist troublemakers who, in the local Oglala context of "his" Reservation, were now out to subvert his authority. The problem was that Wilson had recently been elected by what were, without doubt, some murky procedures and intimidations. Russell Means, one of AIM's leaders who had been prominent in the recent Washington "occupation," was now calling for a properly monitored re-run of that election. Across the reservation he was widely supported. In retaliation, and despite the fact that Means was an Oglala, Wilson ordered his immediate arrest if he should attempt to return to his homeland. In parenthesis, one has to say that, even today, the internal politics—the rivalries, the resentments, the jealousies, the antagonisms, the distrusts, the name-calling—that are endemic on some reservations, and none more so than among the Oglala Sioux of the Pine Ridge Reservation, are incomprehensible to any outsider. If one were foolish enough to attempt even the most basic explanation, one might say that while there are serious tensions between many of the full-bloods and those of mixed blood, those rivalries are relatively mild compared to those that can exist within the community of mixed-bloods. Intra-tribal factionalism is everywhere. Back in 1973 the very personal antagonism, hatred even, that had developed between Dick Wilson and Russell Means was to cost lives.

In that incendiary atmosphere, it was not going to take much to ignite real conflict. The immediate detonator was the killing in the small white community of Buffalo Gap (about 15 miles outside the Reservation) of a 22-year-old Sioux, Bad Heart Bull. But this was not the first time that an Indian had died in a recent encounter with whites; only a few months earlier, a 51-year-old Sioux called Yellow Thunder had died of a head wound inflicted by some drunken rowdies who had been roaming the small Nebraskan town of Gordon looking "to bust an Indian." So tempers on the reservation were already more than merely simmering.

Now from Buffalo Gap came news of this second killing, in a barside brawl. A few days later, in the county seat of Custer, the indictment against Bad Heart Bull's white assailant was announced as manslaughter, because it was judged that the fatal stabbing had been accidental, rather than premeditated. In their fury at what they saw as an entirely inadequate charge, the leaders of AIM and several hundred of their local followers now attempted to storm the snowbound courthouse. The local police, already reinforced by officers from other Black Hills communities, held them off with nightsticks (clubs) and tear gas. The Indians retaliated by torching two police cars. Arrests were made. The next day, the agitation spread to the nearest major town, Rapid City. Bars were sacked and shops damaged. The National Guard was alerted. White communities all through the Black Hills became frightened, some to the point of panic. Across the state, there was a marked increase in the sale of guns.

There must have been relief among those whites when, presently, they heard that the focus of Sioux anger had moved away, back onto Pine Ridge Reservation. Within a single evening, the remote hamlet of Wounded Knee was taken over by an armed force of more than 200 Indians. For the Sioux, the symbolism of the place was powerful. Further, they calculated that, over the days that followed, this same symbolism would be a gift to the writers of the nation's headlines.

Among the Indians digging in at Wounded Knee were Vietnam veterans who well knew how to defend a perimeter. Urged on by Russell Means and other leaders of AIM, they took over and fortified the area around the same low hill on which, 83 years earlier, those Hotchkiss guns had been placed, and where their forebears lay in that mass grave. This was, whatever the rights or wrongs, an armed revolt: the first, some said, since the Civil War. So, given that Dick Wilson's tribal police were too weak and possibly too divided among themselves to contain the insurrection, Federal forces of law and order, namely US marshals aided by FBI personnel, were flown in. They set up armed blocks on the several roads leading in and out of Wounded Knee. Amongst other weapons, heavy machine guns were mounted on a dozen or so Armored Personnel Carriers (APCs) commandeered from a reluctant Army. Despite the urgings of the by-now–paranoid Dick Wilson back in the Pine Ridge Agency that the US marshals should go in, guns blazing, and "eliminate those AIM clowns," the authorities were well aware that news reports, let alone TV footage, of those APCs driving towards a second Wounded Knee confrontation would not play well across the nation, or the world. So over the next few days, then weeks, words like siege, standoff, deadlock, impasse, and stalemate found a central place in the vocabulary of every news report.

The official thinking seems to have been that if the belligerents inside Wounded Knee were "contained"—nothing in, nothing out—they would, within a week or two, crack from boredom, from hunger, and from the realization that they could not win. In short, they would have to surrender. But, among the leaders of AIM and their militant Sioux allies, the thinking was that they could afford to hang on. Provisions and weapons were not an immediate problem; there were hidden paths through the hills by which backpacked necessities could reach them almost every night; there was even a tip-and-run airdrop by three light aircraft. Meanwhile there were demands that they wanted met. These included an urgent federal inquiry into the dubious election and subsequent nepotism of Dick Wilson and his cronies on the Oglala Tribal Council and in the Tribal Police. (Wilson is alleged to have once said that, under tribal law, "there's nothing illegal about nepotism.") Only slightly less immediate was a demand for a full-blown judicial investigation into the Fort Laramie Treaty of 1868 under which the Black Hills had been formally recognized as Sioux territory "forever." When would they be getting their Hills back? Next, and connected with the claim on the Black Hills, they wanted a thorough resolution of Indian sovereignty: Indian rights, tribal and individual, as they applied right across the nation. They wanted more tribal self-determination, in place of what they saw as the raggedy colonialism of Washington's Bureau of Indian Affairs. Lastly, they wanted UN observers flown in, so that the world might know that this was more than an inconsequential spat somewhere deep within "interior America." Many might say that these demands were unrealistic; but that, surely, is rather to miss their point ...

The problem with such confrontations, the world over, is often much the same: governments, despite their usual superiority in resources and weaponry, feel that they cannot afford, with the media looking on, to be too heavy-handed. Yet, at the same time, until the "rebels" have agreed to give up their weapons and hostages (if any), the authorities cannot be seen to have been coerced into negotiations. At Wounded Knee, there was another complication: there were too many rival branches of government, local and national; all of them were jostling to push solutions which ranged from all-out assault to quiet containment. At times this led to a shameful (or farcical) lack of coordination between the FBI, the US Marshals Service, the Bureau of Indian Affairs, the Federal Justice Department, the Governor of South Dakota and, even more locally, the Oglala tribal police and Dick Wilson's Tribal Council. And that says nothing of the lawyers, busybodies, and assorted congressmen and senators who also came helicoptering in to make a contribution.

And all the while, the "rebels" were well aware that, as long as they stayed put, they were a continuing embarrassment to all the relevant arms of the Washington government. But, at the same time, they became aware that they were not making any progress.

Under a white flag, negotiators from Washington's Justice Department eventually took the lead in trying to break the all-around impasse. Watched with some distrust by the other agencies, they passed back and forth between the besieged and the besiegers several times; also, hundreds of live rounds were exchanged. Reports speak of a firefight, big or small, almost every night. Each side always accused the other of having fired the first shots. There were casualties and two deaths among the "rebels."

It is difficult to work out what finally tipped the balance toward capitulation. Perhaps there was no specific catalyst, or perhaps there was a whole range of them. Perhaps, above all, there was the realization by those inside Wounded Knee that as time dragged on and media interest and national support dwindled, so too did their morale. Then inevitably, being Sioux, there was bickering among their leaders about what to do next. Further, the FBI was now across some of those clandestine supply paths. Ammunition inside Wounded Knee was short, and getting shorter. So, despite the fact that the authorities did not offer any amnesty for a long list of alleged offenses, nor did they offer any concessions in terms of that disputed election of the Tribal Council, the end came quickly. A so-called Accord, wherein the government agreed—once the rebels had disarmed—to discuss the 1868 Black Hills Treaty, was signed on May 5. The standoff had lasted 10 weeks.

In the months and years that followed, neither the Black Hills Treaty nor any of the other grievances were ever discussed in an effective way. Nor, in the months and years that followed was there any lessening in the tensions and conflicts across Pine Ridge (Oglala) Reservation. Indeed, instead of being concentrated around Wounded Knee, the contagion of hostility spread into even the remotest settlement. It was a time when scores were settled, sometimes in the most vicious way—by assassinations. Even on a conservative count, over the next two years more than 50 people were shot, beaten or stabbed to death. A few were simply "disappeared." If homicide was the measure, Pine Ridge Reservation became (per head) by far the most violent place in the nation. The majority of the victims were people who, while they had not necessarily been inside the Wounded Knee perimeter during "the troubles," had not held back in supporting those who had been. Dick Wilson's tribal policemen, out of uniform and often working at night, were widely blamed for many of the murders. Even though the identity of many of the assassins was common knowledge, no charges were ever brought. Witnesses were too frightened. But there were deaths on the other side too, most notably two FBI agents who were ambushed and shot while trailing a van of AIM militants. The FBI quickly allocated more than 100 of its agents to track down the culprits. The chief suspect was found in Canada; he was extradited and eventually sentenced to two terms of life imprisonment.

Inevitably, comparisons were made between the energy with which the FBI followed up on the death of two of its own officers, and its lack of zeal in chasing after a number of known killers living on and off the Reservation.

Among the erstwhile occupiers of Wounded Knee and other supporters beyond, more than 500 were apprehended on various state and federal warrants. Of these, 185 were formally charged with crimes that ranged from "assault with deadly weapons" to "crossing a state line to incite a riot." In the end there were just 15 solid convictions, which would seem to point to some skillful defense lawyers or some unconvinced (or unwilling?) juries; or both.

ᕦᔦ

Today, the sad but inescapable fact is that, despite all that happened at Wounded Knee, life for the Oglala Sioux and, as far as I know, their tribal cousins on the other Sioux reservations across South Dakota is as bleak as it ever was. If one wants proof of that assertion, just go and stand on that hill where, once, those Hotchkiss guns were unlimbered. Then look around.

I have been to Wounded Knee four times, both before and after the uprising. When I first made the pilgrimage, back in 1963, there was a small, white clapboard Catholic church on the hillside near the mass grave; it dated back about 50 years. On the flat land below, by the road, there was a one-room general store owned by a rather uncommunicative white couple, Mr. and Mrs. Gildersleeve. One corner of the store was given over to a dusty montage of photographs and bits and pieces derived from that day in 1890. Another corner displayed various pieces of Sioux beadwork for sale. Outside, in summer, there might be a car or two with the out-of-state plates that indicated some tourist visitors. Today, more than 50 years on, the store and the church are long gone; the first was looted, trashed, and then torched during the 1973 confrontation; the latter is said by some to have been set on fire by children playing with matches some days after everyone had gone home. But what, of course, is still there is the mass grave of early 1891. It is as forlorn and derelict as one supposes it has been since the day they shoveled the earth over those frozen corpses. The long rectangle of concrete laid later around the grave is cracked and discolored. Its bordering margin is disjointed and broken. Weeds poke through. At one side, around the base of the small ornate memorial, are a few plastic flowers, ribbons, and feathers. And there is a teddy bear: an almost inevitable part of such places nowadays. Every few years, on the reservation, there is talk of lobbying Washington to declare the hill a national monument and, thereby, to pull Federal funds for a bigger and better memorial, a visitors' center and, who knows, a few scholarships. Nothing has happened; nor will it.

It would be a cliché to say that the state of that mass grave and its memorial serves as a symbol of the reservation as a whole. But, sadly, one does not need to spend much time on Pine Ridge to know that, cliché or not, that observation is near the truth. In parts, this is Third World territory. The Oglala people are, as I have written earlier, at the wrong end of any list that matters. Their reservation, despite considerable injections of federal money, and much hard work by various Oglala self-help groups, is still the poorest corner of America.

∽

Back in 1963 I filmed an interview with an Oglala of about my own age. Since then, I had read that, at various times through the 1970s and 80s, Gerald One Feather had served as a campaigning Chairman of the Tribal Council and, at other times, he had stood against the Dick Wilson regime. Indeed, following the Wounded Knee confrontation in 1973 he was the target of at least two assassination attempts. Over the years, he had won recognition as a leading elder of the Oglala community. So, in the spring of 2011, I went back to see if I could find him. I inquired at the local office of the Bureau of Indian Affairs. Straightaway I noticed a change from my earlier visits: the place was now staffed not by whites, but by Sioux. Surely that was significant. When, with the prompt help of the Bureau, I found Mr. One Feather ("call me Gerald"), he remembered our earlier meeting. Indeed, he joked that we had both lost most of our hair. More importantly, he agreed that his people now had rather more control over their own affairs than when we had first met. And health and life expectancy were improved; but not nearly enough. Housing was better; but not nearly enough: there were still too many homes without running water and reliable electricity, and there were still too many people crowded into broken and leaking trailer homes. Yes, schools and education were more accessible, but, with job opportunities on the reservation so sparse, it was difficult to "incentivize" young people. In short, there was still a long way to go—in every direction. Unemployment, he said, was by far the greatest single problem. Other than work for the Bureau, or the Tribal Council (and its police), or an occasional public-works program (e.g. road building), there were very few jobs. In any case, culturally there was no tradition among the Sioux of regular long-term employment, even if such opportunities existed on the reservation—which they didn't. So, when young Sioux left home to look for work elsewhere, they were too often ill-equipped to compete against white job seekers. They returned discouraged and discontented. Some, to drown their frustrations, even their despair, took to petty crime or drink or drugs. A few killed themselves. The reservation has the highest suicide rate in the nation.

Gerald also talked about the 1868 Fort Laramie Treaty whereby the Sioux were "granted" ownership of their Black Hills "for as long as the grass shall grow." Despite nearly a century of legal actions against the United States, the only real "honoring" of that treaty has been in various offers of cash—most recently a suggested settlement of $750 million. The Sioux point out that, over the years, the value of the gold taken out of the Black Hills by successive generations of miners has been far, far more than that. So they are reluctant to settle; they just want the Black Hills back in their undisputed ownership—as the 1868 Treaty demanded, and still demands.

Towards the end of our conversation, I reminded Gerald of something he had said in that interview of 48 years ago: "We have had to learn to live in two worlds: the white man's world and the Sioux world ... to try to learn each of their values, which are totally different, in order just to survive." He thought that was only slightly less true than it had been in 1963 ...

12

COWBOYS AND COW-TOWNS

"Hell is now in session … murder, lust, highway robbery and whores run the city day and night."
From the Abilene Chronicle in the summer of 1869; the paper seemed to take some pride in the mayhem.

"We didn't have much law in those early days. Fact is we didn't need much— till all the lawyers arrived."
A comment that appears in more than one reminiscence about various cow-towns across Kansas in the early 1880s.

❧

True, it was a long time ago, and I was only in his company for a couple of hours. But for me, even now, over 50 years later, Mr. Roberts is still someone very special. He had lived right through the taking of the West. Indeed, as a young man, he himself had played a part in that "taking." Over the years, I have met and listened to a number of old timers, but Mr. Roberts is the only one who went back that far, back to the days of the pioneers and their covered wagons. I still wonder at my luck.
He was 101. On that hot Colorado afternoon, he tilted his Stetson forward against the glare of the sun and then, in the slow and scratchy voice of a very old man, he told me and the camera about coming west from Iowa

with his father and mother. He reckoned that he was 12 or 13 years old. They had traveled by train as far as North Platte, Nebraska. There they had unloaded their two wagons, hitched their mules and trekked off for a couple of hundred miles toward northern Colorado, to find land for a homestead. He remembered the bad temper of some of the Indians along the way and, later, the bitterness of his parents and other would-be settlers when they learned that the Washington government was intending to issue some of them with guns— in settlement, in his view, of some dubious treaty obligation. His family found their land near Fort Collins; he still lived on the place. He nodded over his shoulder toward the distant Rockies, and recalled that there were still a few buffalo when he had first arrived in those parts. He talked about watching strings of longhorns coming up from Texas and the arguments that his father had with the cowboys to keep the herds off his land. Later, as a young man, he had done some cowboying himself.

Cowboy life: a break for a dip ... (Kansas State Historical Society)

Meeting Mr. Roberts was quite fortuitous. A mile or two further up the road from his place there was a Minuteman missile. That is why we were there, to film a practice refueling. We were making a BBC documentary series about the West, past and present. From the rocket, elevated and upright above its underground bunker, there streamed a feather of liquid oxygen. This was the height of the Cold War, and the missile's destination was exactly fixed on some target on the far side of the world—though it was unknown to the crew in their concrete below. "We don't need to know where that baby's going; we just look after the thing." I remember the crew commander telling me that if the coded signal ever came, the rocket and several dozen others like it spread across Colorado, Wyoming, and the Dakotas could be "on their way" in fewer than six minutes. Inevitably, one reflected that less than a century earlier, quite possibly across that very ground, some belligerent Cheyenne might have sneaked up on a small wagon train, killed the men and made off with the wives and their children.

It was while we were having lunch in a diner after the filming at the rocket site that the waitress (I think she was Mr. Roberts' great-granddaughter) told us about the old man. She made a phone call; we went along and introduced ourselves. He had been three years old when Abraham Lincoln was assassinated; he was 14 when Colonel Custer was killed; he was 28 when Butch Cassidy robbed his first bank; he was far too old to serve in the Great War. His life had spanned the whole history of the settling of the West, from wilderness to weapons programmed for nuclear wipeout.

∽

The Great Plains were the last part of the United States to be settled. Yet once settlement *did* begin, the pace was lightning fast. From wilderness to wallpaper—and the stuff is as good a gauge of domestication as one might find—took just one very short lifetime. For sheer speed, say 40 years, over such a huge spread of country, there has never been anything quite like it.

Until the Civil War, the overland pioneers had only one idea about the plains: to get across them. They were a vast and interrupting nuisance. Except for the Mormons and their Kingdom of the Saints, settlement ended at the Missouri. It did not begin again for another 1,600 miles, until the wagons finally halted in faraway Oregon, or as they rolled down the western slope of the California Sierra. Between the river-line and those distant Utopias lay this huge and, to the whites, empty land. True, ever since the Louisiana Purchase, the nation could claim territorial title to the wilderness, but that was about all it could claim. And even that "ownership" ignored the prior, but ill-defined, rights of a scatter of indigenous inhabitants who, after all, had been Americans for several millennia before the word had even existed. Even today, from eye height, there are some vistas on the Great Plains that look across a land that seems uninhabited. This steppeland stretches unbroken from Texas north to the Canadian prairies, and from the 98th meridian to the Rocky Mountains. Whole empires have been smaller than this.

On official maps printed not much more than 150 years ago, much of this ocean of land was written off under the forbidding title of the "Great American Desert." Yet less than 25 years later, in 1890, the US Census Bureau decided that the vastness had been filled to the extent that the use of the word "frontier" was no longer justified or relevant. The federal statisticians and bureaucrats were more or less right. What had initially been called the Great American Desert, and then a little later the Wild West, would now often be referred to, by the railroads' boosters, as the Garden of America. To be fair, in some of those parts irrigated from the rivers, that was not just Madison Avenue booster talk. Almost the whole process of settlement had taken less than a generation. How?

Well, to start a little before the beginning, the cowboy had something to do with it, though he himself was anything but a settler. His problem, though he did not see it that way, was that he didn't have a wife; he had a horse. As a Frenchman once neatly put it, "*pas de cheval, pas de cowboy.*" Horses are for traveling, wives are for putting down roots and raising families. The cowboy had nothing against wives and children, but he was (and his few true descendants sometimes still are) shy of strong family ties. He was and still is (the few that are left) a drifter with a Castilian pride in his freedom; he doesn't care to plan too far ahead and, until he is into middle age, he does not take easily to being tied down to mortgaged domesticity, least of all to a homestead or a farm. Anyway, he is likely to be bowlegged, and his high-heeled boots are not much good for spade work—for digging wells or irrigation ditches or holes for fence posts. In fact his boots are not much good for anything except riding. Yes, I exaggerate; but not beyond recognition.

So the footloose cowboy looked down on the humble farmer and called him a "sodbuster." Sometimes he still does. I would not want it thought that I do not admire cowboys—though, as I have just implied, there are not many

... and a break for the chuck tent (Kansas State Historical Society)

thoroughbreds left. They are among the straightest men I know. In their heyday—and their dominion was very brief, 30 years at the most—they were the stubble-chinned princes of the plains. And they gave the West something that is still not quite gone: its romance and its style. Those qualities come through today in the Westerner's instant informality: "Howdy, Tim," with a handshake like a vice; and in his walk, his accent, his humor, his hospitality, his sentimental and wonderfully tuneful songs, his sometimes gauche yet always disarming manners, and in his occasionally rather graceless politics.

I am glad that their forebears have, for the rest of us, become the accepted archetype of the West; after all, they opened up a good deal of the place. But the realist in me knows that the cowboys had little to do with the actual settling of it. Indeed, for a few short years they warred contemptuously against the incoming settlers; what the sodbusters wanted to do with the cowboys' open range was not just alien, it was downright hostile. So they fought back. Perhaps, contrary to the myth, the cowboy's Colt or Winchester did not really win the West, not for settlement anyway.

Like many legends, that of the cowboy has several possible beginnings. But as good a place to start as any other would be in Texas just after the Civil War.

Texans straggling home after the collapse of the Confederacy found that, while the half-wild longhorns of the back-country had multiplied "sump'n considerable," there were no local markets for this latent wealth. So a few hardy outfits headed their herds toward the hungry mining camps of the Rocky Mountains, or to army posts and early Indian reservations in Kansas and Nebraska. Others tried to reach northeast all the way to the abattoirs of St. Louis. But the longhorns (though themselves immune) carried a disease, tick fever, which aroused the hostility of the Missouri settlers; they blocked the cowboys, sometimes with guns. They established what they called "deadlines"—indeed, it seems that is where and how the term derives. So the only thing left for the Texan cattlemen was to convert their stringy cattle into mere tallow and hides. But the profits were small. And that, to a Texan, even in those days, was a waste of time.

The solution lay with a certain Joseph McCoy, a 29-year-old cattle merchant from Illinois. He had two older brothers who were also involved in the business, but years later Joseph wrote a book about it all, so he still gets the credit. "This young man," he wrote of himself, "conceived the idea of opening up an outlet for Texas cattle ... a market whereat the southern drover and the northern buyer would meet on equal footing." It was an absurdly simple idea and was to make a great deal of money for the McCoys.

Early in 1867 (only a few months after Colonel and Libbie Custer arrived in Fort Riley), the McCoy brothers looked at a map and saw their opportunity. They would build stockyards somewhere along the Kansas–Pacific railroad, which was then starting to push across the plains of Kansas towards the distant Rockies. Young Joseph was dispatched to get things started. After being turned away from Salina and Junction City—they feared tick fever—he settled on a scatter of shacks and tents called Abilene: "A poor dead place," he later wrote, "consisting of about a dozen huts." He bought the place. Then he sent three or four agents riding down to Texas to spread the word: bring your cattle north to Abilene where they can be shipped by rail all the way back to the meat-hungry towns and cities of the East; everyone will make a packet. There was a last-minute hitch when the Kansas–Pacific Railroad pulled out; the bosses back in St. Louis had decided they did not want tick fever infecting their carts. So McCoy made a quick deal with the smaller Hannibal and St. Joseph railroad; it agreed to haul the cattle in their trucks if the Kansas–Pacific would let them run over the latter's tracks for the first few hundred miles of the journey east. Everyone agreed to this arrangement, but, as a result of the Kansas–Pacific's reluctance to have a bigger part in the deal, St. Louis missed out on the beef trade. Chicago was where the Hannibal and St. Joseph terminated. So Chicago was started on its way to becoming the biggest meat market in the world.

In the first year of McCoy's stockyards, 1867, he shipped about 30,000 longhorns. He thought that he could do better. So, in the fall, he sent more emissaries south. They promised that for every steer delivered to Abilene, Mr. McCoy would pay three times as much as they were then getting from the Texas tallow merchants. The Texans took the bait and in 1868 they came surging up the trail like "wolves who smell summer butter," as someone oddly put it at the time. Through that summer a third of a million cattle were shipped east in 10,000 wagons. And those earlier promises of solid cash were honored immediately, from whence, some folk suggest, we derive that ultimate guarantee of good faith: the Real McCoy.

During the five short shipping seasons of 1867 to 1871, Abilene was probably the wildest town in the West, though it was not without competition. With more than 200 footloose young men in town at any one time, it was "the beautiful, bibulous Babylon of the frontier." Like sailors coming into port after a long and lonely voyage, the cowboys—paid off at the end of a 700-mile trail—set the place ablaze. Sometimes literally. For a week or two, before riding back to Texas, they were unemployed, uninhibited, and totally unrestrained. No wonder that the saloon-keepers, the cardsharps, the storekeepers, and the madams rubbed their hands in anticipation as soon as they saw the first dust clouds coming up from the south. In 1871, three quarters of a million cattle came up from Texas.

In April of that year, the town council, under Mayor McCoy, anxious to bring some order to the place, signed up Wild Bill Hickock as town marshal. He was a dandy with a big reputation, and he demanded an appropriate salary: $150 a month. But he seems to have done his job; the killing rate went down and he himself only shot two men all summer. Perhaps he was so effective that he did himself out of a job; the town council paid him off in the fall and appointed a successor at a mere $50 a month. Perhaps the truth was that, as the last of the trains rattled away to the east that fall, the cattle trade—together with the saloons, cardsharps and the rest—had moved on. With the railroad and branch lines pushing further west, McCoy had shifted his operations to a new and more convenient railhead: Wichita.

The pattern was repeated all through the 1870s as the railroad built out across the plains: Abilene, Salina, Ellsworth, Newton, Wichita, Dodge City. Each reigned briefly as the self-styled Queen City of the Plains until it was succeeded by the next. But Abilene was the first and the original. Incidentally, only a few years later, in quieter times, this was the boyhood home of Dwight D. Eisenhower; the house still stands.

There was a saying "there was no Sunday west of Junction City and no God west of Salina." At this distance in time, it is difficult to sort some of the legend

The cow-town of Stratton in Nebraska celebrates its first anniversary in 1888 (Nebraska State Hist. Soc.)

from the reality. But we know quite enough to judge that in the flux of a Kansas cow-town, life did not count for much. For example, in the first four months of Dodge City's existence, the claim was that "of the 24 people who have been buried, not one has died a natural death, except for a prostitute who shot herself." Whether that claim is half true or merely colorful does not really matter; more than a century later every one of those Kansas cow-towns tells much the same story of itself: proud of its raucous birth, yet, at the same time, coyly embarrassed at its heathen beginnings. After all, this was a society almost entirely made of single males. So, as already implied, the ingredients of mayhem were simple: too many young men on the loose, too many loaded guns, too many gamblers, too much cheap liquor, and too few women—cheap or otherwise.

Glamor has become the legend; dirt, dust and squalor, and not a little disease (particularly what they called "the venereals") are probably nearer the truth. Yet we have not been entirely misled. There *was* a raw courage and even a rough chivalry among many of those people on the cattle frontier, though judging by the number of people shot from behind, or bushwhacked at short range from the shadows, there must have been a number of prudent cowards around too.

Each cow-town grew up around its railroad stockyards. At first, it was not a town at all, just a few false-front saloons, a dance hall, and a rickety general store or two. These were quickly built of canvas and wood; they were frequently burning down. If the place prospered and business was going well, the traders would get together and contract with someone to lay wooden planks in front of their shops—the boardwalk. This saved walking in the mud or dust. Then the traders on the other side of the street (if there *was* another side) would do the same, so that they did not lose out to the competition. Presently someone would start a newspaper, someone else would set up as a lawyer—one did not need any high-flown qualifications. Pretty soon there might be a bank and a post office. By now, a sheriff would have been appointed and, with the income he collected from fines and petty taxes, a jail would be built. Within a few weeks, the place had a name, a mayor and, no doubt, the beginnings of a reputation.

There was always a recognized alleyway of vice. In Abilene one learns that it was called Texas Street, in Ellsworth it was Naunchville, in Newton it was Hide Park. And Dodge City claims to have donated its own particular label—the Red Light district—to the rest of the world. It was, some say, the area surrounding one particular "sporting house" which, rather grander than its neighbors, had red-tinted windows on the ground floor and was, therefore, called the Red Light House. Ellsworth, not to be outdone, has it that when the locomotive men took a few hours off while their trains were being loaded with cattle, they would take the red brake lanterns off their cabooses to hang outside whichever establishment they were visiting, so that they might be found when their train was ready to go. Like so many stories about the early West, you can take your pick.

The joy girls, "everyone a genuine former virgin," were invariably the first women to arrive at the various railheads and, later, at the mining camps. They seem to have had a civilizing effect: men might even take a bath and change their shirts. The new arrivals were known by a variety of inventive soubriquets: prairie nymphs, calico queens, fancies, soiled doves, and Marys (as in Magdalene). Individually, they traded under some appealing pseudonyms: Lonesome Flower, Little Miss Muffet, Lady Jane and, neatest of all, Sue de Nym. No doubt some of them really did have hearts of gold.

"I never seed such a little town with such a mighty name" is the reported comment of one out-of-season traveler when he arrived in Abilene. The *Dodge City Times*, in September 1877, when most of the Texans had hit the trail for home, opined that "our city is relapsing into morality." Then, with nostalgia for times just past, it reported that "at this time of writing there are only seventeen saloons and dance houses, sixty prostitutes, thirty gamblers, and eighty cowboys left in town." It was all good small-town Chamber of Commerce stuff—with no Parent Teacher Association to worry about. But civilization (and much else) had surely arrived when, a few years later, there was formed the Dodge City Dramatic Society; it even put on an abridged performance of *A Midsummer's*

Night's Dream; maybe they played it for laughs. At about the same time, the place got itself its own Cowboy Silver Cornet Band—so that "Dodge City can toot its own horn." Presently the band shipped east and invited itself to play at the inauguration of President Harrison.

Nevertheless, these civilizing touches and that earlier "relapse into morality" were only partial. From the height of the cow-town era of the mid 1870s to the end of the century, and across the frontier as a whole—which would include the many mining camps—it seems (though estimates vary) that as many as 5,000 violent deaths may have occurred. Most would have been by gunshot or hangings (also sometimes referred to as being "jerked to Jesus"). Judged against the rough-and-ready legal code of what has come down to us as the "Wild West," some of that so-called justice might even have been warranted. As someone is reported to have reminisced, "We didn't have much law in those early days. Fact is we didn't need much—till all the lawyers arrived."

❧

The Wild West? Yes, it certainly existed. And if one were to point to a time and place where that universally popular concept was born, the time would be the early 1870s, and the place would be any cow-town.

The cow-towns are still there, but they don't do so much cow-business these days. Mostly it is wheat. Coming into town, past the feedlot, you slow to 30 mph and roll past the Old Corral Trailer Park and the Frontier Filling Station: "Fastest Gas in the West." Then just beyond John Deere Implements and the Town-n-Country One-Stop Mart, the speed limit drops again to a mere 20 mph, and you'd better believe it: they've got radar hereabouts. You start looking for somewhere to bunk down for the night: the Trail Motor Inn, the Western Skies, the Silver Spur, the Longhorn, or the Lariat. But maybe you could find something cheaper at the Lazy U. You check in. The lady stops sniffing her Vicks Inhaler for long enough to run your card through her swipe; she hands you a room key. You take your car round to park in front of your room; you go inside and, depending on the season, you turn down the heat or turn up the cool. Then you "wash up"—after you've unwrapped the soap, *sorted out an assortment of towels, worked out how the faucet at the basin works, and taken the Sanitized-for-Your-Protection label off the seat. All this for $52.50 plus tax, if you're lucky. If you're in Dodge City, there will be a card on the mirror inviting you to "Step downtown and relive the Legend at the Boot Hill and Front Street Museum and Gift Shop." No sir, the cow-towns may not do too much cow-business any more, but they sure can dream.*

Dodge City's Cowboy Band in 1889—formed so that "our city might toot its own horn." (Kansas State Historical Society)

A country school. The building material, earth sod, is clearly visible (Nebraska State Historical Society)

The 1890s — Cheyenne "society," often also known as The Barons. (Wyoming State Historical Society)

13

CATTLE BARONS

"Cattle raising in the western states of America is at the present time one of the most lucrative enterprises in the world."
From the 1882 prospectus for the Wyoming Cattle Ranche Ltd, a British company

"Where is the man that wants to be a cattle king? We venture to say that within ten years his money will fill a boxcar."
From the *Mandan Daily Pioneer* (North Dakota), July 1883

❧

In 1873 the prices at the Kansas railheads were poorer than usual. So some Texan cattlemen, hoping for a better bargain the next year, held their herds back from sale and wintered them on the open plains. It was a mild winter and in the spring the beeves were found to have put on weight; certainly they fetched better prices than the travel-tired animals that shortly arrived from Texas. What had been a temporary solution started to become a permanent answer: the grassy plains of Kansas, then Nebraska and, within a few years, those of Wyoming and Montana and even Alberta became a new home for the cowboys and for the founding fathers of big-money ranches.

Given that there was not a fence between Texas and the tundra, the early cattle spreads, some of them far bigger than mere feudal baronies, had imaginary boundaries, the location of which had much to do with whoever was doing the imagining. Of course there were some sharp disputes, but, for much of the time, the cattle barons got along in an uneasy alliance with each other; they had common interests, the chief of which was "to have and to hold" against the disrespectful latecomer—the small man who had the impertinence to "locate" along some creek or meadowland "belonging" to a baron. "How come that man

219

is running all those new-branded calves? He sure didn't bring them with him when he pulled in last fall. And whose land does he think it is anyway?" The fact that a baron would be claiming exclusive possession of land to which he often had no formal title was, as far as he was concerned, wholly irrelevant.

His brand was his heraldic crest; it marked his property. As in the early days in Texas, a common problem centered on the annual "crop" of unbranded calves. In the mêlée of the spring roundup, it was inevitable that some of those "doggies" would become separated from their branded mothers. And rustlers were becoming increasingly bold. It was too easy, given the enormous size of the some of those early ranches, for thieves to sneak into unguarded corners and drive off 20 or 30 head—and not just maverick calves. Such cattle could be quickly rebranded. It became a very serious offense to be caught with a running iron: an iron rod (rather like a short upside-down walking stick), the crook of which, when red hot, was used by the rustler to "modify" an existing brand to something different. Some men were artists at it. But if caught, they were likely to pay with their lives—jerked for Jesus.

The arithmetic of ranching was simple. It was reckoned to cost $8–$10 to raise a calf over three years. At the end of that period, the full-grown steer might sell at the railhead for between $25 and $30. So, even at a poor showing, there was a theoretical return of, say, 40% a year on capital. Of course, it often did not work out like that. For a start, the calculations took little account of the ups and downs of the market. Further, they ignored the weather which, in a dry summer, could reduce carcass weight by a third; and in a severe winter, when the thermometer dropped well below freezing for weeks on end, could much more than decimate a herd. And yes, there were those rustlers. Nevertheless, despite these problems, the profits were still unusually attractive.

An ex-army officer, General James Brisbin, in the pay of the railroads, had written a book with a seductive title: *The Beef Bonanza or How to Get Rich on the Plains*. Besides having a domestic readership "back East," it sold well in Britain. Indeed, *The Scotsman* newspaper sent a reporter, John Macdonald, on a fact-finding tour of the West. His report, published as *Food from the Far West*, was as enthusiastic as the American booklet. Simultaneously, the high price of meat in Britain was prompting various experiments in crude forms of refrigeration, to permit the import of carcasses from across the Atlantic. The problem was reliability.

It was a New Yorker, John Bate, who came up with the first effective solution. In 1875, he persuaded a shipping company to adapt part of a hold. He loaded just 12 carcasses and several tons of winter ice. Throughout the eight-day crossing to Liverpool, he employed men to turn fans, to drive a steady flow of icy air past the carcasses. The meat arrived in good condition. On the next voyage, the ship-owners provided steam to power bigger fans. Within three years, Liverpool was receiving 1,000 tons of meat every week. And at the same time investors, surveyors, accountants, and long-faced lawyers were buying tickets for places they had never heard of: Ogallala, Missoula, Amarillo, Fargo, Rapid City, Sioux Falls, and Medicine Bow. Joint-stock companies had arrived in the West. The place would never be the same again.

Some of the well-to-do British immigrants came not merely to enlarge their fortunes but to become self-styled "Gentlemen of the Prairie." They brought their hunting pinks with them; they galloped after coyotes; they built baronial ranch houses furnished from New York and London; they became founding members of the Cheyenne Club. Within a few years, the Club's cuisine and cellars would compare with any gentlemen's club in New York or London.

One thing that everyone, from both sides of the Atlantic, had early recognized: if the meat business was going to prosper, the feral Longhorn, more bone and gristle than meat, would have to be replaced. So, the Scots brought in the quicker-fattening and more docile Shorthorn and Angus; the English imported the Hereford. These three breeds have been the mainstay of the American beef industry ever since. Within 20 years the Longhorn was almost extinct.

❧

In confident ignorance I wrote that last sentence in London. A few months later I found myself driving along Kansas Rural Route 14. As I came over a rise I saw two cars stopped about a mile ahead. It seemed that they were held up while some cattle crossed the road. As I approached and then slowed I realized, with surprise, that the cattle were Longhorns. I had never seen any of these legendary creatures before, so I got out to ask someone what was going on. She and her friends had on large sunbonnets and long dresses; their ensembles were straight out of the pioneering 1870s. She explained that next Saturday, Ellsworth (ten miles down the road) would be celebrating its 140th birthday; it had started life as a cattle-shipping town on the newly-arrived Kansas–Pacific Railroad in the summer of 1867. Fortunately, I was able to say that I had heard about that. Those Longhorns crossing the road were part of a "memorial" herd and had been trucked in from Oklahoma to a nearby ranch. Now they were being driven toward Ellsworth, in readiness to be paraded down Main Street as the high spot of the commemorative celebrations. "You oughta come— it'll be a lot of fun."

It was too. On parade was all the joyous hoopla of small-town America: strutting bands and leggy twirlers, cowboys on showy horses, covered wagons, bars open all day and half the night, hot dogs and burgers, raffles (I didn't win a '73 replica Winchester rifle), sideshows, square dancing, and, as something of a finale, those Longhorns came sauntering down Main Street. I was surprised, after all that I had read, that they were so docile. A neighbor explained that, over many years of breeding, they had "been tamed down a bit." He then wondered what a Brit was doing in those parts. I explained. He asked me to convey his polite displeasure to BBC-America (a cable channel): his complaint was that the channel was now no longer showing "One Man and His Dog," a series about competitions between shepherds and their respective dogs. He bred Border Collies, so this was his favorite program. I said that I'd pass on his disappointment. Who would have thought that, in the middle of Kansas, one would find a Stetsoned aficionado of that most pastoral and English of programs? But these strange things occasionally happen.

✃

Through the late 1870s and into the 1880s, British investment played as important a role in the early ranching business as did those three imported breeds. The aristocracy led the charge: Lord Dunmore, Lord Dunraven, the Marquis of Tweeddale, and the Earl of Airlie took up land along the foothills of the Rockies. Even today there are said to be several titled British families who draw dividends from cattle companies started in those early days.

The Cheyenne Club, with its $500 joining fee and $200 annual subscription, its uniformed waiters, its hunting trophies, and its full-dress balls has long gone. But not so some other traces of those Anglo-Americans. One can still come across unexpected echoes: close by Wyoming's Bighorn Mountains there is the IXL Ranch. It was founded by two retired officers of the 9th Lancers; that is what the brand still stands for. And I remember meeting an attorney in Laramie, Wyoming, who subscribed to *The Illustrated London News* and *Punch*—because "the family always has." And, still in Wyoming, there is a ranch where, in the stables, alongside the heavy (almost armchair) Western saddles, one can see two lightweight hunting saddles shipped over from the shires 130 years ago. Then out on the plains of central Kansas, there is the patriotically named town of Victoria; the local high school plays baseball in the George Grant Park, named after a baronet who founded the place. He came West with a party of friends to restore

The Cheyenne Club, reckoned to be the best gentlemen's watering hole west of the Missouri (Wyoming State Archives)

the family fortune. But things did not work out for him or his chums and, after a couple of years, bored by the heat of summer and the icy winds of winter, they all went home. Incidentally, just six miles from Victoria is the town of Catharine, founded by some Russian émigrés and named after *their* queen who, nearly 100 years earlier, had helped their grandparents. (We will come to that story.) And spread right across the West there are scores of other echoing names: Andover, Derby, Glasgow, Kensington, Oxford, Cambridge, Edinburgh, Aberdeen, Midlothian, Nottingham, New Waverly, Albion, Stockton, Westmoreland, Torrington, Newcastle, Plymouth, Winchester, Watford City, and many more.

Ranch life soon mellowed the stiff-necked attitudes of those upper-crust Britons. One such, Horace Plunkett, the younger son of Lord Dunsany, wrote in his diary on his first visit, before he knew better: "Here, there does not seem to be a gentleman—no, not one." After a year or two of rough and tumble he wrote more appreciatively of his American neighbors: "They are to a certain amount clannish and feel our intrusion. The exact feeling they would express thus, 'You compare us with your society. We don't compare favorably perhaps. But we are members of a greater nation than yours and just as good—though you don't know it.' English visitors make themselves and us unpopular by their incapability to adapt themselves to the people."

❦

The captain of one of the teams told me that, as a young man, he had "done a spell at your (sic) Royal Agricultural College at Cirencester." He and his friends played most Sundays through the summer: the Over-the-Hill Boys against the Wolf Creek Crew, the Dutch Creek Outfit versus Sheridan Town. For the rest of the week, the ground doubled as the rancher's airstrip. But, apart from the wind-sock and the Bighorn Mountains behind, the scene—rugs on the grass, and picnics spread out on the tailgates of the station wagons—was not very different to the one below Windsor Castle on a fine July afternoon. Polo arrived in the West with the English m'luds who, well over a century ago, came to find land in this part of Wyoming.

The transatlantic connection still continues, as I found out a few days later when I drove to Sheridan airport (a few miles from that polo field) to pick up some BBC film stock. As soon as the airport manager recognized that I was a Brit, he leaned over the counter and quietly suggested that I might like to pay the $14 that, he explained, the British Embassy had underpaid on the landing-and-parking fee incurred some months earlier by an aircraft "belonging to your Queen." The Queen? Here in Wyoming? Surely not. "Oh yes, you bet." And he pointed to a photograph on the wall. No doubt about it. She was coming down the steps of her aircraft on arrival.

While he explained, I reached for my wallet; after all, it seemed that the nation's credit worthiness (to say nothing of the Queen's) had suddenly become my personal responsibility. Then the manager laughed. "Only joking; and even if it was a few dollars, I wouldn't be chasing you for it. A charming lady—great to have her here." Relief on my part? No, disappointment. After all, I might have found unique fame as the Man who Once Paid the Queen's Parking Ticket.

It had happened the previous autumn: the Queen, at the end of a royal tour of Canada, diverted to put down at Sheridan to stay for a few unofficial days with some old friends, Lord and Lady Porchester. They had (and still have) a small ranch tucked under the lee of the Bighorn Mountains. Lady Porchester's grandfather was the youngest son of the Earl of Portsmouth. As a young man seeking to make his own way in the world, he had come west in 1888 to start a ranch on which to breed horses for the British army. In time he became an American citizen and, in 1908, he ran for and was elected to the Wyoming legislature. Meanwhile his father had died and the title had passed to his eldest brother. Then, over the next decade, his other brothers also died until, unexpectedly, he found himself with a seat in the House of Lords and, at the same time, that place in Wyoming's own small parliament. Rather than renounce the Portsmouth title, he reluctantly gave up his American citizenship. But his children remained Americans. Decades later, his grandson, Malcolm

Wallop, became one of Wyoming's two US Senators (1976-1995), and it was his granddaughter, Jean, who was now the Queen's Wyoming hostess. How come? Well, in 1955 she had married the Queen's racing manager and long-time friend, Lord Porchester. Presumably, "Porchie" (as he seems always to be known) had been telling the Queen about Wyoming for some years and now, at his urging, she had come by to see for herself. By all accounts she had a very good time, and although it was a private visit she acquiesced to public interest and went for several walkabouts to meet the people of Sheridan and the nearby "village" of Bighorn. They still talk about her.

Her VC10 of the Queen's Flight was, and still is, the largest aircraft to have put down at Sheridan's airport, which for some reason has a longer runway than one might normally expect.

℘

But, to return to earlier days ... By the early 1880s the cattle business had reached some kind of high-water mark. Lured by optimistic prospectuses, investment capital was pouring in. Scottish investors were particularly enthusiastic; their jute industry, centered on Dundee, was making large profits, and so there was money to be turned around and put into new enterprises. Even Americans were looking back across the Atlantic for funding, and the English were not to be left behind.

One of the most interesting English "migrants" was an eccentric young man called Moreton Frewen. Fortunately, from his own and other people's reminiscences (some now kept in the archives of the University of Wyoming), we know a good deal about him and his various Western ventures. Mr. Frewen was a keen "follower" of the horses. On a summer afternoon in 1878 at the Doncaster Races, he backed a considerable winner. Thinking that, with luck, he might at least treble his money, he put all his winnings on a horse in the next race. If he won, he would be rich. If he lost, well, he'd go and try his luck in this American cattle "game" about which he had been hearing such enticing rumors. He lost. But his life was lived by two complementary mottoes: winner-take-all, or if things don't work out something else will turn up. So on the eve of his departure he threw a party he could not afford and said his optimistic goodbyes. His friends, presumably amused at Moreton Frewen's happy profligacy, wished him well and rechristened him Mortal Ruin.

A few months later, with just three companions, he was caught deep in the winter snows of the Bighorn Mountains. The temperature was far below freezing and a blizzard was not long past. Even today, the skidoo-mounted locals will tell you that winter is no time to go trekking across their high-country wilderness. But, as one comes to know the man better, there seems to be something characteristic, even admirable, about Mortal Ruin's breezy carelessness. He was ever the optimist: things would work out.

Once through the mountains (he and his English chums drove a small herd of bison to bulldoze a path through the drifts), Frewen looked out eastward; the vastness of the Powder River basin stretched away forever. The land was hardly clear of Indians; the Custer debacle had occurred only three years earlier, just two days' ride to the north. Now, from somewhere just below the snow line, Frewen looked in wonder at what he saw: "Again and again we dismounted to spy out the far distant horizon through our glasses. Never was such a view. To the east was limitless prairie, the course of the Powder River showing its broad belt of cottonwoods fading out in the far distance. Not a human habitation in sight."

I know the scene because, almost 100 years later, from what may have been much the same spot, I filmed a slow panning shot across the same marvelous vastness. Yes, indeed, "Never was such a view." There were still not many "human habitations in sight."

It was that "limitless prairie" that set Mortal Ruin thinking. Here he would make his fortune. He hurried back to England to talk up his project with the people who mattered. He called the enterprise the Powder River Cattle Company; private partnership shares sold quickly to the value of £300,000 (about £18 million or $26 million today). He invited the Duke of Manchester to be the chairman of directors. With the money raised, he hurried back to the Powder River. He now set about establishing himself in the grand manner. He started to build a two-story chateau: the "home ranche." "We selected the site with much care. It was on a flat prairie about a hundred yards from the river and perhaps seventy feet above it. There we rightly judged we would be free of mosquitoes. Nor did it escape us that half-a-mile away was a seam of excellent coal quite seven feet thick."

The building logs had to be hauled 20 miles from the pine forests on the eastern flanks of the Bighorn Mountains. In the same month that construction began, Frewen paid for several thousand Longhorns to be driven 700 miles north from Texas. From New York, Chicago and London he ordered a prefabricated staircase, curtain material, carpets, hardwood paneling, and several four-poster beds. Also on his shopping list were several tons of flour, sugar, lentils, dried peas and soap, and sacks of seed for a vegetable garden. Then there was a sawmill, hardware for a blacksmith and a carpenter's shop, and several cast-iron stoves for cooking and winter heating. And lastly came what he considered to be the other essentials: a piano, sofas, pictures, boxes of quality cigars and fine French wines. Everything had to be hauled from the nearest point on the Union Pacific railroad, 200 miles away.

The ranch was huge: 50 miles in one direction and 50 miles in the other, or 1.6 million acres. Yet none of that land belonged to Moreton Frewen and his aristocratic backers in any legal sense. Some nervous investors asked a London lawyer for an opinion. Looking across the Atlantic, he did his best: "In point of fact … these people put their cattle in common, and if any stranger came in and built a ranche (sic) and put out his cattle we think the place would be, to use a vulgar expression, made 'too hot to hold him'." Exactly. For a decade or so, the system worked.

Within a year, Moreton Frewen doubled the number of cattle. At the same time he was importing Shorthorn and Hereford breeding stock to improve his herds. In the evenings, he wrote to his moneyed and titled friends inviting them to come West and see things for themselves. After all, work on his two-story chateau was now almost finished. The paneling and the staircase were in. The main room on the ground floor was 40 ft square with a large stone fireplace at each end. The dining table could seat 30 people with ease. There was a separate drawing room and, up the stairs, a corridor of large bedrooms. A cook and a butler were in place. The cowboys were agog: they had never seen anything like it; they called it Frewen's Castle. Nor had they seen anything like the guests who now, over the next two and three summers, accepted those invitations. The house parties combined the influential and the famous with the merely double-barreled: Lords Gordon, Granville, Manners, Mayo, Queensbury, Linlithgow, Desborough and Donoughmore, Sir Samuel and Lady Baker (just back from their search for the source of the Nile), Mr. T. Porter-Porter, and Mr. J. Turner-Turner—amongst others.

The guests got off the Union Pacific train at a wayside halt northwest of Laramie; they transferred to a stagecoach sent to meet them. Then they swayed and bumped for two days (and those 200 miles) across the mountains and the prairies. During the summer months, it seems that there was music in the drawing room, al fresco banquets in the bunkhouse and, who knows, croquet on the prairie. Buffalo Bill came by several times to take some of the guests off hunting along the foothills of the Bighorns. The cowboys got confused with all these notables and assumed that everyone coming from "the old country" had a "handle"; they called their boss Sir Frewen.

At a ford further down the Powder he established a post office and a general store for his and other people's cowboys. He called the place Sussex after his home county back in England. Between the store and his Castle, 20 miles upriver, he strung wires for "an electric voice-telephone"; it was said to be the first in Wyoming. History has it that one day he arranged for Plenty Bear at one end and Wolf's Tooth at the other to talk to each other. At first they could not believe their ears. But then, in slow wonderment, as they identified each other's voices, they were persuaded that the white man's talking wires were, indeed, heap-big-medicine.

ᘓ

In the spring of 2007, in the course of that flight with my English friend across the West (already mentioned in the chapter on the Overland Trail), we flew over the Powder River country and the small settlement of Sussex. During our flight planning, we saw that across most of what would once have been Moreton Frewen's ranch, the air chart was marked as an "MOA," a Military Operating Area. Apparently this is where the pilots of A10 (Wart-hog) aircraft practice their low-level attacks before being dispatched to Iraq and Afghanistan. There being no practice that day, we were allowed across. From 2,000 feet, we looked down on the river crossing that is still called Sussex.

Thirty minutes earlier we had flown over some of the largest open-cast coal mines in the world. Mr. Frewen could not know it, but his sevn-foot seam widens (and deepens) to 90 feet only a long day's ride to the north. Statistics vary, but it seems that the coal railed out of Wyoming's Powder River basin is, through the first decade of this twenty-first century, now providing nearly a quarter of all the nation's power-station fuel.

ᘓ

On his frequent journeys to and from England—he made the trip two or three times a year—Moreton Frewen often tarried for a few days in New York in order to court a young woman called Clara Jerome. Clara and her two sisters were the daughters of Leonard Jerome, a rich financier. Some years earlier, Jennie had married Lord Randolph Churchill, second son of the Duke of Marlborough. So, when Clara and Moreton finally married in June 1881, he became an uncle-by-marriage of an eight-year-old lad called Winston.

Moreton took Clara back to Wyoming. She seems to have enjoyed herself, for she wrote to one of her sisters: "This is our real honeymoon. Moreton is the greatest darling. You'd love it here … the air is perfectly delicious and the scenery so beautiful with the snow-capped Bighorn Mountains in the near distance and troops of antelope by our house going down to the river to drink." She went on to tell of the summer house parties and to extol the interesting life that she and her husband were living on the ranch. But, sadly, toward the end of her first pregnancy, she went into premature labor and, though rushed south to Cheyenne (the nearest proper medical help), her baby was stillborn. They buried Jasmine by the Castle. Perhaps the distance (230 miles) and the roughness of the journey made the tragedy almost inevitable. After she had recovered, Clara returned to the family home in New York. She never went West again.

From distant Wyoming, Frewen wrote frequent letters to his wife. For several years, as he later put it, "no cloud was in the sky." Beef prices were high, and he reckoned on the ownership of 45,000 cattle. This was almost certainly a considerable overestimate, but, ever the optimist, he told Clara (and others) something of the next Big Project that he had in mind. He planned to start new ranches further north in Montana and across the border in Canada. In 1884, with these projects in hand, he was confident enough to tell his backers that "we have legitimate cause for congratulation."

Frewen was never short of big ideas. But to raise the financial steam, he found that he had no choice but to turn the ranch into a public company. Years later he wrote, "I fell into line with the company mongering craze … and transferred the Powder River herds to a company." While Frewen retained a large number of shares, he no longer held a controlling majority. In time he found that the directors sitting in London thought they knew better than he did how to run the ranch in Wyoming. For example, at just the time when he was trying to build up some financial reserves to fund that expansion onto the Canadian prairies, the directors decided, without reference to Frewen, to pay out an unsustainable 20% dividend.

Things got worse. Frewen was torn between dashing back to London to persuade the absentee directors to see sense, and staying where he was to reorganize as best he could. Before he could decide which course to take, London telegraphed instructions to the bankers in Cheyenne that the company's accounts were to be frozen, for the time being anyway. As soon as news got out that his credit was suspect, Frewen was paralyzed. He could do nothing. The Powder River Cattle Company began to come apart as he watched. Frewen hurried back to England to bring legal action against some of his fellow directors. But it was too late to put the bits together again. Demoralized, he suddenly seems to have lost interest. In fact, although he could not know it at the time, many of his friends at the Cheyenne Club would be facing their own crises within the next two years.

He left Wyoming in June 1885 and, as he suspected at the time, he never went back. But over the next 30 years, ever the extravagant optimist ("never talk poor," he would say), he made and lost several fortunes funded with other people's money: in Canada, Australia, South Africa, and India. He promoted a rock pulverizer which would release gold in prodigious quantities from abandoned spoil heaps around the world; he trumpeted a grease which was uniquely suited to lubricate the axles of the world's railroad rolling stock; he invested in "an improved disinfecting fluid" he called "Electrozone"; he was on the edge of making a fortune with a new tramway system for Denver; he saw "magnificent investment promise" in the obscure port of Prince Rupert on Canada's Pacific coast; he lobbied for a railroad to be built from the prairies north to Hudson Bay (it would be built, but not for another 40 years); he pushed the highlands of Kenya as a land of limitless opportunity for white settlement; he proposed a monetary union between Canada, the US, and the British Empire. Always he thought of himself "as a rich man in the making." He tried hard, desperately hard, but sadly he never quite made it.

In its obituary, *The Times* called him "a thwarted Elizabethan." Rudyard Kipling, who as a near neighbor in Sussex (England) had known him in later years, wrote: "He was a man who lived in every sense except common sense." Someone else said, "Moreton had a first class mind quite untroubled by second thoughts." Maybe those comments are too harsh. Yes, he was ultimately a failure; indeed, with the bailiffs literally knocking on his Sussex door to take away some furniture, he ended his life as a pauper—but a rather splendid one. And while he lasted those few years on the Powder River, he had put on quite a show.

ↂ

A few months after that flight over Sussex (Wyoming), I drove to the place. There is nothing much to see: a small cattle feedlot, a couple of ranch houses and their stock yards, some irrigated fields of alfalfa, and a road bridge across the Powder River. The general store and the post office are long gone. And 20 miles upstream, there is nothing left of Frewen's Castle either. I was told that, for a few years in the 1890s, its main room had been used as a school. Then a little later it was pulled apart for its timbers by incoming settlers; a mile away is a derelict barn supposedly built with some of those timbers. Where the Castle itself once stood there is nothing but a dimple in the ground; this may be where the well once was. There is no trace of little Jasmine's grave. After a good deal of asking around I was later shown, in a bank 70 miles up the road, a paperweight allegedly fashioned out of one of the balustrades in that staircase. That seems to be all that is left.

The evening after I had been to Sussex and the Castle, I checked in at a motel an hour or two away. Recognizing that I was a Brit, the owner asked where I had been that day, so I explained. He asked if I knew the story about "your Mr. Churchill." Apparently, local legend has it that when Moreton Frewen learned that his young nephew-by-marriage was not performing too well at school (and in his autobiography, Churchill complains that at Harrow "I remained in the Third Fourth three times as long as anyone else"), Frewen suggested to Winston's mother that perhaps, in a few years' time, when he was into his teens, the lad might do worse than to leave school and come out West and learn the cattle business. I have tried to check the tale, but there is no mention of it in any of the several books about Moreton Frewen. But who knows? It is possible—just. Certainly at one time Winston's mother was close to despair: "He is so idle and of course that is conducive to naughtiness ... one can't manage him." Certainly English ranchers of the day used to take on boys in their teens from the "old country" as apprentices; they called them Pups and charged their families $500 for a year's tuition. So, Cattleman Churchill? Might he have succeeded as a rancher where Frewen failed? The possibilities must make this one of the more beguiling (if minor) "what ifs" of history. As such, the story is far too intriguing not to pass on.

❧

If it was the McCoy brothers' good judgment, good luck and self-confidence back in Kansas that had much to do with sparking the cattle business back in 1867, it was other people's poor judgment, bad luck and overconfidence which put the brakes on less than 20 years later. Until then, everyone had been making money out of cattle. The industrializing cities back east and in Britain were a sure and ever-growing market. The boosters continued to claim that a man starting with a relatively small investment could become wealthy in just a few years.

"Where is the man who wants to be a cattle king in western Dakota?" asked the *Mandan Daily Pioneer* in July 1883. "Let him come at once and select a suitable location. We venture to say that within ten years his money will fill a boxcar."

It did not actually work out that way. When the crash came, all the investors—not least those in distant Scotland and England—took a hammering. On the northern plains, where most of their investments had been made with such high promise only a few years before, it was becoming obvious to the people on the spot that every fourth or fifth year there came a winter that was too severe for the cattle to forage for themselves; they needed hay if they were going to be meaty enough to be saleable in the spring.

But the causes of the crash were wider than just a lack of winter feed in the bad years. For some time, more and more investors had been enticed by the rich returns. So there was a deal of over-grazing. The grass and the profits were wearing thin. To disguise the problem, some directors quietly sold off parts of their company's assets—parcels of land and the cattle on that land. The cash thus generated was then used to boost dividends to keep the distant and unsuspecting investors happy and, of course, to entice new investment—one of the oldest tricks in the corporate fraudster's handbook. It worked for a while because cattle numbers (and value) were calculated on what was called the "book count." This was a wholly theoretical calculation dependent on every cow producing a calf every year. It ignored rustlers, disease, the weather and other depredations— to say nothing of those cows (or bulls?) that did not perform as required. The only people not in on the secret seem to have been the investors reading the seductive balance sheets back east and, even further away, in Britain. But, by the mid-1880s the truth began to overtake the fiction; in some cases the book count was found to exceed the reality by 50%.

Then came another blow: the winter of 1886–1887 was unusually hard. It was preceded by a very dry summer, so many cattle were already in poor condition before the storms even arrived. Across the northern plains of Wyoming, Montana, the Dakotas, and down into Nebraska tens of thousands of cattle did not survive.

 ℘

During the year we lived in northwest Nebraska, the first snow fell before the end of September. The temperature had peaked at 100°F only five weeks before; one night in February it fell to 44°F below freezing. That range of more than 110°F was, they told us, "only a little bitty more than usual. What matters is the windchill and the precipitation." I don't know if, back in 1886, they talked about "precipitation," or if they still called it "snow," but by mid-October of that year they were getting plenty. And wind: dry, subzero temperatures are just about endurable to people and to livestock, but it is the wind that makes the difference.

A snow blizzard or, even worse, an ice storm on the High Plains is a thing entirely of its own, beholden to no modifying influence whatsoever. It blows down from the north like a hammer. From the Arctic to the plains it seems that there is nothing bigger than a barn to deflect it. It knocks down trees, buries trains, blows over trucks, turns rivers into solid ice, and even kills people. Hours before the storm arrives, barriers are erected on all the roads leading out of town, to stop anyone who has not heard the news. Schools close (or fill up with stranded travelers), drivers out on the highways head for the nearest refuge, shops shut to send their employees home, and local radios give an almost minute-by-minute countdown. "Right now, it's at Rapid City; weatherman says it'll be coming our way within the hour. More details coming up. Stay tuned."

Every year some motorists don't catch the warnings or are foolish enough to think that they can make a run for it before the storm hits them. Mostly they will be lucky, but not always. They will come to a stop because in the "whiteout" they can't see the road, or are blocked by a drift. If they stay in their cars, they might survive. Sometimes they get out to look for help; sometimes they find it and sometimes, huddled in some roadside gully, their bodies aren't found until the thaw. A blizzard can last for two hours or for two days. They don't happen everywhere every year, but almost every year they happen somewhere. Early in 1887 they seemed to happen "all over."

Nowadays, ranchers have snow fences and shelter belts of trees to protect their cattle from the full force of the storms. Nevertheless, the effect of a sudden blizzard on untended cattle can still be disastrous; a rancher can lose a sizeable proportion of his herd. The animals will drift before the wind until they come to a fence, where their frozen carcasses are later found. Sometimes they will just freeze to death; sometimes the snow builds up inside their nostrils and around their mouths until they suffocate; sometimes they may be blinded by icicles building up on their shaggy forelocks and hanging down over their eyes. Sometimes the survivors will have large areas of their flanks stripped to bare, pink skin where the ice has built up until it is so heavy that it finally falls off, dragging out the hair on which it has frozen.

Ranchers usually reduce the numbers of cattle they will keep through the winter by selling in the fall. Apart from the climatic unpredictability, any cattle remaining will have to be given feed, and there is only a limited amount of that available. Northern ranchers also take the precaution, the previous spring, of running their bulls with the cows a little later than is the practice further south. They do this so that the calves will not be born before the end of April. Even so, an unusually late storm—and they can be as late as mid-May in northern Wyoming, Montana, and the Dakotas— can kill a lot of calves.

∽

Before the winter of 1886–1887 they took none of those precautions. They expected to lose some cattle; they would write the loss off as a necessary overhead. But that winter the so-called "die-up" was worse than ever before. Newspapers tell of blizzards before the end of November. The *Bismarck Tribune* wrote: "The storm of Monday and Tuesday was the worst on record. The snow drifted to a greater extent than ever before and it penetrated buildings wherever it was possible for the wind to find its way." In December the weather moderated a little, but all this did was to melt the surface of the snow which then, when subzero temperatures returned two weeks later, re-froze into a crust of concrete-like ice; the cattle could not break through to reach the grass underneath. Many died of starvation.

It was reckoned that the northern ranchers lost at least 40% of their herds. Some lost twice that many. John Clay, who had been an early English neighbor of Moreton Frewen's in the Powder River country, wrote in his memoirs that "the cowmen were flat broke. Many of them never recovered … most of the Easterners and the Britishers said 'enough' and went away. The summer and fall of 1886 was, to use a western expression, simply a fright. The big guns toppled; the small ones had as much chance as a fly in molasses."

Perhaps Clay was not quite right; a few of the "big guns" picked up the pieces and slowly built their herds again; some of the small guns struggled on. But by the late 1880s the ever-optimistic heyday of the open range was gone. It was prudence, not profligacy that now governed the successful cattleman's strategy. And another thing: a different breed of pioneer was closing up behind— the settler and his family. For most rancher-barons, these late arrivals were to become much more than just a nuisance …

14

RANGE WAR

"We are beset by rustlers ... there is an urgent necessity for a lynching bee."
Major Walcott, a leader of Wyoming's large ranchers, advocating that the sternest measures be taken against all alleged rustlers

"The Johnson County War ... the most notorious event in the history of Wyoming."
A comment by Ray O'Leary and Bob Edwards, in their book *Frontier Wyoming* (2006)

℘

With hired gunmen from Texas, bloody intimidations, vigilante hangings and assassinations, crooked lawyers, and the cavalry cantering onto the scene at the last moment, the story of what is usually known as the Johnson County War has the theatrical sweep of a Hollywood epic. Indeed, the incomparable *Shane* was at least partly based on it; and the three hours of one of the most expensive film flops ever made, *Heaven's Gate*, was almost wholly so. But as a social drama that really happened, it had deeper causes and wider consequences than might have been invented by any mere scriptwriter.

To start at the beginning ... "If you can't beat them, join them." But what if "they" won't let you in? Well, if you had hopes of starting your own small ranch or farm in Wyoming in the late 1880s, you had best be very determined and very well armed. For nearly a decade, the cattle barons had had things very much their own "closed shop" way. They saw no reason to change. By pressuring the state government in Cheyenne they virtually wrote laws in their own favor; by dominating the banks they promoted their own wealth; by leaning on the editors of a chosen newspaper or two they made sure of a favorable press; by legal manipulation they held off latecomers; and by their own self-righteousness they reckoned they could (and should) get away with anything, even murder. But the "Die-up of '87" had weakened them financially, and now a wave of would-be settlers—trespassers who did not give a damn for the careless imperialism of the barons—were nibbling away at them territorially. And there were other, more distant forces to worry them as well.

Starting back east, antagonisms had been growing between "big business" and the individual, between conservative and radical, between speculator and worker, between creditor and debtor. There were clashes in factories, mines, ironworks and slums. The discontent was catching out West. The momentum had gone out of Manifest Destiny: it didn't provide a living; it didn't pay the rent. The railroads, eastern financiers and their banks, big government and politicians— these were the enemies. The would-be farmers, the homesteaders, hit by falling prices and harassed by their creditors, were thoroughly unsympathetic to "big money." In the famous words of a settler wife, it was time to "raise a lot less corn and a lot more hell." It was Populism in the west, Trade Unionism in the east.

The barons of the northern plains, some of them being those English, Scots and Irish m'luds who had managed to hang on through the problems of a few years before, were well aware of the undercurrents. Around the billiard tables and in the smoking room of the Cheyenne Club, the talk was of getting convictions and meaningful penalties against rustlers, of falling cattle prices and the need to cut cowboys' wages. And among some, there was undoubtedly quieter and more sinister talk: buying judges, arranging evidence, and even secret assassinations.

So during the late '80s, battle lines were forming. On the one side were the ranchers of the powerful Wyoming Stock Growers Association, in informal session most evenings in the Cheyenne Club. On the other side was a shifting alliance drawn, at different times, from almost everyone else in the state.

As good a time as any to pick up the narrative is late on the afternoon of October 30, 1891. The place: the town of Buffalo in northeast Wyoming. Then, as now, it was the unofficial "capital" of the Powder River country. Main Street would have been crowded with buckboards and saddle horses tethered to the hitching rails. By early evening the saloons would have been emptying; people were going to a meeting.

First arrivals would have taken all the seats, so others stood around the walls; at the doorway latecomers peered over the shoulders of those in front, straining to catch the run of the proceedings. There are no written records (perhaps deliberately) of who said what. But we can be almost certain that there were angry words, appeals to solidarity, and warnings of the intimidations that would undoubtedly be coming their way. Cheyenne, 250 miles away to the south, was decried as the source of all their problems. By the end of the evening, on a show of hands and loud vocal approval, a number of decisions had been made. None was more important (or more provocative to the cattle barons) than the title that the meeting chose for itself: the Northern Wyoming Farmers and Stock Growers Association. The small ranchers and farmers of the Powder River country reckoned that things would be a little different from now on. For a start, they would now be running their own spring roundups, away from the heavy-handed bullying of the official Cheyenne-based Association. With that decided, everyone shuffled out of the hall and, after the usual sidewalk postmortems, they went back to the saloons or rode home.

Two days later, very early on a frosty morning, the man who, at that Buffalo meeting, had been suggested as the "captain" of the first roundup of the new Association was awakened by a gunshot. It missed. Nate Champion was half out of his bed when from just outside the now-open door a voice called out, "Give up. We've got you this time." The isolated one-room cabin (50 miles south of Buffalo) was very small and its interior would have been much darker than outside. Perhaps, for that reason, the attacker could not see properly and his aim—when he heard Champion moving for his own gun—was poor. The man fired twice in quick succession—and missed again. Champion, whose eyes were accustomed to the gloom, fired and hit the man in the stomach. He and his three companions just beyond the doorway turned and fled. Champion had identified one of the would-be assassins.

It has to be said that Champion was certainly not the embodiment of all Western virtues. On the contrary, he was a self-opinionated Texan. He had come north a few years before to work as a cowboy on one of the big spreads. But at some point he had broken one of the most sacred tenets of the big ranchers' Association by deciding to graze a few cattle of his own. The Association's rule was rigid: no cowboy could possess so much as a calf, because to permit him to do so would be to encourage him to "divert" some of his employer's cattle and then, later, to sell them as his own. Any suspected cowboy was immediately sacked, and from then on he was barred from employment by all the Association members. Anyone thus blackballed could no longer find work as a cowboy—maybe the only trade he knew. So, unless he left the state to find work on the railroads or to drive a freight-wagon, he almost had to become a small-scale rustler. The country of the Powder River, with Buffalo as its center, had more than its share of such men. Owning a few calves (or maybe more than just a few) had become socially acceptable. The region was regarded, by the people who mattered down in Cheyenne, as a breeding ground of petty thieves; plus a few who were not so petty.

So the Association had Champion firmly in its sights; they would make an example of him. No one was ever charged with his attempted murder, even though Champion knew two of his assailants, and one of the others would have needed treatment for that stomach wound. (In fact he died some weeks later, 1,000 miles away in Missouri.) One of the men recognized by Champion was Frank Canton, a so-called "range detective" in the pay of the official Association.

It had happened before. One did not have to be a cattle thief to incur the enmity of the Association. It was enough that you knew your rights and, thereby, that you were a troublemaker. In central Wyoming, 100 miles or more southwest of Powder River country, a couple of years earlier, a posse had kidnapped a man and his common-law wife. They made such an untidy mess of the hangings (the "drop" was allegedly a mere two feet) that the couple slowly strangled on the ropes. The slowly twisting bodies were left as an example. The man, James Averell, had been making life awkward for the Wyoming barons by writing letters to his local newspaper, the *Casper Weekly Mail*, pointing out the illegality of some of their land claims.

Of the barons, he wrote, "They are opposed to anything that would settle and improve the country or make it anything but a cow pasture for Eastern speculators … They advance the idea that a poor man has nothing to say in the affairs of his country … Is it not enough to excite one's prejudice to see the Sweetwater [River] owned, or claimed, for a distance of seventy-five miles from its mouth by just three or four men?" Obviously, he had to be silenced. The woman, Kate Watson, had some calves in her corral; the assassins claimed that the calves were payment by some local cowboys for the lady's favors. No evidence was ever produced to substantiate the allegation. But that did not stop the *Cheyenne Daily Leader*, a newspaper very much in the pocket of the big cattle interests, from referring to Kate Watson as "a brushwood tart of no consequence." Again, the identity of the murderers was an open secret, but no one was ever charged—a fact that would seem to demonstrate the grip that the barons had on Wyoming's judicial processes. Interestingly, even today, one can still start an argument (well, an intriguing discussion) in some parts of the state by suggesting that there is little evidence to think that Averell and Watson had come by their cattle illegally.

By the early 1890s no one in Wyoming was in any doubt about the power of the Association. Yet its ruthless bullying was also its weakness. Once away from its power base in Cheyenne, it was so disliked that it could very seldom get a conviction. Juries, having some sympathy for even the most obvious rogues, would arrive at "not guilty" verdicts. So the barons decided that the time had come to take the law into their own hands. The Powder River country was the region that caused them most pain; the draws and broken hills that had given cover to Sioux war parties only 15 years earlier now gave it to the rustlers. "God's teeth, those people up there in Buffalo have even gotten themselves together and formed their own Association. Damned subversion! It must be stopped–otherwise everyone will be at it." That observation, or something close to it, must have been heard more than once in the dining room of the Cheyenne Club.

Within a few weeks, not only had Nate Champion been attacked, but two other men were murdered as they drove their wagons home from Buffalo shopping trips. The first was Orley Jones, a young cowboy who ran some cattle on a small homestead he had started in the canyon country some 60 miles south of Buffalo. By all accounts, he was an "uppity" fellow, though whether he was a rustler would have depended on whose side you were on. Anyway, Orley Jones' body was found a little way off the wagon track about halfway home. No one knew who the assassin was, but there were some well-informed guesses.

Next was John Tisdale. In Buffalo to buy stores, he was overheard voicing his own well-informed suppositions about the assassin. He too was a Texan who, with some savings, had set up a small ranch a year or two earlier in the same neighborhood as Orley Jones and Nate Champion. He was a well-educated and settled family man; it seems unlikely that he was a rustler—though, like many people in those parts, he probably did not ask questions of those he knew who were. With his wagon loaded, Tisdale set off for home. It would not have been difficult for someone to watch his departure and plan accordingly. He was shot some miles south of town at a place where the track dipped down to cross a small draw called Haywood's Gulch. One can still see the likely spot. Evidently, with the job done, the murderer led the loaded wagon a little way up the gulch and then shot the two horses. The whole business would have taken only a few minutes. Easy. But one thing would have worried the hit man: he knew that he had been seen.

Charlie Basch's subsequent "evidence" was to be muddled, contradictory and, in parts, hardly credible. Obviously, he knew what was good for him. His story was that he had been riding towards Buffalo when, coming over the southern rim of the gulch, he saw a man leading a loaded wagon away from the track. No, he did not recognize the man and, no, he did not realize that a shooting had just occurred. Did he not think to ride over and see what was going on? Well no, if the man had wanted help, would he not have called out? What about the sounds of the shots that would have killed Tisdale, and then those two horses? Shots? What shots?

The fact was that Charlie Basch thought it prudent to wait 44 years—until he heard that the man he had seen that morning had died. In 1935, a very old Charlie

Basch named the murderer as Frank Canton, the same Association "detective" who had been identified by Nate Champion. But back in 1891 the gossip in Buffalo was strong enough that Canton felt forced to demand a court hearing to clear himself. He obviously calculated that he had a solid alibi. He called several corroborating witnesses: the owner of the hardware store, the man who ran the drug store, the steward of the local cattlemen's club (Buffalo had its own scaled-down version of the Cheyenne Club), and the local doctor. Yes, all these people had seen Frank Canton in Buffalo that morning. But strangely, the question of whether he had been in town throughout the morning was never asked. After all, the murder had taken place less than eight miles south of Buffalo. Canton could have ridden that distance in 20 minutes. So he could have left Buffalo as late as 9:30, attended to his business at the gulch—taking, say, a cool 15 minutes to shoot Tisdale and the two horses—and still be back in Buffalo in not much more than a further 20 minutes—an hour, say, in all. Yes, it would have taken a good horse and an iron nerve, but no one has ever doubted that Canton had both. On arrival back in town, Canton presumably made sure that he was seen by one or more of his alibi witnesses. There was no jury. The judge, a known ally of the barons, dismissed the case. There must have been a good deal of muttering as folk left the court.

An obvious question arises: why did no one see Frank Canton riding back into town that morning with a horse which would have looked, at the least, stretched and sweaty? Perhaps, like Charlie Basch, they were too fearful to come forward. In his memoirs, *Frontier Trails*, written 40 year later, Frank Canton covers these various events in a few simple sentences. Why should he do otherwise? After all, as everyone knows, he had nothing to do with the killings:

"In 1891, two rustlers, John Tisdale and Orley Jones, were shot and killed by unknown parties some fifteen miles south of Buffalo. It was whispered among the rustlers and their friends that I was the man who killed them both ... I surrendered to the sheriff, had a trial, and I proved by a large number of the best citizens of the county that I was in Buffalo every hour of the day on which Tisdale was killed. In the Jones case the evidence was exactly the same. The case was dismissed, but the rustlers were not satisfied ... They wanted some excuse for getting me out of the way, and I knew that they intended to do it the first time they got the drop on me."

That "fifteen miles" is revealing; by almost doubling the real distance—and I checked the mileage myself—Canton slyly reinforces his alibi; he is really saying that he could not have ridden 30 miles in the one hour that his witnesses could not vouch for.

Back in 1891 in Buffalo, folk were angry. Anyway, a week after that court hearing, someone persuaded another (more sympathetic?) judge to issue a warrant for Canton's formal arrest. Evidently, under Wyoming law, as the first hearing had been at Canton's own request, the restriction of "double jeopardy" did not apply. But when the deputies knocked on Canton's door to serve a warrant, there was no reply. He had left town only an hour or so before.

In his memoirs, Canton's account of why he left Buffalo is innocence itself: he had decided that it was time to spend some time with his wife's family, nearly 1,000 miles away, back east in Illinois. A week or two later, the sheriff in Buffalo applied for an extradition order to have Canton brought back from Illinois. Constitutionally, the application had to be routed through Wyoming's governor in Cheyenne. He dismissed it.

So far, the Association, the Cheyenne Ring, the Wyoming Old Guard, the Barons (at different times all these labels were applied) had managed to contain things, but only just. Now they were worried. Those folk up around Buffalo were getting out of hand; they were altogether too uppity. Something had to be done … And those gentlemen had a point. They were being robbed to ruination. As they saw it, half the population of Wyoming was at it. They never understood that, by denying any cowboy the right to keep some cattle of his own, by preventing anyone who was not a member of their Association from taking part in the annual roundups, by the blinkered pursuit of their own interests, they were losing (had already lost?) any chance of support from many of Wyoming's population.

Nevertheless, whatever the Association said, not everyone up on the Powder River was a rustler. Some were honest men who never stole anything. Others were small-scale ranchers who, maybe, did a little rustling on the side. Others were small-scale rustlers, who, maybe, did a little ranching on the side. And a handful, the professionals, were full-time thieves who did nothing on the side. So, apart from a man's inherent honesty or the fear of being bushwhacked, there was not too much point in going straight: the barons were likely to say that you were a rustler anyway: look at what had happened to James Averell, Kate Watson, Nate Champion, Orley Jones, and John Tisdale.

In Buffalo, the recently formed Northern Wyoming Stock Growers Association held further open-to-all meetings. At one such gathering it was decided to ignore Cheyenne's "official" spring roundup; they would organize their own a week or two ahead of the big ranchers. The big ranchers, furious at this blasphemy, quickly formed a "war committee," with a fighting fund of $50,000. Both sides, through the newspapers, fired off propaganda salvos. Cheyenne editors wrote about "murderous rustlers going armed to the teeth"; the Buffalo paper declaimed against "paid lickspittles who … have been writing lies about thieves in this locality."

Printed insults were one thing, armed invasion was something else. A Major Walcott was put in charge; he proposed that as soon as the winter snows had melted and cross-country travel became possible, a small army should be dispatched to settle this insufferable Johnson County business once and for all. But, for the time being, because those Buffalo people had their damn spies everywhere, such plans would have to remain very secret.

John Clay, an Englishman, the Association's president and one of the leading cattle barons in the northern part of the state, was as keen as anyone to clean up his domain. All the same, he was leery of getting himself too directly involved. Years later, he wrote about a discussion he had with Major Walcott: "The gallant Major said there was an urgent necessity for a lynching bee, especially in the northern part of the state, and he had developed a plan. At that time, like many other cowmen, I was quite willing to draw a rope on a cattle thief if necessary. Yet his scheme was so bold and open that I told him that, as far as I was concerned, to count me out. I went away to Europe on a long holiday."

So, the gallant Englishman hurried away, leaving the equally gallant Major to get on with organizing his lynching bee. There was one obvious problem: who could be recruited to do the dirty work in the proposed invasion? After all, it would not do, as John Clay had already indicated, for the barons to take to the field themselves. And there would be a marked shortage of volunteers in Wyoming among the cowboys and other lower orders. Also, to beat the recruiting drum around the state would be to give the game away. Problem.

The answer lay 700 miles away in Texas. Agents were sent south to the dusty cow-towns along the Red River. There they recruited a contingent of 22 hired guns. These mercenaries were told that they were needed to put down a gang of dangerous outlaws. Their contracts specified $5 a day and a bonus of $50 for every outlaw captured or killed. They were not to talk to anyone about where they were going, but were told to make their way to Denver, where they were to wait quietly until horses had been collected, wagons found, and munitions purchased. Then there was a train to be arranged; the Powder River country is over 200 miles north of Cheyenne, so if Major Walcott and his mercenary crew could cover part of that distance quickly by train, it would add to the element of surprise.

There was also the awkward matter of Article 19 on the State Constitution. One imagines that the law books came down from their shelves on that one. The Article is specific: "No armed police or detective agency or armed body or unarmed body of men shall ever be brought into this state for the suppression of domestic violence except upon the application of the executive [the Governor] when the legislature itself cannot be convened." Incidentally, four of the cattle barons had been members of the committee which had drafted the very

Constitution they were now about to ignore.

Governor Barber would have known full well what was going on, but a waiver of Article 19 could not be authorized in secret; it would need his formal and open signature. Furthermore, the reasons would have to be recorded. Given that surprise was essential, this posed a real problem. In the end, it seems that everybody in the know connived to look the other way.

The rank-and-file of the expeditionary force were the Texans, now waiting in Denver. Their "officers" were a collection of ranch foremen and range detectives. Frank Canton (back from his in-laws in Illinois) was among them. In command was Major Walcott, manager for a Scottish ranch company, and nearly 30 years earlier a respected officer in the Union Army.

That winter, the final task of the self-appointed Star Chamber in the Cheyenne Club was to draw up a "wanted list" of all the people considered to be the enemy. Many years later a member of the organizing committee said that "when the list was finally completed ... the number stood at an even seventy. It was decided that these must be exterminated by shooting or hanging." The list included Sheriff Angus of Buffalo and three of Johnson County's elected commissioners (councilors). A wide range of small ranchers, a local journalist, and several storekeepers were also set down for "severe treatment." In later years, it became an honor among Wyoming folk to have been on that roll-call. But at the time, the cold nerve of those respectable gentlemen sitting around a table sifting through their death list took some beating. Interestingly, a young cowboy known as Butch Cassidy was also on that list.

In Cheyenne, even at night, a six-carriage train with more than 50 people aboard, plus horses and wagons, comprised far too much of a circus to keep secret. As well as the mercenaries and their "officers," there were wagon drivers, a surgeon, and a two-man press corps: one from the *Cheyenne Sun* and the other, a brash young go-getter from the *Chicago Herald*. Despite a cover story that the expedition was a survey party for a new railroad "somewhere up north," by the time the "special" steamed out of Cheyenne, anyone hanging about the Union Pacific depot would have easily guessed what was going on. Indeed, someone hurried round to the telegraph office to send a coded warning to Buffalo. It never arrived. Presumably, someone had cut the wires.

A little before dawn the engine sighed to a stop on a desolate siding where it was reckoned there were no inquisitive eyes. The train had come 120 miles. It was cold. The wagons were manhandled off the flatcars and loaded with stores. When all was done, Major Walcott ordered the crusade to saddle up and move off. By daylight they were clear of the railroad and hidden in the sagebrush eating breakfast.

If its purpose had not been so cold-blooded, there was more than a touch of the comic about the operation. Before breakfast was over, several horses had broken loose, never to be recovered. There was trouble fitting the untested wagon harness, and the gentlemen who were running the show were thoroughly muddied up with the gummy clay of those parts. As they set off, one of the journalists found that his piles were playing up so badly that he could not ride his horse; he transferred to a wagon. Doubtless, the Texans, as is still the habit with folk from those parts, were not saying much but thinking plenty. But still, at $5 a day ...

It began to snow and, by the afternoon, their northward progress had slowed right down. Instead of reaching a remote and friendly ranch, they had to spend the night in the open. They were so exhausted that when they did reach the ranch house the next day they decided to rest up for 24 hours. Presently an advance man (he who had cut the telegraph wire?) rode in to tell them that two of the men on their death list were living at a one-roomed ranch house just a few hours' ride to the north. Major Walcott decided on a dawn attack. Two or three of the other "officers," led by Frank Canton, pointed out that the delay would cost them the advantage of a surprise arrival at Buffalo, the target that really mattered. The major huffed and puffed and tendered his resignation. For the sake of unity, the dissenters withdrew their objections.

One of the "wanted" men in that cabin was the same Nate Champion who had so effectively defended himself against attack in that same cabin only a few months before; the other was a petty rustler called Nick Ray. There were a couple of other men staying the night as well: out-of-work cowboys who were doing some trapping to eke out a living through the winter. They all slept late that morning, oblivious to the 50 armed men who now lay in cover just 100 yards away.

The major guessed, from the wagons parked outside, that there must be other men inside besides Champion and Ray. To give him credit, he held back from a direct assault—rushing the doors and shooting the men in their bunks—because he did not want to kill anyone who was not on the list. This regard for the niceties of what they were doing was to hold them up for several hours. It was time they could ill afford. Eventually, one of the cowboy-trappers came out to get some water from the nearby stream. They waited till he was out of sight from the house and then quietly jumped him. Presently, the other trapper came out, presumably to see what had happened to his friend. They jumped him too.

A few minutes later a figure recognized as Nick Ray appeared in the doorway; he looked around and began walking toward the stable. He was on the death list. The gunmen waited until at least six of them had a clear shot. The impact of the fusillade, at such short range, would have been colossal—enough to hurl him back several yards, almost to the doorway. He was more dead than alive. Incredibly, Champion, firing with one hand, managed to drag Ray inside with his other hand.

They shouted at Champion to surrender; he replied with shots. Over the next couple of hours they poured shot after shot into the cabin, some say as many as 200. But the walls were too thick. Champion, by changing his position too frequently for the attackers to bring their rifles to bear accurately on the chinks in the wall, kept up a remarkable return fire. For the major it was most frustrating. Eventually, some men were sent off to get some hay from a nearby barn. They would burn Champion out.

During this lull, a man and a boy were distantly seen coming down a track. A posse immediately rode out to capture them: it was vital that the secret of the invasion did not get out. But the two "intruders" had guessed what was happening; they immediately turned and made their escape. It was as well that they did because Jack Flagg (there with his son) was on that death list. One doubts if Paul Revere would have had anything on the speed of their dash to spread news of what they had seen.

Major Walcott now knew that the secret was out. They would have to move much faster. But they had to fix Champion first. They loaded a buggy with hay and a few dry bits of timber. Then, while the best shots among the Texans gave covering fire, the hay was lit and the whole contraption was given a hefty push down a slight slope toward the cabin. The timbers of the cabin took several minutes to catch. Champion now had three choices: he could surrender and end up on the end of a rope, he could be roasted alive, or he could make a dash for it. He waited for a few minutes and then ran nearly 50 yards through the smoke before they got him. It took four shots. They turned him onto his back and someone pinned a note onto his bloody chest: "Cattle Thieves Beware."

There was one small problem: what to do with those two trappers. If released, they might warn people to the north—but that had already happened when Flagg and his son had got away earlier. So, in the end, the major let the trappers go, telling them to ride south and to keep their mouths shut.

In mid-afternoon, the invaders saddled up and moved on. They had to make up lost time, so they rode through the evening and then on into the night. Eventually, sometime in the early hours, they pulled into a remote ranch house, the TA. Here, in quarters provided by an absentee Association member, they reckoned that they could spend a few hours resting before moving on the final 13 miles to "take" Buffalo. The confident and arrogant seldom see much need for haste. But Frank Canton, who undoubtedly had a more realistic appreciation of what Buffalo had in store now that it had almost certainly been warned, would have been frantic with these delays.

Canton's concern was justified. In Buffalo, the rumor was that a murdering gang of at least 100 Cheyenne thugs, with hang-ropes looped over their saddles, was on its way to sack the town, seize all property, and exterminate the leading citizens. In some desperation, Sheriff Angus appealed to the commandant of the nearby US Cavalry base at Fort McKinney. But the colonel said that he could not help in what was obviously a civilian matter without specific orders from much higher up the military ladder.

It was becoming very obvious to the people of Buffalo and Johnson County that they could rely on no one but themselves. Accordingly, Sheriff Angus assembled and then led a large posse out on a sweeping reconnaissance to the south. Within a few hours, drawn on by the smoke from the still-smoldering KC cabin; they found Nate Champion's body and the note on his bloody chest. On their way back to Buffalo they spied what they had been looking for: an unusual amount of activity around the TA ranch house. By the time they got home late that night they had ridden nearly 100 miles. They and their horses were exhausted. Nevertheless, with fresh horses, they were off again well before dawn. But this time the posse had grown to a small cowboy army. It set out for the TA ranch.

As the early light of the morning crisped the surrounding hilltops on that cold April day, the gentlemen from Cheyenne pulled themselves slowly from the snugness of their blankets. Presently, Major Walcott was called to a window. He would have been dumbfounded by what he saw. Skylined, but just beyond rifle range, more than 100 horsemen were silently watching. Through his binoculars he could see that they were all armed; some were dismounted and lying half-hidden on the snowy ground.

Frank Canton was called. Through those binoculars he identified a number of men who were on "the list." He and his companions were surrounded by a siege-line that included many of the very men they had come to hang. Presently, bullets began to thump into the heavy timbers of the ranch house and the nearby barn.

Major Walcott and his "invaders" were luckier than they deserved: the ranch and its cluster of outhouses were built of heavy pine logs. (In the more than 120 years since, nothing much has changed, not even the loopholes cut by those Texan mercenaries.) Provided that no one showed himself unnecessarily, they knew that they could hold off their enemies as long as the food, water, and ammunition lasted. Each man had about 100 rounds, but food was going to be a problem because two of their supply wagons had fallen behind the previous evening and were still somewhere out in the sagebrush. The major and his lieutenants must have decided that when news of their predicament leaked out to their supporters back in Cheyenne, a relief column would be organized. But rescue would take several days. Meanwhile they had best reinforce the ranch with any spare timber that was lying around and then hang on as best they could. One wonders what the Texans made of the whole business. After all, $5 a day was all very well, but ...

In fact, Sheriff Angus and his cowboy army had found those supply wagons some way short of the ranch; under their tarpaulins were food, suitcases of personal baggage, ammunition, and two boxes of dynamite. There must have been some rough humor about the use to which the dynamite might now be put.

By that afternoon, there were nearly 200 men surrounding the ranch. Starting as soon as it was dark, they began to move in closer and dig shallow trenches. Those besieged in the ranch also used the night to strengthen their defenses. The siege was going to be a drawn-out business.

Starting the next morning, rifle fire was directed at the horse corral to deny the invaders any means of escape; their horses were picked off one by one. At the same time, one or two particularly good shots were employed as snipers against the ranch house. Consequently, when one of the "officers" (and a baron in his own right), Bill Irvine, was sitting by a window at the back of the ranch house (where he thought he was safe), he took a direct hit on his big toe, from a range of nearly 400 yards. Elsewhere, well back from the siege-line, men were at work on two of those captured wagons. Roped together, and with a shield of heavy logs hanging on the front and sides, they were converted into a bulletproof fort on wheels. A dozen men, crouching behind the logs, intended to push the whole contraption until they got close enough to throw grenades made with the dynamite found in the wagons the day before. Someone had the notion of wrapping oily sacking around some of the grenades and so turning them into incendiaries.

Meanwhile, far away in Cheyenne, there had been no news from the north for nearly a week. True, the Governor and his friends in the Association had not expected to hear anything for the first few days, but by now they must have been getting uneasy. Had something gone wrong? If so, what? After all, Major Walcott should have reached Buffalo several days ago; he would immediately have ordered the telegraph line to be repaired and then sent some message of his success. The Cheyenne establishment was worried. Maybe they should send someone north to find out what was going on.

By Tuesday evening the rolling fort was complete, for use at first light the next day. Now there were at least 400 men camped in the hills around the TA ranch. Some time on that same evening, a telegram arrived in Cheyenne. It did not come from Buffalo but from Gillette, a small town 70 miles to the east. Who sent it, to whom and what it said is a mystery. But we know exactly what action Governor Barber took when he read it. Within an hour, a flurry of priority telegrams was on its way to the divisional army commander in Omaha, to Wyoming's two senators in Washington and, highest priority of all, to the President:

"An insurrection exists in Johnson County in the State of Wyoming against the government of said state ... Open hostilities exist and large bodies of men are engaged in battle ... United States troops are stationed at Fort McKinney which is about thirteen miles from the scene of the action which is known as the TA Ranch. I apply to you on behalf of the State of Wyoming to direct the US troops to assist in suppressing this insurrection. Lives of a large number of persons are in imminent danger. Amos W. Barber, Governor, Cheyenne."

It was the least the Governor could do for his friends. But Washington's clocks were two hours ahead of those in Cheyenne and by the time the telegram reached the White House, the President had gone to bed. No one was willing to wake him up with a panicky request for help from some politician somewhere out on the god-forsaken prairies more than half a continent away.

When no presidential authorization had come through by midnight, a sleepless Governor Barber telegraphed the Wyoming Senators again. Maybe they had been out that evening, so had not received his first message until they got home. Anyway, as soon as they learned what was happening they hurried round to the White House. They got the President out of bed and persuaded him of his responsibilities. So, sometime before dawn, the silence of the sleeping orderly room at Fort McKinney (outside Buffalo) was broken by the sudden clattering of the telegraph; the line had been restored just a few hours before. Colonel Van Horn was immediately called from his quarters. He read his instructions; he was to cooperate with the state government in "suppressing the rustler disorders." He gave instructions for three troops of his cavalry to muster for departure within 20 minutes.

Meanwhile, back at the ranch (sic!), as the sky lightened, the "invaders" could see and then hear that fortress wagon creaking forward. Obviously, the rustler army was going to try to set fire to the place, just as they themselves had done only two days before at the KC cabin. All they could do was to wait until the wagon was really close and then hit it with such a weight of rifle fire that, somehow, they might halt the thing. But that plan could use most of their remaining ammunition. What then?

Of course, anyone who has seen a few Westerns will already know the answer to that question. If one were writing the screenplay it might run as follows:

"The scene begins with a slow montage of drawn and unshaven/bearded faces; we begin to realize they are peering through rifle slits. We cannot see what they can see, but we begin to *hear* what they can see: a distant creaking and the faint sound of men straining and exhorting each other while pushing something very heavy. The camera just watches the apprehension on those faces. Then it cuts to a high (crane) shot of the ranch house and its neighboring barn; it pans across a corral of dead horses; it continues panning, to pick up an armored wagon being pushed forward foot by foot. Then, if the location geography allows, the camera slowly zooms onto a distant skyline. Like ants, a line of cavalry emerges, pennants flying. Then, with a cut to a mid-shot of the horses and troopers, the soundtrack bursts in to a rousing cavalry air. Intercut hooves and relieved, even smiling faces. Roll credits."

Well, something like that anyway.

In real life it was not quite so straightforward. It seldom is. As soon as the besiegers heard that the cavalry was on its way—the word would have traveled ahead—they began a continuous and rapid fire into the ranch house and the barn. It was an individual and collective act of frustration, to inflict as much damage as possible in the short time remaining. But once the cavalry had actually arrived and halted, Sheriff Angus gave the order to stop firing. It would have taken some minutes before the shooting raggedly died away, leaving only the smell of black powder and a smoky haze drifting off in the wind.

The Sheriff was surprised to be told by the cavalry colonel that his orders had originated all the way from Washington, maybe from the President himself. The sheriff agreed to lift the siege and to allow the military to take the surrender of the invaders, provided that they were all taken into the Army's custody pending their eventual transfer to Wyoming's civil authorities for trial. Then the colonel and a small party, including the sheriff, rode down to the ranch house. Major Walcott emerged; in a thoroughly bad temper, he objected to the presence of the sheriff and made it very clear that he was not surrendering; at most, he was agreeing to give himself and his crew into the protection of the US Army, of which he himself was a retired officer. He demanded safe passage back to Cheyenne as soon as possible. While the details were being worked out, the cowboys on the hills moved forward. They were very angry, but somehow a loose discipline held and no one made a move against "the enemy" who now came out from the ranch house and the barn to give up their weapons to the soldiers. Wagons were brought forward and the invaders, some defiant, some dejected, climbed aboard. One can be almost certain that there would have been, at the very least, some shouted insults from the watching and still-indignant crowd: "murderers, assassins, bastards!"

By ten o'clock, as 400 armed men looked on, the Army wagons were moving off. In two and a half days, despite the thousands of rounds that had been fired, the only casualties were Mr. Irvine's toe and two of the Texans who had both accidentally shot themselves in the foot. The affair at the TA ranch was over. But that is not quite the end of the story.

❧

In 1984 I was making a documentary about the settlement of the high plains. The TA Ranch was still there and, with permission from the owners, we filmed the barn where the Texans had holed up and, more specifically, we focused on the rifle slots which they had hurriedly made in the log walls. After 92 years, except for a car and a pickup truck outside the main ranch house, and the fact that there were more trees, I doubt that very much had changed.

In 2007, 23 years later, I was staying with some friends in Buffalo. We phoned to see if I could revisit the TA Ranch again. It had changed hands, but the new owners, Mr. and Mrs. Madsen, were most welcoming. Surprisingly, they knew something about me because, some years before, they had gotten ahold of a copy of that film. Indeed, they sometimes ran it for their guests. They fed me and asked me to stay the night. They put me in the very room where Billy Irvine had his toe shot off by that distant sniper. I may say that, before getting into bed, it was something more than mere superstition that prompted me to draw the curtain across that window.

❧

"No event in the history of the history of the West has been more flagrantly misrepresented, sometimes with great skill ... by writers ignorant of the ways of the old West."
A comment in *Guardians of the Grassland*, an official history of the Wyoming Stock Growers Association, published by the WSGA in 1971.

The Cheyenne Club is long gone. But the Wyoming Stock Growers Association still exists. Indeed it flourishes, for, as any Wyoming car license plate will tell

you, this is the Cowboy State. In short, beef is still very much "the business."
Today, if one calls at the Association's offices as I did—admittedly over 20
years ago—one will meet a thoroughly welcoming, cooperative, and friendly
bunch. But while they see no need to apologize for the dubious activities of
some of their forebears—after all, it happened a long time ago—one senses
that there is still just a touch of embarrassment about those far-off events.
Maybe it is a case of "least said, long-time mended." Anyway, in an official
history of several thousand words, the Association advances a brief and neatly
neutral rationale of the Powder River "invasion." After mention of various
other early "invasions" into Wyoming, such as that of tick fever, Splenic fever
and sheep (true cattlemen don't much appreciate "woolies"), it comes to the
point:
"Then there was another invasion – the invasion of Johnson County in 1892
which was not unrelated to some of the 'invasions' heretofore mentioned.
Rustling was only the immediate cause of it. It was the tangible cause that
the cattleman could see, and he fought against it. The transition had to be
made from the open-range system to that of managing smaller herds of cattle
on privately owned hay ranches and pastures, but nowhere was the transition
fought so bitterly as in Wyoming. Johnson County was practically bankrupt
after the invasion; cattlemen who took part suffered heavily—their cattle
weren't safe on the ranges. And the Wyoming Stock Growers Association
suffered too."
Fair enough. But it might be even fairer if, instead of just saying that Johnson
County found itself "practically bankrupt after the invasion," it explained
that the County ran its treasury dry in its efforts to bring Major Walcott and
his crew to justice. The fact is that the barons employed every imaginable
legal and quasi-legal maneuver to prevent the whole murky affair from being
dragged into the daylight. The process of obfuscation began as soon as Major
Walcott climbed into one of those cavalry wagons at the TA Ranch.

℃

Long before the wagons were back at Fort McKinney, the major was already
letting the colonel know just what he expected of him. One can conclude that

the major and his lieutenants were in a hurry to get back to the state capital as quickly as possible in order to start generating a smokescreen over any attempt by Sheriff Angus to expose their conduct as being in blatant breach of Wyoming's constitution, to say nothing of their personal involvement in two murders. The major might also have been worried about those two trapper-cowboys he had "released" back at Nate Champion's cabin. Were they even then telling what they knew?

Well, yes, they were. Within a few days of their "release" they were in the town of Casper where, once they heard what had happened to their recent captors, they got drunk and talked to anyone who would listen. They became local celebrities, and got drunk some more.

The dangerous news of these two gossips was reported in Cheyenne at about the same time that Major Walcott and his 44 comrades-in-arms arrived back from Buffalo. Together with their army escort, they had had a rough journey, beginning with a five-day wagon ride through freezing temperatures and blizzards to the nearest railroad at the small town of Douglas. There, a crowd had gathered to shout and jeer. But, still with their cavalry escort, they had boarded a train and a day later pulled into Cheyenne. Now they were confined in some comfort at the local army base, Fort Warren, but not so confined that they could not first pose for a group photograph. Meanwhile, their cronies worked on the problem of the charges that the folk up in Buffalo insisted on bringing against them. The major seems to have been much less concerned with his legal predicament than with revenge for the humiliation he had suffered. Apparently, even on the train he had been boasting that Johnson County would be punished within weeks. "The bloodshed is not yet begun," was his reported comment. He had a plan.

But first there was the need to silence those boozy blabbermouths up in Casper. Maybe a dose of lead poisoning in some bar brawl would be sufficient? But might that be too blatant for anyone to accept as a credible coincidence? Instead, the two men must be removed as far as possible from Wyoming. To this end, emissaries were sent to Casper to explain to the two cowboys where their best interests lay. They were told to sober up, shut up, and mount up—for a ride eastward to Nebraska. They were accompanied by a pistol-toting posse. On their arrival at the Nebraska line, a local Sheriff (a friend of Buffalo's Sheriff Angus), who had been tipped off by telegraph, arrested the two cowboys for theft: a charge he dreamed up to provide a pretext for holding them safe from their trigger-happy escort. The escort was arrested too, on principle. There followed a hectic few days while the telegraph lines ran hot with warrants, counter-warrants, charges, subpoenas, and every legal device that imaginative Western lawyers could dream up.

The invaders in Cheyenne awaiting the trial that never happened. Billy Irvine is fifth from the right. Major Walcott stands to his right (with white cravat), and Frank Canton is seated in front of the major (The Gatchell Memorial Museum, Buffalo)

The upshot of all these dodges was that the two cowboys were taken a little further east to appear before a judge who, advised by friends on the telegraph from Cheyenne, seems to have known his duty. He quickly turned the prisoners over to two Federal Marshals who had just arrived from Omaha with warrants for the two men on charges of having, at some quite unspecified time, sold liquor to some Indians. Being a federal offense, this required that the case be heard in a federal court. The nearest such court was in Omaha, 400 miles further east. Given that it would take time to assemble all the witnesses, the case would obviously take several months to come to court; meanwhile the prisoners would be held in custody and, thereby, unable to spill any damaging beans.

However, unexpectedly, the federal judge in Omaha saw through all these shenanigans; he released the two cowboys on bail of their own recognizance. The Association was most unhappy; Omaha was a mere 600 miles from Wyoming. Not far enough. So now Cheyenne played a trump card. It dispatched a lawyer to persuade the two cowboys that, at the end of just a few more days on a train, untold wealth could be theirs. The lawyer looked after them all the way to Rhode Island on the Atlantic seaboard, where they were each given a carefully post-dated check for $2,500, cashable only at a local bank. So, they would have to remain in Rhode Island in order to collect their money on the day the checks eventually became valid. Some say that the checks bounced. It seems probable.

While the railroading (and one uses the term literally) of those two cowboys had been a purely defensive measure, back in Cheyenne Major Walcott was mounting a major offensive. The plan required the involvement of the Federal Government. The local US Marshal was a man called Rankin who, in the past, seems to have been sympathetic to the problems of the cattle barons. Now the major quietly urged him to send some deputies north to Buffalo to serve warrants for conspiracy on all the rebels. The major knew that anger and resistance were certain, and so, with luck, a federal warrant server might get himself shot at or (with even more luck) killed. That would force a presidential declaration of martial law; the Army would have to be sent into northern Wyoming to enforce the declaration and to quell what would quickly become, with a little encouragement, an open rebellion. When the insurgents had been put down with federal firepower, the major and his crew could return to triumph over his former enemies, if any of them were left. Splendid.

But US Marshal Rankin had doubts. It seems that he was aware of the "disappearance" of those two cowboys. And he did not need second sight to see the bullying major's plan for what it really was: a calculated incitement to violence. He did not like it. He refused to cooperate. The major was furious. He and the Association tried a different tack. Once again the long-distance telegraph called for the help of Wyoming's two state senators in Washington. They were "instructed" to ask the president to authorize the US Department of Justice to suspend its uncooperative man in Cheyenne. But the US Attorney General, perhaps with a recent report from Marshal Rankin on his desk, was suspicious. He sent one of his inspectors out to Cheyenne to take a closer look at what was going on. A few days later, the Association, never an organization of much subtlety, met the inspector off the train and made the mistake of being over-persuasive with offers of assistance. The inspector would have none of it: he didn't need help; he was quite capable of making his own inquiries. He took only a few days to write a damning report about what was afoot, fully upholding US Marshal Rankin:

"I am forced to the conclusion that it was not so much the intention to have the men [of Johnson County] arrested as it was to have them driven out of the country or killed ... it appears that nearly everyone in authority was doing what the representatives of the cattle owners told them to do ..."

Now Major Walcott and his not-so-merry men were not only furious, they were impotent. And their trial was coming up. The authorities in Cheyenne were in deep embarrassment; if they ever allowed the affair to come to court, a whole load of very dirty state washing was going to get aired. So, with legal delays and subterfuge, with adjournments and attempts to change the venue, they did their best. But public opinion in the rest of the state would not let go.

On the other hand, things were not going well for Johnson County. The state's attorney general was charging the County $100 a day to guard, feed and hold the prisoners. And there were all kinds of legal expenses. In another few months the County would be bankrupt. Meanwhile, the taxpayers of northern Wyoming were not getting much for their money; the prisoners were prisoners in name only. True, the Texans were under guard: there were too many of them and they knew too much. But, on any evening, the "gentlemen in custody" could be seen in the downtown saloons or over at the Cheyenne Club. After some months of this near-farce, the local judge decided to let the whole crowd have bail on their own surety. The Texans promptly took the next train south. That was the last Wyoming ever saw of them.

When, in the spring of 1893, the trial was convened, there were 23 defendants. Large crowds turned up at the courthouse; they need not have bothered. More than 500 potential jurors were challenged by the defense or the prosecution. After nearly three weeks, it had not been possible to find the twelve "good men and true" with whom both sides were satisfied. The defense attorneys were particularly long-winded in rejecting anyone who did not fit with their definition of impartiality. This was the last card in the Association's hand. It was enough. Johnson County was now bankrupt with the cost of the never-ending delays. It had debts of $28,000. In the end, a weary attorney for Johnson County had to ask the judge to dismiss the case; his clients could afford no more. The judge complied, and no one was ever tried for the murder of Nate Champion and Nick Ray.

"There was no shout of victory," wrote John Clay, president of the Association and now returned from his timely absence in England. "No unseemly disturbances—a quiet dispersal of this gallant band who had been led into an ill-conceived scheme. There was a mild jollification at the club but it did not touch the bubbling enthusiasm of the old days." Elsewhere in his book, *My Life on the Range*, he described Major Walcott and his immediate crew as "a band of the best, bravest men who ever lived … intelligent beyond the average. This refers of course to the Wyoming men. I do not class the hired bad men from Texas who were with them." (There speaks a solidly class-conscious Englishman.)

No one had won. But, in the dying storm of the conflict, the distant thunder rolled on. There were at least two more murders up in Powder River country, and more cavalrymen were posted to northern Wyoming. Libel actions and injunctions kept the lawyers busy for years. And there is an intriguing postscript involving book-burning and intimidation.

A book with an overlong title, *The Banditti of the Plains, or the Cattlemen's Invasion of Wyoming in 1892—the Crowning Infamy of the Age*, was secretly printed in Denver in 1894. Today, its original edition is one of the rarest books in the US. Indeed, given the efforts of the Cheyenne establishment, it is a wonder that the book was ever published at all. Its author, a Wyoming newspaperman called Asa Mercer, was charged with printing obscenities and then held in prolonged custody. At the same time, the printing plates were smashed.

Curiously, until the Powder River invasion, Mercer had written supportively of the cattlemen's struggle. No one knows why he switched sides. Some have suggested that he sincerely recognized that his earlier stance had been wrong; others imply that he was simply a journalist with an eye for a good story. Does it really matter? Surely, more interesting (and revealing) are the extreme measures that some people felt were needed to destroy the book. As for Mercer's motives, it seems that—like most people who, late in the day, see the light—his conversion made him even more ardent for his newfound cause than the folk who had been there all the time.

Indignation fuels every paragraph. Nowhere does he admit to the merits of understatement. "Nothing," he writes, "so cold-blooded, so brutal and yet so cowardly was ever recoded in the annals of world history." But what matters is that, despite the invective and the undoubted distortions, the story of the cattlemen's invasion is all there. He names names, from the president down. He spares no one. Today, even with the generously loose libel laws of the United States, he would never get away with it. There were plenty of people in Wyoming who tried to stop him getting away with it in 1894. They came within a whisker of success. But enough copies of his book got out for it later (much later) to be reprinted. (See the Bibliography.) Though over-colored, it has become a useful starting point, or end point, for any account of what Mercer called the "Crowning Infamy of the Age."

As a simple narrative, the Johnson County War and its aftermath is as rich a story of rifle-toting conflict and legal trickery as ever came out of the West. But it had a deeper meaning than that. Rustling was what the members of the Association thought it was about. And of course in an immediate sense they were right. Other people thought that it was about the small man's rights and freedoms. They too were right. But, more deeply, given the perspectives of hindsight and history, it was really about the shift from a vast open-range pastoralism to a smaller scale of individual ranching, from free-grass feudalism to settled enclosure. In short, it was about the antagonisms generated by an inevitable process: the domestication of what, only a few years before, had been an almost limitless wilderness. But if, in 1892, you had suggested to Major Walcott that what he and his feudal cronies had been fighting was an aspect of what some, both then and since, have more grandly called "Manifest Destiny," the major would have regarded you with a very strange look indeed.

"Johnson County—We Haven't Trusted Cheyenne since 1892 ... "
A bumper sticker sometimes seen in Johnson County

The Che[yenne]

TWENTY-FIFTH YEAR.

CHEYENNE,

CAUGHT IN A TRAP

The Invading Stockmen Regularly Besieged in a Ranch House in Johnson County.

DRAWING THE COILS SLOWLY BUT SURELY ABOUT THE DEVOTED BAND

Hundreds of Men Flocking to the Scene and the Consequences May be Disastrous.

The Governor Asks the President for the Fort McKinney Troops—Three Rustlers Shot—One of the Invaders Dying at the Hospital.

Definite Details.

Special to the Leader.

DOUGLAS, Wyo., April 12.—Reliable news from the north was received here

McCullough, proprietor of the stage line, had started to Gillette but received word to return to Buffalo. A courier going in hot haste reached a small camp of rustlers

(Wyoming State Archives)

15

BUTCH CASSIDY AND ALL THAT

"If Butch Cassidy didn't come back—if he really was killed in that shoot-out in Bolivia—then what were all those Wyoming old-timers talking about? Damn it, they knew what he looked like! They'd known him before he went off to South America. They didn't get in a huddle to cook up a story—some of them didn't even know each other, yet they all said much the same thing: "Sure, it was Butch." Yes, he'd have been older, but in 20 or 30 years a fellow's looks don't change that much. Anyway, they'd have shared old jokes, old gossip. So, are we meant to believe that those old-timers were all just a bunch of conniving mischief-makers? Or were they just gullible old hayseeds, taken in by some imposter?"

A comment in an interview with Larry Pointer, long-time researcher and then writer of the book *In Search of Butch Cassidy*

❧

The story goes that, by 1933, Butch Cassidy was almost bankrupt; he had lost his livelihood and nearly all his savings in the recent financial crash. So, working under the name William Phillips, which he had used since returning from South America a quarter of a century earlier, he set about writing his autobiography—

in the third person. Eventually, a year later, he sent the manuscript off to Hollywood. He called the rather rambling narrative *The Bandit Invincible: the Story of Butch Cassidy.* He ended his tale with details of a shoot-out in South America from which he (in the third person) was the only survivor. Butch was obviously hoping that some movie-maker would buy the rights, and thus the income would go some way to clear his debts. So he must have been very disappointed, insulted even, when, only a few weeks later, his story was returned as being "too preposterous to be believable." He tried to sell his work elsewhere, to magazines and publishers. But no one was interested. Three years later, Butch died of cancer, penniless. The local Spokane newspaper carried a brief obituary for William Phillips, a one-time local businessman.

In fact, as the world knows, it was another 35 years before Hollywood bought into the many-stranded story of Butch Cassidy and, via Richard Goldman's marvelous screenplay and Burt Bacharach's music and lyrics ("Raindrops," amongst others), fashioned it into one of the most successful movies of all time. It made superstars of Robert Redford and Paul Newman. And everyone fell in love with Katherine Ross, who was cast as Sundance's girl, Etta Place.

It was consequent on the worldwide interest triggered by the film that a copy of *The Bandit Invincible* came to light. The manuscript, initially in the keeping of Mr. Phillips' adopted son, had lain forgotten for nearly 40 years until what one might call "perusal rights" were granted to a Spokane journalist, James Dullenty, and to the historian–author Larry Pointer.

The fact is that, before the film, Butch hardly had a place on the world's roll call of bandit heroes. Even within the US he ranked well below, say, Jesse James, Doc Holliday, Belle Starr, the Dalton Brothers, or Billy the Kid. Yet, within a year or two of the film's release, he had surely become the world's favorite outlaw. While the film certainly takes full advantage of dramatic license, many of its details are essentially true: Butch really was, by almost every account, a good-looking and very likeable rogue, a gentleman who seems to have behaved, except when deeply angry, with a quiet courtesy to almost everyone, even in a hold-up. Until that shoot-out, there seems to be no record that he ever killed anybody. And yes, he really did enjoy the company of children and they, in turn, seemed to adore him, and he really did catch the turn-of-the-century craze for cycling and, further, for doing acrobatics on his machine. Also, he really did play the harmonica, after a fashion. As for Sundance? We know less about him, but, according to most reports, he had the laconic and mordant wit that comes across so powerfully in the film. He was said to be a very mean hand with a shooter and, in terms of his temper, he could also be quick on the draw. He does seem to have really loved Etta; and Etta, neat and beautiful, really did look rather like

Katherine Ross (or should that be the other way around?). Together with other members of the so-called Wild Bunch, Butch and Sundance really did get away with holding up a succession of banks and with blasting their way into a series of railroad bullion cars. Also, there really was a relentless Pinkerton detective who, ploddingly, seemed to be getting ever closer. Plus the Union Pacific railroad, in some desperation, really did put together a posse that held itself in a state of almost permanent pursuit-readiness. So when, in the end, things just got too hot, the three of them really did take off for South America. But there is just one rather important aspect, perhaps the *most* important (certainly the most intriguing) aspect in which the film may have got things seriously wrong ...

More than 30 years ago, while making a documentary for the BBC, I interviewed a veteran Montana rancher called Boyd Charter. He told me that his father, as a very young man back in the late 1890s, had been one of Butch Cassidy's getaway men; he had held the horses while Butch and others went into banks to make what Mr. Charter told me were "some cash withdrawals." No less interesting was his account of how one summer in the early 1920s, when he was aged 17, he and his sister became friends with a man who had turned up unannounced at their father's Wyoming ranch; the stranger unloaded a tent from a T-Model Ford (with a small trailer) and then, for a week or two, made himself comfortable camping down by the river. Apparently, Boyd's father greeted the visitor warmly. It was obvious that they were old buddies, but they were both quite unforthcoming about the origin and history of their friendship. At the time, young Boyd learned only that the visitor's name was Bill Phillips. Even then, his father warned him and his sister not to talk about their visitor to the neighbors or when they went to town. Only much later did their father tell them something of his earlier acquaintance with their guest, whom he then revealed was a certain Mr. Cassidy.

I believed Boyd Charter—which means that if anybody was killed in some Bolivian shoot-out, then it can't have been Butch Cassidy. I believe he came back, and so do many others who have been much better informed than me. The fact is that less than a lifetime ago there were still living at least a dozen old men and women—ranchers, cowboys, lawmen, store keepers, garage mechanics, and others—who, like Boyd Charter's father, had known Butch when they were all young men in central Wyoming through the 1890s, and who two or three decades later still easily recognized and greeted (but, one imagines, with some surprise) the man they had known back in those earlier days. As author Larry Pointer's comment at the top of this chapter makes very clear, they could not all have been "just gullible old hayseeds" taken in by some clever imposter.

☙

Incidentally, on Larry Pointer's suggestion, we filmed that interview in an entirely appropriate location: the remote Hole-in-the-Wall valley of the Bighorn Mountains in central Wyoming; it was appropriate because that valley was one of several hideouts across the West used by Butch Cassidy and his crew when, after a bank raid, they wanted to lie low for a while. Yet, despite the legends, it was not a place that was particularly difficult to get into. Rather, it was the remoteness and geography of the place that would give any outlaw plenty of warning of an approaching posse of lawmen. And certainly, in its remoter draws and gulches, even today, one could hide herds of cattle or horses—or outlaws.

☙

The real-life story began in 1866, when Cassidy was born and christened as Robert LeRoy Parker, the first of 13 children of a Mormon family—though, it seems, not a polygamous one. Just ten years earlier, his father Maximillian Parker, then a lad of about 12, had helped *his* father (another Robert) and his mother push a handcart, loaded with everything that they owned, from a railhead in Iowa across more than 1,000 miles of prairie and mountain to the Mormons' New Jerusalem. Grandfather Robert had been a cotton worker in the Lancashire town of Accrington, when, as an early convert, he had been drawn across the Atlantic with his wife and young son in answer to Brigham Young's call for pilgrim-artisans to join his flock in a faraway Promised Land.

When that young son Maximillian was grown to 21, he married Ann Gillies; she had not long arrived from England (maybe from Newcastle), and Robert Leroy was born the following year. Presently, the Parkers took up some rough farming land just outside the small Mormon settlement of Circleville, nearly 200 miles south of Salt Lake City. The family grew: a baby arrived every 18 months. So money was scarce, and by the time young Robert LeRoy was 13 he had to leave school and work full-time on a nearby ranch. During this time, he had two experiences that, some say, planted the seeds of a cynicism toward authority that was to stay with him, one way and another, for the rest of his life. The first incident allegedly happened when the lad rode into town to buy some new overalls, only to find that for some reason the local store was shut. Night was coming on and he wanted to get home. So he climbed in, helped himself, and left a signed note saying that he, Robert LeRoy Parker, would be back with the money before the end of the week. But the store owner, on opening up the next morning, took a dim view of the break-in and reported the boy to the town's Mormon authorities. He was sent for and reprimanded and, though it went no further, one supposes that, as a 13-year-old, he would have been deeply humiliated, and would surely have resented the imputation that he was less than straight and honest. The second of those experiences occurred a little later: his father lost a tract of land to which he was sure that he had rightful title; it was taken from him and given to a disputatious neighbor on the decision of the local Mormon elders. Their judgment seems to have been prompted less by the legalities of the matter than by the fact that Mr. Parker's church attendance was deemed to be too infrequent.

One day a young itinerant cowboy called Mike Cassidy came by, and was taken on as a temporary hand alongside LeRoy on the ranch. He was obviously a likeable, though rascally, character. For the young LeRoy, already skeptical of the law, that seems to have been part of his attraction. After all, his new friend knew a maverick when he saw one; he knew how to use a running iron; he knew some interestingly shady characters; he knew how to shoot straight; he knew how to break a feral horse; and, no doubt, he knew how to say the right things to the girls. Presently, he gave young LeRoy an old six-shooter, and then some lessons on how to use it. That was probably not all he taught him. In time, when his drifter friend moved on, LeRoy wanted to go with him, but his mother prevailed. Nevertheless, it was only a matter of time before the young man, now growing into his late teens, would cut loose.

When LeRoy did go, some months later, he appears to have left in a hurry; he had almost certainly gotten too close to some of those interestingly shady characters who seemed to make a living by selling other people's cattle and horses. Anyway, whatever the reason, he said some quick goodbyes and rode off east, 250 miles through the Rockies, to the mining town of Telluride in the mountains of Colorado. There he got a job as a muleteer, hauling gold and silver ore from various small "high country" mines down to the central Telluride smelt-mill. Before he was 18, he was accused of stealing a horse. He was eventually acquitted, but the experience almost certainly reinforced his doubts about the law. Perhaps he was beginning to think that, if people were going to suspect him anyway, he might as well give substance to those suspicions, if and when a worthwhile opportunity came along.

From *The Bandit Invincible*, we learn that at some point he joined up with two other drifters, Matt Warner and Tom McCarty. Together, they set up a horse-racing venture. Traveling from town to town, they would bet that their horse—a particularly fast filly called Betty—could outrun anything the locals could produce. Betty seldom let them down. As a sideline, the partners also dabbled in the business of buying and selling horses, a risky occupation in a country where the legitimacy of any such deals was always likely to be questioned.

An exact log of his wanderings in those early years is not too important; it seems that he and his friends went hither and thither across Colorado, Wyoming, and Nebraska as the spirit moved them. But we can pick up their trail more accurately a year or two later (which is more than a pursuing posse was able to do) when the threesome galloped away, $20,000 better off, from the San Miguel Bank of Telluride on a June afternoon in 1889. It was a classic armed hold-up, over in minutes. It had been temptingly easy. LeRoy was just 23.

In later years he became renowned for the care with which, on behalf of his crew, he planned their various hold-ups and, more specifically, their getaways. Evidently, the Telluride venture was something of a prototype. Some days before the raid, the gang had quietly "planted" three or four fresh horses every 20–25 miles along their planned escape route. The horses and their minders—to be well rewarded if things went well—were hidden away in remote draws and canyons or on thickly timbered mountain slopes. Coming away from Telluride, it seems that Bert Charter, Boyd's father, was one of these minders. Anyway, thus organized, the robbers would be able to outride any pursuing posse who, even if it could find and follow the robbers' trail, lacked the advantage of fresh mounts every few hours. And the horses used in the initial getaway? Usually, they would be driven ahead of those just swapped at the relay; without the weight of saddles and riders they could make the pace.

It was a technique used again and again in the years to come. By means of such relays, and often traveling through the night (thus making their trail more difficult to follow), the robbers could cover more than 150 miles in the first 24 hours. After that, probably twisting and turning along little-known tracks, they might ride more gently, but ever watchfully, for another day or two until they pulled into some remote valley where, shielded by friendly rustlers, assorted ne'er-do-wells, and even small ranchers who did not ask too many questions, they could sort out the loot and rest, safe from pursuit.

The Telluride crew rode for more than 200 miles before they finally dismounted in a remote Colorado valley called Brown's Park: even today, it is one of the loneliest tracts of country anywhere in the West. (In Colorado, valleys are still called "parks.") Here, for several weeks, they relaxed and partied with the thin scatter of inhabitants who could be trusted to keep quiet. Then, with winter coming on, George Cassidy (he had now given himself the cover of a new name) emerged; he headed for central Wyoming and the small towns of Rock Springs and Lander where, as *The Bandit Invincible* has it, "there was plenty of hard men but Verry [sic] few bad ones." He must, one supposes, have been relieved to hear the saloon gossip that one of those robbers away south in Telluride was thought to be some Utah boy called Robert LeRoy Parker—obviously nothing to do with him.

Now he got a job butchering the carcasses of cattle at a small meat works. (Although there is some debate, it seems probable that this new occupation prompted the nickname "Butch.") It was likely that in time, tempted by the smell of easy money, he developed a sideline of quietly slaughtering and cutting up animals brought to him by some small-time rustlers. We certainly know that it was not too long before he was arrested and accused of knowingly receiving stolen goods: specifically three horses—though it could just as easily have been cattle. Not surprisingly, he was found guilty, and was taken off to the Wyoming state prison in Laramie for two years of hard labor. Butch always maintained that those horses were, in effect, a trap set by some big ranchers (Englishmen amongst them) to get him, an alleged rustler, out of the way. As his third-person comment in *The Bandit Invincible* has it: "Butch was the goat in that deal and inocent [sic] of the trap he was placed in." He may have been right.

Despite his bitterness, Butch behaved himself in jail and, if the tale is true, it is said that after a year he got a message through to the Governor of Wyoming; with admirable chutzpah, he suggested that if he promised not to commit any more robberies within Wyoming, he might be pardoned and released early. Strangely, the Governor agreed. As far as Wyoming banks were concerned, Butch would keep his promise. But, as events over the next few years would show, he obviously reckoned that railroads were not part of the deal. Perhaps, as trains started and finished their journeys far beyond the bounds of Wyoming, he decided that they were fair game.

Anyway, on release he headed back to central Wyoming. But those earlier enemies, the big ranchers, had evidently heard of his return and "he found that he was on the black list in earnest and every place he went there were no hands wanted." In short, he could find no work—not even as a butcher. In *The Bandit Invincible*, he is reported as telling an old acquaintance, "I want to go straight if they will let me. It is the stock mans [sic] move and if they move in the wrong direction I will give them plenty to chase me for." In other words, "If that's the way the ranching barons and their cronies want it, then I'll give as good as I get ..."

Within a few weeks, Butch was taking the first steps toward fulfilling his threat. He contacted some helpers: Ellsworth Lay and Bub Meeks. Elzy (as he was always known) was a quietly spoken cowboy whom Butch had first met when, after the Telluride raid, he had gone into hiding in the remoteness of Brown's Park. Bub Meeks is a rather shadowy figure, but we know that he (like Butch) came from a Mormon family; maybe he too had found domestic life too dull.

Butch's target would be a bank—what else? But mindful of that promise to the Governor, it would have to be a bank outside Wyoming. With the warmer weather of spring, he rode west and, after quietly observing several small-town banks in southeast Idaho, he decided that the one in Montpelier met his criteria. The deciding factor seems to have been that there was a good escape route. As at Telluride, there was nothing haphazard about Butch's planning. First, he and his two colleagues got work on a ranch just out of town. Then, riding into town separately over several days, so as not to arouse suspicion, they examined the layout of the bank and the habits of its staff. Once again, a chain of relay horses was put in place. Additionally, the gang made sets of leather "boots" that could be slipped over their horses' hooves—an old Indian trick to make a trail more difficult to follow. Then, when all was ready, the outlaws headed into town. Dismounting outside the bank, they pulled up their neck scarves, drew their revolvers and, while Bub held the horses, the other two went inside.

Everything worked as planned. Customers and staff were lined up, safes were unlocked, notes and coin were dumped into the several sacks that they had brought with them There was no shooting and only minor violence: Butch is said to have told Elzy to relax when he saw that he was about to cuff a hesitant cashier with his pistol butt. Within a very few minutes, the outlaws were mounted and galloping off.

It took time to put a sheriff's posse together—too much time. Butch, Elzy, and Bub got clean away. When one recognizes that, in those days, even a cowboy in full-time employment would have been lucky to make $400 in a year, a haul of $25,000 was a huge sum. Subsequent accounts about where Butch and company eventually came to rest are confused, even contradictory—which, one supposes, is just the way they would have wanted it. But if *The Bandit Invincible* is to be believed, Butch Cassidy made a secret visit to see his sweetheart, a girl called Mary Boyd who lived near Lander in central Wyoming. Then the narrative goes on to tell how he got out of the West altogether, by train for more than 1,000 miles to Chicago, and then on beyond to Michigan.

As far as the world knew, he had disappeared, until an April afternoon when, in the small Utah coal-mining town of Castle Gate, he quietly stuck a revolver in the ribs of a payroll clerk. The poor man was walking back from the nearby railroad depot where he had been to collect a heavy satchel. The satchel was bulging with two weeks' pay for the employees of the local coal mine. Within seconds, Butch and Elzy Lay were galloping away down the street, heading for the hills. Once again, they had left little to chance. For example, Butch and Elzy must have made it worthwhile for someone to tip them off about which train would be carrying that satchel. Further, when someone ran across to the depot to telegraph other towns to send out posses, they found that the wires had been cut. And as usual the escape route had been worked out, with backup teams (probably including Bert Charter and Bub Meeks) and fresh horses waiting at convenient points.

The haul came to over $8,000. The next month or two were spent in the wild and many-canyoned sanctuary of the aptly named Robbers' Roost. Their likely presence in those parts, along with other outlaws, was probably no secret. But, as far as any lawman's posse was concerned, the risks of ambush in such broken country were too great; so they kept clear. The law would just have to wait.

About now, Cassidy found himself at the center of a small band of like-minded pirates. He was not their leader in any formal sense, but he certainly seemed to set the pace and the tone. Today, we would talk about "charisma." Riding alongside him, sometimes literally, were Elzy Lay and Bub Meeks. Other "notables" among the crew were his Telluride friend Matt Warner, Harvey "Kid Curry" Logan, "Flat Nose" George Curry, Ben "Tall Texan" Kilpatrick, young Bert Charter and, of course, Harry Longabough. The last, while still in his teens, had served a sentence of hard labor (for horse stealing) in the small Wyoming town of Sundance. So from then on he was usually known as the Sundance Kid. Collectively, this rough-hewn crew was just that: an informal "collective" dedicated to a life outside the law. Soon they would be known as the Wild Bunch; indeed, it was not long before even the American Bankers' Association, meeting in distant Chicago, would be using that label in one of its annual reports.

The next robbery, at the small Dakota town of Belle Fourche, nearly 500 miles east of Castle Gate, came later in that same summer of 1897. For some reason Butch Cassidy did not take part; maybe he was visiting Mary Boyd. Anyway, apart from the fact that no one was killed, the raid was a small disaster. They should have had Butch along.

The raiders, six of them, decided that four would go inside while the other two would hold the horses. Early on, before the bank's safe had even been opened, someone on the other side of the street realized what was happening and started shouting. The raiders, nervous and alarmed, came tumbling out of the bank, threw themselves on their horses, and everyone headed for the hills.

It was said that they found their way within a few days to the Hole-in-the-Wall country, 160 miles away. It turned out that their total profit was just $97, taken from the pocket of one of the bank's customers right at the start of the raid. One can only guess what Butch had to say.

It is difficult to avoid writing about Butch Cassidy and his Merry Men in admiring terms (the analogy with Robin Hood is an obvious one). Like any bunch of brigands who "get away with it," and who thereby cock a snook at authority without killing anyone in the process, they become endowed with a patina of bravado and glamor. But the fact is that by the late 1890s a growing number of people in Wyoming were beginning to take a less tolerant view of what one of them neatly termed "all this unnecessary lawlessness."

Perhaps Butch Cassidy sensed the change. There is an attractive story that, with the outbreak of the Spanish–American war (following the blowing up of the battleship *Maine* in Havana Harbor), Cassidy put it to his immediate confrères that they should join one of the cavalry regiments, like Teddy Roosevelt's Rough Riders, which was then being formed of volunteer cowboys. Maybe Cassidy was moved by patriotism, along with the hope that military service would bring a subsequent amnesty. In the event, the plan came to nothing; the Governors of Wyoming and Colorado, who through discreet intermediaries would have been approached, were unsympathetic. Indeed, they authorized the funding of bounty hunters to be set on the Wild Bunch's trail. Cassidy's reaction was typical: snubbed by the authorities who were obviously out to get him anyway, he might as well give the bastards a (literal) run for their money ...

Very early on a Friday in June 1899, while it was still dark, one of the Union Pacific's crack trains, the Overland Express, was slowly hauling itself up an incline toward a place called Wilcox in eastern Wyoming. Presently, the engineer saw a red lantern flashing on the track ahead: danger on the line. Then, even as he was slowing his locomotive, he and his fireman were surprised by several masked men who had come clambering over the tender to take the crew from behind. The engineer was ordered to take the train on beyond a small bridge which, with pre-positioned charges, was then blown up. Now, when the clerks inside the mail car refused to open up, a small charge was used to blast their door off its hinges. Then, with the train crew and the clerks held at gunpoint, the robbers used bigger charges to open two safes; in the process (as the photograph taken a day or two later clearly shows) they blew out the wooden sides and most of the roof of the mail car. The gunmen scooped up all the money (mostly notes) that had not been wafted away on the night air. Then they were gone.

It was later claimed that the total haul from the Wilcox hold-up was more than $60,000. While, of course, the Union Pacific did not admit to losing such

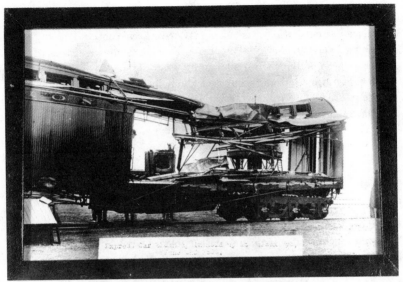

A Union Pacific mail car after being visited by the Wild Bunch (The UP Railroad)

a huge sum, it was quick to offer a reward of $18,000 for the capture of the outlaws. It also put together what, today, would be called "a rapid response unit": a well-armed posse on almost permanent standby with its own dedicated locomotive and horse wagons. Yet further, it suggested that the Army should get involved, and there was talk of bringing in bloodhounds. Whatever the means to be employed, the hunt was really on—though the standby posse, which would first have to be railed to the scene of any hold-up, would seem to have been a particularly futile notion.

Trying to unravel the movements of the different members of the Wild Bunch across the vastness of the West, especially after a robbery, is almost impossible. Not only does each of the many historians of the period have his/her own theory (sometimes supported by impressive but conflicting research), but, to muddle things further, the outlaws themselves used any number of aliases and disguises. Nevertheless, it does seem that, after the Wilcox adventure, Butch Cassidy and Elzy Lay eventually decided to lie low as mere cowboys on a far-away ranch in southern New Mexico. They became Jim Lowe and Mac McGinnis.

The WS Ranch was managed and part-owned by an Englishman, William French. Despite the fact that Low and McGinnis were hardworking and likeable, the part-owner had his suspicions. Further, with rumors that a Pinkerton detective had arrived to ask questions in nearby towns, he became worried that he himself might be implicated for harboring two cowboys whom, it might be claimed, he must have suspected or even known were outlaws. On the evidence available, it seems that Cassidy too may have been concerned that he was becoming an embarrassment to an obviously understanding employer. He may even have been prompted to think that it was worth making one more attempt to go straight, to return in peace to his family in Utah. Anyway, we know that he soon made his way north to Salt Lake City. There, he asked a lawyer to approach the Governor of Utah to see if he might be granted an amnesty if he promised to behave himself. The lawyer pointed out that even if the Governor were receptive, he would not be able to speak for the Governors of the other states—Colorado, Wyoming, and Idaho—where Cassidy was wanted for armed robbery. Further, it would be unrealistic to suppose that the Union Pacific would allow bygones to be bygones. Perhaps in response to that last point, Cassidy (in despair or optimism?) came up with another idea: if he promised not to organize any more train hold-ups, maybe the UP would drop all charges against him. He even suggested that, with his considerable expertise (to say nothing of his chutzpah), he might become what today would be called a "security consultant" to the UP: advising the company on how best to avoid future depredations. Amazingly, the UP seems to have thought that there might be merit in the idea. Accordingly, arrangements were made that Cassidy would rendezvous with railroad representatives at a remote spot in deepest Wyoming. On the agreed day, but wary of a trap, Cassidy watched the meeting point from a distance. He waited all day. Then, when still no one came, he left a note saying that he had been double-crossed and that "the UP can go to hell." In fact, the railroad negotiators had been delayed by the weather.

Shortly afterwards, following up on the wish that the UP might indeed "go to hell," Cassidy sent word to the Wild Bunch's inner circle. According to *The Bandit Invincible,* he told them what he had in mind: "Say, fellows, I understand the UP is looking for more trouble. They tell me that they have a bunch all lined up and ready for the emergency. [Presumably this referred to that rapid response unit.] What do you say if we give them a little exercise?"

The team evidently thought well of the proposal and a few weeks later, at a place called Tipton, on August 29, 1900, the Union Pacific was relieved of $55,000. The hold-up was an almost exact rerun of the previous summer's robbery at Wilcox. Once again, Cassidy and his crew made their escape along a well-planned route; once again, relays of fresh horses were waiting for them; once again, the Union Pacific stuck to an established and modest formula: it admitted to a loss of just $54.

The Bandit Invincible tells us that, in getting away from Tipton, "Butch was quite happy that they so complitly out witted the posies [sic]." The narrative then moves on to outline the plans for the next raid, which would come just three weeks later: 500 miles away at a small mining town far out in the semi-desert of central Nevada. Winnemucca's First National Bank was chosen because it was "in that part of the country where they was not much known and every body was hunting for them in other parts of the world." Once again, Cassidy, Sundance, Harvey Logan, and Will Carver took their time with the preparations:

"The Hold up being so thorough and quiet they were well out of town and heading for the hills before any one was ware of the hold up ... the boys were fifty miles away in the cotton wood range of the hills by night fall ... they divided the money between the 4 of them which was $32,000; after a short rest for men and horses they rode all night."

That account, written more than 30 years later, might have added that the robbery was so far from the normal stamping ground of the Wild Bunch that it was several days before they were even suspected of having been the culprits. By that time they were in Texas, more than 1,000 miles away.

Nearly 80 years later, some Western historians came up with a theory that the Wild Bunch had nothing to do with the Winnemucca raid. How, they asked, could Butch and Co., in just three weeks, not only ride across the 500 miles of mountains and semi-desert that separate Winnemucca from Tipton, but also then have the time to carry out the unhurried reconnaissance that was so much a hallmark of the way they worked? Not possible. So obviously this must have been the work of an altogether different crew, a much more local bunch of bandits. Winnemucca's merchants, led by the town's mayor and council, the Chamber of Commerce, and the recently renovated Buckaroo Hall of Fame, would have nothing to do with such a stupid theory. After all, since that movie, Butch Cassidy had become the town's big draw, its leading tourist attraction. Now, if those pesky history people got away with such a blasphemy, it could be the end of all the hoopla (and dollars?) that came together during the holiday season, and more especially during the town's annual Butch Cassidy Days. Probably half the motels and bars, including the one called The Hole-in-the-Wall, would be out of business. Disaster.

In fact, those history know-it-alls were only turning up the volume on a whisper that had been around since the beginning. But what if Butch and Co., traveling separately and incognito, had made most of the journey by train? Then, reunited, and while some distance, they bought the best horses they could find. There is strong evidence that this is just what happened: the crew bought a bunch of strong, fast horses from an understanding rancher in southern Idaho, 100 miles away. After the raid, the rancher conveniently waited several weeks before disclosing the sale. So, it seems that the Chamber of Commerce and all the other merchants in Winnemucca can rest easy ...

The distant Texas rendezvous was to celebrate the marriage of Will Carver to a Fort Worth girl; he wanted his friends in on the celebrations. Butch and the crew hardly needed the excuse: they must have reckoned that it was high time they started to enjoy the proceeds of their various exertions. Where better than Fort Worth? It was renowned as a "good time" town or, as a newspaper described it, "a bibulous Babylon of bars, bordellos and, no doubt, brotherly love." It seems probable that, in the run-up to the wedding, the bridegroom and his three thirsty friends enjoyed themselves too enthusiastically; why else would they now make a quite uncharacteristically careless move? Together with one other Wild Bunch arrival, they rolled down the street and had their photograph taken. It has become a famous picture. There they sit, duded up like a bunch of self-satisfied bankers: shoes polished, ties knotted, watch chains dangling, derbies tilted, mustachios neatly trimmed.

It is said that the photographer, impressed by the largesse of these visiting high-rollers, put a framed copy of the photograph in his studio window. A well-informed passerby recognized one or more of the men in the window and

The famous 1900 Fort Worth photograph; from left to right: Sundance, Bill Carver, Ben Kilpatrick, Harvey Logan, and Butch (Denver Public Library)

quickly alerted the authorities. One can reckon that, within a week, copies of that photo were on the wall of every lawman's office across the West. Pinkerton detectives rushed to Fort Worth—but the birds had flown.

Perhaps Butch and Sundance now decided that the West, for outlaws, was no longer the user-friendly environment that it had been only a few years before. Dammit, bigger and bigger rewards were being offered for the capture of any train robber, alive or even dead! The UP had even taken to building its mail cars of reinforced steel, and its safes too were getting heavier and more difficult. It was putting extra guards on valued cargoes; there were even rumors of Gatling guns. Clearly, it was time to be thinking of an easier and safer life.

So, one asks if this is when they hatched a plan to take off for South America? Probably. Certainly we know that Sundance and his lover, Etta Place, were in New York within a few weeks of leaving Fort Worth. We know this from a photo of the couple taken at a fashionable Broadway studio. They posed (in both senses of the word) as Mr. and Mrs. Harry Place. Presently, Butch arrived. He let it be known that he was Etta's brother. Sure of their anonymity, the threesome saw the sights, went to theatres, shopped in Tiffany's and, no doubt, dined at the best restaurants. Money was not a problem. Then, if *The Bandit Invincible* is to be believed, James Ryan (Etta's "brother") bade a temporary farewell to Mr. and Mrs. Place; he would join them later. So while they took ship for Buenos Aires, he headed back to the West.

On July 3, 1901, the *Coast Flyer*, on its way to the Pacific, was stopped in broad daylight on a lonely stretch of track in northern Montana, up near the Canadian border. The bandits used the same procedures that they had used so successfully in the past. Some accounts say that they rode away with more than $60,000. Posses gave chase but soon lost the trail. *The Bandit Invincible* closes the episode with "Butch suggested they split the bunch and make their way in pairs and after shaking hands, separated for the last time ..."

Although that hold-up was the last adventure of the Wild Bunch, individual members of the gang would continue to live by the gun (or the threat of it) for a few more years, or rather for *only* a few more years. Consider the fates of the three men who, in 1900, stood with Butch and Sundance for that Fort Worth photo: Will Carver went down to a sheriff's bullet in Sonora, Texas; Harvey Logan was shot and killed trying to rob a train of the Denver and Rio Grande Railroad; Ben Kilpatrick lasted until 1912 when he was shot dead by a clerk during a bungled raid on a Southern Pacific mail car.

But back to Butch ... After that Montana raid, he returned to the east coast. Evidently he found that it would be several weeks before a ship was due to sail for South America, so he was advised that his best course would be to take passage

Sundance and Etta Place in New York, just before leaving for South America (Larry Pointer)

across to Liverpool. From there, with the burgeoning trade between Argentina and Britain (meat coming in, manufactured goods going out), he would easily be able to get a ship to his final destination. Again, *The Bandit Invincible* implies that Butch had several days to kill in Liverpool before the next ship left for South America. It is surely difficult to imagine that he just checked into some dockside rooming house and sat chatting with the landlady. Maybe he took a trip to London? Here are intriguing possibilities for a novelist with imagination.

When, eventually, Butch joined Sundance and Etta in South America, they headed south for nearly 1,000 miles to the remoteness of Patagonia. There, in the foothills of the Andes, after they had looked for the right spot, they filed for ownership of 25,000 acres of empty public land. They began stocking the place with sheep and cattle; they built themselves a small ranch house; they employed several gauchos to help with the livestock; they made friends with a scatter of distant neighbors; they settled to a life of well-behaved and rather lonely pastoral pioneers. Perhaps, being so far away from anywhere that knew their past, they became complacent and may even have let slip their real names. Anyway, in time, the Pinkerton Agency back in New York worked out their whereabouts. The agency suggested to the UP that for $5,000 (much less than that earlier dead-or-alive reward) an expedition could be mounted that would bring the criminals back to the US. The UP was not responsive. Why, it may have reasoned, bring them back when there was no chance that the railroad would ever recover any of the stolen money? And anyway, once home the fugitives would certainly try to escape, and if successful, the railroad would just be faced with yet more robberies; better to leave them where they were, well out of the way.

If Butch Cassidy was indeed the author of *The Bandit Invincible*, he explains why, after three years of peaceful living, he and Sundance decided to return to a life outside the law. In 1905 a stock buyer called Apfield was passing through their corner of Argentina. "He had at one time been a sheriff in Wyoming and he had known Cassidy quite well. Apfield thinking that he might be able to collect part of the large reward began negotiations for the arrest of Cassidy and Maxwell [Sundance sometimes used yet another name]. Realizing that there was little chance of peace for them in any part of the world they decided to resume their life of banditry."

That last sentence makes it sound as if there may have been some reluctance to return to the risks (and excitements?) of the old days. Maybe there was. Or maybe they had become bored with the quiet and nothing-much-happening life? Another theory is that they abandoned their ranch when they heard they were under suspicion for a bank raid in the extreme south of Patagonia, a raid they had not committed. The fact is that we will never really know what turned them back to their old ways.

Likewise, we will never know which of a succession of bank raids, railroad hold-ups, and highway robberies that took place across the huge spread of Argentina between 1905 and 1907 can reasonably be charged against Cassidy, Sundance, and Etta. There were, at the time, at least three other bands of *bandidos yanqui*, to say nothing of a slew of home-grown villains on the loose in Argentina. But that our duo (trio?) *did* target banks and railroads is not in doubt. *The Bandit Invincible* admits, with some pride, to several successful heists: banks, trains and, in the mountains, mule trains. But the robbery that really matters happened not in Argentina but away to the north, in neighboring Bolivia ...

Sometime toward the end of 1906, Butch and Sundance (now calling themselves Santiago Maxwell and Enrique Brown) turned up looking for a "straight" job at a tin mine, the Concordia, high in the Bolivian Andes. They must have impressed the manager, for they were both taken on. Indeed, within a few weeks they were entrusted with the job of riding to La Paz, 75 miles away, to collect the mine's monthly payroll. But it was only a matter of time before their true identities became known; it is said that someone, while on vacation from the mine, had seen a "wanted" notice over in Argentina. Even so, they were still trusted and, evidently, they honored that trust. Indeed, the mine's under-manager at the time, an American called Percy Siebert, is reported in a 1930 edition of the American *Elks Magazine* as saying that although he knew their background, "they were scrupulously honest as far as we were concerned ... Butch Cassidy was an agreeable and pleasant person ... he allowed no other bandits to interfere ... I never had the slightest trouble getting along with them." He also recalled that, in the end, Butch told him that, because their true background was now widely known among the mine's management, they would have to move on. "There's always an informer around. Once you have started, you have to keep going, that's all. The safest way is to keep moving all the time."

While there is no certainty, it is quite possible that over the next few months Parker and Longabough (let's go back to their real names) were the *bandidos yanquis* who pulled off several hold-ups in the high country of Bolivia and Peru: a stagecoach and at least two mule-trains carrying supplies and cash to a mine. It was with one of those mule-trains that the much-debated dénouement begins.

On November 8, 1908, somewhere on a rough mountain track, two masked and well-armed men ambushed a small convoy of mules. The man in charge, the paymaster of the nearby Aramayo mine, would later report that the bandits spoke American–English. They relieved him of a sizeable bundle, containing the mine's wages. Then, taking one of the mules with them (to carry the loot?), they made off. Three days later, that paymaster and the manager of the Aramayo mine received a message to say that the two *bandidos* had been killed in a shoot-out with a detachment of Bolivian gendarmerie in a lonely mountain village called San Vicente; the missing money had been recovered. But that brief narrative contains about as much as we know for sure. Beyond that all is conjecture, and conjecture that not merely allows debate but positively generates it.

Most of the ingredients, true or enhanced, that constitute the legend of Butch and Sundance (of which the above is an outline and on which the Hollywood film is based) are found in that 1930 article in the *Elks Magazine*. The author, Arthur Chapman, a freelance journalist who had never been to South America, had talked at length to the mine manager, Percy Siebert, who by that time was retired and living back in the US. How far Chapman enhanced what he was told we do not know. But there are some curious elements of his account that have become embedded in the Butch Cassidy legend.

First, if those two bandits were indeed Butch and Sundance, it seems totally uncharacteristic that, in three days, they had only bothered to make less than 80 miles from the scene of the hold-up. Further, whoever they were, they were surely foolhardy in the extreme to arrive well-armed and seeking overnight accommodation in a village where it was quite likely that the inhabitants would already have heard rumors of a recent hold-up and would obviously be suspicious of incoming strangers, especially American ones. Finally, arriving with a "borrowed" mule which carried the brand of the Aramayo mine would immediately suggest that the animal was not traveling with its legitimate owners. In short, if we are to believe Chapman's account, those two *bandidos* were totally inept—complete beginners. So one has to doubt that they really were Cassidy and Longabough. One's skepticism is reinforced by yet one more anomaly …

As might be expected, a villager did indeed alert a nearby detachment of gendarmerie; they quickly mounted up and rode into the village. When they called on the *bandidos* to surrender, the reply came in several well-aimed revolver shots; one of the detachment was killed. But, incredibly, according to the standard version of events (and the movie), the *bandidos* had left their main weaponry, their Winchester lever-action repeating rifles and ammunition, on the far side of the courtyard from the room in which they were now besieged. Again, this was wholly uncharacteristic. Of course, in trying to reach their rifles those *bandidos* were shot down. Their bodies, it seems, were quickly bundled into a grave; there was no attempt at a formal identification. It was enough that the robbers were dead and the loot had been recovered. But could it be that, within a day or two, Percy Siebert deliberately put it about that the corpses were those of his two ex-employees—his friends who had told him that if they had the chance, they wanted to go straight? Was he, by saying that they were now buried in San Vicente, giving them that chance? It is an attractive possibility; one can go no further.

Needless to say, the author of *The Bandit Invincible* tells a quite different story. Immediately after they had ambushed a mule-train, Cassidy, Sundance, and two others, referred to only as Billings and Haines (where had they come from?), were surprised by a detachment of mounted gendarmerie that was patrolling along the same rough track. In the shoot-out that follows, Sundance and the other two are fatally wounded, but Cassidy manages to escape. "After everything became silent in the darkness ... for an hour he crawled on his hands & knees so he could not be seen or heard so easily." The narrative goes on to detail how he caught his horse and made his way out of the mountains. "He alone survived the terrible battle." Eventually, and without going into any detail, he reached the coast and found a ship to England. From there he went to Paris where "he entered a private hospital where he submitted to several minor operations. Three weeks [later] left the hospital he could see Verry little trace of his old self in the mirror, so clever had the transformation worked out." The narrative ends by saying that "the various governments of North & South America accepted their [the gendarmerie's] story as authentic and the name of Butch Cassidy became only a memory."

Perhaps one can understand why Hollywood found the whole tale "too preposterous to be believable."

❦

So did Butch Cassidy come back to the United States?

First, let's examine the evidence that he *did* return. First and foremost is the fact that there were at least a dozen people across Wyoming and Utah who, through the 1920s and 30s, claimed to have recognized the man they had known as Butch Cassidy two and three decades before. Concerning that surgery: it is worth remembering that "recognition" is not just about faces; it also depends on recalling and sharing old jokes, long-ago experiences, and gossip about mutual friends and enemies. Additionally, there has come down to us some strong, written support about those old-timers. Consider, for example, two 1936 letters which reportedly rest in the Utah State Archives; they are from the State Treasurer of Wyoming who, presumably, was a responsible man in a responsible job. In Treasurer Christensen's letter to a Utah historian, Charles Kelly, he respectfully suggests that Kelly's recently published account of Cassidy's death in a Bolivian shoot-out is ill-founded. He writes that as late as 1934, only two years earlier, Cassidy, while visiting one of his old Wyoming haunts, had spent time with "three old friends whom I know personally and whose veracity and memory I do not question for a moment. He [Cassidy] goes by the name of William Phillips ... and resides in Spokane." Those "three old friends" were, first, Ed Farlow who had been a mayor of Lander; second, Harry Baldwin who was a Lander storekeeper from whom Cassidy had often bought supplies; and third, Hank Boedeker who was the sheriff who had taken the young and handcuffed Cassidy to Wyoming's State Penitentiary back in 1894. When historian Kelly dismissively rejected this information, Christensen got rather cross. He wrote a second time, "The men I have named are reputable, well-known and responsible citizens and not the type who would exploit any kind of story for publicity or for gossiping purposes. They knew Butch Cassidy well and are not mistaken in this whole matter." If author Kelly now had second thoughts and decided to go to Spokane and seek out Cassidy/Phillips, he had left it too late; Cassidy/Phillips died in July 1937. Further, there is no record that Kelly took himself off to Wyoming to meet those acquaintances of Butch's in Lander. Maybe he did not want to spoil his story.

And there were other Wyoming citizens who were sure that they recognized the man they had once known as Cassidy. In Rock Springs, a garage man, John Taylor, remembered the day in the mid-1920s when Cassidy pulled in to have some work done on his Model-T Ford; he was pulling a trailer loaded with camping gear. Similarly, an old-timer called Tom Welch remembered that same Model-T and trailer. And there was Boyd Charter who (in that BBC interview and elsewhere) told of his father's warm greeting for the visitor who had unloaded his car and trailer to make camp on their ranch. It seems unlikely that Taylor, Welch, and Charter decided to get together to cook up an agreed story that included the detail of that trailer. Why, and to what end, would they do so? Then, down near the Colorado line, the Mayor of Baggs (a one-time favorite haunt of the Wild Bunch) was also clear in his assertion that the man he once knew as Butch Cassidy had recently come by.

In parenthesis, one might ask, "Yes, but what was Cassidy/Phillips actually *doing* traveling around Wyoming?" Why did he return, several times over the years, to his old haunts? He surely did not come back just to renew old acquaintances. At the time, he told anyone who asked that he had come to do a little recreational hunting. Then he would disappear for a week or two into the

Wind River Mountains. Most likely he was trying to find some of the loot that he had buried more than 30 years before, but he must have been unsuccessful. At least one forest fire had destroyed some of his possible landmarks ...

In a further parenthesis, one might also ask what Cassidy/Phillips was doing when he was "at home" between those trips to Wyoming. It seems that by the early 1920s, after perhaps trying his luck in Alaska, he had come to rest in Spokane. There he set up a small machine shop. He did engineering work for an outfit called the Riblet Tramway Company. For a few years he prospered, but with the Depression, Riblet lost money until it went under. Cassidy/Phillip's machine shop followed—which is when he started writing *The Bandit Invincible*.

But to return to another of those old Wyoming acquaintances ... What about Mary Boyd, Cassidy's girlfriend back in the days when they were both in their mid-20s? More than 30 years later, now a widow, she met Cassidy again. Later, she was to say that she had never been in any doubt who William Phillips really was. When he got back home to Spokane, they exchanged letters; he even sent her, as a memento of their time together in those early days, a ring he had

Is this Butch Cassidy as William Phillips, residing in Spokane? (Larry Pointer)

worn for many years. The ring was inscribed "Geo C to Mary B." Of course, like all the other "evidence," none of this can be taken as a guarantee that William Phillips and Butch Cassidy *were* the same person. Maybe Mary Boyd was making it up. But if so, why? Perhaps we get closer when examples of handwriting are compared. Larry Pointer, in chasing every possible lead for his remarkable book, *In Search of Butch Cassidy*, had the idea of engaging a graphologist to determine if there were similarities between the writing that was known to be Cassidy's when he was in South America, and Phillips' writing 25 years later. A letter that Butch was known to have written from Argentina was found in the Utah State Archives; it was compared with one that the man who called himself Phillips wrote (30 years later) in Spokane to Mary Boyd. Graphology is not an exact science, but the verdict was that, in this case, the similarities were too many to be merely coincidental; and, perhaps more revealing, there were also likenesses in the style, grammar, and misspellings. Larry Pointer explored another possibility: did the photographs of Cassidy and Phillips show any facial similarities? It has to be said that if one compares the prison mugshot of Butch (1894) and a good photo of Phillips more than 20 years later (*c.*1916), no obvious similarity leaps off the page. But might that plastic surgery in Paris have made a difference?

Lastly, there is at least one other witness to Butch's return whom one cannot ignore: his youngest sister. Being born just after Butch left home, Lula Betenson (her married name) did not meet her brother until 1925 when, she says, he came for two weeks to be with his father and those other members of the family (including herself) who still lived in Circleville. (Butch's mother had died in 1905.) In 1977, when Mrs. Betenson was 92 and the last sibling still alive, she gave a long filmed interview to Britain's best-known traveling TV reporter, Alan Whicker. (The finished film, in the series *Whicker's World*, is available from Amazon.) In that interview, the old lady was impressively articulate and firm in her recollections; at no point did she give the impression that she might be dissembling. Yes, it is true that she had not long finished co-authoring a book, *Butch Cassidy—My Brother*, and some skeptics have suggested that, in the interests of boosting sales, she may have colored some details of the story. We will never know. But on one thing, she was very specific: Butch came back and stayed with the family in 1925. Unfortunately and uncharacteristically, Alan Whicker did not ask her why he made no subsequent visits to his ageing father, brothers and sisters, given that he lived for another 12 years. Surely it is what one might expect of a dutiful son? But there *is* a possible reason why Butch never revisited his family: several of his brothers and sisters were devout and law-abiding Mormons, and it is said that they found Butch's outlaw lifestyle (even in its past tense) an embarrassment. Maybe, after that one reunion, being sensitive to their discomfort, he deliberately spared them any further shame by keeping his distance. One might argue that was the decision of a truly thoughtful son.

So let's now look at other points made by those skeptics. What is the evidence the other way, that Butch Cassidy did *not* come back, that he *was* killed in Bolivia? And what about the Sundance Kid and Etta Place?

In any examination of the "killed-in-Bolivia" thesis, one must start with a husband-and-wife team, Anne Meadows and Dan Buck. Their book, *Digging Up Butch and Sundance*, is essential reading. Over the years they have traveled to Argentina and Bolivia at least three times; they have combed the archives from La Paz to London, from Salt Lake City to Dublin; they have spent thousands of hours in research; in their book, they acknowledge the help of nearly 400 organizations and individuals. At one point, they even remortgaged their house to fund their work. So, obviously, they have left no pebble unturned. In the end they conclude, without any significant doubts, that Sundance and Butch were both killed and then buried at San Vicente. Many of the arguments they advance are straightforward contradictions of the opinions of the "Butch-came-back" lobby. Some of those rebuttals seem wholly reasonable, others less so. They reject that graphologist's conclusion about the handwriting, and cite in their support the opposing findings of another graphologist. They suggest that the "identification" of Butch by those Wyoming old-timers was mistaken; after all, they say, he would have aged so much in the intervening 25–30 years that those later assertions must be unreliable. But one might have thought that the time gap would make the old-timers *more* careful, not less, in affirming that their unexpected visitor was indeed the same person they had known in the old days. And certainly identification depends on mutual reminiscences as much as it does on facial recognition.

Anne Meadows and Dan Buck further maintain that the "Geo C ring" sent to Mary Boyd was an imposter's forgery. They point to undoubted inaccuracies in some of the names, places and events in *The Bandit Invincible*. This may be unfair: the writer of that biography (autobiography?) claims right at the beginning that his "mistakes" are deliberate, in order to shield outlaws as well as law-abiding friends, some of whom were still alive at the time of his writing. On the other hand, yes, those inaccuracies could be due to the fact that the writer was nowhere near some of the events he describes and therefore has to rely on his imagination. Again, these two arch-skeptics are unconvinced (reasonably) by any alleged similarities in those photographs. They are critical of Lula Betenson, and seem to suggest that she was suffering from a mild form of age-related wishful thinking. But watching and listening to the old lady in that long TV interview, one doubts that she is suffering from age-related anything; she positively sparkles with matter-of-fact normality.

Meadows and Buck, the leading skeptics, also point to the fact that William Phillips' wife, after his death, denied that her husband was Butch Cassidy. But the "he-did-return" lobby make the counterpoint that the marriage had long come apart, and additionally the estranged wife probably feared that, although many years had gone by, the Pinkerton Agency and/or the UP Railroad might still be interested enough in Butch Cassidy to try to extract some monetary redress from his widow. In short, it might have been in her interests not to acknowledge that Phillips and Cassidy were one and the same person.

It soon becomes obvious that for every argument supporting the contention that Butch came back, there is an equal and opposite one that he did not. Impasse. Then, in the early 1990s, there came a possible breakthrough: Meadows and Buck were contacted by an unusually experienced forensic anthropologist, Dr. Clyde Snow. Over the years, having spent time in both Argentina and Chile investigating "the disappeared," he too had become fascinated by the riddle of Butch Cassidy and Sundance. His proposal was simple: if the Bolivian authorities would allow it, why not exhume the bodies of the two *bandido yanquis* that were known to have been buried at San Vicente? Who could tell what might by revealed by bones, scraps of clothing and even DNA? Dr. Snow—"I've been in the bone business thirty years"—was persuasive. Further, given that his plan might have the makings of an intriguing documentary film, it soon attracted funding from one of the US's leading public (i.e. non-commercial) TV stations, WGBH of Boston.

Within a few months, a team of archaeologists, led by Dr. Snow with Anne Meadows, Dan Buck and a film crew close behind, was on its way to San Vicente, 14,500 feet up in the Andes.

❧

I had read about the involvement of WGBH-TV in one of the several books that I have about the Wild Bunch. Then I remembered that, more than 30 years earlier, I had worked alongside an American TV producer who was on a 12-month attachment with the BBC. I knew that, when he had returned to his "home" TV station in Boston, WGBH, he had started a science-based series called Nova. Now, it seemed a fair bet that if WGBH had commissioned a film involving exhumation

by a forensic anthropologist, it would have been produced under the Nova banner.
Although we had not met for over 20 years, I still had the phone number of my friend.
Within minutes we were talking to each other. Yes indeed, Nova had funded that
film. Although he had long since retired, he immediately gave me the number of the
right person at WGBH. Within four days of those two phone calls, I was viewing a
DVD of that film at home in Wimbledon. Marvelous. (Thank you, Mike Ambrosino
and Melanie Wallace.) Now I was virtually transported to Bolivia, to the alto plano,
to the cemetery; I could watch Clyde Snow directing operations; I could hear and see
the pick-and-shovel men; I could listen to Dan Buck; I could sense the excitement
when the team found a skull and some bones that might be relevant; I could follow
the subsequent analysis of the forensic problems. Then, on the film's end credits, I
saw that the man who had made the film was an old BBC colleague who had been
working with WGBH at the time. I phoned him. We had a long, interesting, and
informative discussion. Small world.

❧

The cemetery at San Vicente is crammed, higgledy-piggledy, with hundreds of
graves. Many are unmarked. With a shortage of properly consecrated ground,
the dead are often crowded in, one on top of another. So the first problem was to
find the right graves or, at least, the most likely ones. The task was complicated
by the fact that, at about the same time as the burial of the two *bandidos yanqui*,
two other gringos had also been interred: a Swede who had apparently shot
himself getting off his mule, and a German mining engineer who had carelessly
blown himself up. But even though the identifying gravestone has disappeared,
the keeper of the cemetery—the job had been in his family for two generations—
thought he knew where the *yanquis* were. They started digging.

By the second day, the local pick-and-shovel men had opened up a sizeable
trench and were down to what, in prospecting terms, would be called "the pay
dirt." Now it was the turn of the archaeologists to go down with trowels and
brushes. It is not surprising that Clyde Snow, given his long experience in this
kind of thing, was the top honcho. Under an ancient trilby and with a cigarillo
permanently clenched between his teeth, he gave encouragement from above.
"What have you got down there? A mandible! Well, take it out real gentle …

284

Hey, I reckon we have a male mandible here ... at the age range of the two fellows we are looking for. And, say, this is quality dental work ... gold fillings ... this isn't curb-side dentistry. Whoever this is, he could afford real good dental work." Then, turning to the camera, "Bones and teeth make good witnesses: they don't lie, they don't forget."

By the fourth day, they had extracted most of the rest of that skeleton. The skull was that of a Caucasian, and the skeleton itself was about the right height and build to "fit" Sundance. But these remains could also have been those of the Swede or the German, about neither of whom had the team any information on height and build. They would have to take the bones back to the US for detailed tests. Now they started to look for Butch Cassidy. Presumably he was lying alongside the bones that they thought just might be those of Sundance. But there was a problem. Only recently, a baby had been buried right over the spot where they reckoned that Butch might be. They found the mother and asked if she would allow the re-burying of her child, so that the diggers could have clear access to the ground underneath. She refused. So now the team tried tunneling under the baby. It was very slow work because they had to shore up the over-burden as they went. As Dr. Snow put it, "We've had to turn an archaeological dig into a mining operation." But by now time and money were running out; it was a four-hour drive down to the railhead and, from there, the once-a-week train took 14 hours for the 400 miles back to La Paz. From La Paz—a flight home. They suddenly realized that the weekly train came and went the next day. So they worked all through the night. The haul was disappointing; they found only a jumble of bones and five non-Caucasian skulls. The best that could be said was, as Dr. Snow succinctly put it, "With four gringos buried around here, we've definitely got one of them." But which one?

Not surprisingly, this narrative (and Nova's documentary) now switches to Dr. Snow's laboratory in Oklahoma. Part of that Caucasian skull was missing; is that because it was blown away by gunshot? They take X-rays to see if there are any tiny metal particles embedded in the skull, left by a bullet as it passed through the bone. Yes, there are some metallic specks. That rules out the German, who did not die of a gunshot wound. They commission some complex comparisons of the skull shape with a photograph of Sundance; the match is a reasonable one. What about a rumor that Sundance had once had a gunshot wound in the leg? Reassuringly, a consultant podiatrist identifies a minute nick in the skeleton's left shinbone. Those gold fillings are identified by a dental expert as having probably been made around the turn of the century, maybe in Chicago; that would seem to eliminate the Swede. Then they try to get a DNA match with a known relative; they get Sundance's nearest present-day relatives to agree to an exhumation of a long-dead uncle, buried in Pennsylvania. When, eventually, they get a usable specimen, it does not match the DNA from San Vicente. But this, it is optimistically suggested, may be due to some contamination(s) picked up during the exhumation or in the acidic soil of Pennsylvania. In any case and at that time, DNA matching was most reliable via the female line; it seems that the female Longabough "line" had long died out. Nevertheless, the height and build of the skeleton both seem to coincide with those of Sundance. Second, the skull "fits" with the photo of Sundance and, lastly, the nick in the shinbone seems to point to the probability that the skeleton was that of Sundance. But the word "probability" seems about as far as one can go. And even then one is left with those actions before and during the Vicente shoot-out which seem so uncharacteristic of our duo.

And what about Butch? Certainly, there is a lack of any solid evidence that he was killed in Bolivia. Equally, there is a lack of solid, 100% evidence that he came back. Nevertheless, it is surely difficult to fault Larry Pointer's comment at the top of this chapter in which he asks if that collection of Wyoming old-timers back in the 1930s were just a bunch of "gullible old hayseeds taken in by some imposter." Maybe I am guilty of the same wishful thinking of which, in the preface, I accuse others: writing not merely about what I *think* happened, but writing about what I *want* to think happened. Yes, I want to think that Butch came back. It makes a much better story ...

But there are still a few more questions: if Butch came back, did he really live out his days as William T. Phillips? If not, then Phillips must have been an imposter. In which case, one must ask once again, how did an imposter fool all those old-timers?

And what about the beautiful Etta? The short answer is that, beyond what we know about her during those few years that she was with Sundance (which is not much), everything else is an enticing mystery. One theory is that, before Sundance came along, she was a Texas call girl; another says that she was a schoolteacher. While the two professions are not mutually exclusive (though difficult to practice simultaneously), most people seem to prefer her to have been a schoolteacher. Everyone who met her seems to have thought her "a lady of class," educated and very well-spoken. Could that support the contention that she was the daughter of a George Capel, the illegitimate son of the 6th Earl of Essex? After all, her surname, Place, is an anagram of Capel. If so, how did she wind up in Texas where she met Sundance? One of the few certainties about the lady is that before Butch and Sundance had moved on to Bolivia, she had returned to the US. Some say that she returned to Denver to have a baby; others say that she shipped out from Chile to San Francisco and was hardly off the boat

The Union Pacific's "rapid response unit" ready to chase after Butch Cassidy and the Wild Bunch (The UP Railroad)

when she was killed in the famous earthquake. The fact is that we will never know where Etta Place came from and where she wound up. Maybe she would want it that way.

One last question: if that really was Butch Cassidy traveling around Wyoming during the 1920s and 30s, he was surely taking a very considerable risk that someone who knew who he really was would not report him to the authorities. After all, although his crimes against those banks and the UP Railroad dated from 25 or more years before, he could not assume that the banks, the railroads, and Pinkertons would have forgotten or forgiven him. They certainly would not have looked the other way if he had found that loot in the Wind River Mountains, and the news had become known. Nor would he have been protected from criminal prosecution by the seven-year statute of limitations; that statute (in both federal and state law) can apply in civil cases, but it does not apply in criminal cases, nor if deception has been involved. The fact that Butch had been using a false name would have been more than enough to constitute that deception. This, to me, is the weakest link in the "Yes, Butch-did-come-back" thesis …

So, a summary: Sundance was most likely killed in South America; Butch Cassidy most likely died in Spokane in 1937. Finally, may I invoke the thought with which this book began? I believe that everything in this chapter is true; and even if it isn't, it *could* be.

16

THE SOD-HOUSE FRONTIER

"When Dorothy stood in the doorway and looked around, she could see nothing but the great gray prairie. Not a tree or a house broke the broad sweep of flat country that reached the edge of the sky in all directions."

From *The Wonderful Wizard of Oz*, set in Kansas, and written in 1900 by Frank Baum

ↄ

Explorers, trappers, miners, soldiers, and cowboys might be the criss-crossing pathfinders out ahead, but out on the Great Plains it was the farmer who was always the agent of actual settlement. He and, perhaps even more, his wife or his woman were the would-be homemakers; they became, to modify a cliché, "the domesticators of someone else's wilderness"—the "someone else" being, of course, the Native American.

The pattern had begun Way Back East more than two centuries earlier. With a few animals and some simple tools—an axe, a plow, a mattock, and a gun—the first settlers had cleared an acre or two along the edge of the forest, built a crude cabin of logs, shot or trapped game for meat and hides, gathered wild fruits, scattered pumpkin and corn seed in the early spring, and then hopefully waited through the summer for a crop. In time, if things went well, the family might buy a second cow, another mule or a brace of oxen, and some more chickens. They would plough more land; they would split more logs to build a barn and to lay some fences.

Then, after a few years, they would watch other people moving past to open up new land further west. For some, the temptation might be too much, and, if they could find a buyer, they would sell out and join those other pioneers on their way to the greener and more fertile lands which always seemed to lie "on the far side of the hill." It was a creeping process that had taken the frontier of settlement a third of the way across the continent. Then in the middle of the nineteenth century there was a pause; the pattern faltered.

The convulsions immediately before and during the Civil War had a good deal to do with the slowing down; so did the prevalence of malaria along the flatlands of the Missouri. But there was something else; it was as if the yeoman farmer and his family became afraid of pushing on much further. In fact, they *were* afraid or, at the least, they were apprehensive. Behind them lay the familiar forests and clearings through which they had come during the preceding 200 years. True, the trees had been a nuisance which first had to be cleared, but, once felled, they gave timber for shelter, fuel, and fencing; the clearings and riverine meadows were fertile (for a while) and the soil could be turned with a mule- or ox-drawn plow. The farmer's musket had range enough for shooting forest game. It was a life hard in its simplicities, but at least the pioneer farmer and family understood their environment and were reasonably easy in it. They and their tools were adapted to the habitat. They worked.

Before the Civil War, some hundreds of farmers had crossed the Missouri River and reached into what would become the eastern margins of Kansas and Nebraska. This was still a fertile, reasonably watered terrain; it had enough trees to give the settlers what they needed, but not enough to make life too tedious. But now, more than 1,000 miles from the sea where the whole process had started, a different and very unfamiliar land began. It was as simple as that. Westward, the trees thinned and gave way to the Great Plains; they were as endless and windswept as an ocean. Out there, there was very little timber, no easily turned soil, no shelter, no fuel. With less rain (under 20 inches a year), the grass became shorter and more wiry; the summers grew hotter; the winters longer and colder. Even today, once away from the now-irrigated margins of the few rivers, the transition is as clear as it ever was: just drive northwest across Nebraska from Grand Island along State Highway 2 and, somewhere beyond the 99th meridian, one crosses a visible natural frontier—from the trees and green of the Midwest (corn-belt country) to the short grassland of the Great Plains. And, of course, 150 years ago there were the still-feral tribes. At best they were irritable, at worst they were deadly. After all, this was their land.

So, in the face of this alien and windswept geography, the farmers hung back; they were worried about things they did not understand. Maybe, they thought, this is as far as the business of farming and permanent settlement was meant to go. After all, some of the maps showed that these almost treeless plains ran out into what was marked on the maps as a desert. One doubts that people literally turned to each other to ask, "What now?" But the result was as if they had. They hesitated, waiting for answers.

Just as the problems were varied, so, when they came, were the solutions. But they did not all come at once. The first, not only in its timing but in effect, was the Homestead Act. Signed by President Lincoln in 1862, it gave land, in 160-acre lots (a quarter of one square mile), to anyone who wanted it. All you had to do was to find a 160-acre plot that was not already claimed by someone else, stake your boundary out with markers or a plowed line, pay a small registration fee at the nearest Land Office, and then live on the land for the next five years. Or *say* that you had lived on it for five years. Free land, especially for emigrants from Europe, was a dream. (Until a few years ago it was *still* possible to "homestead," though the only free land left was in Alaska, the very last frontier.)

A Homestead Bill had been talked about for years, but it had long been opposed by the southern states; they feared that it would entice droves of non-slave–owning northerners to settle the new land in the West, particularly in Kansas. Kansas would then, they argued, be quickly admitted to the Union and thus upset the delicate balance between "free" states and "slave" states. The southerners were right. Bloody Kansas was one of the incendiaries that would ignite and then burn right through the Civil War.

Lincoln's signature was not long dry when, at a minute or two past midnight on New Year's Day 1863, the door of one of the first western Land Offices opened for just three minutes: long enough to allow one man to file the very first claim for a homestead under the new act. He was a Union soldier on furlough; he had "located" on a stream near the small Nebraskan settlement of Beatrice (pronounced Bee-atriss). One wonders how much his being a Union soldier and, even more, his name, Daniel Freeman, had to do with his selection. Was it a deliberate flaunting by the local Unionists aimed at the Confederates a few miles to the south in Kansas?

Today the farm is a national monument with neat displays of implements, frontier furniture and journals. Despite my supposition that Freeman's name had something to do with his selection, there was no official confirmation of it. The curator smiled and thought that it was a "neat" idea—one, he said, that had occurred to any number of people before me. Of course.

After the Civil War it did not matter much what southerners thought; hundreds more would-be homesteaders moved to "locate" beyond the Missouri. The lure of free land was powerful enough to overcome their earlier hesitations.

But as they pushed onto the plains of Nebraska and Kansas, alongside the advancing railroads, they soon found that a farm of 160 acres was not nearly big enough to support a family in this new, drier land. Back in the more fertile country that they had left behind, 80 acres were sometimes sufficient. But here, on the climatically uncertain plains, a family needed at least 300 acres. Even if a man illegally registered his wife for her own 160 acres, and thereby managed to accumulate a larger holding (a fairly standard procedure), there was then the question of how one man, his wife, some growing children, and an ox or two could cultivate even a part of so much land. (To plow one acre with a single furrow, a farmer would need to trudge backwards and forwards behind his team for something like six miles.) Even if somehow the family did manage, there was little they could grow that could compete with the produce coming off farms back east; not only were those farms on better land, but they were much nearer the growing urban markets. Out west, it was at best subsistence farming—not what those first pioneer farmers had hoped.

For those who persevered, the Homestead Act had its share of legal loopholes, and the small-town lawyers were quick to come up with their interpretations of the small print. There was the "commutation" clause under which a farmer did not have to wait the full five years to gain absolute freehold of his land. Any time after the first six months he could, by paying a little over $1 an acre, take full possession. Now crafty men came along and, seeing an over-ambitious settler or one in difficulty, would quietly offer to lend the cash necessary to complete payment on the homestead. But there was always a catch: the interest rate would be almost impossibly high, with the farm held as collateral in the event of the farmer failing to meet that rate. Or there might be an "arrangement" whereby the speculator came into partnership with the farmer. Later, the cuckoo might take over the nest—to rent the holding back to the original homesteader. So, in the very regions it was meant to populate, there were problems with the Homestead Act. Some families managed to struggle through the first and most difficult years; but for others, debt and the harsh environment were too much. By the late 1870s, a steady trickle of broken families were going back eastward across the Missouri.

Nevertheless, as time went by, whatever its failings, what really mattered about the Homestead Act was its seductive promise. And there were other inducements. Through the early 1870s, the Union Pacific Railroad (through Nebraska) and the Kansas Pacific and the Santa Fe (through Kansas) were trying to populate their massive grants of government land. They set up "colonization bureaux" and, back east, the newspapers carried their advertisements extolling the easy life on the plains. "An invitation is here extended to everyone desiring

Collecting "meadow muffins" for fuel (Kansas State Historical Society)

a choice home in the Finest Country in the world. Come to Kansas and locate in the State that is always in front. Bring your family to the State that offers you Fertile Lands, Prosperous Towns, Plenty of Churches and Schools and no Saloons." Enticing. But the truth was rather different.

Once onto the treeless plains, farming in ways the newcomers brought with them did not work. Ordinary plows were almost useless in coping with the matted grass sod whose tangle of roots, looking for moisture, could reach down two feet or more. Surface water was scarce and, until a well could be dug, had to be hauled from the infrequent streams. There were few trees to provide timber for building homes, or for fences, or for feeding the settlers' stoves through the long winters. The more determined newcomers struggled as best they could; they probably had no money to get back home anyway. So they built their one-roomed, dirt-floored dwellings with what they called "prairie marble"—slabs of earth cut out of the prairie. They would stretch a canvas wagon cover for a roof until they could make the journey to a railroad town for a few lengths of timber to make a ridgepole and rafters, to support a roof of sod and thatch. They dug wells and then put together crude wooden windmills to draw up the often-brackish water. They scratched with mattocks until a scrap of land was broken for sowing some vegetables. Then they went into debt to buy one of the newfangled plows devised by an Illinois blacksmith called John Deere; its sharp point and its smooth steel meant that it could cope with the matted prairie—something quite beyond the older, blunter wooden or cast iron plows they might have brought with them. They planted thorn hedges or built walls of sod to keep the cattlemen's herds off their windblown seedlings, because, of course, they were pushing into the domain of the cattlemen.

They collected sun-dried droppings of cattle or buffalo, "meadow muffins," for fuel. They watched and waited to see how their first year's crop would come through. If there was spring hail, or summer drought, or grasshoppers, the plantings would fail and everything would have been wasted. Some had not the resources, mental, physical or financial, to start all over again. That was the time when some friendly fellow would come by and offer to buy out the homesteader. Often it seemed better to cut their losses for those few dollars; at least they would pay the way home. It was a recurring pattern. "In God we trusted, in Kansas we busted."

If the settlers who hung on were not hardened when they started, they soon got that way. For the women, the real home-makers, life was particularly difficult. Almost always, sometimes for years, there was a lack of almost everything that would go to make even the most rudimentary home. There was the loneliness, the seemingly vicious climate, puddles on the floor when it rained and, just as inevitably, dirt and dust between times. There were coyotes, snakes, mice, cockroaches, and fleas. The children might be crying, sometimes merely fractious, sometimes sick or even dying of dysentery, measles, whooping cough, pneumonia, or diphtheria. No advice, no doctors, no companionship. Their men were often away for days or even weeks at a time trying to earn a few extra dollars: digging someone else's well or working on the railroad. And over all, there was the starkness of the plains, the constant wind, the awful emptiness of the sky. These things tightened on their undernourished minds, and some of them became deranged. They called it "cabin fever." Sometimes, despair or sheer heartbreak led to suicide.

If one looks at early photographs of families standing outside their "soddies," one hardly ever sees a smile on their bony faces. They look tired; the women particularly seem pinched and hungry, like people who have not quite given up but are forlornly waiting for something, anything, better to turn up. For the photographer, they have brought out their most treasured possessions: the family

Bible, a sewing machine, an accordion, even a bird in a cage. The children are often barefoot. No Hollywood Western was ever like this; John Wayne or Kevin Costner never played an early Kansan or Nebraskan homesteader; no dimpled starlet looks right as a pioneer wife; the heroics were altogether too gray, too grim.

Nevertheless, although it took time, life could slowly improve for the homesteaders who hung on and persevered. They had learned new ways of farming. Gradually, with more people taking up land, there was less isolation. The towns were growing; there were churches, schools, and even a few simple hospitals. And the years of the mid-1880s were blessed with better rainfall than usual, so the crops—those that escaped the grasshoppers or the sudden hailstorms—did not wither in the ground. There were good years amongst the bad.

Through those same years, the Western railroads sent their recruiting teams across the Atlantic. In Britain alone, more than 50 agents spread out with magic lanterns, brochures, and sales talk. Elsewhere across Europe, farmers who could never hope to be more than landlorded tenants would listen to the promise of owning their own land across the ocean. Even though the railroads were seldom giving their land away for nothing, their message was seductive. Oppressed but industrious farming communities, such as Mennonites, Moravians, and Bohemians, were the most eager. Sometimes the railroads would pay all expenses for one or two chosen men to cross the Atlantic to look for themselves. Then, if these advance guards were satisfied, the message would go back: whole villages would uproot to make the long journey to the New World.

Some of these communities still exist, though they are less tight-knit than once they were. A few years back, I stopped for a meal in North Dakota; paralleling the menu in English was one in Swedish. Near Hemingford in western Nebraska there is a small colony of wheat farmers originally from Bohemia. And one wonders about the first settlers in the towns of Malmo or Gothenburg or Belgrade. In Kansas, Russian and English migrants named the towns of Catherine and Victoria after their Queens. Until a couple of decades ago, in the foothills west of Laramie, the timber workers spoke Norwegian among themselves. And further north, the radio station in Buffalo put out a daily program in Basque for the sheepherders in the nearby Bighorn Mountains. But one has to be careful. There are no dreaming spires in Nebraska's Oxford and Cambridge, nor are there onion domes in Kremlin (Montana) or in Moscow (Texas). And there are no massed choirs in Welsh (Oklahoma), nor angels in Paradise (Montana).

Much of the human geography of Western settlement is still clear on the ground. Fly over Nebraska, Kansas, or Oklahoma and you can see the precise geometry of the early surveyors. They went ahead of the homesteaders and superimposed an exact quilt of one-mile squares. Each square was, and still is, known as a "section"; 160 acres is thus a "quarter section"—an original homestead. If you ask a farmer how much land he owns, he will invariably answer you in terms of sections. "Got a half section right here, where my great gran'daddy and his brother homesteaded, and then there's a section three miles south on the east side of the county road which used to belong to my wife's folks. Got most of that under wheat present time." If you are interested (and how could you not be?), he will show you the site of his great gran'daddy's sod house, and then go on to tell you stories of the Depression and the subsequent slow and often difficult progression to some kind of eventual prosperity. From the earliest sod house days, it may well have taken his family more than a century.

Today, as you fly at 3,000–4,000 feet through the bumpy summer air of, say, western Kansas, you look out over hundreds of square miles of ripening wheat. This is part of one of the world's great granaries. Perhaps, below, you will see echelons of combine harvesters. They will chew their way northward all summer, following the migration of the sun whose ripening warmth creeps up the map at a rate of 12 miles a day. So the combines start down in Texas in May; they finish 1,500 miles away on the prairies of Canada in late September, often in the first light flurries of snow.

ᘒ

"It's eighteen hours a day, and the only way we know it's Sunday is if one of the crew takes an hour out to get to church." Dale Starks was the boss; he started traveling the wheat trail in the 1950s with a bank loan and one small secondhand combine. By the time I met him 25 years later (I was making a documentary about the wheat harvest) he owned nine combines and employed 20 young men to drive them and their attendant fleet of trucks and pickups. He and a hundred or more other harvest bosses and their crews were contracted by farmers from one year to the next, from Texas to Alberta.

A farmer with, say, 1,000 acres of ripening wheat wants it harvested the moment it is ready, against the risk of summer hailstorms which can hammer down from nowhere and flatten the man's bank balance in a few catastrophic minutes. Only the very biggest farms can afford to have enough combines to do the job themselves, and even then, what would the combines be doing for the rest of the year? Hence the system of contracted harvest crews.

When I first knew him, Dale was everyone's idea of the direct and laconic Westerner. Booted and Stetsoned, he might have been the Marlboro man's elder brother.

"How," I asked him, "have things changed since you started 'contract cutting' all those years ago?"

"Combines growed a lot bigger."

"Is that all?"

"Well, I guess the highways have improved some."

A man of very few words, Dale was trainer, manager, accountant, and chief mechanic: the complete master of his trade. Sometimes at nearly midnight one would find him deep in the guts of one of his machines, making adjustments or repairs. In the heat of noon, listening to the drone of a combine half a mile away, he would reach for the two-way radio in his pickup truck and tell the distant driver that he better make a fractional change to one of the control settings, "pronto." He could glance at a field of wheat and estimate the yield per acre to within a bushel. He knew as much about wheat, combines, and the backroads of the West as any man alive. And his wife, Margie, knew as much as any woman. She was quartermaster to the whole circus: food, fuel, and spare parts. She kept a motherly eye on the young bachelors in the cutting crew; she looked after the married couples and, if needs be, she could drive a combine better than anyone except Dale. As they moved northward through the summer, four days at this farm, ten at the next, their camp was a cluster of mobile homes, pickups, and old school buses—bunkhouses for the cutting crew. Electricity and water were laid on by the farmer.

You can't cut damp wheat. So the cutting day begins as soon as the sun has burned off the overnight dew—about 9 o'clock. It finishes, under headlights, anything up to 15–16 hours later when the dew returns. If there is a wind there will be no dew, so the cutting can go on till 2–3 a.m. In the early weeks, some of the new recruits cannot stand the pace and they drop out. But the rest will keep it up for five months until, up in Canada, they are racing against the forecasts of incoming snow. By that time Dale Starks and his nine combines will have harvested enough wheat to keep the whole of England in bread for about five days. And some of that wheat may well be exported to England; or to India or Brazil or Egypt; or, when the harvest on the steppes has failed (as it did several times in the 1970s and 1980s), even to Russia. And there is some irony in that—given that Russia is where this strain of wheat came from in the first place.

❧

Over 140 years ago, the first wheat planted on the Great Plains withered in the summer heat, its long stems tangled in the wind. The first wave of settler-farmers were dismayed; they were forced to conclude that this would never be wheat country. It was a band of immigrants from Russia, with the help of the Santa Fe Railroad, who began to change all that. Theirs is a tale worth telling.

In 1872, a man called Bernard Warkentin came to the United States; he was an advance agent for a colony of Russian-Mennonites. Four generations earlier, their ancestors had left their original homes on the north German plains to escape religious persecution. Catherine the Great gave them a home. Indeed, she encouraged these industrious farmers to come and take up land in the Crimea and on the steppes, and thereby to set an example to her own less industrious peasants. She offered the Mennonites reduced taxation, plus the educational and religious tolerance they sought. And she promised that their descendants would be exempt from military conscription for the next 100 years. But nearly a century later, with their royal sponsor long gone, the Mennonites were increasingly subjected to the very restrictions that they had once escaped. And Tsar Alexander was about to revoke that military exemption. So they appointed Warkentin and a couple of others to start searching out a new home.

The story varies in some of its details, but it seems that the European agents of the Santa Fe Railroad heard of the plan (maybe they were in on it from the start) and alerted their head office. Anyway, Warkentin was brought across the Atlantic and then taken out to Kansas; he was offered 60,000 acres of railroad land for $250,000 in gold. Further, his hosts offered to build temporary barracks to house the potential immigrants through the first difficult years. The advance man liked what he saw; indeed, the country was very similar to that back home.

The first Mennonites, nearly 800 of them, arrived in New York in 1874. They brought with them their gold, smuggled past the Tsar's police. They are also said to have smuggled (in trunks and sacks) some tons of a short-stemmed and hardy strain of wheat that they had developed over the years to withstand the difficult climate of the steppes. One legend has it that some of the Mennonite women left Russia with additional grain (nowadays it is known as Turkey Red) hidden in their voluminous pantaloons. Who knows, it could be true. What is more certain is that, mixed with the grain, were inevitably some weeds; chief among them was Russian Thistle. In time, it would spread all over the West: tumbleweed. Yes, the stuff came from Russia.

Once arrived in Kansas, the new arrivals impressed *The Topeka Commonwealth*. "They are the most peaceable foreigners that arrive on our shores. In their colonies there are no quarrellings, no fightings, no murders, no lawsuits, no lawyers, no juries, no courts, no police, no officers, no governors, and crimes even of the smallest character are of the rarest occurrence. They are dressed in primitive homespun garments of coarse wool. The women and children have funny old handkerchiefs tied around their heads, and certainly no Broadway milliner ever supplied one of the quaint bonnets which the fair Mennonite beauties wear." As well as the Mennonites, there were soon other Russian immigrants, Roman Catholics, coming into Kansas. They too had been wooed by the railroad.

Of course the Rooshans, as they became collectively known, recognized the steppe-like plains immediately. And, even more significantly, so did their wheat. It flourished where earlier strains had struggled. It could stand the climate and, being short-stemmed, it was not flattened by the fierce prairie winds. With Turkey Red and the hybrids that quickly followed, the seeds of the plain's future were sown, almost literally. Of course, it did not all happen at once; the full spread of that wheat across the plains took more than a decade.

At first, and almost inevitably, the earlier homesteaders were suspicious. After all, drought, wind, and the disease of rust had too often ravaged the best

As life improved, the sodbusters were able to move from a house of "prairie marble" to one of wood (Nebraska State Historical Society)

that they could grow. So why should these strangely dressed newcomers know better? But once the skeptics saw for themselves, they quickly became converts. Additionally, a farming lecturer from Kansas went back to Russia and, near Kharkov, found other strains which ripened in an even shorter growing season than Turkey Red. Now wheat could be (and would be) successfully grown right up through the Dakotas and onto the short-summered prairies of Canada.

It is interesting to contrast two early reports by the embryonic Kansas Board of Agriculture. In 1872 it wrote, "Wheat is the least profitable of crops." Yet, just four years later, it found "that on new ground, no crop is more certain than wheat." The arrival of the Rooshans (by 1876 there were over 4,000 of them and more arriving every year) had made the difference. Many years later, near the site of their first church, the Kansas-Rooshans put up a roadside marker saying that they had established themselves in those parts "By the Grace of God, and with the Aid and Assistance of the Acheson, Topeka and Santa Fe Railroad." Surely, no railroad could ask for more than to share credit with the Almighty. Incidentally, by 1910, according to the census of that year, there were over 100,000 Rooshans on the plains; almost all of them were wheat farmers. They are still there, from Kansas to Alberta.

❧

If the hard Russian wheat arrived ready-made for the plains, it was one of the few things that did. Heating was certainly not easy. Obviously those "meadow muffins" around a sod house would not last long for cooking and winter warmth. What then? The settlers had to turn to anything that would burn: corncobs, sunflower stalks and, above all, hay. It was said to take "two men and a boy" to gather enough hay to keep a fire going through a freezing night. But, in time, someone devised a special stove which only required the full-time efforts of the boy.

That hay-burner was just one of the many newfangled tools that helped the settler families to improve their lives. One does not need to know by what precise means the need for other contrivances, newly designed or merely adapted, was recognized back in the factories and workshops of the east. But through the 1870s and 80s, as well as developing the sodbusters' plow and the hay-burning stove, the nation's tinkerer-mechanics (a subspecies of *homo sapiens* that still seems to exist in greater numbers in America than anywhere else in the world) came up with ever more contraptions and machines to ease the farmers' work: corn planters, drills for deep wells, self-governing wind pumps, reaper-binders, threshing machines and, not least, barbed wire. Most of these things could be ordered via another invention of those times: the mail-order catalogue. For many years it was, along with the family Bible, the most important book on Western farms. Indeed, by 1899 you could even order a wooden house (in bits) for $1,499 from Sears-Roebuck in Chicago; a sewing machine cost $12.75; a Smith and Wesson revolver $9.75; or for $6.80 you could buy an Ezeeoff—a gadget for castrating calves.

Of all the inventions, barbed wire was one of the simplest while also one of the most important. Livestock and crops are mutually exclusive; unless they are kept apart, the stock will trample and eat the crops. So where there was no timber for split-rail fencing, barbed wire quickly became the farmer's vital friend. Today we take the simplicity of the stuff for granted. But 140 years ago one might have had to guess what it was for. Folklore says that back in Illinois in 1874 a certain farmer, Henry Rose, owned an athletic cow that kept breaking through a split-rail fence into Mrs. Rose's pea patch. So, to deter the animal, Mr. and Mrs. Rose drove some sharp wire points into the top rail. It worked so well that, proud of their ingenuity, they took a length of the rail along to the local county fair to show their friends and neighbors. That much is the folklore of the story. What is more certain is that two of the Roses' neighbors were sufficiently impressed to go home and try their own experiments. They both hit on the same basic idea: to dispense with the wooden rail and, instead, to wrap short bits of twisted wire directly onto a long strand of wire. They decided to combine their efforts, and partners Joseph Glidden and Isaac Elwood fought patent battles against all comers for the next 20 years. The problem was how to stop the small twists (the barbs) from merely sliding along the wire. The solution lay in using a coffee grinder to twist two strands together, so that the barbs were wrapped around one strand and held in position by the other encircling strand. In 80% of the wire made today, that idea has not changed.

Farmers were soon lining up for this invention at the hardware stores. It cost about $150 a mile: enough to run a single strand around a 160-acre homestead. By 1880, with more than 20 manufacturers, the business had become a full-blown industry. By 1900 more than 400 US patents had been filed: some for variations on the wire itself, some for particular configurations of the barbs, some for the machinery to make the stuff. There is a kind of rural poetry in the different designs: Kennedy Barb, Split Diamond, Twist Oval, Lazy Plate,

Crandall's Link, Merril Twist, Burnell's Four Point, Brotherton Barb, Champion Zig-zag and, most descriptive of all, Billings Vicious. It has been said that, because of barbed wire, patent law became, for a few years, the most lucrative branch of the American legal trade; certainly the lawyers made millions. There is no record of whether Mr. and Mrs. Rose with their awkward cow made anything.

જી

The museum was shut when I got there, but there was a note on the door telling any would-be visitor to phone someone called Lee. So I did as I was told, and Lee Shank was with me inside ten minutes; he had been having an early lunch. In this small mid-Kansas town of La Crosse they take barbed wire seriously. Indeed, they will tell you that this is the Barbed Wire Capital of the World. Certainly, with a museum and a library dedicated to the stuff, one would not want to doubt their claim.

You might suppose that if you have seen one piece of barbed wire, you have seen them all. But that would be before you had been inside the museum. Arrayed along the walls and in glass cases are more than 3,000 varieties; they have been collected from all over the world and range from the most modern varieties (including several made of plastic) back to the earliest types from the 1870s. A good example of the latter, perhaps no more than 18 inches long, can fetch at least $200 from a devotee at the annual "Swap'n'Sell Fair." I was too late for the 2007 jamboree, but Lee reckoned that over 1,000 collectors had turned up. Each year they have auctions, seminars, and contests to find the world's fastest wire splicer. I think they elect a Barbed Wire Queen. Certainly, there is a Barbed Wire Hall of Fame, a collectors' magazine and a flourishing internet site at Rush County: Barbed Wire Museum. Lee encouraged me to turn the handle on a replica of Mrs. Glidden's coffee grinder, to twist some wire together. He explained an array of fencing tools, and he talked, as only an enthusiast can, about the whole history of barbed wire. The afternoon was quickly gone; I would not have missed it—it was an education. Lee, thank you.

જી

Fights between herdsman and cultivator go back at least to the Old Testament. Now, with his wire, the farmer on the plains had the means of defending what was his. The cattlemen fought back with wire cutters, bloody intimidation, and lawsuits. But, in the end, the sodbusters won; there were just too many of them. Indeed, one might say that barbed wire had at least as much to do with "the winning of the West" as did all the Colts and Winchesters that ever fired a shot. One might also say that barbed wire provides one of the best examples in history of a simple technology changing geography forever; it re-drew the map physically, economically, and socially.

Another seemingly simple device, viewed from this distance in time, is the sodbusting plow. Adaptations of it are now used in mechanized farming all over the world. But before the mid-nineteenth century the plow had not changed very much since Biblical times. Thomas Jefferson, who used his ingenuity on everything from the Declaration of Independence to a folding bed, had ideas for the plow's improvement. He designed a wooden mold-board with an iron tip; he sent the thing to Paris and won a gold medal at an agricultural show. Later, seeking further improvements, others came up with a *steel* mold-board with sometimes a sharp vertical disc up front. It was heavy and, when breaking virgin soil, it needed two or three oxen to pull it. Because of this and its cost, it did not immediately catch on out on the plains. But when the homesteaders found that the plows they had brought with them did no more than scratch the surface, they had no choice but to save up (or go into debt) to buy one.

The plow took some pulling. Tractors costing $250,000 or more do the job now, sometimes dragging 8–12 plows at once. In the biggest of these "rigs" the driver sits high up in an air-conditioned cab with power steering, power brakes, ten forward gears, and a stereo tape deck. As well as his cell phone, he has a two-way radio to keep in direct touch with his mate who may be driving a similar "rig" on the far side of a 640-acre field. And he'll have an ice cooler containing another American invention: iced tea. His radio will be tuned to keep up with hog prices in Kansas City, wheat futures in Chicago, what is for lunch today at the local high school, and who has been discharged from the local hospital. Plus, of course, the weather.

Back in the early days, it was soon recognized that a farming family on the plains needed more than the statutory 160 acres. At the same time, the ancient belief that cultivation brought an increase in rainfall was given formal support by Washington. The popular slogan was "Rain follows the plow." Trees encouraged rain too. So the Timber Culture Act of 1873 combined the two targets of giving the settler more land and of increasing the rainfall. This gave a further 160 acres to a homesteader if he undertook to plant trees on 40 acres of his new land.

Any number of people hurried down to the local land office to claim more land. Some even got around to planting some young trees, if they could find any. Others stuck a few twigs in the ground. Others didn't bother either way. After all, if there was anything to this rain theory, why not let your neighbor put in the trees? The resultant clouds were as likely to break over your land as over his. A humorist of the day suggested that any disputes might be settled in a Court of Nebulous Claims.

Strangely, a few years after the passing of that act, there really was an improvement in the rainfall. The seven years ending in 1885 were unusually moist, and even the skeptics had to admit that something, somewhere, was making a difference. If it was not the almost nonexistent planting of trees, then perhaps it was the discharge of "earth electricity" which allegedly flowed up and down the steel rails of the newly built railroads. The professional rain-makers denied both these possibilities and put it about that it was all due to their own scientific powers. They were persuasive. For a handsome fee from a syndicate of farmers, they would fire small cannons and play about with lengths of copper wire and hand-cranked dynamos. Preachers simply explained that the better weather was the result of prayer and the considerate response of the Almighty. The fact was that the Great Plains, like most parts of the world, have a naturally varying cycle of climate. But in those days, climatology was no more understood than electricity.

In time there came better years for those who earlier had struggled just to survive. Not only had they had learned how to farm on the plains, but, to their relief, the price of wheat was rising; demand was growing. In both the US and Europe, industrialization meant that there now were urban millions who had to be fed; industry and its workers depended on wheat and meat as much as on iron ore and coal. On top of this, Europe had suffered several poor harvests and was being denied its usual imports from Russia: trouble between Russia and Turkey had closed the wheat ports of the Crimea. So prairie wheat went up to more than $1 a bushel (a bushel being 60 lbs.) On their increased income, some of the settlers could now afford to move out of their houses of "prairie marble" into something bigger, better, and built of wood.

Some historians suggest that, prompted by the needs of the sodbusters out on the plains, the last two decades of the century saw an agricultural revolution at least as profound as the one that had occurred a hundred years earlier in the British Isles. They may be right. By some mechanical equivalent of Darwinism, the more efficient contrivances survived to prosper, together with the people who made them. Some of the manufacturing names from that era are still very much in business; one thinks of McCormick, Case, Deere, and Massey-Harris.

And still there is the ever-present symbol of the plains: the wind-pump. Wind, after all, is the one resource of which the Western farmer was (and is) never short. Indeed, in settling the plains, wind-pumps were as important as barbed wire, or those sod-busting plows, or of course the railroads.

Techniques had changed too. Above all came the realization that "dry farming" was the answer to the problem of low rainfall. At its simplest, two years' precipitation (rain and snow) was/is used to grow one year's crop. That way, the soil absorbs enough moisture (what is not lost to evaporation) over two years to sustain one crop. Of course it means that, at any one time, half a farmer's land is unseeded, or lying fallow. And that, in turn, means that a farming family needs at least a section of land (640 acres or one square mile) to begin to make even a meager living.

In the celebrated Rogers and Hammerstein musical, *Oklahoma*, there is the chorus that tells us that "the wavin' wheat can sure smell sweet when the wind comes right behind the rain." But the truth about Oklahoma, one of the last parts of the Great Plains to be settled, was rather different. While there was never much doubt about the constancy of the wind, there came years when the rains might fail and then the farmers' wheat would shrivel before if got anywhere near wavin' or smellin' sweet. But the first homesteaders into those parts could not know that …

By the late 1880s, most of the Great Plains were "pretty much settled out"; such virgin lands as were left were either pockets of infertility that the whites did not want or they were treaty-lands occupied by the tribes. Nowhere was this more apparent than across most of what is today's Oklahoma. On maps, this last, vast stretch of land was labeled as Indian Territory or sometimes, more cynically, as the (as yet) Unassigned Lands. In effect, this was one enormous reservation of 50 million acres (about 300 x 250 miles). For several decades the native inhabitants, some of whom were known as the Five Civilized Tribes, had been well-behaved and peaceful; some had even become farmers. But once it became apparent that they were sitting on land, particularly along the valleys of the Washita, the Red, and the Arkansas rivers, that the whites now wanted, the Indians' good behavior did not count. Indeed, untroubled by any last-minute qualms, in March 1889 President Cleveland signed the aptly named Indian Appropriation Act under which, with a minimum of consultation, two of the tribes (the rest would be forced to follow within a few years) were compulsorily bought out for a few million dollars.

Now, with the land appropriately "appropriated," there was the question of how the government should parcel it out among the thousands of hopeful homesteaders. It was decided that, held back by posses of quickly

Newfangled equipment: a reaper-binder (Kansas State Historical Society)

appointed marshals, all settlers would be barred until a specifically appointed moment. Accordingly, at exactly noon on April 22, 1889, guns were fired simultaneously at various points around the long perimeter of the "new" land. This was the signal for thousands of men to leap to their horses or buggies or bicycles to race for the choicest pieces of land: first come, first served. Within hours, marker stakes were being hammered down as far as 40 miles "inland" from that start line. Within a day, over 10,000 settlers had claimed nearly two million acres. This was the first of Oklahoma's Land Rushes. In one afternoon, a tent-town calling itself Guthrie sprang up; by nightfall it had a population of over 5,000. By the next morning it had declared itself to be the capital of the whole territory.

As one might expect, there were a number of men who had secretly "jumped the gun"; they had collared some of the best locations. Among these "sooners" (as they became known) were some of those policing marshals. And, as one might further expect, platoons of disputatious lawyers came swooping quickly onto the scene.

Over the next decade, as more and more Indian lands were appropriated, there were more land rushes, each as hectic as the one before. By the end of the century, with a population of nearly a third of a million, Oklahoma Territory was said to be "all filled up." Within a few years, the place had become a state with Oklahoma City as its capital. And, to this day, the state's citizens take pride in being known as Sooners.

Now, it had long been more than just whispered that the grasslands along the southwestern margins of the Great Plains had a particularly uncertain climate. Yes, sure, there would be the occasional droughty times, but, hell, these were anomalies that would pass. After all, everyone knew that rain followed the plow. So, the more settlement, the more rain! Anyway, wheat prices across the world were going up. Indeed, in the years during and after the Great War they more than doubled. Drawn on by those prices and, as always, the need to pay off the banks (who were charging usurious rates on mortgages and loans for tractors, wind-pumps, barbed wire, and a dozen other bits of machinery), farmers out on the western fringes of Oklahoma became ever more vigorous in their methods. Why run cattle on your land when you could plow it up for wheat? What was the point in wasting a recently harvested field by putting it to fallow? Why bother with those newfangled theories about crop rotation, windbreaks, and shelterbelts?

The fact is that some farmers and their plows had been tempted further west than they had any right to go. Those droughty years were not anomalies: they came back; they were part of the climatic cycle. The native grasses of the southwestern plains were never meant to be turned over; their deep and tangled roots had held the fragile soil together for millennia. But the sharp-nosed plow changed all that. When the drought years came back in the early 1930s, the topsoil was literally rootless. Dry and friable, it just blew away in the wind: millions of tons of it. Sometimes visibility was down to a few yards. The skies in distant Chicago were darkened. In far-away New York people remarked on the beautiful sunsets.

While western Oklahoma was the epicenter of what became known as the Dust Bowl, bordering regions in other states—Kansas, Nebraska, Colorado, and northern Texas—were not much less devastated. Hundreds, then thousands of farms were abandoned. Banks went bust. Towns became derelict. Old people and children died on the choking dust. In three years, more than two million people abandoned the country of the Dust Bowl. Destitute, the Okies (as they became known) piled their possessions into old jalopies and puttered off west to look for work in California. But these were the Depression years; there was no work. Many of those refugees never recovered; they died paupers.

With time, of course, techniques changed. They had to. Above all, there was the growing realization that "dry farming" was, at least, a partial answer to the problem of low and chancy rainfall. As mentioned a couple of pages ago, two years' rain (and snow) is used to grow one year's crop. After any "precipitation," the soil is quickly turned—to hold the moisture against evaporation. So, in most years, the soil will absorb enough water over two years to sustain one year's crop.

Of course it means that, at any one time, half a farmer's land is unproductive. And that, in turn, means that a farming family needs at least a section of land (640 acres or one square mile) to begin to make a reasonable living. So it is not surprising that, over the last 50–60 years, farms right across the Great Plains have become much bigger. Yes, there are still family farms, but they are becoming ever fewer. Increasingly, by means of amalgamation, partnerships, rentals, sales, and purchasing, the farms have become more and more extensive. Increasingly, corporate farming seems to be the rule.

As I have already hinted, by far the quickest way to appreciate the immensity of what has been achieved on the Great Plains over the last 150 years is to fly from, say, Omaha to Denver. Get yourself a window seat and then, for 500 miles, you will be looking across the slow heart of the continent and over what is undoubtedly one of the broadest and most productive granaries in the world. Yet, back when Abraham Lincoln signed that Homestead Bill, this was still buffalo country. On the Great Plains, the homesteader and his family deserve the accolades. Without really knowing it, they tamed what many had called the Wild West. They, more than anyone, began the process of settlement, of home-making, of domestication. From mean and difficult beginnings in their soddies, they had hung on—always hoping. They made the difference. Everyone and everything else followed, from that day to this.

A final thought: if it is the actual settlement of the West that we are talking about, quite apart from the often overlooked fact that this was the last part of the United States to be peopled, the story contains a deep and intriguing irony. Run your eye along the book shelves of almost any aficionado of "the West," and you will notice there are fewer books, far fewer, about the folk who finally and permanently *settled* the place than there are about almost everyone else. The early explorers and the pathfinders get their detailed literary due. So do the cowboys and the miners, the tribes and the Army, the gunmen and the conmen, the cardsharps and the saloon-keepers, the madams and the joy-girls, the bankers and the lawyers, the railroad magnates and the engineers, the cattle barons and the range detectives. But the sodbusters, the homesteaders, the grangers, the farmers? Where are they?

Yes, of course, there are some splendid books (and chapters within books) about the men who finally domesticated the place, and, just as important, about their women too—women who, leaning against a constant and windswept loneliness, ultimately took the place from wilderness to wallpaper. But the fact still remains that there really *are* many more books about, for example, Colonel Custer, than there are (or ever will be) about the hundreds (thousands?) of brave and modest mothers who raised their barefoot children in leaky dwellings made of sod, and who, together with their menfolk, withstood blizzards, droughts, locusts, and near penury in the hope that, one day, life might get better. Similarly, there is more written about the Colt and Winchester than about barbed wire and wind-pumps; there are more words expended on Calamity Jane or Billy the Kid than on the achievements of all those nameless women; there are more TV Westerns about the cowboys and their cattle trails than there are about the sodbusters and their acres; there is probably as much published about the shoot-out at the OK Corral as there is on the ramifications of the Homestead Act—some of which are still with us.

Yes, I am conscious that I too am guilty of this misbalance: I have just one chapter on the homesteaders, but a dozen or so on everyone else. So, in some shame, I can only offer the weak excuse that the colorful and the dramatic will most usually win against the merely admirable and the grimly stoic. They are just easier to write about. Yes, as I say, it is a weak excuse.

Anyway, like I said, go get yourself that window seat.

∽

"We sure must have been dumb to have come out here, but we soon got smart enough to survive."
The reported comment of an old-timer reflecting on his early days of homesteading on the Great Plains

Alistair Cooke and Tim Slessor, the director, dicussing a railroad sequence during the filming of Alistair Cooke's BBC *America* series. (David Evans)

17

LAST THINGS LAST

From the sidewalk, I could see that a wide dimple in the grass was the only trace of the small, three-room house in which we had once spent some of the happiest days of our lives. Back then, we had been all together. Now, I was by myself. Memories—inevitably. And a few tears. My wife, Janet, who had gently generated so much of that happiness, was gone. Our two children, Jeremy and Kate, then just four and two, were now into their fifties with teenaged children of their own.

After 50 years, I was back in Chadron. Apart from our missing house, the place did not seem to have changed much.

In fact, over the years, I had been back several times, but, on those occasions, I was just driving through—time enough to call on my old boss and his wife, and then to hurry on. Now I had been invited back for rather longer. How come? Well, on the last of those fleeting visits, I met someone from the college where, all those years ago, I had tried to teach. Hardly thinking, I had commented that it would be interesting, even fun, to come back for a few days; perhaps I might talk to a journalism class about documentary film-making or the differences between American and British newspapers or the BBC. Anyway, a little later, via a few trans-Atlantic e-mails, the College took me up on the idea—but for eight weeks. So here I was. My brief, besides spending some time with that journalism class was to go off to give talks or, as they called them, "presentations," at various other colleges, high schools and public libraries across Nebraska and, further, into neighboring Wyoming. The college organized my schedule and, via a charitable and broad-minded foundation, I was provided with my airfares to and from London, a car, a mobile phone, and a stipend to cover my food, motel rooms, and all other outgoings.

My brief was a loose one. "We don't get too many Brits in these parts, so we'll be interested in most anything you want to tell us." Ridiculous—but flattering and welcoming. So what *did* I talk about? I decided to lead off by trying to explain what it was that, over a span of more than half a century, had kept me coming back. After all, though I have lost count, I reckon that over the years I must have journeyed west of the Missouri at least 20 times. Of course, many of those sorties were paid for by my employer, the BBC. But latterly, since my retirement, I have been self-propelled. So, what is it about the place? Why? Perhaps, now that I (or *we*—if, gentle reader, you are still with me) have almost reached the end of this book, I might here briefly re-run my several fascinations—as I did in those talks. They also explain why I began this book in the first place.

First, dating from my very first sortie out West, I have always been spellbound, almost hypnotized, by the geographical vastness of the place. I can think of a number of remote spots on various highways where, perhaps cresting a rise, the horizon is suddenly so broad, and the sky so immense, that I have to pull over to the verge, turn off the engine and just sit and wonder. I can see 80 or 90 miles. I think I can even see the curve of the earth. Perhaps only those lucky few who have been launched into space can, looking back, have had a wider view of our planet.

Integral with the vastness of the West is, of course, its emptiness. Consider: Wyoming is slightly larger than Great Britain; its population is about the same as that of Bristol or Belfast. Western Nebraska is not much different. Along with such striking disparity, there are our contrasting senses of Distance. In most parts of Britain, a drive of, say, 150 miles is—especially if you have an appointment at the other end—a fairly serious business. If you are wise you will allow at least an extra hour for possible delays. But, out West, if need be, you can—driving at 70 mph along almost empty roads—easily cover those 150 miles before breakfast. When we lived in Chadron we would, with friends, drive 95 miles to Scottsbluff for an evening of ten-pin bowling, followed by a pizza. Then we'd drive home. On my most recent sojourn, several of my "presentations" involved a 250-mile round-trip. In eight weeks I drove more than 7,000 miles. On one occasion, out of interest, I asked my GPS to give me a route from Omaha to Cheyenne. I was told to "Take Interstate 80—493 miles to Exit 36." What it did not think worth mentioning was that there are no traffic lights anywhere along those 493 miles. Indeed, if you could stay awake and your car had a big enough gas tank (and you had a big enough bladder) the US system of interstate highways (two lanes in each direction) would allow you to drive the 2,902 miles from New York to San Francisco at 70 mph without pause.

So, as a Brit, a core ingredient of my fascination is the contrast between life in our own small and crowded island, and life in the vast and empty West. It is inevitable that we have different ways of looking at things—and not just at our vastly differing geographies. Just as far apart are our historical perspectives. For example, out West, while a journey of 150 miles is a just "a run down the road," an event of 150 *years* ago is (as I remarked nearly 300 pages back) so long gone as to be, in a westerner's time-scale, only a little this side of Magna Carta. After all, back in 1865 this part of America was quite unsettled; it was still home to vast herds of buffalo; the Civil War was hardly finished; the war with the Plains Indians had hardly begun; the building of the first trans-continental railroad had only just started, and another decade would pass before Custer would pay the price. To Europeans, the history of the place is all so recent. On a personal level I think back to the time when I interviewed a Sioux elder who, as a boy in 1890, had watched the 7th Cavalry ride out to Wounded Knee—the last "battle" with the tribes. Or, I remember a conversation with a centenarian who, born before the Civil War, had arrived in a wagon with his parents to take up land in Colorado in the mid-1870s. To today's born'n'bred westerners, all those things are so long ago that they might as well be prehistoric.

What else? Well, for me, even more than the geography and the history of the West are the people. Their friendship or, at the least, their kindness and courtesy are almost immediate. I can think of many examples …

So, yes, the road ahead seemed empty to the horizon and I had been speeding. But a Highway Patrol car came up from nowhere and pulled me over. He came to the window, "You in some kinda hurry?" "Well, not really officer, but I was sort of paying my dues to the folk who built this fine road." Even as I said it, I regretted my bumptious idiocy. But, with the faintest of smiles, he just looked at me. "Never heard *that* line before." Then, examining my license with slow puzzlement, "So you're a Brit. What you doin' in these parts?" I explained. "Well now," he asked, "what would a patrolman back in *your* country do with you?" Lying through my teeth, I told him that I would probably be given a good talking to, told not to do it again, and then sent on my way. "Well, Mr. Timothy, we've got limits hereabouts—you know that. I ought to give you a ticket. But you're a visitor. So consider yourself talked to, and mind you don't do it again." He paused and smiled. "Now … on your way." And, as he turned away, "Oh—and have a good day." Unbelievable? No, it really happened. I called out to ask his name: Patrolman Brady. I was going to write to his boss in appreciation. And admiration. But then I thought better of it: perhaps his boss would think that Patrolman Brady had been altogether too generous.

I used to tell that story as part of my "presentation"; it always raised an appreciative chuckle. What else? Well, I have long found it worth putting a GB sticker on the back of my car. Often, at gas stations or motels or supermarket parking lots, people will come over to talk. Why was I here? Where had I been? Where was I going? Sometimes they would remember that they had some distant cousins in Okehampton or Carlisle. They all love the Queen—"some lady, that." Sometimes they would invite me to go with them for a pizza or a steak that evening. All Americans are hospitable, but none more so than the folk out West.

Anyway, back to those "presentations." After talking for a few minutes about those fascinations, I would turn to a few of the many things our two nations share. One thinks of Democracy, the Law, our Freedoms—but as I was quite unqualified to talk about what one might call Those Big Fundamentals, I would hurry on to the "everyday" fundamental that we all use all the time: our language. Yes, there are some interesting differences, but I would suggest that very few of them justify that well-known but overly clever assertion that we are two nations "separated by the same language." On the contrary … Nevertheless, as I have just said, there *are* differences. For example, some words and usages that the earliest settlers took with them to the New World have long since disappeared back in the country where they originated. When was the last time one heard a Brit talking about a faucet or a skillet or the fall? And when we say that someone is as mad as a hatter, most Americans would not suppose that the hatter had behaved strangely, rather that he is very angry. What about the common Americanism, "gotten"—as in "I've gotten some real good exam results"? One will find the verb in Chaucer but, in today's Britain (and for the last several centuries), it seems only to exist in "forgotten" and in "ill-gotten gains." Then there are American inventions that have come back to us across the Atlantic; they are now so common that we Brits think that they have always been with us: commuter, teenager, gimmick, hangover, stunt, countdown, hold-up, breakup, ripoff, top-up, cocktail, jackpot, and several dozen more. And there are the Americanisms that we understand easily enough but which we do not normally use: trash, sidewalk, platter, overpass, candy, cookies … Americans don't have front gardens, they have yards; they don't have cupboards, they have closets; they don't buy things in shops, they buy them in stores; they don't have dressing gowns, they have bath robes; they don't keep their trousers up with braces, they keep their pants up with suspenders. Their first floor is our ground floor—now *that* can cause confusion. Their rocks are our stones; their apartments are our flats; their diapers are our nappies. They visit *with* people, and they don't know anything about fortnights. I could go on …

Sometimes, particularly in high schools, we would discuss where English, our shared language (and one shared worldwide) came from. I found that a useful starting point lay in the creed of "Life, liberty, and the pursuit of happiness": two of those words come from Norman French, two from Anglo-Saxon. Likewise, was I giving a "talk" or a "presentation"? Again, same difference, different roots. In short, Anglisch (as it once was) is a crossbreed, a mongrel and, like most hybrids, the stronger for it. Then I would lead on to the thought that, for some time now, America has been the leading generator of new phrases and sayings. Appropriately (given my audience), some of them come out of the West. So,

314

from the gold rush we get, "Let's see how things pan out" and "Let's hope that we strike it rich." From the West's bad old days, we get "He's rather too quick on the draw" or "She's inclined to shoot from the hip." Someone has suggested that "to jump the gun" comes not from athletics but from the Oklahoma land rush. Spreading the net more widely, we use several metaphors derived from baseball—a game we don't even play. Listen to a political discussion on the BBC and soon enough someone will observe that "It's high time that someone stood up to the plate on that." Wait a while further and you'll get "We're getting into a whole new ball game." Or "I'll give you a ballpark figure on that." And what about "playing hardball"? Or, my favorite (and recently heard on a discussion about MP's expenses), "Oh, I'm going to have to plead the Fifth on that." Everyday American conversation has any number of pithy and useful admonitions; I think of "Wise up," "Get real," and "Go figure."

And I haven't even touched on the differences in spelling. Maybe it is enough to say that the American spelling is more logical.

Given that I was talking in a state that lies well within the bounds of what was once the French-claimed territory of La Louisiane, it seemed appropriate sometimes to move on to the background story of the Louisiana Purchase. Sacrificing tact in the interests of a wider truth (as I see it), I would point out that *if* (and I am always intrigued by historical "ifs") it had not been for Admiral Nelson's victory at the Battle of the Nile (Aboukir Bay, 1798), America's history might have developed differently. Who knows, but I might have even been giving "ma présentation en francais." Unlikely, mais possible. After all, when Jefferson learned that Napoleon was hatching plans to build a French empire out of New Orleans, he let it be known that if any French soldiers *did* land at that port, then the Americans would have to "marry" themselves "to the British fleet and nation." Given that only a few years before, when Napoleon had landed 20,000 troops to establish a French empire in Egypt and the Levant, he had seen his grand design totally cannon-balled by Admiral Nelson at Aboukir Bay, it was hardly likely that the French emperor would now go looking for a repetition of that disaster in the waters off New Orleans. Once bitten by the Royal Navy, twice shy? In any case, the last thing Napoleon wanted was an alliance between the Americans and the British. So, on hearing of Jefferson's threat, he quit. He withdrew 25,000 troops (his invasion force) from their way station on Santo Domingo (today's Haiti). Then, within days, he signed away La Louisiane. Most American versions of the story are rather different: Napoleon, they say, changed his mind because he was losing too many of those troops in Santo Domingo to yellow fever and to a slave revolt. There is truth in that—as far as it goes. But was that the main reason he quit on his imperial designs? It depends on whose history books you are reading.

Of course, there is more to it than that (there usually is), but that limited narrative often sparked (as I designed it to) an interesting discussion on the way our two nations view the same events from different perspectives. As implied, American history books are a little short on the role of the Royal Navy—and not only in the instance just mentioned. For example, it can be argued that the successful imposition of the Monroe Doctrine across the Americas owed almost as much to the British navy as it did to the American. In an opposite direction, British histories are sometimes one-sided on aspects of the War of 1812 or the details of our two-faced support of both the Union and the slave-owning Confederacy through the Civil War. And, moving much closer to the present day, we sometimes like to think that we played the major role in winning World War II. Surely that achievement really lies with the US and Russia. But what *we* did was just as important: through 1940 and 1941, we didn't *lose* the war in the first place; we hung on until those other more powerful nations joined us. In my talks I would use the analogy of American football where there are, within the same team, a defensive and an offensive squad; if the former collapses, the latter has a very difficult task in subsequently regaining the initiative, let alone making a winning score. Britain and her Commonwealth allies did not collapse. Important.

At the end of my talks there was usually time for Questions. One that came up several times derived from my uncompromising (well, almost) enthusiasm for America. So was there, I would be asked, anything that I did *not* like about their country? That was a difficult one. As a guest, one does not want to give offense. But (unwisely?) I would take a risk and point to what many foreigners, and some Americans, see as an extraordinary level of polarization that exists in parts of the nation's politics. There can be a hostility towards someone from "the other side" which goes far beyond mere dislike or distrust; it is close to hatred. It has to be said that this execration is more often directed by far-right Republicans towards "liberal" Democrats than the other way. Consider a recent diatribe by Clint Eastwood—in a widely circulated e-mail marked "pass it on." At 84, he writes a piece called "My Twilight Years." After a simple, even moving, 120-word passage which, in effect, celebrates life, he ends thus, "So, just in case I'm gone tomorrow, please know this: I voted against that incompetent, lying, flip-flopping, insincere, double-talking radical socialist, terrorist-excusing, bleeding heart, narcissistic, economic moron currently in the White House." Beyond my saying Mr. Eastwood's rant is not unique, the comment seems superfluous. But I hope he credits me for having, in a small way, "passed it on."

On a lighter note, I would, with as straight a face as I could muster, turn to the way too many Americans make their tea—by dunking a tea bag in a cup of allegedly hot, but sometimes merely tepid, water. No. As the rest of the world knows (well, most of it), the water must be boiling, or within a very few seconds of being so. And the tea bag must be allowed to diffuse for a minute or two. But then, as I would remark, Americans have long had a problem with the proper handling of Tea; it goes all the way back to the beginning of their nation. Mostly they would smile indulgently at what, I admit, was a pretty feeble joke. All the same, I am still unsure that, once home, they brought their water to a proper boil.

What else? Indeed, how to end?

Well, perhaps I might finish with something I had long forgotten—until I found it a few days ago in a proverbial bottom drawer. I wrote it about thirty years ago as part of a book which did not then get written—not at that time, anyway. Yes, maybe it is a bit of a ramble, but it does sum up a number of my thoughts about the West. So, here goes …

Only 125 years ago, in 1890, the Census Bureau in Washington, applying some formula based on the number of settlers per square mile, declared that the concept of The Frontier was finished. By chance, the timing was entirely appropriate: in the December snows of that year, the most famous of all Indian warriors was shot; Sitting Bull was not long home from a starring role in Buffalo Bill's Wild West Circus. Two weeks later, at Wounded Knee, over 200 Sioux were killed by a detachment of the regiment that had served under Colonel Custer 14 years earlier. It was the last incident—one could hardly call it a battle—of the last campaign against the "Native Americans." Then, less than 18 months later, the open-range feudalism of Wyoming's cattle barons fractured when their well-armed, but ill-judged "invasion" of mercenary gunmen came up against an equally well-armed posse of settlers. In the decade that followed, western women won the vote (in their states), the Mormons gave up polygamy, the mail-order catalog was invented and, in the Oklahoma land rushes, some of the last unfenced land was "released" to would-be settlers. Only a few years later, those attractive rogues, Butch and Sundance, decided that the fun had gone out of life and, anyway, some Pinkerton men were getting too close. They took off for South America.

So, one way and another, it would seem that the bureaucrats back in Washington had it about right: the Old West probably *was* finished.

If today's westerners think about it at all, they are likely to regard "all that history stuff" as of very little contemporary relevance. And who is to blame them? After all, if they drive past an intercontinental missile site, it is hard for them to realize that only two longish lifetimes ago, that very ground was grazed by buffalo. Between the Missouri and the Mountains, so much has happened in so short a time.

These days, many of the Sioux who still live around Wounded Knee are near-destitute; they shuffle in once a month to collect their welfare checks. Except for a few protected herds, the buffalo is long gone. The beavers and the wolves too. The eagles and the coyotes are trapped as vermin. Across too many acres, the topsoil has been plowed up and blown away. Whole mountain sides have been stripped of trees. Rivers have been dammed and diverted. Where once there were teepees, there are feedlots and junk yards; where once the fur-seeking mountain men gathered for their Rendezvous, there are ski lifts and resort motels.

Sometimes, the rest of the nation can be strangely dismissive of the West: in superior tones, East Coast sophisticates talk about the place as The Sticks, The Boonies, The Empty Quarter, The Fly-Over Country. To them, it is what slides by, mostly unseen from 30,000 feet, as they jet to and from California. Or if, as vacationers, they are driving to see the faces at Mount Rushmore or to wonder at the geysers of Yellowstone Park, the West is sometimes not much more than the seemingly empty miles between last night's motel room and the next gas station.

And yet …

Some things have not changed. If you get off the superhighways and away into the back-country, you can still find something of the Old West., The sky, bigger and bluer than any other, cannot have changed. Or the wind-blown silence. Or a winter blizzard coming down from the Arctic like a hammer. Or the summer thunder with hail as hard as marbles. Or the short arcadian spring. Or the grass—where it has not been plowed under.

And there are the places too. Go to Hole-in-the-Wall and you will plainly see why Butch Cassidy and his friends chose this remote valley for a hideout. And in the Red Desert of Wyoming, far from any road, you can still find the occasional wagon-rut of the Overland Trail. At Register Cliff, you can see where the Forty-Niners left their passing graffiti. In Deadwood, under some plastic lilies of purity, lies Calamity Jane. Near South Pass, the hills are pocked by derelict gold mines with names like Some Hope and Wish Me Luck. A few miles south of Buffalo, one of the most archetypal of western towns, in the wooden walls of a still-used barn, you can see rifle slots hurriedly cut by a small army of besieged Texas gunmen; they were in the pay of the cattle barons.

And the people? Of course, there is no one left who was "there at the time." But only sixty years ago, there were still a few old-timers who remembered some of these things: the last covered wagons, the last buffaloes, the last bloody confrontation with the Sioux, the last bank robbery, the last railroad hold-up.

The West, to its devotees (like me), has always been much more than an area marked off on a map. To us, it was, and still is, a certain style, a state of mind. And it is in their way of doing things, their manner, that one can most clearly identify today's true Westerners. They even stand in a certain way. Their upright and up-front style has much to do with their heritage. Of course, in cities like

Denver, there are any number of dudes—bankers, traveling shoe salesmen, and lawyers-on-the-make. They wear black string ties; their belt buckles and their Stetsons are too big; their boots are too pointy. To find the real thing you need to get out of town (preferably in a pickup truck) to find what the locals would call "the real, no shit, no stop lights West." Out there, who knows, you might still be able to find a genuine cowboy.

Although there are not many real cowboys left, the world has long seen them as the archetypal Westerners. Their forebears, drifting up from Texas with their longhorns, gave them—and by cultural osmosis, much of the rest of the West—qualities which are not quite gone yet: an instant but rather cautious informality, a slow humor, a love of firearms and of sentimental music. The cowboy is often a big man; he thinks big too: difficulties are either to be ignored or to be "fixed"; they are not to be much pondered. Distance means very little; he will drive 200 miles to see a friend, share a burger or two, drink a few weak beers, then drive home again. If he *does* say "Howdy pardner" it will be because he is not above a little role playing—if he senses that it is expected of him. He has become a Living Legend. And he knows it. So too, if he is riding one, does his horse.

One last thought—and then I'll shut up. In the perspective of history, all of the US has been The West at one time or another. Whether it was just up the beach from Plymouth Rock, or later in the woods of Ohio, or, much later, in the high country of Wyoming or Montana, the tempting promise of "movin' west" has always been the same: new land, new hope, the chance to "start over." Down at least three centuries, even if that promise might sometimes have been broken, its existence has surely been a most particular influence in the evolution of what the rest of us have come to recognize as the American spirit. In short, in the story of all the successive Wests lies a major part of the story of America. Rather to this point, more than a century ago, a touring English diplomat, Lord Bryce, wrote, "The West is the most distinctly American part of America because the points in which it differs from the East are the points in which America as a whole differs from Europe." Or, as someone else said, "The West *is* America—only more so." To me, both those comments are as true today as on the day they were written.

So, finally, to all my friends Out West, thank you for all you have given me. So much. So much.

ACKNOWLEDGEMENTS

Way back at the start, in my Preface, I implied that an important motive in my writing this book was a wish to put together an homage, a sort of "thank you," to those many Westerners who, for more than 50 years, have always made me welcome. So, now that I have just about finished the thing, I hope that all those warm and genial friends will regard this book as an informal recognition of my gratitude. But, of course, besides that rather general expression of indebtedness, I should also be more specific in terms of those people who have very directly helped me with encouragement and/or many of the actual details in this book.

I owe a very special debt to John Gottschalk and his wife, Carmen, of Omaha. I have known John since he was 19 and working his way through college; 50 years on he is the recently retired CEO of the *Omaha World-Herald*, and a whole lot else besides. He and Carmen always look after me from the moment I land in Omaha; they are my anchors. John was one of the first people to tell me, on the strength of a couple of chapters, that I ought to persevere. And there is one other person in the US to whom I am particularly grateful: Larry Pointer, the author of the first significant book about Butch Cassidy; he has always been most generous in allowing me to pick his brains and seek his advice.

Among other American friends with whom I have been (and will continue to be) in touch for help of one kind or another, I must list Mike Ambrosino of Boston's WGBH-TV; Arlene Buffington of Mitchell; Don and Diane Cooper of Billings; Bob Edwards, lately of Buffalo's Gatchell Museum; Doug Ganz and his mother, Eleanor, both of Lincoln; Dorset Graves of Chadron State College (he was my boss for the year I spent working in Nebraska); Donna Grimm of Lincoln; Jerry Jasmer and other staff at the Little Bighorn Visitors Center; Barbara and Earl Madsen of Wyoming's TA Ranch; Gerald One Feather of the Oglala Sioux; Emerson Scott Jr. of Dayton; Walter Scott of Omaha; Lee Shank of the Barbed Wire Museum; Bob and Donna Swaim of Tucson; Colin Taylor of Casper and Hole-in-the-Wall; Melanie Wallace of WGBH-TV; Jeff and Sandra Wood of Golden; Charlie and Suzi Wright of Lincoln, and Dennis Zitterkopf of the American Society of Germans from Russia. I must also thank the folk at Wyoming's State Archives in Cheyenne, and those at the Nebraska and Kansas State Historical Societies in Lincoln and Topeka. Lastly, I am grateful to Randy Kane of Crawford who put me right on several factual details.

Now I must turn to friends who, sadly, are no longer with us. First must come Jim Hull; he was the managing editor of the *Laramie Boomerang* when I, a young and very innocent Brit, called to ask his advice over 50 years ago; he was my first real Westerner and, as such, an initial inspiration. A little later, I met another small-town newspaperman, Phil Gottschalk. He and his family kept the warmest of open-houses for me and my BBC crew when, each evening for a week, we returned to a motel in Rushville—after a day's filming on the nearby Sioux reservation of Pine Ridge. It was the beginning of a warm and enduring friendship; it was Phil who found me that teaching job; it is his son, John, to whom I refer above. Then there were Retta and Glenn Elliott (Gran'ma and Gran'pa) who adopted the four of us (the Slessor family) during the year we lived in Nebraska. Later there was Alistair Cooke who took a good deal of wry but always encouraging amusement at this Englishman's interest in Western history. I worked with him for nearly a year on his TV series, *America*; I learned more than I can tell. Later still came Bob Murray: he was a retired National Park historian, and what he didn't know about the Indian Wars and the country of Wyoming's Powder River was not worth knowing; he must have given me days, even weeks, of his time. Then there's Dale and Margie Starks of the wheat-cutting crew. More recently, in Buffalo, Emerson Scott always allowed me unlimited access to his wonderful library of Western history; he also gave me a bed on many occasions and drove me many guided miles in his pickup. I still get a warm welcome from his wife, Ann, every time I pull into Buffalo—which, incidentally, is my favorite western town.

In England, I must thank my publisher James Ferguson, who, since he took on this book, has shown a sharp interest in its development. I have been very fortunate in his choice of an editor to work with me: Brenda Stones has been firm yet understanding in her advice and her occasional criticisms; the book is hugely better for that input. In the same way, I must thank Tora Kelly, the Production Editor for her patience with me and, also, Emilie Ferguson and Kate Seabra for the hard work they put into drawing up the very thorough index. Then there's Rob White of Norfolk, Nick Ross of Notting Hill, and Moira Lovegrove of ING-Barings Bank. Also, I am very grateful to a friend and near neighbor, right here in Wimbledon: Janice Everitt understands the mysteries of computers. I know almost nothing of these things. Without her frequent "rescues," this book might never have happened.

Lastly, I thank my son, Jeremy, and my daughter, Katy, for their encouragement and interest. And though she has been gone these last 14 years, my wife, Janet. She was as fascinated by the West as I was (and still am).

BIBLIOGRAPHY

This bibliography is arranged in two sections: first a chapter-by-chapter commentary on sources I have found useful (in some cases, essential); and second an alphabetical listing of titles and publishers for reference. The alphabetical listing refers to both American and British publishers, not entirely systematically; and the dates of publication may include both the original date and the recent date of reprint. There are of course numerous other titles on the subject, which for reasons of space cannot all be included.

Chapter 1. First Things First

As this is an entirely personal chapter, and there are no sources other than my own memory and various notes and letters written at the time.

Chapter 2. La Vente de La Louisiane

The story of the Louisiana Purchase is found in varying detail in almost every American history book that covers the relevant period. But, as implied in my chapter, only a few of those books mention the role of the British in terms of both the payment arrangements and the naval threat as invoked by President Jefferson. Most authors, in their accounts of Napoleon abandoning his plans to restart a mainland American empire (via New Orleans), concentrate on the deaths caused by yellow fever on the expeditionary force he had dispatched to Santo Domingo (Haiti), and the simultaneous losses suffered by that force in fighting a slave revolt. A few authors (including at least one anonymous entry in Wikipedia) recognize that there were what one calls "other additional factors" in Napoleon's change of mind. One of the very few detailed accounts of the financial arrangements is contained in a booklet, *The Financing of the Louisiana Purchase,* published in 2004 (the Purchase's bicentennial) by ING Bank. A useful overview of the thinking and negotiations is found in what would seem to be a school textbook: *The Louisiana Purchase* by James P. Barry; likewise, *The Letters of Robert R. Livingston: The Diplomatic Story of the Louisiana Purchase* by Edward Parsons. A lengthy and detailed narrative covering the dominance of Britain's fighting fleet throughout the era in question is the subject of *The Command of the Oceans: A Naval History of Britain, 1649–1815* by N.A.M. Rogers.

Chapter 3. Lewis and Clark

The out-and-back journey of the Lewis and Clark expedition was to become so significant to the young nation's growing knowledge of itself that it is mentioned, at varying length, in every history about those times. A detailed, almost day-to-day account of the enterprise, with many diary extracts, excellent maps, and contemporary illustrations, is found in David Holloway's *Lewis and Clark and the Crossing of North America*. Likewise, *Lewis and Clark* by Dayton Duncan and Ken Burns is an informative book with many excellent illustrations. Other very useful sources are a lengthy chapter in John H. Hawgood's *America's Western Frontier* and, likewise, in Jeannette Mirsky's *The Westward Crossings*. Other books which, at varying length, carry informative accounts include David Lavender's *The American West*, Bernard De Voto's *Westward the Course of Empire* and *The West: Contemporary Records of Expansion across the Continent: 1807–1890* edited by Bayard Still. Lastly, a surprisingly sour and critical assessment of Lewis and Clark's achievements occurs in Walter Prescott Webb's classic *The Great Plains*.

Chapter 4. Mountain Men

For a full-length account of the mountain men and their trade, one should read Don Berry's marvelously researched *A Majority of Scoundrels*. Its equal is *The Beaver Men* by the prolific and renowned Nebraskan, Mari Sandoz. John Hawgood, Bernard de Voto, and Jeanette Mirsky, as listed just above, all include informative chapters about the fur trade. A variety of historians contribute to *The Oxford History of the American West*, which contains several sections on different aspects of the fur trade, including a discussion of the rendezvous system. Robert Athearn's *High Country Empire* includes a chapter on the mountain men; likewise, *The American West: An Appraisal* edited by Robert Ferris, and Everett Dick's *Vanguards of the Frontier*. Of a more specific nature is *Jedediah Smith and the Opening of the West* by Dale Morgan. *A Nation Moving West*, edited by Robert Richmond, contains a number of contemporary eyewitness accounts by various travelers during the heyday of the mountain fur trade. For a critical assessment of the exploitive nature of the whole business, particularly where the Indians were concerned, one should read the relevant chapter in *Land Grab* by John Terrell. Lastly, *The Mountain Men* by John Neilhardt is a book written entirely in verse about the exploits of various mountain men, including Jedediah Smith and Hugh Glass.

Chapter 5. The Overland Trail

Obviously, most books about the history of the West contain at least a chapter on the California and Oregon Trails. Books which are more specifically given to the story of the overland trails include *Wagons West* by Frank McLynn, *The California Trail* by George Stewart, and *The Great River Road* by Merrill Mates. For a full account of the ill-fated Donner Party one should read *Ordeal By Hunger* by George Stewart; additionally, one should include *The Forty-Niners* by William Johnson. Francis Parkman's classic *The Oregon Trail*, first published in the late 1840s, while fascinating, is only concerned with the first third of the trail; Parkman journeyed no further west than Fort Laramie. Wallace Stegner's *The Gathering of Zion* is, of course, mainly concerned with what the author calls "the Mormon trail."

Chapter 6. The Gold Rush

A most enterprising and entertaining book is *Gold Fever* by Steve Boggan; in 2013 this London-based journalist took himself off to California—to pan for any gold that he could find (not much) and, at the same time, to pan through the local history of the stuff. Further, as one might expect, Alistair Cooke in his *America* covers the era in intriguing detail. *The West: Contemporary Records* edited by Bayrd Still contains diary accounts and reflections by a number of Forty-Niners and those who came soon after. *Wagons West* by Frank McLynn concentrates (though not exclusively) on the adventures of the Argonauts in overlanding to California. Scattered through *The Oxford History of the American West* are numerous informative narratives and analyses. Lastly, for further nuggets, it is worth prospecting through the index of almost any general history of the West—for example, John A. Hawgood's *America's Western Frontier*.

Chapters 7 and 8. The Hostiles and the Military, No Survivors

Given that the Fetterman Massacre was one of the two worst disasters suffered by the Army on the Western plains (the other one, nine-and-a-half years later, was the even greater Custer debacle), there is no shortage of books and articles which include accounts, long and short, of the events at Fort Kearny in 1866. But if one had to choose three books of thoroughly researched detail and absorbing narrative they would have to be Dee Brown's *The Fetterman Massacre*, *Where a Hundred Men were Slain* by John Monnet, and *Give Me Eighty Men* by Shannon Smith. Most interestingly, Ms. Smith explores the possibility that Captain Fetterman has been subtly denigrated in a process started by Colonel

Carrington's two successive wives. His first wife, Margaret, died four years after the massacre but not before she had written a book about events at Fort Kearny. A few years later, the colonel married Frances Grummond, the widow of the officer who, leading his cavalry detachment, had raced ahead of Fetterman on the fatal day. In sequence, both women evidently decided that their husband, the colonel, had been unfairly condemned by his superior officers. So, in their books, they sought to "correct" the record by delicately shifting the blame onto Fetterman; they both imply that he was a gentlemanly but headstrong officer who, in disobeying their husband's careful orders, was the major cause of the disaster. There must obviously be the possibility that the colonel was sitting beside his wives … Anyway, their blaming the disaster on Fetterman has long been the generator of the accepted version of events. Shannon Smith finds a good deal of contrary evidence and, thereby, points to the possibility (or probability?) that Captain Fetterman was a much better officer than he appears to be in most of the standard accounts. She also questions the authenticity of Fetterman's boastful declaration, "Give me eighty men and I will ride through the whole Sioux nation." Did he ever say it? The wives' books, held in the archive section of some Western libraries, are *Absaraka, Home of the Crows* by Margaret Carrington and *My Army Life* by Frances Carrington. Another interesting account of events at Fort Kearny forms a chapter of Geoffrey Grinnell's *The Fighting Cheyenne*.

Elsewhere, there is a whole slew of absorbing narratives in which each comes at the story from a slightly different angle—though nearly all are critical, to a greater or lesser degree, of Fetterman. Amongst these accounts, one should include *Crimsoned Prairie* by General S.L.A. Marshall, *Frontier Regulars, 1866-91* by Robert Utley, *War Cries on Horseback* by Stephen Longstreet, *Forked Tongues and Broken Treaties* edited by Donald Worcester, and *The Long Death* by Ralph Andrist. Lastly, in an absorbing work of fiction (though it is entirely convincing in all its widely researched detail), one learns a great deal from *Where the Rivers Run North* by Sam Morton.

Chapter 9. The Railroad

There are a number of books that devote themselves entirely to the building of the first transcontinental railroad, and there are other, more wide-ranging histories which include sections on that particular story. In the first category, one should list *The Great Iron Road* by Robert Howard, *High Road to Promontory* by George Kraus, and *Iron Horses to Promontory* by Gerald Best. Among books with more general accounts of Western railroads are *The Story Of Western Railroads* by Robert Riegal, *Hear That Lonesome Whistle Blow* by Dee Brown, *The Big Four* by Oscar Lewis, *Railroads of America* by Oliver Jensen, and *Blood, Iron and Gold* by Christian Wolmar.

Chapter 10. Custer and Little Bighorn

Given that George Armstrong Custer is the most written-about man in all the military history of the United States, it would be wrong of me, as a layman, to suggest that any particular books are markedly superior to any of the others. So the following, all informative, are simply the ones with which I am most familiar: *The Sioux War of 1876* by John Gray, *The Custer Album* by Lawrence Frost, *The Custer Myth* by Col. W. Graham, *The Custer Reader* edited by Paul Hutton, *The Custer Companion* by Thom Hatch, *A Terrible Glory* by James Donovan, *Custerology* by Michael Elliott, *The Last Stand* by Nathaniel Philbrick, *To Hell With Honor* by Larry Sklenar, *Custer's Luck* by Edgar Stewart, *Glory Hunter* by Frederick Van de Water, *Custer* by Jay Monaghan, *Son of Morning Star* by Evans Connell, *The General Custer Story* by Lauran Paine, and *Soldiers Falling into Camp* by Robert Kammer and Frederick Lefthand. Interesting accounts of recent archaeological discoveries (following the grass fires of the mid-1980s) are found in *They Died with Custer* by Scott, Willey, and Connor and *Archaeology, History and Custer's Last Battle* by Richard Fox. Additionally, there are a number of booklets that are well worth studying; they include *The Custer Adventure* compiled by Richard Upton, *The Custer Battlefield* by Robert Utley, *Custer Made a Good Decision* by Major Robert Morris, and *Army Failures against the Sioux in 1876* by Francis Taunton in the British Custeriana series. Books that come at the story with less detail and/or from a slightly different perspective include *Crazy Horse and Custer* by Stephen Ambrose and *Crazy Horse* by Kingsley Bray. That last book, by an Englishman, is deeply impressive in terms of both its scope and detail. No less notable is Robert Utley's wonderfully researched *Sitting Bull: The Life and Times of an American Patriot*; in which he covers far more than the biography of the Sioux chief. For a critical analysis of the weaponry carried by Custer's cavalrymen, read *The "Trap-door" Springfield in Service* by Colonel Philip Shockley. As mentioned in the main text, both Custer and his wife wrote books which have the added interest of being written from a personal viewpoint and more or less contemporaneously with the events they describe: *My Life on the Plains* by General George Custer and *Boots and Saddles* by Elizabeth Custer. Lastly, *The Court-Martial of George Armstrong Custer* by Douglas Jones is an interesting novel that hypothesizes about what might have happened had Custer survived.

Chapter 11. Wounded Knee

As its title implies, *The Last Days of the Sioux Nation* by Robert Utley is almost entirely devoted to an account of the Wounded Knee engagement and all the events that led up to it; Mr. Utley returns to the story, though at much shorter length, in his *Frontier Regulars*. Then, as one might expect, Dee Brown's book *Bury My Heart At Wounded Knee* ends with two very informative chapters on the Ghost Dance and the subsequent events at Wounded Knee itself. Likewise, there are useful pages of text and several impressive photographs in *The West* by Geoffrey Ward, Ken Burns, and Duncan Dayton. Other worthwhile sources are in General S.L.A. Marshall's *Crimson Prairie* and in Ralph Andrist's *The Long Death*. For an unequivocally "army" version of events, one should read *The Wounded Knee and Drexel Mission Fights* by Major L. McCormick, who was the 7th Cavalry's adjutant at the time. A fictionalized (but not necessarily inaccurate) version of events is *Ghost Dance* by John Norman.

The 1973 hostilities generated a stream of print and broadcast copy at the time. But the first book to examine the long-standing roots of the 1973 "revolt" was *The Road to Wounded Knee*; written by Robert Burnette (President of the Rosebud Sioux Tribal Council) and John Koster (a white journalist); it argues the Indian cause with passion—though not, as far as one can tell, at the expense of accuracy. In 2000, 27 years after the events it examines, there came *Wounded Knee 2* by Rolland Dewing, a thoroughly researched narrative and analysis which seems to raise all the relevant political questions and, where possible, to point to most of the answers. Ten years earlier, the 1973 Superintendent of the Pine Ridge Reservation's office of the Bureau of Indian Affairs, Stanley Lyman, published *Wounded Knee 1973: A Personal Account*. I have read a 5,000-word essay by Sonya Scott entitled *Wounded Knee: Intratribal Conflict or Response to Federal Policies?*, and the full transcript of a TV documentary, *We Shall Remain*, made for the Public Broadcasting Service; this includes revealing contributions from, amongst others, the leader of the US Marshals, from Russell Means of AIM and from the "disputed" President of the Oglala Tribal Council, Dick Wilson. There is also a good website at www.woundedkneemuseum.org.

The books listed above cover the 1890 and 1973 "confrontations" at Wounded Knee in some detail. But for an account which is both broader and more personal in its historical perspective, do read Joe Starita's *The Dull Knives of Pine Ridge: a Lakota Odyssey*. In poignant detail, the author follows the hopes, frustrations, and despairs of a leading Sioux family across 150 years and five generations—from the Custer battle to Wounded Knee (1890), then on via both World Wars, to Vietnam and Wounded Knee (1973); or, as the author puts it, "from Custer to Saddam Hussein, from the Sun Dance to Holy Communion, from buffalo meat to pizza." By the same author comes *I Am A Man*, which tells the moving story of the Ponca people's mistreatment down the years, and of their Chief Standing Bear's long search for justice.

Chapter 12. Cowboys and Cow-towns

Again, I list the books I know best: *The Cattle Towns* by Robert Dykstra, *Prairie Trails and Cowtowns* by Floyd Streeter, *Vanguards of the Frontier* by Everett Dick, *A Nation Moving West* edited by Robert Richmond and Robert Mardock, *Cow Country* by Edward Dale, *The Cattlemen* by Mari Sandoz, *Cowboys and Cattlemen* edited by Michael Kennedy, and *Nothing But Prairie and Sky* by Walker Wyman. *The American West: An Appraisal* edited by Robert Ferris contains an interesting chapter called *The Cowboy: Then and Now*. Likewise, Walter Prescott Webb's *The Great Plains* has a chapter called "The Cattle Kingdom". Lastly, *The Cowboys* by William Forbis is a detailed and marvelously illustrated part-work with scores of early photographs.

Chapter 13. The Cattle Barons

Most of the books listed for the last chapter also cover, often in depth, the era of the cattle barons. For example, *Cowboys and Cattlemen* (see above) has several chapters grouped under the section "Rangeland Royalty"; one of those chapters features Moreton Frewen. Additionally, I would point to *The Beef Bonanza* by James Brisbin, *Land Grab* by John Terrell, and *The Swan Land and Cattle Company* by Harmon Mothershead. Lastly, *Moreton Frewen's Western Adventures* by L. Milton Woods is both impressively researched and an entertainingly good read.

Chapter 14. Range War

The story of the Johnson County War is told, at varying length, in a range of Western histories. But three full-length and thoroughly researched accounts (though varying in some details) are *The War on Powder River* by Helena Huntington Smith, *The Johnson County War* by Bill O'Neil, and, most recently, *Wyoming Range War* by John Davis. For an absorbing collection of accounts (40 of them in over 120 pages) written by some of the actual participants (on both sides) and observers of the "invasion" and its aftermath, there is nothing to compare with *The Powder River Country* edited by Margaret Brock Hanson. In *The Johnson County War: A Pack of Lies* the author, Jack Gage, has had the inventive idea of writing what amounts to two quite contrasting books within the same cover: the first tells the story entirely from the perspective of the barons and their mercenaries; the second from that of the settlers and would-be small ranchers. Additionally, there is an interesting biography of a leader of the "invasion" and one of Wyoming's most notorious range detectives/assassins in Robert DeArment's *Alias Frank Canton*. Other relevant books include *The Wyoming Lynching of Cattle Kate, 1889* by George Hufsmith and *The Banditti of the Plains: The Crowning Infamy of the Ages* by A.S. Mercer; this was the book that was virtually banned when first published in the mid-1890s.

Interesting accounts of the conflict are found in the issues of two local newspapers through most of 1892: both are available at the Wyoming State Archives and at the public libraries in Buffalo and Cheyenne. *The Cheyenne Daily Leader* presents the story from the cattle barons' viewpoint; *The Buffalo Bulletin* takes the opposing stance.

Chapter 15. Butch Cassidy and all that

Since the famous film, the lives of Butch, Sundance, and Etta have spawned scores of articles in magazines and journals of Western history. But among full-length books there are three which seem to lead the way. First is Larry Pointer's *In Search of Butch Cassidy*; in this readable and informative account, Pointer convincingly argues that Butch came back to live out his days under the pseudonym of William Phillips. Taking a direct and interestingly contrary view is *Digging Up Butch Cassidy* by Anne Meadows. Last, most recent and impressively researched is *Butch Cassidy: A Biography* by Richard Patterson, who seems undecided about Butch's alleged return; or perhaps he has decided that the evidence in each direction is equally convincing. Following closely on the three books just listed is one co-authored by Butch's sister: *Butch Cassidy, My Brother* by Lula Betensin. One of Butch's associates in the Wild Bunch, Matt Warner, eventually went straight and even became a deputy sheriff; in 1938 he co-wrote *The Last of the Bandit Riders*, which contains a number of interesting reflections on Butch Cassidy and his colleagues. Also in 1938, the Utah author referred to in my main text, Charles Kelly, wrote *The Outlaw Trail: The Story of Butch Cassidy*. Twenty years later, with further research, he wrote a revised edition which, particularly in its details of the alleged Bolivian shoot-out, must surely have inspired the climax of William Goldman's famous 1969 film. The published screenplay, as one might expect, makes a quirky and entertaining read.

Chapter 16. The Sod-house Frontier

Given that the farming homesteaders were the first people to really settle the Great Plains, it is not surprising that aspects of their story occur in a wide variety of books, ranging from academic treatises through popular histories to privately published family reminiscences. A number of authors have contributed individual and informative chapters about the development of Western farming to *The Oxford History of the American West*. Everett Dick's *The Sod-House Frontier* tells the story, but only up to 1890. Another interesting book is *Nebraska* by Frederick Luebke. Pioneers' diary entries and their letters back home (in the original spelling) feature in *900 Miles from Nowhere: Voices from the Homestead Frontier* by Steven Kinsella. Equally personal and engaging is *Western Story: The Recollections of Charley O'Kieffe, 1884-98*. Another personal account, reaching through to the hard times of the Great Depression, is George Shepherd's *West Of Yesterday*. As one might expect, Dee Brown's *The Settlers' West* contains an informative chapter about early farming. Likewise, Walter Prescott Webb deals in some detail with the problems faced by the homesteaders (water, fencing, markets, transport, climate) in his *The Great Plains*.

There are a number of good texts on women's experiences. The Nebraskan author Mari Sandoz has several informative "farming" chapters in her *Love Song to the Plains*, as does Martha McKeown in *Them was the Days*. *Pioneer Women* by Joanna Stratton is both a thorough and very readable book about the role and many hardships faced by Kansas pioneering women; it contains a short but entertaining chapter on the English families who founded the town of Victoria. Also to be recommended are *Grit and Grace: Eleven Women who Shaped the American West* by Glenda Riley and Richard Etulain, and *The Women* by Joan Reiter, with particularly good photographs. A fascinating anthology of diaries, letters and reminiscences by pioneering women is *Staking Her Claim: Women Homesteading the West* by Marcia Hensley.

The English author Jonathan Raban (now living in Seattle) did detailed research into the lives and hard times experienced by one of the last waves of homesteading farmers in eastern Montana, presented in the very informative *Bad Lands*. Another review of lives and hard times, particularly during the Depression years of the Dust Bowl in Oklahoma, is the prize-winning *The Worst Hard Time* by Timothy Egan. Of course the best known novel to come out of the Dust Bowl years is John Steinbeck's Pulitzer prize-winning *The Grapes of Wrath*. More idiosyncratic is the detailed history of barbed wire and the way it changed the West, in *The Wire that Fenced the West* by Henry and Frances McCallum. Finally, the Oklahoma Dust Bowl is the subject of a famous documentary film of those times: *The Plow that Broke the Plains*, directed by Pare Lorenz in 1936; and I made a documentary myself for the BBC's "World About Us" series called *Yellow Trail from Texas*, on the American wheat harvest, from Texas to Alberta.

Chapter 17. Last Things Last

As with Chapter 1, this is a largely personal chapter. So there are really no sources other than my recollections.

REFERENCE LISTING

Ambrose, Stephen. *Crazy Horse and Custer.* Doubleday, 1975.

Andrist, Ralph. *The Long Death (The Indian Wars).* Macmillan, 1964.

Athearn, Robert. *Westward the Briton.* Bison Books, 1953.

    High Country Empire. Bison Books, 1965.

Barry, James. *The Louisiana Purchase.* Franklin Watts Inc., 1973.

Best, Gerald. *Iron Horses to Promontory.* Golden West Books, 1969.

Berry, Don. *A Majority of Scoundrels, 1822–1834.* Ballantine, 1961.

Betenson, Lula. *Butch Cassidy, My Brother.* Brigham Young University, 1975.

Bird, Isabella. *A Lady's Life in the Rocky Mountains.* Western Frontier Library, 1967/1879.

Boatright, Mody. *Folk Laughter on the Frontier.* Collier Books, 1961.

Bonney, Edward. *The Banditti of the Prairies.* Western Frontier Library, 1963/1850.

Boorstin, Daniel. *The Americans: The Colonial Experience.* Penguin Books, 1963.

    The Americans: The National Experience. Penguin Books, 1969.

Bray, Kingsley. *Crazy Horse.* University of Oklahoma Press, 2006.

Brown, Dee. *Hear that Lonesome Whistle Blow.* Chatto & Windus, 1977.

    The Fetterman Massacre. Barrie & Jenkins, 1977.

    Bury My Heart at Wounded Knee. Henry Holt Publishing, 1970.

    Wondrous Times on the Frontier. Random House, 1994.

    The American West. Simon & Schuster, 1994.

Burnette, Robert and Koster, John. *The Road to Wounded Knee.* Bantam Books, 1974.

Brisbin, James. *The Beef Bonanza.* Western Frontier Library, 1959/1881.

Bryson, Bill. *Made in America.* Secker & Warburg, 1994.

Burton, Sir Richard. *The Look of the West in 1860.* Bison Books, 1963.

Casson, Simon. *Riding the Outlaw Trail.* Eye Books, 2004.

Cather, Willa. *O Pioneers!* Houghton Mifflin, 1995.

Catton, Bruce. *The Penguin Book of the Civil War.* Penguin, 1966.

Chapman, Arthur. "Butch Cassidy." *Elks Magazine*, April, 1930.

Chilton, Charles. *Discovery of the American West.* Hamlyn, 1970.

Clay, John. *My Life on the Range.* University of Oklahoma Press, 1962.

Connell, Evan. *Son of Morning Star.* Harper & Row, 1984.

Cooke, Alistair. *America.* BBC, 1973.

Cooke, John Byrne. *South of the Border.* Bantam, 1989.

Costain, Thomas. *The White and the Gold.* Doubleday (Canada), 1954.
Custer, Elizabeth. *Boots and Saddles.* University of Oklahoma Press, 1961.
Custer, George. *My Life on the Plains.* Bison Books, 1966.
Dale, Edward. *Cow Country.* Western Frontier Library, 1968.
       Frontier Trails: The Life of Frank Canton. University of Oklahoma, 1972.
Davis, John. *Wyoming Range War.* University of Oklahoma Press, 2010.
Davis, William. *The American Frontier.* Salamander Books, 2002.
DeArment, Robert. *Alias Frank Canton.* University of Oklahoma, 1996.
Deloria, Vine. *Custer Died For Your Sins.* Avon Books, 1969.
DeVoto, Bernard. *Westward the Course of Empire.* Eyre & Spottiswoode, 1954.
Dewing, Rolland. *Wounded Knee: 1973.* Great Plains Network, 2000.
Dick, Everett. *Tales of the Frontier.* Bison Books, 1963.
       The Sod-House Frontier. Bison Books, 2008.
Donovan, James. *A Terrible Glory.* Back Bay Books, 2009.
Dunn, J.P. *Massacres of the Mountains.* Eyre & Spottiswoode, 1963/1863.
Dykstra, Robert. *The Cattle Towns.* Alfred Knopf, 1970.
Edwards, Robert. *Guns of the Garchell.* Gatchell Museum Press, 2009.
Edwards, Robert and O'Leary, Ray. *Frontier Wyoming.* Gatchell Museum Press, 2006.
Egan, Timothy. *The Worst Hard Time.* Houghton Mifflin, 2006.
Ehrlich, Gretel. *The Solace of Open Spaces.* Penguin, 1985.
Elliott, Michael. *Custerology.* University of Chicago Press, 2007.
Emrich, Duncan. *It's an Old Wild West Custom.* Worlds Work, 1951.
Everett, Dick. *Vanguards of the Frontier.* Bison Books, 1941.
Farb, Peter. *Man's Rise to Civilization.* Secker & Warburg, 1969.
Ferris, Robert. *The American West: An Appraisal.* Museum of New Mexico, 1963.
Finerty, John. *Warpath and Bivouac.* Western Frontier Library, 1961/1890.
Fox, Richard. *Archaeology, History, and Custer's Last Battle.* University of Oklahoma, 1993.
Frost, Lawrence. *The Custer Album.* Superior Publishing Co., 1965.
Graham, W.A. *The Custer Myth.* Bonanza Books, 1953.
Gray, John. *The Sioux War of 1876.* University of Oklahoma, 1988.
Graybill, Andrew. *Policing the Great Plains.* Bison Books, 2007.
Greenleaf, Barbara. *America Fever.* Mentor Books, 1970.
Gage, Jack. *The Johnson County War.* Flintlock Publishing (Cheyenne), 1967.
Handlin, Oscar. *The American People.* Hutchinson, 1963.
Hanson, Margaret Brock. *The Powder River Country* (pub. by the author), 1980.

Hassrick, *Royal Cowboys.* Octopus Books, 1974.

Hawgood, John. *America's Western Frontier.* Alfred Knopf, 1967.

Henry, Will. *From Where the Sun Now Stands.* Corgi, 1963.

Hensley, Marcia. *Staking her Claim: Women Homesteaders.* High Plains Press, 2008.

Hollon, Eugene. *Frontier Violence.* Oxford University Press, 1974.

Holloway, David. *Lewis and Clark (Great Explorer Series).* Purnell Books, 1974.

Horan, James. *A Pictorial History of the Old West.* Spring Books, 1962.

Howard, Robert. *The Great Iron Trail.* Bonanza Books, 1962.

Hulsmith, George. *The Lynching of Cattle Kate.* High Plains Press, 1993.

Hutton, Paul. *The Custer Reader.* University of Oklahoma, 2004.

Hyde, George. *Indians of the High Plains.* University of Oklahoma, 1959.

ING-Baring. *The Financing of the Louisiana Purchase.* ING, 2004.

Jensen, Oliver. *Railroads of America.* Random House, 1992.

Jones, Douglas. *The Court Martial of George Armstrong Custer.* Scribner, 1976.

Kammer, Robert and Lefthand, Frederick. *Soldiers Falling into Camp.* Affiliated Writers of America, 1992.

Katz, Loren. *The Black West.* Doubleday-Anchor, 1973.

Kelly, Charles. *The Outlaw Trail: A History of Butch Cassidy.* Bonanza Books, 1959.

Kennedy, Michael (ed.). *Cowboys and Cattlemen.* Hastings House, 1964.

King, Charles. *Campaigning with Crook.* Western Frontier Library, 1967/1880.

Kinsella, Steven. *900 Miles from Nowhere.* Minnesota Historical Society, 2006.

Knight, Oliver. *Following The Indian Wars.* University of Oklahoma, 1960.

Kraus, George. *High Road to Promontory.* American West Publishing, 1969.

La Farge, Oliver. *A Pictorial History of the American Indian.* Spring Books, 1962.

Laighton, Margaret. *Comanche of the Seventh.* Berkeley Publishing, 1972.

Lavender, David. *The American West.* American Heritage Publishing, 1965.

Lewis, Oscar. *The Big Four (Central Pacific R.R.).* Ballantine Books, 1966.

Sea Routes to the Goldfields. Ballantine Books, 1971.

Longstreet, Stephen. *War Cries on Horseback.* W.H. Allen, 1970.

Luebke, Frederick. *Nebraska.* Bison Books, 1995.

Lyman, George. *The Saga of the Comstock Lode.* Ballantine, 1971.

Macewan, Grant. *Harvest of Bread.* Prairie Books, Saskatoon, 1969.

Marshall, Slam. *Crimsoned Prairie.* Scribner's Sons, 1972.

Marshall, Sprague. *Money Mountain: The Story of Cripple Creek.* Ballantine, 1953.

Mattes, Merrill. *The Great River Road.* Nebraska State Historical Society, 1969.

McCallum, Henry & Frances. *The Wire that Fenced the West.* University of Oklahoma, 1969.

McCormick, L.S. "The Wounded Knee and Drexel Fights." *Journal of American Military History,* January, 1975.

McKeown, Martha. *Them Was the Days.* Bison Books, 1961.

McLynn, Frank. *Wagons West.* Pimlico/Random House, 2003.

McMinty, Larry. "Sacagawea's Nickname." *New York Review of Books,* 2001.

McPhee, John. *Coming into the Country (Alaska).* Bantam Books, 1980.

Meadows, Anne. *Digging up Butch and Sundance.* Bison Books, 1994.

Mercer, A.S. *The Banditti of the Plains.* Western Frontier Library, 1968/1894.

Michno, Gregory. *Lakota Noon.* Mountain Press, 2001.

Millard, Joseph. *The Cheyenne Wars.* Monarch Books, 1964.

Miller, Nyle and Snell, Joseph. *Why the West was Wild.* Kansas State Historical Society, 1963.

Miller, William. *A New History of the United States.* Dell Publishing, 1958.

Milner, Clyde (ed.). *The Oxford History of the American West.* Oxford University Press, 1994.

Mirsky, Jeanette. *The Westward Crossings.* Allan Wingate, 1951.

Monnet, John. *Where a Hundred Men were Slain.* University of New Mexico, 2008.

Morris, Robert. *Custer's Defeat and Other Conflicts.* Sunflower Press, 1979.

Morton, Sam. *Where the Rivers Run North.* Sheridan County Historical Society, 2007.

Mothershead, Harmon. *The Swan Land and Cattle Company.* University of Oklahoma, 1971.

Murray, Robert. *The Army on the Powder River.* Old Army Press, 1972.
    Fort Laramie. Old Army Press, 1974.

Myers, Jay. *Red Chiefs and White Challengers.* Washington Square Press, 1971.

Neihardt, John. *The Mountain Men.* Bison Books, 1971.

Nevis, Allan. *A Pocket History of the US.* Washington Square Press, 1942.

Norman, John. *Ghost Dance.* Sphere Books, 1970.

Nye, R.B. and Morpurgo, J.E. *The Birth of the USA.* Penguin, 1955.
    The Growth of the USA. Penguin, 1955.

O'Kieffe. *The Western Story.* Bison Books, 1960.

O'Neal, Bill. *The Johnson County War.* Eakin Press, 2004.

Paine, Lauran. *The General Custer Story.* Foulsham and Co., 1960.

Parsons, Edward. *The Louisiana Purchase.* American Antiquarian Society, 1943.

Patterson, Richard. *Butch Cassidy: A Biography.* Bison Books, 1998.

Penrose, Charles. *The Rustler Business.* Gatchell Museum, 1914.

Philbrick, Nathaniel. *The Last Stand.* Bodley Head, 2010.

Phillips, David. *The West: An American Experience.* A. & W. Visual, 1975.

Pointer, Larry. *In Search of Butch Cassidy.* University of Oklahoma,1977.

Prucha, Francis (ed.). *Army Life on the Western Frontier.* University of Oklahoma, 1958.

Raban, Jonathan. *Bad Land.* Picador Macmillan, 1996.

Reedstrom, Lisle. *Apache Wars.* Sterling Publishing, 1990.

Rhodes, Richard. *The Inland Ground.* Atheneum, 1970.

Richmond, Robert (ed.). *A Nation Moving West.* Bison Books, 1966.

Rickey, Don. *Forty Miles a Day on Beans and Hay.* University of Oklahoma, 1960.

Riegal, Robert. *The Story of Western Railroads.* Bison Books, 1964.

Riley, Glenda and Etulain, Richard. *By Grit and by Grace.* Fulcrum Publishing, 1997.

Sandoz, Mari. *Crazy Horse; The Buffalo Hunters; Love Song to the Plains.* All Bison Books, 1961.

    The Cattlemen. Bison Books, 1978.

Saul, Norman. *The Russian-Germans to Kansas.* Kansas Historical Society, 1974.

Schmitt, Martin with Dee Brown. *The Settlers' West.* Scribner, 1955.

Schofield, Brian. *Selling Your Father's Bones.* Harper Press, 2008.

Scott, Willey and Connor. *They Died with Custer.* University of Oklahoma, 1998.

Shepherd, George. *The West of Yesterday.* McClelland & Stewart, 1965.

Shockley, Philip. *The "Trap-door" Springfield.* World Wide Gun Report, 1958.

Shorris, James. *The Death of the Great Spirit.* Simon & Schuster, 1971.

Silverberg, Robert. *Ghost Towns of the American West.* Ballantine Books, 1968.

Sklenar, Larry. *To Hell with Honor.* University of Oklahoma, 2000.

Slessor, Tim. *Yellow Trail from Texas.* Old Pond, 1976.

Smith, Helena. *The War on Powder River.* McGraw Hill, 1966.

Smith, Shannon. *Give Me Eighty Men.* Bison Books, 2008.

Smith, Sherry. *The View from Officer's Row.* University of Arizona, 1995.

Starita, Joe. *The Dull Knives of Pine Ridge: A Lakota Odyssey.* Putnam, 1995.

    I Am A Man: Standing Bear's Search for Justice, St. Martin's Press, 2008.

Stegner, Wallace. *The Gathering of Zion (The Mormons).* McGraw Hill, 1971.

Steinbeck, John. *The Grapes of Wrath.* Viking, 1939 and Penguin Classics, 1980.

Steiner, Stan. *The New Indians.* Dell Publishing, 1968.

Stewart, Edgar. *Custer's Luck.* University of Oklahoma, 1955.

Stewart, George. *The California Trail.* Eyre & Spottiswoode, 1964.

Ordeal by Hunger. Eyre & Spottiswoode, 1962.

Still, Bayard. *Contemporary Records, 1607–1890.* Capricorn Books, 1961.

Stone, Irving. *Men to Match My Mountains.* Corgi, 1971.

Stratton, Joanna. *Pioneer Women of Kansas.* Simon & Schuster, 1981.

Streeter, Lloyd. *Prairie Trails and Cowtowns.* Chapman & Grimes, 1936.

Taunton, Francis. *Army Failures in 1876,* British Westerners Series, 2005.

Terrell, John. *Land Grab: The Truth about 'Winning the West'.* Dial Press, 1972.

Time-Life Books. *A set of 25 illustrated and informative part-works about almost every aspect of the West.* Published through the mid-1970s,

Twain, Mark. *Roughing It.* Harper & Row, 1962.

Upton, Richard. *The Custer Adventure.* Old Army Press, 1975.

Utley, Robert. *Frontier Regulars.* Macmillan, 1973.

    The Last Days of the Sioux Nation. Yale University Press, 1963.

    A Guide to the Custer Battlefield. The National Park Service, 1994.

    Custer and the Great Controversy. Bison Books, 1998

    After Lewis and Clark. Bison Books, 2004.

    Sitting Bull: The life of an American Patriot, Henry Holt, 1998.

Van de Water, Frederick. *Glory Hunter: General Custer.* Bison Books, 1934.

Ward, Geoffrey. *The West: An Illustrated History.* Weidenfeld & Nicolson, 1996.

Watts, Peter. *A Dictionary of the Old West.* Alfred Knopf, 1977.

Webb, Walter Prescott. *The Great Plains.* Bison Books, 1981.

Wellman, Paul. *The Blazing South-West.* Tandem, 1973.

Werner, Fred. *The Dull Knife Battle.* Werner Publications, 1981.

Wexler, Alan. *Atlas of Westward Expansion.* Facts on File, 1995.

White, Jon. *The Great American Desert.* Allen & Unwin, 1977.

White, Robert. *Stark's Harvesters.* Old Pond Publishing, 2010.

Winter, Dylan. *A Hack Goes West.* Old Pond Publishing, 2007.

Wolmar, Christian. *Blood, Iron, and Gold.* Atlantic Books, 2010.

Woods, Lawrence. *British Gentlemen in the Wild West.* Free Press, 1981.

Woods, Milton. *Moreton Frewen's Western Adventures.* University of Wyoming, 1986.

Worcester, Donald (ed.). *Forked Tongues and Broken Treaties.* Caxton, 1975.

Wyman, Walker. *Nothing But Prairie and Sky.* University of Oklahoma, 1954.

INDEX